BARE KNUCKLES AND BACK ROOMS

ED ROLLINS
WITH TOM DEFRANK

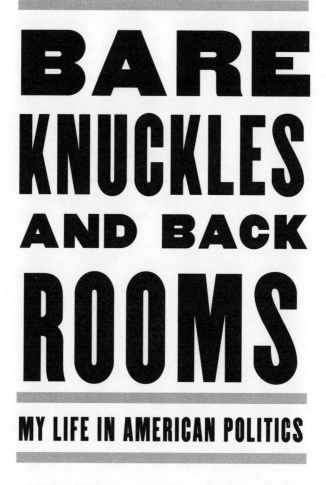

BARE KNUCKLES AND BACK ROOMS

MY LIFE IN AMERICAN POLITICS

BROADWAY BOOKS   NEW YORK

BROADWAY

BARE KNUCKLES AND BACK ROOMS:
MY LIFE IN AMERICAN POLITICS
Copyright © 1996 by Ed Rollins. All rights reserved.
Printed in the United States of America. No part of
this book may be reproduced or transmitted in any
form or by any means, electronic or mechanical,
including photocopying, recording, or by any
information storage and retrieval system, without
written permission from the publisher. For
information address Broadway Books, a division of
Bantam Doubleday Dell Publishing Group, Inc.,
1540 Broadway, New York, NY 10036.

Broadway Books titles may be purchased for business
or promotional use or for special sales. For
information, please write to: Special Markets
Department, Bantam Doubleday Dell Publishing
Group, Inc., 1540 Broadway, New York, NY 10036.

BROADWAY BOOKS and its logo, a letter B
bisected on the diagonal, are trademarks of Broadway
Books, a division of Bantam Doubleday Dell
Publishing Group, Inc.

Library of Congress Cataloging-in-Publication Data
Rollins, Ed.
Bare knuckles and back rooms : my life in American
politics / Ed Rollins with Tom DeFrank.
— 1st ed.
p. cm.
Includes index.
ISBN 0-553-06724-9
1. Rollins, Ed.   2. United States—Politics and
government—1981–1989.   3. United States—Politics
and government—1989–1993.   4. Political
consultants—United States—Biography.
I. DeFrank, Thomas M.   II. Title.
E840.8.R597A3   1996
320.973—dc20   96-19723
                                                      CIP

*Photo insert researched, edited, and designed by
Vincent Virga*
All photos that are not credited are from the
author's collection.

96 97 98 99 00 10 9 8 7 6 5 4 3 2 1

FIRST EDITION

To my wife, Sherrie,
who sometimes wishes my commentary was a little blander,
but whose love and support are constant

And to our daughter, Lily,
who has added so much richness and joy to our lives

CONTENTS

BARE KNUCKLES AND BACK ROOMS

PROLOGUE

POLITICS IS A crazy goddamn business, I reminded myself. I loathed this campaign and had wanted to bail out for weeks. But I'm not a quitter—I'm a masochist. In three decades as a political junkie, I'd never worked a more miserable, depressing, rotten race. Compared to Michael and Arianna Huffington, Ross Perot had been St. Francis of Assisi. And yet, incredibly, I was feeling something close to euphoria. For the past couple of months, I'd been at the top of my game, bobbing and weaving, punching and counter-punching as well as I ever had. I was juiced, I was on, I was high on the knowledge that I'd miraculously managed to resuscitate my candidate's moribund prospects—and my own.

It was Wednesday morning, October 26, 1994. I was sitting at my desk in a corner of the war room, the conference room–turned nerve center of our second-floor headquarters in an upscale Costa Mesa office complex. The nightly tracking polls had just come in, and I could hardly believe the story they told.

In July, when I'd taken over Michael Huffington's senatorial campaign, the carpetbagging megamillionaire from Santa Barbara by way of Houston was eighteen points down. Nobody gave us a snowball's chance in Orange County of catching incumbent Dianne Feinstein, the most popular Democrat in California and an icon of the liberal Democratic establishment. Michael's personal checkbook, Larry Mc-

Carthy's brilliant attack ads, and America's disdain for President Bill Clinton and his unpopular wife had steadily shrunk the gap. By early October, the race was dead even. Now, with two weeks to go, we'd actually blown past Feinstein. We were scoring with haymaker negative ads: Many of the same people who loved her when we started this campaign now hated her. As of this morning, our private polls showed us holding a strong eight-point lead; equally important, Feinstein's negative rating had soared to over 50 percent.

Drinking my third cup of coffee and poring over the numbers, I allowed myself a dangerous thought: We're going to win this mother. The pleasure inspired by this notion was hardly selfless. After four years in my party's doghouse, I'd soon be riding high in the water again. If I pulled this out, the doubters could go fuck themselves. In life, living well may be the best revenge. In politics, it's winning. "The controversial political consultant Ed Rollins"—which the press had decided was my full legal name—was about to knock off the formidable Senator Feinstein, one of the mandarins of the brie-and-Chablis set.

I could almost see the morning-after headlines about our victory—then reality set in. This thing was far from over. Too many times, I'd knocked out an opponent who was leading in the closing minutes of a fight. I'd also learned long ago that overnight is a lifetime in politics, and this race had thirteen days to go. True, I liked our chances, but I was still nervous as hell. For the first time in my career, I knew next to nothing about my candidate.

When I take on a campaign, I always begin by running a vulnerability study on my own side. I tell my candidates, "Pretend I'm your priest. Confess all your sins to me, and I'll tell you whether they're mortal or venial." I tried to have this conversation with Huffington more than once; each time he steadfastly refused.

"I'm not going to spend my money to investigate myself," he'd say. "I know what I've done, and there's nothing there."

I was never persuaded—especially after an old friend in the Reagan White House personnel office tipped me that when Michael was up for an administration job, the FBI field investigation unearthed a couple of potential skeletons sufficiently worrisome to keep him from getting a presidential appointment that required Senate confirmation.

As a consequence of his stonewalling, the opposition had a better fix on Michael Huffington than any of his advisers. And his wife, the scheming Arianna—well, she was proving to be a major liability herself. Her ties to a cult minister had become an embarrassment, and the more she talked about herself and some of her wacko ideas, the worse we fared. My staff and I were flying blind, knowing that every major media outlet in the country was trying to find dirt on the pair of them. Rumors were everywhere. So far, nothing had emerged from the whispers, but for weeks, my gut had been queasy about some nuclear-tipped warhead out there, waiting to vaporize us in the final days.

I put down my coffee cup just as the phone rang. It was David Lesher, the *Los Angeles Times* reporter covering the campaign.

"Ed, your candidate's got a nanny problem, and I'm breaking the story tomorrow morning." Lesher paused for dramatic effect, then asked smugly, "Would you like to comment?"

I declined his generous offer, saying I knew nothing about it but would check the story out and get back to him.

"Her name's Marsella," Lesher added, "and she worked for them for over five years. And Rollins, just to add to your misery, your candidate made a flat-out denial when asked about it an hour ago in San Diego. Of course, you know he was in San Diego campaigning for Prop 187, don't you? Oh, by the way, my deadline's five o'clock." Lesher, like almost everyone else at the *Times,* hated the Huffingtons. The bastard was enjoying his exclusive just a little too much.

I can't say I was shocked. One of the biggest rumors going around was that Feinstein's camp knew the Huffingtons had illegal workers on their payroll and would time this nasty revelation for maximum devastation. If true, we were in big trouble; Huffington had just endorsed Proposition 187, the controversial ballot initiative cutting off state benefits to illegal workers. I'd asked them about it several times, but each time I pressed them on this rumor, they'd retreat into full denial.

After Lesher's call, I walked twenty feet down the hall and found Arianna, who was sitting in her secretary's tiny office. I shut the door and told her what the *Times* had.

She was indignant, and emphatically stonewalled me yet again.

"How many times do I have to deny these rumors?" she complained.

"Arianna, let's quit bullshitting each other. The *Times* has all the facts. The reporter has her *name,* for Christ's sake. They're running the goddamn story in tomorrow's paper."

Stunned that her secret had finally been exposed, Arianna broke down and started to cry.

Fuck me, I said to myself, the wheels are really coming off now.

After getting Arianna to calm down a little, I made her tell me the whole story. Marsella was Guatemalan and had worked for them for four or five years. Arianna claimed they hadn't known she was illegal when they hired her. I didn't believe her for a minute.

"We did it for the children," she said, sobbing again. "The children loved her."

It took fifteen minutes to reach the candidate in San Diego, where he was making one of his few public campaign appearances. I told him we had an extremely serious problem on our hands, and he must avoid the press at all costs until we came up with a strategy to contain the damage.

"I knew this was a problem," he said. "I *told* her it would be a problem. It's not my problem, it's Arianna's problem. The nanny worked for *her*."

I didn't bother to remind him that she wasn't the only Huffington who'd lied to me about Marsella, or that he'd lied about it again to the press only a couple of hours ago.

"It's *our* problem, Michael," I said. "This can be a fatal wound. It's really critical how we handle it. We have to get back on the offensive as quickly as possible. But first we have to know what the facts are and put them out." I told him we needed to meet as soon as he got back from San Diego.

Throughout the conversation, he spoke in a normal tone of voice. But I could tell he was shaken. Maybe he realized that the Senate seat he thought he could buy with $28 million of his own money had been flushed down the toilet.

Because that's what had just happened. The tag line of one Feinstein spot—"The Texas Millionaire Californians Can't Trust"—was about to take on lethal new meaning, for them and for me. Barring a miracle, the race was over.

In any other campaign, I would have responded to this bombshell by heading straight into full crisis mode and lobbing hand grenades back out of the bunker. Instead, I got up, shut my door, and sat quietly at my desk for a few minutes. The euphoria I'd felt a mere half-hour ago now seemed like the cruel joke I deserved. And the justice of it made me face some hard truths. The bullshit—mine included—would stop right here.

Since early July, I'd been working for two of the most unprincipled political creatures I'd ever encountered. One was such a complete cipher he gave empty suits a bad name. But his wife was even worse—a domineering Greek Rasputin determined to ride her husband's wealth to political glory at any cost. These two didn't deserve the time of day from the good people of my home state, much less their vote.

On a good day, I could almost feel sorry for Michael Huffington.

He was a colorless man, the kind who would bore you to tears if you were unlucky enough to be stuck next to him at a Georgetown dinner party. He was so dull that if he hadn't inherited several hundred million dollars from his oilman father, he'd never have made it through the door of those parties.

But he wasn't a malevolent guy, and matched up against his new-age wife, he seemed almost harmless. Arianna Huffington had charmed me out of my socks to get me to manage her husband's campaign. But in a few short months, I'd come to realize that she was the most ruthless, unscrupulous, and ambitious person I'd met in thirty years in national politics—not to mention that she sometimes seemed truly pathological. Her allure and style were only a veneer; the soul of a wily sorceress lurked beneath. Now, in her obsession with making her husband president some day, she had destroyed him.

In some ways, these past few weeks reminded me of my short, unhappy life with another rich Texan. Ross Perot was a paranoid lunatic on an ego trip, a short man with a tall appetite for attention. At least he believed in something. The Huffingtons, by contrast, believed in nothing except the pursuit of raw power. But the worst sin was my own. I hadn't just bought into their game because I'd needed their money. After my self-immolation in New Jersey the previous year, I wanted the redemption that only a death-defying victory can bring. In the process, I'd almost gotten both of them—Michael and his Svengali—elected to the United States Senate.

I SHOULD have quit on the spot.

Instead, I opened my door and went back to work. I was a professional, and whatever my personal feelings, I wouldn't abandon the ship now.

The drill was obvious. This wasn't the first time I'd taken a direct hit in the last ten days of a campaign. I assembled my staff and began mapping out a response. We had to make a full and immediate disclosure of the facts combined with a mea culpa—a mea *maxima* culpa, to be precise. However, we now knew our candidate was perceived as a liar, so we couldn't compound the damage by letting him talk to the press.

When Michael returned in midafternoon, I reassembled the troops in the war room and we presented our recommendations to the Huffingtons. Put out a press release with all the facts, we told them; eat a twenty-five-pound crow and try to change the subject.

They thought we were crazy. They were positive a press conference was the only way to salvage this disaster. Arianna always thought she could talk her way out of anything. We told them as politely as we could that they were nuts. Arianna then came up with the bright idea of doing the press conference in Santa Barbara, where she thought it wouldn't attract as much attention. We all argued that a press conference anywhere would give the story legs. The only way to make it a one-day hit was to hunker down. Having reached an impasse, we agreed to talk about it more the next day.

Later that evening, I was astonished to see Michael doing an interview with KCAL-TV in which he dumped the whole mess on Arianna. He said he'd been living in Texas when she had hired the woman. For good measure, he turned the tables and charged that Feinstein had herself hired two illegals.

Shortly after I watched this idiotic performance, an early edition of the *Times* was delivered to my hotel room. The headline—"ILLE-GAL IMMIGRANT WORKED 5 YEARS AT HUFFINGTON HOME"—was brutal. The story was worse. Feinstein's camp had clearly known about the nanny for some time. When Huffington endorsed Prop 187, the trap was set. It was obvious to me from all the detail in Lesher's piece that he hadn't worked up a sweat to get *this* exclusive. Lesher was a close friend of Kam Kuwata, Feinstein's campaign manager. It was almost certainly a classic spoon-fed job.

Next morning, the piece exploded with all the force of a torpedo below the waterline. The juxtaposition of Marsella and Prop 187 made Huffington look like a total hypocrite, which in fact he was.

I later learned something else they hadn't told me. After his election to Congress in 1992, Huffington picked up Arianna and the kids at the airport in Washington, D.C. He nearly passed out when he saw Marsella, and sent her packing back to California. He'd been astute enough to realize nearly two years ago that she was a problem, and had still chosen to lie about it to me.

Once we'd all gathered at headquarters, we met again with the candidate and his wife. I repeated our unanimous recommendation that anything more than an apologetic, full-disclosure press release would be suicidal. We had to confess our sins, tough it out, and try to shift the focus back to Feinstein.

"Let us save you," I told them. "We can do it, but you have to listen to me."

They didn't. With the race squarely on the line, they panicked, and we were melting down by the hour.

No doubt because she understood she was the guilty party, Arianna was hysterical. She began babbling about the need for a counterattack.

"We have to find this woman who worked for Feinstein," she shrieked. "We must do this for Michael."

Oh shit, I thought, time to get the waders out. I knew where she was heading. Seizing on an item turned up by our opposition research team—known in campaign parlance as "Oppo"—Arianna was convinced Feinstein had also employed an illegal housekeeper. Now she'd deluded her husband and herself into believing that if we could prove Feinstein had an illegal worker too, the whole shitstorm would simply disappear.

Before deciding to ignore all of us and drive to Santa Barbara for a press conference, Michael called Larry McCarthy, who was back east in his production studio, and directed him to put together a new attack spot saying Feinstein was a liar because she had her own illegal. The Huffingtons also ordered me to scramble the jets to find the woman. At the same time, Arianna dispatched Dana Kierstead, chief former security for the Huffington family oil business in Houston, who was now working out of our headquarters and was in charge of security for the campaign, to head up a separate investigation.

That afternoon, my staff and I watched the press conference in the war room. It was even worse than we'd feared. Not only did the state press turn out in full force, but Michael and Arianna scheduled it so it could be carried live on the local evening news in Los Angeles. Huffington did everything wrong. His demeanor was hostile, not apologetic. He blamed it all on Arianna, making her an even bigger issue. For good measure, he compared the transgression to "running a stop sign." Once again, he said he knew for a fact that Feinstein had two illegals herself; this time he promised to produce the evidence shortly. Michael had managed to do precisely what we couldn't afford—keep this miserable story alive.

"Those fucking idiots," said a senior adviser sitting next to me. It could not have gone worse if we'd scripted it. In a bizarre way, we *had* scripted it. Everything we told them not to do, they did. Now, the candidate had not only poured gasoline into our foxhole, he'd lit the match.

I turned to Jamie Moore, the campaign manager. "Just the campaign I've always wanted to run," I said in disgust. "The Battle of the Illegals."

Now the situation was truly hopeless. Michael's negatives blasted through the stratosphere. Literally overnight, our lead evaporated. But I still owed them my paycheck, so I asked my counsellor Bruce Nestande, an old friend and twenty-year veteran of California's internecine Republican wars, to fly north to see what he could learn about Feinstein's illegal.

After a day of checking his sources, Nestande reported in from San Francisco. "You're not going to believe what these crazy people are doing," he said. "It's right out of the Keystone Kops."

According to Bruce, Arianna's rogue operation had pulled together a team of about a dozen security operatives to find the housekeeper at all costs. They set up a command post in a San Francisco hotel, changing locations every day or two to keep from getting caught by hotel security. They used the standard tools of the surveillance trade—stakeouts, detectives sleeping in cars outside suspicious houses, car chases, cameras hidden in vans.

After hearing this story, I decided the wisest response was to do nothing. This was Arianna's operation, and I couldn't stop it. The outing of Feinstein's housekeeper had taken on mystical proportions; probably she perceived it as the only way to exorcise her own culpability. Arianna was utterly out of control, incapable of listening to me or anyone.

Meanwhile, we did what we had to do. We tried to get back on the offensive. We added another direct-mail firebomb in the final week and started running McCarthy's liar spot. But we never got any traction. The story was still Michael, Arianna, and Marsella.

Arianna made matters much worse by booking herself on every news show she could, manically trying to explain it all away. I was canceling these appearances as fast as she booked them, but she got on a few shows without my knowledge. Finally, I got Michael to order her to cease and desist.

Four days before the election, on Friday, November 4, Nestande called again, this time to announce that he was getting the hell out of San Francisco before The Great Illegal Nanny Chase caught him in the backblast. "You don't want to know what they've done," he said. Reluctantly, I said I did, and then he told me the story.

Armed with a name from an old newspaper clipping turned up in a Sacramento library by John Nelson, the campaign Oppo director, Arianna's operatives had tracked down the housekeeper's husband. They staked out his house, and eventually he unwittingly led them to the home of a friend where his wife was hiding until after the election. Two of the private eyes had talked their way into the housekeeper's hideaway by fraudulently posing as a lawyer and an insurance agent. They claimed a deceased relative in Guatemala had left her $30,000. Once she showed them some identification, they explained, the money would be sent to her in a matter of days. Excited by this happy news, the poor woman not only allowed her benefactors to photograph her immigration papers, she even served them coffee.

This was worse than stupid—it was ethically appalling to me. It also wasn't the first time that Arianna had gone off the books and hired private investigators. A few weeks earlier, I'd heard that she had hired a detective to scrutinize the private life of a prominent magazine reporter who was working on a profile of her. The idea, I gathered, was to come up with dirt for a leak to the news media. (Of course, she denied everything when I confronted her after finding out about the scheme.) But now she'd finally crossed the line even by *her* minimal standards of human decency.

I haven't been an altar boy in forty years. There's not much of a market for them in my line of work. As they say, politics ain't beanbag. I've observed and occasionally participated in activities that don't make me proud. Even the most honorable candidates are sometimes betrayed by their subordinates; years after the fact, for instance, I learned that a well-known Washington lobbyist who was involved in the 1984 Reagan campaign—a campaign I'd managed— had pocketed an illegal $10 million campaign contribution from a foreign government. But the magnitude of Arianna Huffington's lust for power was beyond the pale even for me. For the sake of her husband's political survival, she didn't care that her private eyes had perpetrated a disgraceful fraud on an innocent housekeeper from Guatemala whose only sin was standing in the way of the Huffingtons' obsession. And I'd been utterly powerless to stop it.

A few minutes after the conversation with Nestande, I walked down the hall and found Arianna in her office.

"I know about your little stunt with Feinstein's housekeeper," I said in a voice more calm than I felt. "Do you realize the consequences of what you've done? This is fraud, committed by your agents. You've violated federal election law at the very least, and probably a few state ones as well." The truth is, I didn't have a clue as to whether what had been done was illegal. But I was so pissed off I didn't care.

"It was necessary," Arianna insisted, without a sliver of repentance. "It's my problem. We had to do this for Michael."

I stood in the doorway to her office, looking down at her. I don't think I've ever felt so much disdain for anyone.

"Reporters are all over San Francisco looking for this same woman after Michael promised them she exists," I said. "If somebody finds her and learns what you've done, Michael will be destroyed and somebody will go to jail."

"They're not going to find out. It had to be done."

I couldn't believe that anyone could be so craven. Arianna and her husband were beyond contempt. I was ashamed to be associated with them. I didn't want to wake up one more morning having to work for them.

"I'm going to Spokane to help a candidate I care about," I said.

Arianna freaked out. "You can't leave," she pleaded. "We desperately need you. You've got to call your friends in Washington and put pressure on the INS."

"There isn't shit I can do here now." It was true. We had no get-out-the-vote operation; except for the attack ads, the campaign was a hollow shell. Thanks to my two candidates, staying in California would have been pointless anyway. I was history, and so were they.

Late the next morning, I flew out of John Wayne Orange County Airport for Spokane, desperate for a disinfectant considerably stronger than the crisp Pacific Northwest air I'd soon be breathing.

As I settled into my seat, I tried to understand why I felt so Godawful sleazy on this sunny Saturday morning. In a couple of hours, I'd be helping one of my closest friends try to pull off an upset in the bellwether congressional race of the year. He and his wife were the kind of people who *deserved* to be in Washington, and in between stints for the Huffingtons, my team and I had given them a shot at winning. At least I have one decent campaign left to work, I consoled myself.

But as my thoughts turned back to the campaign I'd just left, I couldn't stop wrestling with the same troubling questions. Is this what politics has come to? Am I really a party to this? What does that say about me? The answers were dispiriting, and made me even more melancholy. Somehow not even the New Jersey firestorm, where I'd risen from the dead only to set myself ablaze, felt as personally grievous as the scalding wound I'd just inflicted on myself. New Jersey was inadvertent; this was malice aforethought.

And I couldn't plead ignorance. Friends in New York and California who knew Arianna and Michael had warned me to steer clear of them. Maybe it had been my goddamn ego talking: You're so good, Rollins, you can take these idiots and defeat the most important Democrat in California.

Now, as the voters of my native state prepared to render their judgment on Michael and Arianna Huffington, I flew north secure in the rationalization that at least they wouldn't win. I felt good about that. Such a thought was blasphemy of the first order, but for the first time in nearly three decades working the political game, I actually wanted my candidate to lose.

Unfortunately, my confidence that Huffington would be defeated was cold comfort. Every campaign manager knows this mantra by heart: If Only They'd Listened to Me. But I knew that if they *had* listened to me and my professionals, the Huffingtons would have won. And it made me ashamed to admit it, even to myself.

They hadn't made me work for them. I *wanted* to do their race. A Huffington victory might be the fifty-first vote that returned the Senate to the Republican column, and that was reason enough. But I was also looking to repair the estrangement between my party and me. And frankly, I badly needed the money they offered. For the first time in my political career, I'd sold out; I'd become a whore. I felt dirty being around them, and disgusted with myself for having to take their money.

It was such a far cry from my first campaign, when as a starry-eyed young Democrat, I'd worked for Robert Kennedy across the same Northern California terrain that now lay directly below me. I'd experienced the peaks and the valleys of my trade in the decades since Bobby's death, but this California race had scraped the bottom of the barrel.

At least I knew it would be my last. It was finally time to hang up the gloves.

MY DREAMS OF being an Olympic boxer were snuffed out in 1967, when I lost my last fight by a TKO. Now, I'm finished with the other great passion of my life—politics.

I've been a practitioner for nearly three decades, playing the game at the highest levels. I've been privileged to serve three presidents, and others who should have been. I've worked in the White House and two cabinet agencies. I've held the top political job in the country. I've managed the most successful presidential campaign since George Washington ran unopposed for a second term. I've helped defeat many good people, in particular House Speaker Tom Foley. I've worked for candidates, like Ross Perot, who could have won but fortunately didn't. I've hurt a lot of people; I've been betrayed by friends; and more than once, I've shot myself in the head.

At the end of the day, like that cool rainy night many years ago when my first career, boxing, ended so abruptly, I ask myself the same question: Was it worth it? As I reflect back on my life as a Kennedy Democrat–turned Reagan Revolutionary, a life that has been so full and has exceeded every expectation, the answer comes with the swiftness of one of my youthful left hooks. Absolutely—but I just wish there weren't so damn much scar tissue on my soul.

ROUND I

SON OF A SHIPYARD

THEY SAY YOU can't go home again. I say: Bullshit. I lived in Washington for twenty years, yet it was never really home. Home was always the shipyard town of Vallejo, California, a scruffy, scrappy, lunch-pail kind of place that has zero tolerance for anyone with pretensions. I left Vallejo in 1965, but I carried it with me everywhere I went. It's in my marrow; there's a piece of it in every drop of blood in my body, and I go home again every time I hear the beat of my heart.

In June of 1982, I went back to the place itself. My old friend John Herrington, the Assistant Secretary of the Navy, invited me to join him on an official inspection tour of the Mare Island Naval Shipyard. As if I needed any encouragement, in a wonderful gesture John arranged for my father, who spent nearly three decades working at Mare Island, to join us for the day. And a great day it was: Of all the memories I have from my years working for Ronald Reagan, I treasure this one the most.

The secretary's party arrived at ten o'clock in the morning, drove across the short drawbridge over the Mare Island Strait, and was met at the main gate by Captain Ernest Scheyder, the base commander. The shipyard had been spruced up for the arrival of a Navy big shot from Washington, but the ganglia of cranes and drydocks, the bustle of new construction, the roar of heavy equipment, and the view of

San Francisco Bay to the south looked precisely the same as it did the first time I'd seen it as a kid.

We began at the administration building, where my father's personnel records had been pulled so we could see the name of every ship he'd help build. Then we were issued hard hats and set off on a tour of a place I knew by heart. We visited a submarine under construction in drydock, then were hosted for lunch at Quarters A, the turn-of-the-century colonial residence of the base commander.

I was embarrassed when Captain Scheyder introduced me as the highest-ranking government official in history to have grown up in Vallejo. I'm sure that several Dominican nuns and a few members of the Vallejo Police Department's juvenile division would have been shocked and surprised by such accolades.

After lunch, our party boarded the nuclear attack submarine USS *Skipjack,* which was being overhauled. Bustling with workmen, the interior was dark, noisy, dusty, and incredibly congested. This must be what it's like to work in a coal mine, I thought. It's what my dad had done for nearly thirty years: wiring submarines. I walked off the sub so much more appreciative of what he'd done for his family—and even more grateful he'd insisted I not follow in his footsteps.

Continuing our tour, we drove by a very familiar sight. I asked the commander if we could detour for a moment and take a look inside the old base gymnasium.

It hadn't changed at all in the two decades since I'd first swaggered through the front door as a streetwise fifteen-year-old. I walked across the basketball court to a corner I knew as well as my parents' home. As I took a few punches at the heavy leather bag, I could hear the voice of my old coach Mike Denton bellowing in my ears: "Keep the jab up, keep the chin down."

When we ended our tour, each member of our party was presented with a handsome mahogany plaque. As usual, my dad got in the last word. "I spent thirty years here," he said. "You spent five hours, and you got a fancier plaque."

But I didn't need a piece of wood to commemorate my visit to this place. As I turned for a final look at the forest of cranes and other maritime equipment that jutted into the clear California sky, I sensed the sort of simple peace you can only feel when you're home. I thought to myself: I live in the nation's capital. I work for the President of the United States. But what really matters is this—my father's home, my home, the place that made me who I am.

BUT BEFORE VALLEJO, there was Boston, the city of my birth. I was born into a blue-collar Irish Catholic household during a snowstorm in 1943. It was March 19, St. Joseph's Day. I was named after my father, who was stationed in the Aleutians and could do no more than register his objections long distance. My mother wanted to keep his name because she was afraid he'd never return, but my father didn't think any kid should be stuck with being called Junior. Unlike the Brahmin strongholds on the other side of town, the rough-and-tumble neighborhood of Roxbury didn't boast many Juniors, Thirds, and Fourths.

Much to the delight of James Francis Henehan, I was the first grandchild on my mother's side of the family. In 1912, at age twenty-two, Big Jim had immigrated to East Boston from County Roscommon, Ireland. He took a job as a streetcar conductor, and three years later married Anna Bridget Timmins, a waitress at a small restaurant along his streetcar route who'd recently emigrated from County Cavan. Eventually they settled in Roxbury and had six children; my mother, Mary Elizabeth, was their eldest. Big Jim, like so many of his friends and neighbors, was a staunch New Deal Democrat and a union man to his core.

My paternal great-grandfather, William Pierce Rollins, was an inventor and a colleague of Thomas Edison. His son Walter—the grandfather I came to know as Pa Rollins—dropped out of school after the third grade and by his teens was one of Boston's first electricians. He was twenty when he married Ellen Jennings, who'd recently arrived from County Roscommon and was a nanny for a wealthy Boston family. My father was the fifth of their eight children, the youngest of four boys. All were trained by their father as electricians, spent summers wiring carnivals throughout the Northeast, and worked in the family electrical business the rest of the year.

My dad was a brawny man who played semi-pro football after high school. He was strong and tough, but underneath that rugged exterior was a gentle and generous nature. He started seeing my mother when he was nineteen. With her flaming red hair and light complexion, she was the most gorgeous woman he'd ever seen. He never dated anyone else.

In February 1939, he joined the First Corps of Cadets, Boston's elite National Guard unit. His outfit got called up on September 16, 1940, and shipped out to Camp Hulen in Texas. Thirteen months later, he and my mom were married during a one-week furlough shortly before his unit deployed to a secret location in the Philippines. And had it not been for a little-known episode in American history, I might not be here to tell this story.

The day after the attack on Pearl Harbor, just after sunset, a squadron of Japanese planes flew off a carrier inland over unprotected airspace near San Francisco. Turning north, they flew over Vallejo and the blacked-out naval installation at Mare Island, the largest submarine base on the West Coast. The planes returned after midnight and again before dawn, but dropped no bombs. The psychological trauma of the incident reverberated all the way to the War Department. Even after Pearl Harbor, nobody dreamed the West Coast of the United States could be in danger from an enemy nation more than five thousand miles away.

My father's antiaircraft battalion was already on its way west by train when the Japanese fighters buzzed the Bay Area. Instead of continuing on to the Pacific, his battalion was diverted to Vallejo to defend against another aerial invasion. A different unit was sent on to the Philippines in its place; when the Japanese captured the Pacific Islands, that replacement unit was virtually annihilated.

My father's battalion stayed on in Vallejo, and in May 1942, my newlywed mother took the train from Boston and joined him. She went to work at Benicia Arsenal, a nearby Army base. But their second honeymoon lasted only three months; in August, after the Japanese bombed Dutch Harbor in Alaska, my father's unit was reassigned to the Aleutian Islands. My mother, pregnant with yours truly, went back to Boston in November 1942 to await my arrival. My father wouldn't return until I was fourteen months old.

As it turned out, there wasn't much fighting in the Aleutians. My dad spent twenty-two frigid months operating a searchlight unit and thinking about sunny California. While stationed in Vallejo, he'd been impressed by what he'd heard about California's educational system, especially the fact that every kid in the state could go to college for free. He made up his mind to return to California as soon as possible.

My father was discharged from the service in 1945, and in August 1947 my parents moved back to Vallejo. I was four years old. It was a courageous move on their part, since my father hadn't lined up a new job or a place to live. He took three weeks' vacation from his job as an electrician with the Boston Edison Company, and bought round-trip train tickets for the three of us. If he couldn't find a job in three weeks, we'd go home. Luckily, he found work immediately as an electrician in the naval shipyard; he never left, and by the time he retired he'd put in thirty-two years of federal service.

My dad worked in New Ship Construction, where they built the submarines. It was dirty, hard work in dark, claustrophobic spaces. The early subs were over four hundred feet long but only fifteen feet wide. The electricians were among the first workers on board after the steel hull was laid, and they worked side by side with the welders, sheetmetal workers, and pipe fitters. He often worked twelve-hour shifts and six- or seven-day weeks—sometimes for thirty days straight. Every bit of overtime he could get was needed for his growing family.

He hardly ever missed a day of work, but the job took its toll. Several years ago, when he was facing heart-bypass surgery, my dad was told by his doctor that he had to quit smoking. In fact, he'd never smoked a cigarette in his life, but thanks to the asbestos used to line the pipes and wiring in the early subs, his lungs were scarred like a six-pack-a-day man.

My dad is a simple, quiet man, blessed with great wisdom. He taught me two great life lessons. The first was humility. "If you're good," he'd say, "you don't have to tell the world about it. If you're no good, all the bragging in the world won't make you good." And from the moment I could talk, he told me to always tell the truth.

"I don't care what you've done," he'd say, "but lying about it is worse. I may punish you if you've done something bad. But you'll *always* get a worse punishment if I catch you lying."

Like all kids, there's a lot of stuff I never told him. But to this day, I've never lied to him. My father felt there was no more important trait in a man than honesty. He's the most ethical and honest man I've ever known, and his judgment and values are very important to me.

Home was a housing project called Federal Terrace, one of several such projects built in Vallejo for civilian workers during the war, when the base swelled with fifty thousand military and civilian employees. The town became quite notorious during this period. In a two-block stretch of Georgia Avenue, the main street adjacent to the shipyard, more than one hundred bars and several whorehouses awaited the men coming off their shifts and the off-duty sailors and Marines.

I loved living in "The Terrace." There was a baseball field across the street, and a half-block away, next to the firehouse with the first television in town, there was a public recreation center with a fully equipped gym. It was there I put on my first pair of boxing gloves and got my first bloody nose.

Even though I came from a family of electricians, my father was bound and determined I was not going to follow him into the family trade or work in the shipyard. I was going to college. That was his dream, but there were many times he must have doubted I could make it come true.

At St. Vincent Ferrer Grammar and High School, I loved to read, and was always placed in the advanced groups. But I was a B student at best. The Dominican nuns rolled their eyes heavenward and told my parents how smart I was—if only I would apply myself. What they didn't know was that I *was* applying myself plenty. It was hard work playing every possible sport, watching as much television as I could sneak in, and studying as little as possible to get by.

My class had a reputation as the worst in St. Vincent's century-old history, and since I was the best schoolyard fighter and fastest runner, I was viewed by the nuns as one of its ringleaders. Even then, I took my role as a class leader seriously. I expressed opinions on matters the nuns thought were none of my business: how they taught, how much homework they assigned, and whether their punishments for bad behavior were appropriate. But the nuns didn't think these were suitable matters for debate, especially not by a student who didn't study, didn't do homework, and wouldn't respond to discipline.

Unfortunately, both my second- and fifth-grade teachers went to meet their Maker while teaching our class. To add to our troubles, one of them had taken sadistic delight in warning us, "If I die, it will be because of you." From then on, we were known as the "Nun Killers."

Our reputation was further tarnished when, in the fourth grade, our class lined up in the first row of the parade route and booed the great war hero Dwight D. Eisenhower, the 1952 Republican candidate for president, who was making a campaign appearance in Vallejo. The nuns were appalled, and those arbitrarily tagged as the culprits each received an F in Deportment for un-Catholic discourtesy. It was my first F and created enormous trauma on the home front. In my family, the nuns were always right. If you were punished at school, you knew you were going to get it again at home. It didn't help that we'd cheered loudly at a similar appearance by Adlai Stevenson a few weeks earlier. I'm convinced the first Republicans I ever met were hidden behind those black-and-white habits.

Meanwhile, our family was expanding: I now had a brother and three sisters, and I took my role as big brother very seriously. The two-bedroom, one-bath apartment at Federal Terrace wasn't adequate for all of us, so my parents scraped and saved enough that, with the help of a GI Bill loan, they were able to buy our first home. It was a brand-new $7,000 three-bedroom, one-bath, flat-roofed tract house on the outer edge of South Vallejo.

It looked like a matchbox, but we were all mighty proud of our new house. It didn't have a ball field across the street or a gym half a block away, but it had hundreds of acres of farmland close by. Some of my fondest boyhood memories are of hiking in the hills every day after school, alone with my dog Duke. San Francisco Bay was just a little over a mile from our house, and I spent many hours every week, sitting on the cliffs overlooking the Carquinez Strait, watching the great tankers come into Standard Oil or the sugar ships arriving at C&H Sugar's big processing plants across the straits. I always thought how wonderful it would be to sail off to Hawaii or beyond. Even then, I was a dreamer and a real loner. From my earliest years, dogs have been some of my closest companions.

My first real interest in politics surfaced in the summer of 1956 during the Democratic Convention in Chicago. I watched the entire proceedings on television, fascinated with John Kennedy's bid to become Stevenson's running mate. As a fellow Boston Irish Catholic, Kennedy was the candidate for me. I was deeply disappointed when he lost out to Estes Kefauver. But the convention hooked me on politics and my new hero: JFK. Over the next four years, I read everything I could about him, and there wasn't a happier kid in Vallejo when he was elected president in 1960. Ironically, a dozen years later I'd be working for the guy Kennedy beat that year: Richard Nixon.

My mother was the best mom a kid could have. Having raised her five siblings from the age of sixteen after the death of their mother, she knew every parenting trick in the book. I was her first child, and we were always very close. My father was an extremely hardworking man, but he always had time for his children. And I can't blame my foul mouth on him; incredibly for a shipyard worker, he never swore, or at least not around me.

Nothing in either of my parent's lives came ahead of their five kids. They were devout Catholics and raised us accordingly. They had great inner strength; they taught us to take care of each other; and they always struck the right balance between love and discipline.

Much later in life, I would work in campaigns where "family values" was used as a potent code phrase, a weapon that could make just about any opponent seem morally deficient. But to me, it was never an abstract or cynical concept. My family—as loving and close-knit as anyone could ask for—gave me all the best values I have.

FOR AS LONG as I can remember, fighting has dominated my life. From ages thirteen to twenty-three, I was an amateur boxer. During those years, I was as disciplined as I've ever been. I thought of myself as a fighter, I acted like a fighter, and I was respected for being a fighter. I won several major West Coast amateur titles and had many offers to turn pro. I never took the plunge, mainly because I knew I wouldn't be able to play college sports if I did.

My first coach was a cop named Andy Myers. Andy ran the police department's juvenile division and had been a great amateur fighter in his day. He saw me win a schoolyard fight in seventh grade and decided to teach me to box. He worked with me for a couple of months, teaching me the fundamentals. I had a terrible temper as a kid, and he taught me to control it. An angry fighter is out of control, he used to tell me, a pushover to beat. From Andy I learned to fight with a cool head.

"Wait for your shot."

"Don't swing back when you're first hurt."

"Be patient and wait for your opening."

Those were Andy's rules, and they worked.

After grammar school, over the intense objections of my parents, who thought I was too young to enter the seminary, I went off to St. Joseph's, a junior seminary at Mountain View, sixty miles south of home not far from San Jose. I stuck it out for a year before returning to Vallejo and St. Vincent's, but it was there that I found my first real boxing coach.

He was a big-hearted Catholic priest who will remain anonymous here because he used to sneak me out of the seminary when I was fourteen and take me to San Francisco for Catholic Youth Organization and Police Athletic League bouts. He'd once been the New York State CYO champion, and he was a great coach. Despite my parents' hopes, the good father wasn't working on my spiritual life as much as my jab. That wonderful priest really got me into boxing, and for better or for worse, the influence of the sport stayed with me a hell of a lot longer than the influence of the seminary.

Back at St. Vincent's, I plunged into high school activities big time. I was starting fullback on the varsity football team, ran the 100- and 220-yard dashes on the track team, and wrestled. I was class president and held a few other offices—none of which means a damn today but seemed terribly important at the time. Because I was an athlete, I didn't drink, smoke, or use drugs. (I'd be surprised if anyone else in the school did drugs, either.) Sex was also taboo, but I can't blame that on sports. The nuns kept those girls pretty well intimidated, and the mere thought of sex was grounds for eternal damnation.

Most important, though, my boxing career started up again under the tutelage of one of the toughest men I've ever known. Mike Denton was a rugged little man then in his sixties, with a body and fists that were still rock hard. He'd come to the States as a young man after a career as a professional boxer in Europe, including a stint as lightweight champion in the twenties. When I met him, he was the athletic director at Mare Island Naval Shipyard and coached all the Navy sports teams. His true love was boxing, and his teams were always championship caliber—well disciplined and superbly conditioned. Mike used to say, "Fights aren't won in the ring; they're won by running hundreds of miles in the early-morning darkness."

I was introduced to Denton when one of my classmates whose father was a Navy captain invited me to work out at the Mare Island gym. Watching me pound the heavy bag, Mike decided he saw great promise, and offered to coach me. I was fifteen, and never had a tougher taskmaster, before or since.

With Coach Denton, you did it his way or you didn't play. I'd been boxing for about two years and was undefeated in twenty bouts when I began to train alongside the sailors and Marines who fought on his teams. Even though I was only a sophomore in high school, Mike would make me spar with the toughest guys he could find. I tried never to show it, but when you're still just a kid, fighting guys ten years older than yourself is damn intimidating. The service guys pulled no punches. In fact, they tried to knock me around a little more than usual so no one would rag them about fighting a kid. Over time, my confidence and skills grew. After a while, nobody screwed with the kid any more.

One day, Mike asked if I could go over to the naval station at Treasure Island that night and box with the team. His middleweight had gotten hurt in a shipboard accident, and he wanted to sneak me in just this once to fight for the Navy.

On the ride over, we thought up an alias for me. That night, Eddie O'Hara was in the ring with the toughest guy I'd ever fought. I got the daylights kicked out of me the first two rounds. Back in my corner, Mike said, "I'm proud of you, kid, but you're losing." The news came as no surprise.

"Listen, the only way you can win is to knock this guy out. If you don't think you can do it, just tie him up and try not to get hurt. But if you think you can hold out for three more minutes—and if you want to win—work his body for the first part of the round." My head was beginning to clear, and I hung on Mike's every word.

"When he starts to bring his hands down to protect his body, go to the head." The bell sounded, and I got to my feet.

I followed Mike's instructions to the letter. When my opponent dropped his hands late in the round, I got lucky and landed a killer shot that put him down. I jumped on him as soon as he got up and sent him down again. The referee stopped the fight. So began my naval boxing career.

It wasn't until the drive home that Mike informed me the sailor I'd just beaten was the Twelfth Naval District defending champion and had been the runner-up in the Pacific Fleet championships. I was ten feet off the ground. The other guys on the team were all over me with congrats. One of them started calling me "The Sandman"— " 'Cuz when you hits 'em, kid, they goes to sleep."

Mike was careful to use me sparingly. If he got caught boxing a high school kid, it would have cost him his job. In those days, California law said you couldn't fight until eighteen.

The Mare Island team fought other military teams, college teams from California and Nevada, and prison teams from Folsom, San Quentin, and Vacaville. Mike let me fight the college boys, as he called them, and occasionally in the prisons. Of course, there weren't any traveling squads out of San Quentin, so we fought inside the walls. One of my worst experiences as a boxer was a bout at the Vacaville state facility for the mentally insane. I didn't like going to the prisons and especially didn't like Vacaville, where Charlie Manson and other wackos are incarcerated. One night, my nutcase opponent broke out into a weird, goofy laugh every time I hit him. He scared the hell out of me, so I tried to finish him off fast. After I smashed him with a really good right, he started grinning, spit out his mouthpiece, jumped me, and bit my shoulder. The ref and my corner guys pulled him away and stopped it, but I had deep bite marks on my shoulder. I found out later he was in for murdering his ex-wife and her lover. No more prisons, I told Mike on the way home. To this day, I can't drive through Vacaville without thinking about that crazy bastard who bit me like a dog.

In my senior year, I hurt my back playing football and couldn't train like before. Mike thought I wasn't training hard enough. In fairness to him, he probably didn't know the extent of my injuries. But I wasn't willing to take his constant riding any longer.

By now, I'd been honing my boxing technique on the mean streets of Vallejo. I was muscular, strong, and fast, but I wasn't a big kid and didn't look intimidating. For several years the local kids knew my reputation or had seen me box, so they wanted no part of me. But there were always plenty of service guys, out-of-towners, and drunks.

Every few weeks, a new group of Marines would arrive for sixteen weeks of combat training. Fresh from basic training at Parris Island, South Carolina, these kids were always looking for opportunities to test their new skills on the townies, and we were only too willing to oblige. Nearly every weekend, a brawl could be had for the asking. Unlike today, where every punk kid over the age of fourteen has a gun or switchblade, the boys and men of Vallejo fought with their fists. You could get hurt badly, but you didn't get killed. Every so often somebody would pull a chain or knife, but a gun was rare. I never started a fight, but I never walked away from one, either. And once I got into one, I fought to win.

I guess I still do: More than twenty-five years later, for instance, I was working in the White House for Don Regan, the crusty chief of staff and ex-Marine officer. One day he said to me, "The problem with you, Rollins, is you weren't a Marine. A little Marine training would have taught you to follow orders."

Convinced my job was to give counsel to the president, not follow orders blindly, I arrogantly replied, "Don, when I was in high school, I made a career out of kicking the shit out of Marines. I trained *them.*" I don't think he ever forgave me.

Mike Denton taught me two invaluable lessons, in the ring and out. Number one: "The guy who lands the first good punch usually wins." To help me be that guy, he taught me to throw a left hook. Executed well, the left hook is the most deadly punch there is. It's especially valuable when some idiot tries to hit you with a lead overhand right. The counter left hook will always beat him to the punch.

Number two: "Every fighter gets knocked down. A bad fighter doesn't get up. A good fighter jumps right back up and starts swinging. A great fighter gets up on one knee, takes an eight count, clears his head, thinks about what he's going to do next, then stands up and starts fighting again with a plan to survive."

Old Mike's been dead for a number of years now, but his advice has always stood me in good stead.

AFTER LEAVING MIKE, I started training under Johnny Murray, who owned Vallejo's only boxing gym. Johnny was a wiry, craggy-faced guy, a former pro boxer who looked like he'd taken every punch thrown at him square in the face. He managed a number of professional fighters around the Bay Area, and from the moment I turned eighteen, Johnny was hot for me to turn pro. He was convinced he could groom me into a serious professional and make lots of money for both of us. I kept resisting. I was thinking about what Mike Denton had said to me: "Kid, stay in school, go to college. This sport, no matter how good you are, always leads to a dead end. Fight for a while and then get out before you get hurt. No matter how good you are, there's always someone in that next gym or that next town who's tougher than you are." Besides, I knew it would break my mother's heart.

Johnny said I had three things going for me: I was a heavy puncher; I could take a beating; and I was white. To his mind, the last was my greatest asset. There weren't many good white boxers at the time, and promoters believed white fighters were a bigger draw. They don't admit it, but they're still looking for the Great White Hope.

If Mike Denton showed me the clean side of the sport, Johnny Murray exposed me to its dark side. His gym was across from the old city hall and police station, in the basement of a ramshackle office building. It was little more than a sixteen- by sixteen-foot ring in a furnace room, which always made it hotter than hell. The heavy aroma of sweat permeated the air, whether anyone was working out or not. It had a heavy bag and a few speed bags, but nothing like you'd find in a modern gym today. Except for the cops who worked out there after their shifts, I usually had the place to myself.

Even though I wouldn't turn pro, Johnny still fought me for money. To keep my amateur status, he paid me under the table. He'd book me every couple of weeks into private smokers, and I'd earn a couple of hundred bucks to fight some ex-pro or some up-and-coming local hotshot. Gambling was the main entertainment of the evening; thousands of dollars were bet illegally on the fights.

I fought in rented halls all around the Bay Area: Richmond, Oakland, San Jose. The crowds were small, drunk, and rowdy, and bouts were longer than my three-round amateur contests. Most were four rounds of three minutes each, and the main event was usually six to eight rounds. The gloves were smaller and the referees let it get a little rougher than usual. They weren't inclined to stop a fight over blood or technicalities until one man was out. The length of the round didn't always matter: When two guys were really going at it, the bell never seemed to ring until the action stopped.

One day, after I'd won five or six of these matches by knockout, Johnny was sitting next to me in the steambath after a workout. Smelling of booze as he always did, he said, "You know, kid, you could make a lot more money if you'd go down in one of these fights and not get up."

I was now fighting main events, and big bets were laid on my winning. In other words, if I took a dive, gamblers in the know could make a lot of dough.

I blew up and called him every name in the book. I came very close to punching his lights out. He told me to calm down and think about it. He claimed he could probably get me a thousand bucks, a small fortune to a nineteen-year-old kid. I told him to go fuck himself, and stayed away from the gym a few weeks. When I came back, the incident was never mentioned again by either of us, but he started charging me $15 a month to work out. There were never more than two or three guys in there at a time, so I figured Johnny needed the dough. I also quit doing the smokers for a while and just fought regular amateur cards.

A few months later, Johnny's gym burned to the ground. The firefighters said it was arson. They also told me it was strange no equipment was found inside the gym after the fire. Nobody was ever charged, but I never saw Johnny again. I went back to Mike Denton, and he accepted me like a prodigal son.

I learned a hell of a lot about life from boxing. It taught me how to live with fear. I can't imagine many things more fearful than climbing into a ring to face a man whose sole goal is to hurt you. Every time I sat in a locker room waiting for a bout, I felt that rush of fear. But no matter how often I asked myself what I was doing there, no matter how often I told myself I hated the fucking sport, I always went into the ring ready to fight.

It also taught me to live with pain. I've fought on after being knocked semiconscious. I've kept on fighting when my nose was broken, my eye was swollen closed or gashed open, or my mouth was full of my own blood. I've dragged myself to the shower not knowing whether I'd won or lost, or anything that happened in the last round.

Boxing taught me a lot about people. When you fight a man, you develop a relationship unlike any other. You either hate him or respect him, but a bond develops that's deep and shared. It's elementary: When two men face off against each other, armed with nothing more than a pair of eight- to ten-ounce gloves, rubber mouthpiece, and a protective cup, the last thing they think about is education, race, religion, or nationality. What they *do* think about is how tough the other bastard is and how hard can he hit. You learn to watch men's faces. You look for pain or fear in their eyes. You watch their nostrils and mouths for signs they're gasping for breath. You look for energy or despair within the scars and creases of their faces, because that can spell the difference between defeat or victory.

I also learned that quitting is never an option. Before a fight, you always think you can lose or be seriously hurt. But you also know you can win. No matter how often I swore the next fight would be my last, the chance of winning kept me coming back for more. Because when it's over and you've won, there's no greater thrill.

I scored a lot of knockouts in my day, and as barbaric as it seems to me today, I know that hitting someone and knocking them down gives me a rush unlike anything I've ever experienced. That magic moment when you know you've won a campaign comes close to that rush, but it's a shared experience and it's fleeting. The next day your candidate goes off to govern and you look for the next challenge. But a victory in the ring, or in the street or a bar, is something else, and yours alone.

So are the defeats. I won over 160 fights in my boxing career, but they're all a blur: the faces, the arenas, the towns all forgotten. But I remember every detail—every punch, every pain, every mistake—of my two losses. With politics, I vividly remember both the victories and the defeats, but I tend to replay the campaigns I've lost, especially the close ones.

Most days I feel older than my biological age. A nose broken six times, five concussions, numerous shattered bones in my hands and fingers, too many stitches to count, and a stroke brought on by a boxing injury to my carotid artery over a quarter century ago are the physical tolls of my career. It's been more than twenty-five years since my last bout, and I certainly don't have a fighter's body anymore. But I still have a fighter's heart. My love-hate relationship with boxing molded me, toughened me, and made me a survivor. Mike Denton's school of hard knocks was the basic training for the big leagues of American politics.

ANY DREAMS I had of going off to a brand-name college on a sports scholarship collapsed in the third football game of my senior year. I was the starting fullback, and we were on the way to an undefeated season. I was trying to spin out of a tackle when a linebacker planted his helmet square in the middle of my back.

I knew I was hurt bad, but when you're young and stupid, you think you're indestructible. I played the rest of the season with three broken vertebrae in my lower spine and two protruding disks. Despite severe back and leg pains, I played five more games shot up with Novocain and cortisone. My brother Michael, with whom I shared a room, pulled my legs out of bed, stood me up each morning, and helped dress me. This was early training for his future career in nursing.

The first of the six back operations I've had in my life was performed the day after I graduated from high school in 1961. While my classmates went off to the beach, I began the longest and most miserable summer of my life, flat on my back in Kaiser Hospital. The first operation gave me no relief from constant pain, so I had a second surgery in September. Instead of starting college, I spent the next several months in the hospital and recuperating at home, immobilized in a body cast from my neck to knees, while my weight dropped from 175 to 135. After I was discharged, I wore a full steel and leather brace for another year.

My orthopedic surgeon told me I'd never play sports again and should be damn grateful I could still walk. I was determined to prove him wrong. Going away to school was a dream I had to postpone. I enrolled at the local junior college a year behind my class and started the long process of rebuilding myself physically and emotionally. I had a third operation eighteen months later, and three more in later life. But giving up sports was never an option for me. Two days after coming home from the hospital after my first operation, my mother came home from work and caught me lifting weights in the garage. The pain and anger in her Irish eyes is something I'll never forget.

I was active in student government in junior college and became student body president my sophomore year. I belonged to the Greek Letter Society, a small fraternity of thirty guys that included Tug McGraw, the All-Star major league relief pitcher and World Series hero, and Sylvester "Sly" Stewart, better known as the lead singer of Sly and the Family Stone. It was 1964, and I was having a hell of a lot better time than so many of my friends who were shipped off to Vietnam to fight a war nobody understood.

I was a war supporter. Hell, it was easy for me. Because of my back, I had a medical deferment. I was pretty upset when I flunked my Selective Service physical, scotching any plans I had to enlist in the Marines. But in hindsight, being a Marine grunt in those days was a one-way ticket to the toughest fighting in Vietnam, and I'm sure I was blessed in not having to go. Still, I felt guilty being in college playing sports when my friends were going off to Vietnam. Back home, a lot of boys were getting drafted. Most of the folks in Vallejo supported the war. How could you not in a Navy town where almost everyone's father was building Polaris submarines armed with nuclear missiles? If the president and those smart guys back in Washington said we needed to be there, then by God, we needed to be there.

Travis Air Force Base in nearby Fairfield was a major staging area for troops and equipment going to Vietnam. Each week, thousands of troops would fly out of Travis for Saigon, and hundreds of body bags would come back. The coffins would be stacked up on the runway to be sent on for burial. There always seemed to be a picture of those coffins in the Friday edition of the *Vallejo Times Herald*, along with the body count of how many kids and Viet Cong had died that week.

The war *really* came home to me when one of my fraternity brothers, Fred Frome, also from Boston, flunked out and was drafted. Fred was my drinking buddy, and a bigger screw-off never lived. It was bad enough to be drafted, but Fred was drafted into the Marines. After his basic training, I was an usher in his wedding. Seven months later, I was one of his pallbearers. Fred actually got shot twice in the same day. After the first time, they patched him up and sent him back into battle to die that afternoon. The first set of Marines came to his mother's house to tell her he'd been wounded. Three hours later, another set came to tell her he was dead.

In 1965, after completing my associate degree at Vallejo Junior College, I transferred to San Jose State. I'd been offered a boxing scholarship there when I was in high school. San Jose State had one of the best programs in the country in the fifties but had dropped boxing in 1960 after one of its fighters killed his opponent at the NCAA championships. Many other colleges followed suit. I thought I could play football, and San Jose State was still a good place to get an education.

Because of my back injury, I flunked the football physical. So, after one semester, I transferred to California State University at Chico, which still had a boxing team. It was one of the best moves I've ever made in my life. Chico was a wonderful place to go to school. I loved the small town in the northern part of the state. The campus was beautiful—and it was the friendliest environment I've ever experienced.

And it was *some* party school. As a matter of fact, *Playboy* magazine has picked it as one of the top party schools in the country for three decades now. I did my part by reading *Playboy* every month and partying like hell whenever the opportunity arose. I certainly recognized there's a lot more to college than parties and sports. It's just what I did better than anything else.

Chico was where I found myself, and the man who had the greatest influence on me was a professor named Willie Simmons, who became my mentor, coach, and special friend. Willie was a small, sinewy Irishman from Providence, Rhode Island, who headed up the phys. ed. department and was the varsity boxing coach. He had a doctorate in education, but woe to anyone who called him Dr. Simmons. To students and faculty alike, he was just Willie.

My first week on campus, I went to see him about boxing on his team. He remembered that I'd fought for the Navy against one of his kids several years earlier. After I laid out my boxing career, he told me I had too much experience for the college level. After the 1960 tragedy, kids who'd fought in the Golden Gloves or had more than a few fights weren't allowed to compete against less experienced college boxers. But Willie asked me to help him coach the team. It was a troubled time for me. I was still struggling with the aftermath of the back injuries, and unsure of my future. Willie settled me down, focused my energies, and made me believe in myself. He was more surrogate father than coach.

I can never repay him for all he did for me. He trained me for my last fight, and ironically he was the guy who brought my career to an inglorious end by throwing in the towel.

In the fall of 1966, I decided to resume competitive boxing. Helping Willie coach reminded me just how much I missed the fight game. My back was fully healed now, and I'd finished most of my course work for graduation. My goal was to make the 1968 Olympic team. I'd been fighting at near-Olympic caliber when I'd stopped. I thought I had a legitimate shot.

I also needed to exorcise a demon. In my last fight in 1964, I missed a punch at the end of the second round and threw out my back. At the end of the one-minute rest period, I couldn't get up from my stool. The referee took one look at me and stopped the fight. I'd won the first two rounds on points, but the fight went into the record books as a TKO. My opponent was the defending 178-pound national champion, and he went on to make the Olympic team. I went on to another back operation. My last fight had been my first and only loss. I didn't want to go out a loser.

Under Willie's watchful eye, I plunged into the most grueling training regimen of my career. For six months, I ran three to four miles every morning before sunlight and did it again every evening. I spent a good three hours a day in the gym pounding the bags and sparring. I lost fifteen pounds, and didn't have a drink the entire six months.

By February 1967, I was ready. Willie entered me in the Pacific Coast AAU championships. Because of my previous experience, I was seeded into the open middleweight semifinals. It was Valentine's Day. But what I did that night was no game for lovers.

It was the worst mismatch of my career. My body was ready, but my psyche wasn't. My opponent was a tall left-hander, who for three years had been the national collegiate champion and was on his way to becoming the national amateur champ. In the first exchange of the fight, I caught my thumb on his elbow and broke my right hand. Against a left-hander, the right is crucial. I could barely defend myself the rest of the way. But like all fighters who don't know when to quit, I wanted to fight on. I was still convinced I could finish the fight on my feet and if lucky take him out with one good shot, the way Mike Denton had taught me.

That's not the way it happened. Almost from the opening bell, I was little more than a punching bag, knocked into the ropes repeatedly and battered unmercifully in my corner. Willie stopped the fight in the second round. My boxing career was over.

The two-and-a-half-hour ride back to Chico was the longest of my life. We stopped in my old hometown to grab a quick dinner at Terry's, the late-night hangout off Interstate 80. By the time I got there, I was burning up with fever and sweating profusely.

By the time our food arrived, so had the all-too-familiar signs of a concussion: screaming headache, nausea, blurred vision, white flashes. I excused myself to begin the vomiting I knew would continue for several hours. I went out to the car and lay down in the back seat. Willie wanted to take me to the nearest hospital. I couldn't stand the thought of ending my career in a Vallejo hospital where word would quickly spread among my friends. I also didn't want my parents to know I was fighting again.

"No way," I barked through my pain. "Get me to Chico."

I was admitted late that night to Enloe Community Hospital in Chico with a severe concussion, broken right hand, broken thumb, and the most serious injury of all, shattered pride.

The next morning, the neurosurgeon told me another shot to the head could be life-threatening and my days of contact sports were finished. But I knew that already. As we'd driven north through the darkness the night before, I realized Willie had been right to stop the fight. I was furious with him when he did it. I knew I was hurt, but I thought he'd panicked. Now I realized I would never fight again. I was nearly twenty-four years old, about to graduate from college with a degree in political science. It was time for another focus in my life—a new passion that would turn out to be just as cruel and fickle a master.

LIKE MOST INSTITUTIONS of higher learning, Chico State had its share of characters on the faculty. One of them, Ben Franklin, was my favorite professor. A crusty old bastard, Ben was a dyed-in-the-wool FDR liberal, and one of the founders of Americans for Democratic Action. Ben would start his political science class each semester by asking students their political persuasion. First he'd ask if there were any Republicans, and would suggest they drop his class because they'd probably flunk anyway. He then made everyone else define what kind of Democrat they were. Pat Brown Democrats could expect C's. Alan Cranston Democrats could expect B's. And Jess Unruh Democrats could expect to ace the course. At the time, I was still a Democrat, and even though I was never sure if he really meant it, having already taken one of Ben's classes, I knew enough to define myself as an Unruh Democrat.

Chico State had a first-rate political science department headed by Jim Gregg, who'd been the education adviser to Governor Pat Brown. Gregg developed a special internship program for Chico State students in the state legislature that was superb.

I can't remember whether it was Ben Franklin or Jim Gregg who got me my internship with Jess Unruh, the legendary Speaker of the state assembly. I started in 1967, working three days a week for the better part of my last two college years. I did what all gofers do— clipping, speechwriting, constituent mail, and occasionally traveling with the boss.

Jesse "Big Daddy" Unruh was a genuine piece of work. He weighed nearly 300 pounds. His robust appetites for food, liquor, fancy clothes, money, and most of all women are still the stuff of legend in Sacramento. And he was able to indulge those vices to the fullest in his position as the most powerful assembly Speaker in California history. He was one of the most mesmerizing figures I've ever known in politics.

Jess was elected to the assembly on his third try in 1954. Only seven years later, at the tender age of thirty-nine, he was selected assembly Speaker, second only in power to the governor.

Unruh's creed of governing was deceptively simple. "Every man has a price," he loved to bellow. "For some men it's booze. For some men it's money. For others it's women.

"Every so often, you find one that's different. They can drink your booze, take your money, fuck your women, and then vote their conscience. But my secret is to make their conscience say, 'I better do what old Jess wants.' Those are the ones you can't buy for any price, but you can usually rent them for a while. You, young man, have to decide whether you're going to be for rent or for sale."

The life-style of a California legislator in the sixties was wild and freewheeling. It wasn't bad being a legislative staffer, either. Unruh had almost unlimited power as Speaker, and he used and abused it for good and ill alike. He sponsored the most far-reaching civil rights package in state history. He transformed the legislature into a full-time body with huge permanent staffs and made it the most professional and effective in the country.

On the other hand, Jess manipulated the spoils system with the gusto of a Tammany Hall boss. Early on, he figured out how to tap into the largesse of what was known as the legislature's "Third House"—the lobbyists. Before long, the special interests learned that the price for not doing Jess's bidding was too horrible to contemplate. To an unprecedented degree, Unruh controlled campaign contributions from lobbyists, and that allowed him to pick and choose who got to run for office. Many of Unruh's lieutenants, for example, were former aides elected to the assembly from districts in which they never lived. Once in office, they eagerly did his bidding.

It was an exhilarating time for me, my first real taste of political power. It was also disillusioning. I'd expected all the legislators I worked around to be serious, bright, and principled. In fact, most had the same foibles as the jocks and frat boys I knew at Chico State. Getting drunk and chasing broads was an agenda pursued as relentlessly as any piece of legislation. On any given day, the priority of many legislators was seeing how many naked women they could entice into the Speaker's shower. I was young and impressionable, filled with the idealism of youth, and the personal excesses of Sacramento bothered me. It was the beginning of a cynicism that would steadily grow over the next quarter century.

One of the more valuable truths I learned from Jess Unruh is that good deeds are often the products of less than perfect people. Whatever the motivation or the morality behind them, the good deeds stand. And who the hell am I to judge anyone else's morals? Those quickest to condemn, I've learned, are often the greatest hypocrites of all.

More than anything else, Jess Unruh tutored me in the game—how it's really played, and how you win it. In later life, Unruh liked to brag that he'd made every good legislator in the Capitol and trained every good Democratic political operative in the state. He'd even done his bit for Affirmative Action, he liked to add, by training the only good Republican operative in the state—me.

Another important thing Jess did for me was to get me involved in Robert Kennedy's 1968 presidential campaign. Unruh was a Kennedy guy through and through. He'd been the Southern California chairman for Jack Kennedy in 1960, and was Bobby's state chairman during the 1968 primaries. Unruh's political machine was crucial to Bobby's chances. Without it, even a president as unpopular as Lyndon Johnson would have crushed him in California. Jess got me started as a part-time campus coordinator in the winter of 1968. When I finished school in early May, I went to work full time as a Northern California operative.

I met Robert Kennedy a week before the primary election, which was the first Tuesday in June. He was coming to San Francisco and had asked to visit Hunters Point, a housing project near the airport. His advisers thought his time could be better spent elsewhere; most of the residents didn't vote, and he already had the ones who did. Bobby didn't care. His campaign was about people and their problems, and he wanted to hear about their lives firsthand.

I met him in a small office at the project being used as a holding room. He was rail-thin, and had the Kennedy hair and features. But there was something else—an energy that radiated from his tired and bloodshot eyes.

Over a brown-bag lunch, he asked me how the college kids would vote. I reassured him that he had great support on the campuses; the only problem, I said, was that it was hard to tell with school out how many kids would actually vote. He was very direct in reply.

"I need those kids," he told me. "I can't win without them. I know you'll help me get them."

He asked where I'd gone to school, and what it was like there. As he left, I said to myself, This man really cares about me. I'm sure everyone he ever met felt the same way. It was an unforgettable encounter with a vibrant and passionate man. I left there that day absolutely determined to work harder than ever—and to get those college kids to turn out.

On election day, I was working on getting out the vote in the Bay Area. Unruh had invited me to the victory celebration at the Ambassador Hotel in Los Angeles and a private party afterwards at a nightclub called The Factory. My field boss vetoed the idea. There would be plenty of time to celebrate later, he told me.

An hour after the polls closed at 8:00 P.M., I hit the road north for Chico. I stopped in Vallejo to get a quick dinner at Terry's and catch some election returns. One newscast was predicting Bobby would beat Gene McCarthy by a margin of 46 to 42 percent and was also projecting he'd win the South Dakota primary. I was ecstatic. The California winner-take-all primary would give Kennedy 198 delegates and a huge psychological advantage. The next big test was New York, where he'd surely do well as an incumbent senator. We're going to do it, I told myself. We're going to win this thing.

I decided against spending the night with my parents and got back on the road to Chico. Somewhere on a back road shortly after midnight, I listened to Bobby's victory speech live from the Ambassador. Among the last words I heard were these: "I think we can end the divisions within the United States, the violence."

I switched the dial to a music station. Ten minutes later, a bulletin cut in with the news that Bobby Kennedy had been shot. The announcer said he'd been critically wounded in the head. I pulled over to the side of the road and sobbed uncontrollably for what seemed like an hour. I drove the rest of the way to Chico in a daze, pulled into a bar near campus, and drank myself into oblivion.

The television was blaring special reports. Sirhan Sirhan, the assassin, had been captured by former Olympic decathlon champion Rafer Johnson and Roosevelt Grier, an all-pro defensive lineman for the Los Angeles Rams, who had been Bobby's personal bodyguard during the campaign. In one of the crowd scenes I saw Jess Unruh leaning over his friend, who was bleeding profusely from a head wound. Then I saw shots of the police dragging Sirhan out of the hotel past inflamed spectators.

"Kill the bastard," I screamed at the television. The next day's newspaper accounts reported that one man in authority had yelled at the cops, "I want him alive. I want him alive." The man whose words helped calm the mob was Speaker Unruh. My own anger masked a sorrow as deep as any I've ever felt in my life. It was as though someone in my own family had been struck down.

Robert Francis Kennedy held on to life for another 25 hours and 27 minutes. He died at 1:44 A.M. on June 6, 1968. Had he lived, he surely would have altered America profoundly for the better. Had he won the presidency, I almost certainly would never have become a Republican.

Sixteen years later, I sat next to Roosevelt Grier on Air Force One during the closing days of Ronald Reagan's 1984 campaign. Rosey was now an ordained minister and antidrug crusader. I was Reagan's campaign manager; he was the national co-chairman of Democrats for Reagan. At one point, I told him my first presidential primary had been Bobby's; he seemed surprised at first, then talked freely about what Bobby had meant to him.

As we recalled one of the worst nights of our lives, he said, simply: "Will you bow your head with me and say a prayer for Bobby's soul?" For a silent minute, two Kennedy Democrats prayed for Robert Kennedy aboard Ronald Reagan's presidential aircraft.

ROUND 2

A TALE OF TWO CULTURES

I GRADUATED FROM Chico State in the spring of 1968 at the age of twenty-five with a degree in political science and a feeling it was time to get on with my life. Boxing was history. My Olympic aspirations were in the ash can. I was unemployed and broke. I'd spent six years going to college and getting my back repaired. The time for soaring with the eagles had come and gone.

I spent the summer marking time as an assistant to the college president and plotting career moves. Unruh's people had promised me a job, but they couldn't do anything for me until after the November elections.

Lyndon Johnson had bowed out of another term, saying he had a war to win and couldn't stop to campaign for reelection. When the dust cleared after Bobby Kennedy's assassination and the Democratic Convention debacle in Chicago, Richard Nixon was duking it out with Hubert Humphrey. It was anybody's guess who'd end up in Washington, and how much that would affect the outcome in Sacramento.

The best path for me in the meantime, I decided, was to angle for a Civil Service job. I took and passed two highly competitive entrance exams, which got me on an "eligible and qualified" list circulated throughout the state. If a legislative job didn't come through, I figured I'd latch onto something as an assistant city manager or junior bureaucrat somewhere.

In August, the state offered me a position as a budget analyst in Sacramento. I knew nothing about budgets, but my academic adviser told me that mastering the numbers was power. Besides, it was the best offer on the table and might lead to something better. I saw it as a ticket inside the tent, nothing else. I reported for work in September, and hated every boring second of it. I counted the days until the election, when I hoped Big Daddy would deliver me from purgatory.

It never happened. Nixon's 220,000-vote margin over Humphrey in California provided just enough of a coattail to screw me over. Republicans won a razor-thin 41–39 majority in the state assembly, and pulled even in the state Senate. With Republican Lieutenant Governor Bob Finch breaking the 20–20 tie, the GOP controlled Sacramento for the first time in decades. Ronald Reagan was ending his second year as governor, and I'd discovered that I liked the man and his message more than I'd expected. The legendary Jess Unruh was now *former* Speaker of the assembly, stripped of his elegant office and virtually all of his patronage. Thanks to the voters of California, not to mention an unpopular war and an even more unpopular outgoing Democratic president, I was frozen at square one in a dead-end job that was driving me nuts.

Shortly after the election, I interviewed for an assistant city manager's job in Eureka and was offered the post. I went over to the Capitol to say farewell to Unruh and his staffers. As I was leaving his far less palatial new office, I noticed a familiar name on the doorway directly across the hall: Assemblyman Ray Johnson, R-Chico, Rules Committee. I decided to drop in and say hello.

Each of the eighty assembly offices had a different size and shape, reflecting the occupant's importance. This suite was a good deal larger than most. Only the Speaker wielded more power than the seven-person Rules Committee, which had life-and-death power over all the staff and perks of the legislature.

I walked across the thick carpeted reception area into Johnson's sumptuous private office. It must have been twenty feet square, its mahogany paneled walls covered with awards and grip-and-grin photos of the assemblyman with the high and mighty, including the new president and Governor Ronald Reagan. Floor-to-ceiling windows looked out over Capitol Park. A massive desk dominated the room: crafted of a rich dark wood inlaid with hand-tooled forest green leather, it was one of only eighty such desks in the world, for members of the California State Assembly. The whole room looked and smelled of power. To any visitor, its ambience expressed the clout of its proprietor.

Sitting in a matching leather chair behind the desk was a tall, gray-haired man in his mid-fifties, who had a stern, serious look on his face but greeted me warmly.

I'd met Assemblyman Johnson when I was student body president at Chico State and trying to get an ROTC unit onto campus. Yes, I know, getting ROTC *off* campus was what most college kids were doing back then. But sitting out the war was gnawing at my gut, and inviting the military to Chico was my way of assuaging my noncombatant's guilt. I felt I was cheating the system. Thousands of young men were being drafted to fight and die, and I was free to box and play sports, thanks to my medical deferment. In my heart, I knew I could serve in some capacity, and I felt like a hypocrite.

At a time when antiwar demonstrations were ripping college campuses apart, ROTC programs were a prime target. As it happened, Chico State didn't have an ROTC unit—or many antiwar protesters, either. I figured that if all those other schools didn't want ROTC, I'd try to get one for us.

Assemblyman Johnson heard about my proposal and offered to help. His son was a helicopter pilot who'd just volunteered for his third tour of duty in Vietnam. We met in the student government office on campus and war-gamed a strategy to persuade the Army to come to Chico. In the end, the Army decided to hunker down and chose not to expand ROTC anywhere.

Nevertheless, I got something else out of the whole experience that came in handy later. I was appointed chairman of a joint committee of student body presidents and faculty chairmen at state schools, which put together a report on campus unrest for the governor and legislature.

It all seemed like a very long time ago as we sat reminiscing in the green leather chairs facing his desk. He asked me what I was going to do with my life. I told him about the Eureka offer. He said that seemed like a sensible course under the circumstances, wished me well, and asked me to stay in touch.

Later that day, my receptionist came in and excitedly announced, "There's an assemblyman on the phone!" In the insular world of Sacramento, legislators were pretty important people and didn't call state offices very often. It was Johnson, and he wanted me to come back over and have a drink after work. To my shock and amazement, he offered me a job as his administrative assistant.

"Mr. Johnson," I said, "I'm very flattered. But I'm a Democrat and you're a pretty conservative Republican."

"Ed, I've always liked you, and I trust you. I checked you out with Unruh after you left here today and he gave you high marks. Recommended you very highly. Besides, I also think you're a lot more conservative than you think." Johnson knew how to read me better than I read myself. Lobbying for an ROTC unit when most kids my age were trying to run them out of town must have sent him a message loud and clear.

"All I ask is loyalty. You can argue with me on any issue behind these doors, but once my decision is made, you've got to remember, I'm the guy that got elected and I'm the one with the vote."

It didn't take a rocket scientist to realize that a priceless opportunity had just been dropped into my lap. I slept on it, but in the morning I still couldn't see a downside. I was back in the ring again.

Johnson's staff consisted of three people: a receptionist, an executive secretary, and me. As the administrative assistant, I was the chief of staff, legislative aide, press secretary, and official surrogate. I drafted bills, attended committee meetings, and stood in for Johnson at functions back home. I got a crash course in how government really works. It was exhilarating.

College had been great fun, but now I was learning *and* partying, and I didn't have to study. Sacramento was a wild and wonderful place for a bachelor. I met a lot of interesting women, and more than a few interesting men. My best pal during those days was Bob White, assistant to the freshman member from San Diego, Pete Wilson. He was Johnson's office neighbor and I liked him instinctively—he was easygoing, with an open style and progressive ideology. Now Pete's governor of California and Bob's his chief of staff. They're among my oldest political friends.

Sacramento was a more bipartisan place then. The new Speaker, Bob Monagan, was fairly progressive by Republican standards. In the spirit of accommodation, Monagan decided to retain several of Jess Unruh's staffers because he needed their institutional expertise and believed they were professional enough to place the common good over partisan interests. One of these holdovers was Congressman Vic Fazio, now the number-three Democratic leader in the House.

In the days before lobbying reform and spending limits, you didn't spend a lot on food or entertainment when you worked for the California legislature. On scores of occasions, when I was having lunch or dinner with a date at one of the favorite legislative watering holes like Fat's or Posy's, the check never came. Some lobbyist at the bar would simply put it on his tab. If I wanted to go to Lake Tahoe for gambling and a show, tickets and complimentary hotel rooms were always available. Nevada lived in fear that legalized gambling would take business across the border someday, so the gambling interests spent a small fortune schmoozing anyone even remotely connected to the legislative process.

Ray Johnson was the best possible mentor, and like Jess Unruh, he taught me that in politics, things are never just black and white. Johnson's money and power had come out of Chico. He'd been in the tree and nursery business and owned a lot of land adjoining his orchards on the edge of town. As Chico expanded, the price of land skyrocketed, and with it Johnson's wealth and power in the community. He started out with several years on the school board, then was elected to the assembly. Before retiring, he would be a state senator.

He was one of the finest men I've ever known, in or out of politics. He was a religious man, who began each workday with a prayer in the office. He cared deeply about his family and his community, and lived an exemplary life in every respect. He was wonderful to me. His son and I shared the same birthday, and I always felt he considered me a surrogate son. He even looked and talked a lot like Jimmy Stewart.

One morning early in my tenure with him, Johnson met with three businessmen and their chief lobbyist. Johnson was the senior member on the Agriculture Committee, and they were pleading their case on a major agricultural issue to be decided soon. One of them handed him an envelope.

"A little something for your campaign," he smiled.

Johnson opened the envelope, and his face flushed with anger. Inside was a small wad of crisp hundred-dollar bills, more than enough to cover my salary for a month. He threw the cash at the lobbyists.

"You know better!" he stormed in that Jimmy Stewart voice. "I've never taken a dime from you, and I never will. I was with you on this issue anyway, and now you've insulted me. Get the hell out of my office!" As he escorted them out, he said to Dorothy Kaney, his longtime executive secretary, "Make sure it's a cold day in hell before you let these guys into my office again."

When he'd cooled down, we had a talk.

"Do you know why they offered me that money? Republicans are now the majority around here. But the lobbyists are going to find out that the Republicans are not for sale." Then he set his jaw and said to me firmly, "And, Ed, neither are their staffs. I don't care if somebody buys you a drink or lunch or dinner. But always remember, if they can't get to me, they'll try to get to you. Don't do anything that I wouldn't do." It was not for nothing that they called him "Mr. Integrity" throughout his political life.

But as the game changed, lobbying techniques also changed, and lobbyists worked to find a new way to get to him.

Ray had introduced a bill to change the way counties could tax mobile homes. At the time, there were no property taxes on mobile homes, just a modest vehicle tax. It made no sense; they were homes, not vehicles. A county in our district had asked Johnson to sponsor a bill allowing it to tax the permanent trailers like houses.

The mobile-home-park industry's fixer was a veteran Sacramento lobbyist named Kent Redwine. He also represented the movie lobby. Shortly after I'd researched and helped draft a bill that had merit, Ray and his wife, Loraine, were invited to the 1969 Academy Awards ceremony, dinner, and ball, courtesy of Redwine. It was always one of the toughest tickets in the state. The movie lobby flew the Johnsons down to Los Angeles. They couldn't stop talking about their good fortune for days afterwards.

A few days later, Redwine stopped by to talk about the mobile-home bill. After he left, Ray walked into my office.

"Ed, that bill's got some problems in it," he said. "I think we ought to pull it from committee and study it for a while. Maybe we can fix it up for next year."

I was so shocked that I couldn't find the presence of mind to argue. Was this the same man who'd turned down cash for his vote? I remembered what Jess Unruh had told me when I was his intern: "Every so often, you find one that's different. . . . Those are the ones you can't buy for any price," he'd said, that big belly heaving with laughter. "But you can usually rent them for a while."

Ray Johnson, Mr. Integrity, had his price. I still respect him as much as anyone I've ever known in politics, but I think he rented out for two tickets to the Oscars and probably didn't even realize it. I found myself wondering if *I* had a price, and whether I'd know it when the time came.

UNFORTUNATELY FOR JOHNSON and his Republican colleagues, Governor Reagan's hope of pushing through a new agenda based on restoring fiscal integrity to state government had run into trouble early. The narrow margin in both houses meant a single Republican defection could be fatal. Ironically, it was the new president, a son of California, who toppled the house of cards.

Predictably, Nixon turned to his native state to populate his new administration. One of his first cabinet appointments was Lieutenant Governor Bob Finch, his longtime friend and former administrative assistant, who was named Secretary of Health, Education and Welfare. Until Reagan named a new lieutenant governor to break tie votes, his agenda stalled in the state Senate. Then Finch stole away Jack Veneman, an extremely able member of the assembly, to be his undersecretary. When another Republican member died in April, Reagan lost his majority. Special elections to fill those seats took away much of the focus of that year.

Matters were further complicated by lingering mistrust between the governor and his own legislative troops, most of whom hadn't supported him when he ran for governor in 1966. Neither side was ever able to make peace with the other. In November 1970, the Democrats would recapture both houses, relegating the Republicans to the back benches for decades to come. In the end, Reagan's dreams for a Republican Revolution were thwarted by his own party.

Even as far back as 1968, I realized that an important battle had been lost. I began to discover that much of what I believed in fit Reagan's brand of conservatism. I was an old-fashioned Democrat on most social issues, and still am on some. But the more I learned about the inner workings of state government, the more I became a fiscal conservative. In Sacramento, I saw millions of dollars being wasted on pork-barrel projects, legislative boondoggles, and special tax breaks for the privileged. Like all middle-class taxpayers, I knew my taxes were too damn high. Now I understood why. Reagan wanted to balance the state budget, which when he took over was spending $1 million a day it didn't have. It made perfect sense to me. By the time he left office in 1974, the state budget had a $550 million surplus.

Like Reagan, I'd always been a believer in a strong national defense. It wasn't just that I'd grown up in a town whose primary industry was building nuclear missile submarines with nuclear-tipped ballistic missiles. I was genuinely worried about the Red Menace, and believed the United States should be a bulwark against Communism. On the home front, I applauded Reagan's hard line against student protesters on state campuses, particularly at Berkeley. True, I was a Democrat, like my father and his father before him. Gradually, however, I came to realize that whatever I called myself, my core values weren't that far from Republican thinking.

In June 1969, Dr. John Whiteley, the vice chancellor of Washington University in St. Louis, called me with a job offer. He wanted me to run a new program designed to introduce students to urban problems, and to teach one of the courses. The job didn't come exactly out of the blue. I'd met Whiteley a year earlier when he'd interviewed for the dean of students' job at Chico. He knew I'd chaired the joint committee on student unrest and been active in campus government during my college years. He was intrigued by my blue-collar background and thought I could bring something special to his new program.

Whiteley was a psychologist and protégé of B. F. Skinner, the celebrated Harvard behaviorist. John became a good friend, but Skinner would have been proud of his pupil's snow job to entice me to say yes. He promised me free tuition to law school and a rent-free apartment on campus. He offered me more money than I was making in Sacramento, and threw in two season tickets on the forty-yard line for St. Louis Cardinals games.

My gut instinct was overwhelmingly negative. I loved Sacramento, loved politics, and hated academics. Why go teach at a university two thousand miles away, in a town where I didn't know a soul?

On a practical level, the offer had more appeal. A law degree would help my career, especially one from a school as prestigious as Washington University. I'd also concluded that while I liked what I was doing, my job was a bit of a dead end. I didn't want to spend the rest of my career living on reflected power and bouncing from one staff job to another. I already knew I never wanted to run for office myself. I would never subject myself to the phony life members had to live. I would never tolerate the kind of trashing I'd seen candidates take. I knew my talent was in functioning behind the scenes.

In the end, it was the job Whiteley offered that turned me on. The Danforth Foundation had given the university a grant for an innovative urban studies program. Ten percent of the freshman class, about one hundred kids a year, would follow a different curriculum that would expose them to inner-city culture. They'd study black writers for freshman English and the development of St. Louis for their American History course, then be force-fed subjects like health care delivery to the poor, public housing, education, and the criminal justice system in urban cities. They'd be put into real-life situations radically different from anything they'd ever experienced. The idea wasn't to create more urban studies majors, but to take kids and show them a part of life alien to most of them.

The program appealed to my Democratic social conscience. Maybe I *could* make a difference with these kids. After kicking it around for a couple of weeks, I called Whiteley back and told him I'd be in St. Louis for the fall semester. I didn't realize it at the time, of course, but this decision turned out to be the first in a series of high-risk ventures for me. I was walking away from a safe and secure situation and into something unknown. I wasn't a surfer, but I believed in their code: Jump on the wildest wave out there, and see where it takes you.

As MY GREEN Camaro Rally Sport raced across the Great Salt Lake Desert, I felt like I could slam-dunk any challenges stupid enough to get in my way. The big Chevy V-8 engine was cruising along at 80 miles per hour, pulling a six-foot U-Haul trailer. The car was my first purchase as a college graduate, a treat to myself for finally finishing school.

Everything I owned was in that trailer. A big stereo, color television, my clothes, and books. I was driving two thousand miles east to a city I'd visited only once before in my life, to interview for the job I was about to begin.

I'd been driving for nearly ten hours now, but my mind was still racing. I wasn't really certain this made any sense. I reflected back on my last year in Sacramento. I'd learned so much about people, much of it dispiriting. Yet even the disappointments, born of my naivete, were valuable lessons. In one year of real work, I'd absorbed volumes more than I had in any classrooms. I'd seen the reality of politics, as opposed to the textbook version.

My three-day journey ended with the final mile through Forest Park, site of the 1904 World's Fair. Finally, I caught sight of the castle, the university landmark. From a distance, its entrance looked like a medieval fortress built of ancient bricks. The university itself had been the venue for the 1904 Olympics.

It wasn't until I walked up the front steps to the administration building that I realized how inadequate I felt. Here I was, walking into one of the better universities in the country, armed with nothing more than a bachelor's degree from a state college and a few years of street smarts. I was going to be teaching in a school I couldn't have gotten into as a student. I've never felt less prepared for anything in my life.

I quickly learned that the rough and tumble of statehouse politics were foreplay compared to academic politics. Moreover, as the antiwar movement built to a crescendo in the late sixties and early seventies, there was no more chaotic place to be than a university campus. To top it off, there aren't many places in America hotter or more humid than St. Louis in the summer, or as arctic in the winter.

I soon discovered that Whiteley had glossed over several particulars of what he'd described as my personal nirvana. In fact, I'd been had. The law school was a full-time day program; I was a full-time employee. My free tuition was worthless. The free apartment turned out to be the remodeled first-floor lounge of Beaumont Hall, an all-freshman men's dormitory. It had every comfort of home except a kitchen, which meant I had to eat three meals a day in the cafeteria with two thousand kids. I was also under constant surveillance by 150 horny teenagers checking in at all hours of the day and night to see if I was getting laid. When they weren't looking in my windows, they were banging on my door wanting to talk or watch television. Except for the preppies, who'd obviously spent their summers at flute camp or playing Little League polo, the rest of them had never been away from their mommies.

I'd lived off-campus at Chico because dorm life had no appeal to me. My Sacramento roommate wasn't thrilled about the new digs, either. Sampson, my 200-pound, eighteen-month-old St. Bernard, was not about to be cooped up in a dorm room all day. Every morning, I'd let him out and he'd wander the campus to his heart's content. The only problem was that Sampson constantly invited himself into the cafeteria and took his meals with the kids, to the dismay of the old bag who ran the food service. In the year I ate there, I lost ten pounds and Sampson gained forty.

Many's the night I sat in my fish bowl of a room asking myself, What the hell am I doing here? Washington U. was different from any place I'd ever been. And that may have been a lot of my problem.

The fact is, Chico State and Washington U. could have faced off in the Super Bowl of Culture Clash. All they had in common were their enrollments—under ten thousand students. My classmates came from working-class backgrounds, and most had gone to California public schools. For the vast majority, Chico was their first and only choice, and like me they were thrilled to be there. Half the student body played intramural sports, and athletic events were heavily attended. In every respect, Chico was Normal U.

Washington, on the other hand, drew students from all over the country. Many of them were preppies from wealthy families, and it was not everyone's first choice. Despite a ranking in the top two dozen schools in the country, it was the backup choice for Ivy League rejects. A spirit of failure hung over the place. The kids never seemed happy to me. Nobody went to Washington Bears athletic events—a big crowd was five hundred for football, one hundred for basketball. Instead, they spent their weekends in the dorms, studying for exams they were sure they would fail. Mind you, there was plenty of screwing around and smoking dope—it was the sixties, after all—but no one seemed to be having any fun. It was clear to me that the social environment needed serious remedial work.

I was in a marginally suitable position to do something about that in my thankless capacity as a member of both the Office of Student Affairs (OSA) and the Council of Masters, an eight-member faculty body that supervised dorm life. (Only in academia could you get away with such a bullshit title.) Looking back, I spent a lot more time and energy—and shed a hell of a lot more blood, sweat, and tears— on the extracurricular lives of my charges than I did in the classroom.

As the only male on the OSA staff, the fraternities were my assignment. I wasn't a frat man myself, so all the Greek gobbledygook seemed dopey to me. I was supposed to visit a different frat house every night of the week for a meeting or dinner. I established a new tradition: Forget it. Instead, I dropped by each house and told them I'd let them know if I ever wanted another invite. That was more than okay with them, too.

What wasn't okay was their pledge policy. All the houses were lily-white and Christian, which clearly didn't reflect the campus population. They claimed black and Jewish students weren't interested in joining and never pledged. I knew that was crap. I told each fraternity that the next time I visited I wanted to see some cultural and religious diversity, or else. The "or else" was that the university owned the houses and could evict them on my recommendation.

They all hollered to their national headquarters and demanded I be removed. I was hoping for a compromise: The administration would open up the fraternities, then fire me as a consolation prize for the kids. I got half a loaf; the fraternities had to stop discriminating, and I stayed in the miserable job.

Just to keep things surrealistic, a group of black students came to see me a few weeks after my arrival. They wanted their own dorm: blacks only.

"Excuse me, ladies and gentlemen," I said, "but haven't we just spent about two hundred years getting schools like this one to integrate the dorms?"

As a compromise, I agreed to turn over one student lounge for their exclusive use, but they weren't pleased. I thought to myself, I'm trying to make the frat boys integrate their segregated fraternities while the black kids want to segregate their integrated dorms. What the hell am I doing here?

THE EVENTS THAT would profoundly change my personal philosophy occurred a few months after I arrived. Like many other American campuses, Washington U. erupted in turmoil in the spring of 1970. Our disturbances started a little earlier, and not over such weighty issues as the war in Vietnam or the plight of the urban poor, but the reinstatement of curfews in the girls' dorms. My fellow Masters and I found ourselves at ground zero when the campus blew up.

When I arrived, a twenty-four-hour open-house policy was in effect. Boys were in and out of girls' rooms all hours of the day and night, and nonstudents prowled the halls at will. The local drug lords were selling dope on campus to a regular clientele. Local police came on campus only if called by the university. The campus police force was useless, a handful of unarmed guys in blue blazers who patrolled the sprawling campus with one police cruiser and three unmarked bicycles.

Two of my council colleagues, John Duvall and Julius Hunter, were my principal comrades in arms. We all came from working-class backgrounds, and none of us had graduate degrees. J.D. was a Washington U. grad who'd been working on a doctorate before he got bored and gave it up. Julius was a graduate of Harris Teachers College in St. Louis, a predominantly black state school where he'd been the student body president. He'd been an advertising executive in Chicago before returning to run the student volunteerism program at Washington U.

Concerned that the situation in the dorms was getting out of hand, the council voted to reinstate visiting hours early in the 1970 spring semester. My recollection is that the new rules were still pretty lenient: guys out by 1:00 A.M. on school nights and 4:00 A.M. on weekends. But the little brats went batshit. Nightly protests bordered on small riots. You'd have thought we cut off their air, water, and birth-control pills. Soon the local gendarmes were called to hose down the mob. That in turn set off other protests. I always wondered why kids with 1,300 SAT scores couldn't come up with a better slogan than "Pigs Off Campus." Before long, the faculty joined the outcry against the police presence.

The dorm exercise was just a tuneup. As the protests got bigger, the issues shifted, and eventually Washington U. was swept up into the tide of a national antiwar movement. After a while, cops marching onto campus shadowed by TV camera crews became part of the daily ritual. Classes were canceled left and right, which just gave the students more time with nothing to do.

When the library closed at 10:00 P.M., a large group of protesters usually gathered in some university building. J.D., Julius, and I were the designated university representatives at such gatherings.

The self-appointed ringleaders would decide what to protest that night. The menu ranged from the new dorm hours to bad cafeteria food and sloppy janitorial work. Then they'd move on to more pressing global issues like allowing Red China into the United Nations or letting Castro's Cuba live free. In the end, it always shifted back to the war in Vietnam, and the rhetoric would get more heated.

The first item of debate each evening was a vote on whether to throw Julius, J.D., and me out of the hall so they could carry on their enlightened discourse without the campus pigs, as we were so affectionately called. I'd carefully explain that they *couldn't* throw us out because we were in charge. That never stopped them from taking a vote that was always about 585–0 in favor of throwing us out. This was usually followed by twenty minutes of debate about what shits all administrators were, particularly us. They'd ask us to leave voluntarily and we'd tell them to go screw themselves. Then they'd debate whether advocates of nonviolence could resort to violence and physically throw us out. I was always hoping they'd try. I was twenty-six, still in great shape, and only a few years past my boxing prime. Most of these kids had plenty more A's on their high school transcripts, but there were a lot more K.O.'s on mine.

After about two weeks of their threats, on a night when the crowd was really getting ugly and pushy, I took up a position with my back to a wall (a technique I'd perfected as a bar-room brawler in Vallejo) as they surrounded the three of us. In a loud voice, I reminded them *I'd* taken no pledges of nonviolence. I said that any little shits who laid a hand on me were going to have to explain to their mothers what had happened to the perfectly capped white teeth their parents had spent ten grand getting straightened, which were now missing. I added that when they finished that explanation, they could start the longer one of why they'd been expelled from college. That in turn would be excellent practice for the even longer explanation they'd soon have to make to their local draft board entitled, "Since I'm no longer in college, why shouldn't I go to Vietnam and fight for my country?" I said I also knew I spoke for my two companions, Mr. Hunter and Mr. Duvall. The logic of my arguments carried the night. After that, they ignored us and held no more votes on our presence.

The students usually left the hall about 1:00 A.M., then marched to Chancellor Thomas H. Eliot's house, where they'd yell in unison, "Fuck you, Tom Eliot," and other pithy phrases. That lasted until old Tom woke from his slumber, stuck his head out a second-story window, and yelled back, "Fuck *you,* you little bastards, and get your asses back to the dorms." Then he'd call our boss, the vice chancellor, and demand to know why we allowed the little bastards to be out so late. Undaunted, the kids would march to the ROTC building and throw rocks at the windows before turning in for the night.

Any administrator who behaved like that in the current era of political correctness would be looking for work, but Tom Eliot was a crusty old bird and didn't take a lot of crap. A wonderful man in his late sixties, Tom was a die-hard liberal, a former Boston congressman who went on to be part of Franklin D. Roosevelt's Brain Trust. He was a cousin of T. S. Eliot, the famous poet, whose grandfather had founded the school back in 1853. Tom couldn't understand what was happening to his beloved campus, and he definitely couldn't fathom the new breed of students. He was retiring at the end of the year because these "damned kids" were driving him crazy.

During this period of lunacy, he and his wife were walking across campus late one February evening when one of the protesters threw a rock through a library window. The library was a frequent target because it had been named after John Olin of Olin Chemical Corporation, which made chemicals being used in Vietnam. Old Tom ran after the perpetrator and made a beautiful open-field tackle, then sat on the kid's chest until the campus cops arrived. I think it was one of his proudest moments.

J.D. and I lost Julius around this time. The local television stations were on the campus every day looking for stories. One station interviewed Julius and was so impressed they offered him a job. Amazingly, St. Louis had never had a black television correspondent, despite its large minority population. He later became the city's first black anchorman and remains today—twenty-six years later—one of the top-rated newscasters and a local hero.

I missed him terribly. Julius was my drinking buddy. Every afternoon around four o'clock, we'd have a few belts to fortify us for the long night ahead. After a while, we escalated to pints. I'd drink scotch, Julius would down Jack Daniel's. The thought of going through the student revolution half-sober scared the hell out of me. J.D. wasn't much of a drinker, and I was never one to drink alone.

By mid-February, matters started getting bigger and uglier. A student informer told us the protesters were plotting to take over the administration building and occupy Eliot's office. I sat through one of the most absurd meetings in my life as the chancellor's staff and the deans planned what to do. One of the deans wanted to let them have the building. "When they get tired, they'll go back home," he assured us. His only concern was protecting student records, and he suggested we move them out in the afternoon. Other faculty officials were equally lenient. "If we treat them like children," somebody said, "after a while they'll get bored."

I was the hard-liner. "The moment they break down the door, we arrest the little bastards," I argued, "just like you would if they were breaking into a home across the street from campus." I said I'd seen all this before in California, and if we gave in, they'd be emboldened.

If we cracked down like Governor Reagan had, we could bring it to a quick stop. I was speaking to the deaf and dumb. Only Eliot agreed, but he was reluctant to bring the police on campus before a break-in.

That night, February 23, all hell broke loose. The students took over the administration building and trashed Eliot's office. They busted a bunch of windows in the library and tried to torch the ROTC building.

That did it for old Tom Eliot. He ordered university lawyers into circuit court the next day to get a restraining order forbidding students to assemble to disrupt or plan to disrupt the peace of the campus. Every student was served a copy. At our regular evening love-ins, J.D., I, or the campus police chief would recite the order and tell the gathering they had ten minutes to disperse before being held in contempt of court. Photographers would then shoot the crowd for evidence. When the students didn't disperse, the ringleaders were identified by the pictures and hauled into court the next day. The judge would then find them in contempt and lock them up immediately. A number of them got a whole new appreciation of how tough the jails in St. Louis County were, and how much the regular inmates enjoyed their campus visitors. It wasn't long before our homegrown revolution came to a roaring halt.

At the same time, Attorney General John Mitchell ordered the FBI to investigate the attempted arson at the ROTC building. The campus was soon crawling with federal agents. There were so many of them that we organized a Faculty-Feds softball game that spring— won by the G-Men, as I remember it. They didn't drink and got stronger in the later innings. Much to my delight, their presence had a chilling effect, and relative calm settled over the campus. By then, I'd turned into a card-carrying reactionary. I'd come to St. Louis thinking I could do some good for these kids. Now I told myself what they really needed was a strong dose of corporal punishment and a haircut.

THE CAMPUS WAS blessedly quiet for a few weeks, but then Richard Nixon bombed Cambodia and the Ohio National Guard killed four students at Kent State University. Those sparks ignited protests that were far more incendiary. This time, thousands of students and many faculty members joined in. The nightly ten o'clock assembly was now held outside because the crowds wouldn't fit in any campus building other than the field house. The ranks were swelled by curiosity seekers and students from nearby campuses. The throw-the-pigs-out threats had escalated to a point that J.D. and I had police escorts.

On May 4, 1970, one of the Chicago Seven defendants visited our campus. He spoke to a crowd at the football stadium estimated at five to eight thousand people. Too bad home games didn't draw as many fans. Inflamed by his rhetoric, they marched down Euclid Street to the ROTC complex. The mob storming down that street scared the living shit out of me. J.D. and I both knew violence was coming and there wasn't a damn thing we could do about it. My thoughts were very basic: I hope nobody gets killed. Especially me. And the fucking cops better get here quick.

The mob smashed every window in the place. Several students broke down the doors and swarmed through the main building, turning over file cabinets. Then, in an image I'll never forget, I saw red cans and a bright flash. I was maybe ten or fifteen feet from the entrance—close enough to smell the gas and identify the perpetrators.

Suddenly, an explosion ripped through the building. The heat and smoke drove me back. The roar of the fire and the screams of the crowd were deafening. In moments, the fire was blazing out of control, tongues of flames shooting from every window.

The blare of police and fire sirens seemed to come from every direction. As they converged on the scene, the students in the street blocked their approach and threw rocks at the firefighters. The fury on the faces of the mob, which is what the kids had now become, was as menacing as anything I've ever seen. Gathered on a small hill adjacent to the scene, demonstrators were pelting the police and firemen with rocks and bottles. As fast as the cops cleared a path for the fire trucks, the students cut their water hoses with knives. Out of nowhere, two kids raced up to the firefighter nearest the flames. One of them flung a rock, smashing him in the groin. He went down instantly, screaming in pain, but still trying to hold his hose on the blaze. As he lay writhing, the other little creep struck him in the head with a rock. Then both of them kicked him as he lay defenseless. The high-pressure hose sprayed wildly out of control, sending a torrent of water into the crowd. I went after them, but they disappeared into the mob. I grabbed the fireman and dragged him back from the edge of the blaze as the rocks and bottles flew. He was bleeding from a head wound. After we loaded him in an ambulance, J.D. and I searched the crowd in vain for the two gutless rock throwers. If I could have found the little bastards, I would have beaten the crap out of them.

For the next several hours, the blaze raged out of control. By morning, the entire ROTC complex had burned to the ground. The games were over for me and my charges. Early that morning, Duvall and I reported to the chancellor. Eliot had had enough: Those kids were terrorists and he wanted them in jail. He ordered us to cooperate fully with the police. "Get the little bastards out of here and send them home," he said.

As I walked out, a department head in social sciences ran up to me and started screaming. "You incited them, you made them do this," he shrieked. "You could have stopped it before now. You made my students do this!" The inmates were taking over this asylum. I lost my cool and grabbed him by the lapels. I don't remember what I said, but I kept telling myself, Don't hit him, don't hit him. Fortunately, Duvall and a couple of others pulled me off.

I was nearly ready to say fuck it and go back to Sacramento. But I couldn't leave; I had to stick around for the investigations and trials that would surely follow. Duvall and I had been subpoenaed by a federal grand jury. We argued with the U.S. attorney that we'd never be able to work with students again if we testified against them in court. But he told us we had no choice. If we refused, he'd get a judge to hold us in contempt of court and throw *us* in jail.

In the end, seven students were indicted for destruction of federal property in a time of national emergency. All were charged with felonies. Five were convicted and sentenced to terms of varying lengths in federal prison. Duvall and I were the principal witnesses.

When I saw those kids in court, I couldn't believe how young they looked. Dressed in suits and ties and all cleaned up, shorn of their stringy hair and scraggly beards, they looked like ordinary college students. Seeing the anguish on their parents' faces day after day in court was heartbreaking. They thought they'd turned their children over to us to teach and care for them, not to make criminals of them. After more than six months of nightly demonstrations, I thought I knew these kids. At some point, they'd become my enemies. But it wasn't that simple anymore.

We'd all been caught up in something really ugly. I knew as well as anyone how a mob mentality can distort emotions and actions. I'd been ready to smash in teeth, and even heads, on more than one occasion. I'd almost done it to a tenured professor the day after the fire, and I still shudder to think what I would have done if I'd found the punks who stoned the firefighter.

But these kids were still wrong, and they'd done great harm. There was no way to rationalize torching buildings. They had put lives in jeopardy in the name of anarchy. And now they were facing the consequences. The whole thing left a bitterness in my mouth I can taste to this day.

It had been the worst year of my life. I'd come to St. Louis to teach, and ended up being a campus cop. For the first time in my life, I questioned my entire value system. I'd been scared and insecure before. I'd made my share of mistakes, God knows. I'd done things I wasn't proud of. But I'd never wondered who I was or what I believed. Suddenly, I wasn't sure. More adrift than I could ever remember, I began a relationship with a cute little Delta stewardess, drank a lot of scotch, and quit going to church. I ran the urban program for one more year, quit teaching, and ran the student affairs office full time. I resigned in December 1971, effective at the end of the school year, and spent the last six months learning to play golf with Dick Martin, the football coach.

By the end of my first year at Washington U., I thought the students and faculty were all pretty much head cases. A year later, I was beginning to ask myself, How can *everybody* here be screwed up? Maybe I'm the one who's weird. By the end of my third year, I decided I definitely wasn't crazy and maybe some of them were okay too, but it was their place and not mine.

My sojourn in St. Louis was a three-year detour in the road at that point in my life. Nothing I did there advanced my career. I've never taught or played golf since, though reports occasionally surface that I still drink a little scotch.

On the other hand, I learned that I could play in the big leagues. I loved Chico State, but Stanford it wasn't. Washington U. was my first real exposure to the ivory tower world of education. I came away convinced I could deal with anyone on the same intellectual level.

And there's no question it was a defining experience. My evolution from Kennedy Democrat to Reagan Republican may have begun in the halls of Sacramento, but that journey was completed during my years as an underpaid, overworked, and generally bummed-out college administrator and professor in St. Louis.

I didn't set foot on the campus again for twenty years. By coincidence, the first of the 1992 presidential debates was held in the spanking-new gym on October 11. I'd been hired as a commentator for CBS television. I called my old pals, and we planned a reunion. Julius Hunter was the news anchor for KMOV, the CBS affiliate in St. Louis. John Duvall drove up from Lexington, Kentucky, where he was president and general manager of the NBC affiliate. It was quite a reunion.

The campus was as pretty as ever, the castle still as imposing. On this visit, however, it all seemed utterly normal. The basketball program had been revived and was drawing overflow crowds to a new gymnasium. The kids were fresh scrubbed, well dressed, and looked like they were having fun. I doubt more than a handful of them knew a thing about the turmoil that had consumed my years there and transformed my political convictions.

As I arrived at the gym to begin prepping for the debate, a bittersweet wave washed over me. Like a phoenix, the gym rose over the burnt-out grounds of the old ROTC building. Soon I'd be watching the three contenders for the most powerful office on earth debate the great issues of the day on the very spot where I'd stood nearly twenty-three years earlier, dodging rocks and bottles. The more things change, I thought, the more they stay the same.

ROUND 3

LEARNING THE TRADE

I RETURNED TO California in June of 1972 humbler, wiser, and, for the first time since college, unemployed. When I'd left for St. Louis, my hot 1968 Camaro was a statement. I arrived back in Sacramento in a used 1968 Volkswagen Bug. A car was now just transportation. I was hoping that wasn't a metaphor for the state of my career.

Originally, I'd intended to find work running some assembly races for Republicans in the fall, hoping that would lead back to a job in the legislature. Before heading west, I'd talked to Bob Monagan, the former assembly Speaker and now the minority leader. He said he'd find me something somewhere. As it turned out, he was true to his word. By July 1, I was working for Richard Nixon's reelection campaign. In my family, this was equivalent to the Pope becoming a fourth-degree Mason.

I'd been a Kennedy man, and to Kennedy Democrats, Richard Nixon was the devil incarnate. True, I was now comfortable with the California Republicans. I knew and trusted them. I'd even voted for Ronald Reagan by absentee ballot when he ran for his second term as governor in 1970. Particularly because of the way he'd stuck it to the campus radicals, I admired the man.

But Nixon was another story. Still, he had one great thing going for him: He wasn't George McGovern. McGovern was way off the radar screen as far as I was concerned, and if the Democrats were hellbent on nominating a peacenik, they would have to do it without my support.

Governor Reagan was Nixon's state chairman, and Bob Monagan was a co-chairman. Monagan, whom I'd known from my previous tour in Sacramento, was responsible for all of Northern and Central California, including the critical swing area of the Central Valley, where close California elections are always decided. The majority of the voters in that vast region—stretching almost three hundred miles from Sacramento to Bakersfield—are Democrats, but very conservative. Monagan wanted me to work the Central Valley.

I didn't have to think about the offer for long. Bob Monagan was one of the best people I've ever met in politics. He was a prince of a human being. If everyone in government were as honest and decent, voters would feel a hell of a lot better about their government these days.

Bob had grown up in Vallejo like me, went to College of the Pacific in Stockton on a basketball scholarship, and had stayed in the community after graduation. He worked for the local congressman, became mayor of Tracy, and was elected to the assembly in 1960. He quickly became the Republican leader, and was Speaker from 1969 to 1971, succeeding Jess Unruh. If it weren't for him, my political career would have been over before it started. He befriended me, taught me how to think strategically, and was one of my most important mentors. Now he was giving my political career a jumpstart after the three-year idle in St. Louis.

I rented an apartment in Stockton, which was roughly in the center of my area of operations. After being away for three years, I needed to reregister to vote in California. I walked into the county registrar's office in Stockton one morning and asked for the paperwork.

I knew I wasn't a Democrat any longer, but I wasn't sure I was a full-fledged Republican yet, either. As I pondered registering as an independent, the county clerk, who'd seen my picture in the paper as the local Nixon guy, decided the issue for me.

"I guess I don't have to ask *you* what party you want," she said, marking me down as a newly registered Republican. The die was cast. It's a move I've never regretted.

My father felt differently. When I told him I was organizing the San Joaquin Valley for Nixon, he couldn't believe it.

Despite being a lifelong Democrat, he'd voted for Nixon against Helen Gahagan Douglas in the 1950 Senate race. He believed Nixon when he said she was a Communist sympathizer. When the truth came out after the election that she'd been framed, my dad never forgave Nixon for one of the worst smear campaigns in the history of American politics. Now, his son was trying to elect Tricky Dick President of the United States. It caused one of the most heated arguments he and I ever had.

If I could work for Nixon, my dad said with disgust, I'd obviously abandoned my roots in St. Louis, along with my faith and my sanity. He didn't think Nixon was an honest man. "He fooled me once," he vowed, "but he won't fool me again."

There's never been a presidential campaign like Nixon's 1972 effort, and there will never be another like it. It was far and away the most expensive and wasteful campaign in American history. McGovern was so far out on the left wing that Nixon could have beaten him with a handful of yard signs. But he wanted the biggest victory ever to assure his place in history. He got half his wish. His election margin fell short of the record, but he did assure his place in history—as the first American president to resign the office.

The abuses of that campaign spawned the Federal Elections Commission, public campaign funding, and spending limits on presidential races—not to mention a bunch of overeager White House and campaign aides who added "convicted felon" and "unindicted co-conspirator" to their résumés. The irony of it all is that Nixon could have beaten anybody. His vast financial resources and huge organization could have been used to help other Republicans win, giving the nation a new Republican majority. Instead, he gave us Watergate.

The operation was run from Washington, top down, by a bunch of guys who'd never been near a campaign. CREEP was the preferred acronym, used by friends and foes alike. As a field operative, I quickly learned that the job requirements at CREEP (Committee to Reelect the President) national headquarters consisted of a total lack of campaign experience, zero common sense, and a knack for irritating even the most loyal Nixon supporters and staffers by being a total asshole.

The campaign did have some first-rate operatives at the field level, but they were hamstrung by CREEP's insistence that everything be dictated from Washington. The truth is, presidential elections are a series of state elections held under a national banner. Other than national media advertising and scheduling the candidate, everything else should be delegated to the state level.

Despite CREEP's best efforts, California was pretty much an independent fiefdom. That was a tribute to the man who ran the California operation, Franklyn C. Nofziger.

Lyn is a character straight out of Damon Runyon. He dresses like the newsman he once was—poorly. Buttoning a shirt at the neck is obviously against his religion. He convened a meeting once by tossing his sports jacket in the general direction of a chair. When it sailed past, Lyn left it crumpled on the floor for the next two hours. His humor is irrepressible, and his puns are the stuff of legend. He's utterly irreverent and totally incorrigible, but his puckish wit and mild manner mask a steel-trap mind and first-rate political skills. Lyn makes the best friend in all the world—and absolutely the worst enemy.

Lyn had worked as a White House aide in the first Nixon term, and was deputy chairman of the Republican National Committee under Senator Bob Dole before returning to California to head up the Nixon effort. After college, he'd started out as a reporter for the Copley newspaper chain, and in 1965 was hired as campaign press secretary for Ronald Reagan's first gubernatorial race. Lyn was absolutely devoted to Reagan, and he and the future president became very close. He once asked Reagan why he hired a press secretary before anyone else in the campaign.

"Everyone knows that in the movies the first person any actor hires is his press agent," Reagan replied. "Lyn, you're my press agent." Lyn became far more—a confidant, humorist, and counsellor whose instincts Reagan could trust. I've never known anyone more loyal to Ronald Reagan than Lyn Nofziger.

After Reagan's election, Lyn became director of communications in Sacramento, a fancy title for press secretary, and he was one of the key players during the first two years. Despite his Reagan connection, President-elect Nixon was smart enough to know he needed Lyn on his White House team.

When Nixon asked Reagan to chair his California reelection effort, Reagan tapped Lyn to run the show. There was a lot of suspicion between Nixon's California mafia and the Reagan people. The one guy trusted by both sides was Nofziger. He'd developed a reputation as an honest broker, and would be loyal to both men.

Nixon was always nervous about California, even though it was his home state. He'd been elected to two terms in the House and one in the Senate, before going on to be Eisenhower's vice president for two terms. He'd never tasted defeat in California until he lost the presidency in 1960. Hoping for political redemption in 1962, Nixon ran for governor but was abandoned by his own, who reelected Edmund G. ("Pat") Brown. It was a kick in the groin he never forgot or forgave. Stung by this rejection, he moved to New York in 1963 to begin his long climb back.

Now he was president, but California belonged to Reagan. Nixon knew he needed California, and he needed Reagan. What he didn't know was whether Reagan needed him. Nixon was morbidly fascinated by Reagan, who was everything he desperately wanted to be and wasn't: handsome, articulate, charming, and, most of all, able to communicate on television. Reagan was the conservative version of the man who'd defeated Nixon in 1960 and under whose shadow he would always stand: John F. Kennedy.

Like Jess Unruh, Nixon had to control anyone he needed. But Reagan needed no one, except for Nancy. And he had his finger on the pulse of California.

I got my first taste of the Nixon staff mentality during the 1972 campaign. To them, locals were yokels. A few weeks after I'd started working for Lyn, I had a run-in with the CREEP crowd over a fund-raiser we'd proposed for the Fresno area. It was Democrat territory and they had never voted for a Republican presidential candidate. That's the sort of thing locals know.

Nixon did very little campaigning himself. Instead, CREEP had an elaborate surrogate program, deploying cabinet members and the Nixon family as the stars. They were going to send one of the Nixon daughters out for the Fresno event, and they wanted to draw a thousand people at $100 a person.

A campaign advance guy showed up from Washington one day and demanded a progress report on the fundraiser. I tried to explain the demographic realities of Central California to this blockhead, but he wasn't interested. I figured that the only way to get his attention was with a wisecrack.

"We couldn't get a thousand people at that price in Fresno," I told him, "if you sent me both Nixon girls to dance topless."

Major mistake on my part. By the time my attempt at humor got back east it sounded like I'd insulted the president and his family to the *Los Angeles Times*. Some asshole White House advance guy called and reamed me out. The next time he was in California, he vowed, he was going to come to Stockton and defend the First Family's honor by kicking my butt. "Come on out any time," I responded.

I was a hell of a lot more nervous than my bravado suggested, so I called Lyn at his Wilshire Boulevard headquarters in L.A. He thought the whole thing was hilarious.

"The only thing that pisses me off," he chuckled, "is that you're passing false information back to those bastards. You *know* we could get one thousand people to see Julie and Tricia dance topless. I can bus up a couple of hundred from L.A. alone."

Lyn's irreverence emboldened me, and taught me bad habits for life.

The upshot was that CREEP pulled the Nixon daughter idea and sent some nonentity from the White House staff named John Mc-Laughlin instead. I did some research and learned that my talent for the evening was the Reverend John McLaughlin, S.J., a controversial Jesuit priest and White House aide who wrote speeches for Nixon that nobody understood because they always included theological references to people like Pierre Teilhard de Chardin and other thinkers not exactly in the mainstream of contemporary political discourse. Perfect for the farmers of the Central Valley.

John ruined a great cocktail party by speaking for nearly an hour on the morality of Richard Nixon. His timing was impeccable: It was about three weeks after evidence of the Watergate coverup had begun to surface. The event was an unmitigated disaster. Looking back, it was a pretty good way for CREEP to get even with me.

I remind Father John of his first big flop every time I see him. He pretends he doesn't remember. John is now an ex-priest, and *The McLaughlin Group* is seen on television from coast to coast. I'm sure he could draw a thousand in Fresno today—but not if he talks about the morality of Richard Nixon.

The lessons I took away from my first Republican presidential campaign have served me throughout my career. The most important lesson I learned was simple: Never do it their way. When I was putting together Reagan's 1984 campaign, I tried to recreate the precise opposite of the 1972 Nixon apparatus. My campaign organization was as bottom up as I could make it. The state chairmen got to run their operations their way; national headquarters was there to help, not harass. We put our energy into electing Republicans across the board, and more than three hundred new legislative seats were won in 1984. Unlike Nixon's campaign, Reagan-Bush '84 made no effort to turn out Democrats unless our phone bank operation told us they supported other Republicans as well as the president.

The last run-in I had with the CREEP boys was during the closing weekend of the campaign. I had bet a case of Cutty Sark against a case of Nofziger's beloved Bombay Gin that I could win all the Central Valley counties. I was well on the way to collecting until the last weekend, when the geniuses back at headquarters decided to send Vice President Spiro Agnew out to do airport rallies in several of my counties. I called Lyn and told him that if Agnew showed up we'd have protesters everywhere and that the McClatchy papers in Sacramento, Modesto, and Fresno would blast our asses to kingdom come.

"Are you sure you're going to win?" he asked.

"How the fuck do I know? We've got no polls, but it feels good to me. What do *your* polls say?"

He laughed. "I don't have any polls, either." They were all locked up in a vault back in Washington, to be seen only by guys with short haircuts who knew nothing about California. To Lyn's credit, he got CREEP to keep Agnew out. We carried California by over a million votes, thanks to the ineptitude of the McGovern campaign and despite the hamhanded arrogance of CREEP. I got my scotch—one bottle. The rest, Lyn tells me, I'll get one drink at a time.

NIXON GOT HIS California, but Bob Monagan and his staff were devastated. They'd worked hard for Nixon, but their real goal was to ride his coattails to a Republican majority in the legislature. Instead, they'd lost nine assembly seats. After the campaign, Monagan put me on his assembly staff in Sacramento, and I was content to be home and back in politics. My new boss was far from content, however. After twelve years in the legislature, his hopes of being Speaker again were dashed, and he started looking at other options. He decided to give up the assembly and go to Washington to serve in Nixon's second term. He was an old friend of the president's, and they were glad to find a place for him.

The White House offered him the post of assistant secretary for congressional affairs in the Department of Transportation. After his return from Nixon's inaugural in January 1973, Bob walked into my office and asked if I wanted to go along as his deputy. I jumped at the chance.

Washington is the National Football League of politics—you need to be drafted to play. You also need a mentor to survive. Bob was my mentor, and I came to town on his ticket. I'd never have gotten there on my own. The only credit I give myself is that I was willing to take the risk.

So, for the second time in four years, I set off for parts unknown. Unlike the St. Louis detour, however, this move left me with no doubts. Politics was a disease to which I knew I'd succumbed.

I rented an unfurnished apartment in Southwest. I didn't bring a stick of furniture with me, so I bought a lawn chair and a sleeping bag from Sears. I didn't know a soul in Washington and had never even been there before. One night at dinner a few days after we'd arrived, Bob was surprised to hear me say this was my first visit to the nation's capital. He never said this to me, but I think that one of the reasons he'd tapped me instead of several other more able colleagues was that he knew I'd taught at Washington University. Like many folks, he didn't know it's in St. Louis, not the District of Columbia.

I arrived in Washington on the eve of a bloody purge. Nixon's campaign slogan had been "Four More Years," but that didn't include many of the senior appointees from the previous four. The day after the election, the president asked for resignation letters from his cabinet, White House staff, and about two thousand other political appointees. In his first term, Nixon had appointed governors and individuals of prominence to the cabinet, each with his own power base. After the purge, he stocked his new administration with Nixon loyalists. It was a serious blunder. Any president has a right to his own team, but the firing squad finesse left hundreds of loyal Republicans feeling betrayed. Nixon would need those loyalists again in the turbulent months ahead, and they wouldn't be there.

The lack of sensitivity to morale that I'd noticed during the campaign—the almost intentional injection of insecurity and paranoia—was alive and well in Washington. Even new hires got a taste of it. When I arrived at Transportation, I was instructed to write and sign an undated letter of resignation to be kept on file in the White House. That way, Nixon's handlers could "reluctantly accept" my resignation whenever it suited them. At least they were efficient in their ruthlessness.

The first time I observed the hallowed halls of Congress, I walked away disappointed. I'd been on the job only a few weeks when Monagan and I took up seats in the House Executive Gallery, a space reserved for administration officials, to watch a floor debate. These were pre–C-SPAN days, so I had no idea what to expect. I assumed it would be a lot like the assembly floor in Sacramento, only with five times as many members. What I saw appalled me.

The doorkeeper announced in a booming voice, "Mr. Speaker," and in walked a little guy who couldn't have been over five feet tall. Carl Albert ascended the podium. Ten minutes later he was sound asleep, head slumped onto the desk. Speaker Albert was a notorious drinker and, I learned, this after-lunch pose wasn't unusual for him. In those days, drinking to excess was a way of life on the Hill. At least half the members and many of their aides would be counseled today to find the nearest Alcoholics Anonymous chapter in hopes of saving their health and careers.

That day, most of the members were missing from the floor during the debate. A number of those who *were* on hand were playing grab-ass or other childish games. Everybody was talking, and no one was paying attention to the arguments for and against the bill about to be voted on the floor.

Then a couple of emaciated old men, who were clearly senile and would surely be carried off by vultures if left alone for an instant, were wheeled into the chamber by aides. The geezers were covered up with blankets for their afternoon naps. When it came time to vote, bells and whistles went off everywhere and a great procession of members marched in from their offices, the gym, or the cloakrooms. If I'd given a buck to every member who'd read the bill before voting on it, I'd have gotten back change from a twenty. As they filed in, party whips would tell them how to vote. Then the members would walk up and put their voting cards into a machine. A green or red light—for aye or nay—would light up next to their name on the huge electronic tote board on the wall. Pretty soon someone came over to the old guys, took their cards from their pockets without disturbing their slumber, and voted on their behalf.

"What a fucking zoo it is down there," I said to my boss. The scene before us made the California Assembly look like the House of Lords. I was expecting the best and the brightest; what I saw was more like a ship of fools. Bob, who had been a congressional aide in the fifties, smiled at my innocence.

"The House is a representative body," he reminded me. "If you had 435 brilliant orators or perfect members down there, they wouldn't represent the people in the country. Like the country, ten percent are very bright and ten percent very stupid. The rest are somewhere in between."

Bob's analysis made perfect sense at the time, and I've never forgotten it. After more than twenty years of dealing with Congress myself, however, I now think he may have underreported the "very stupid" category.

That spring, I had a firsthand encounter with the Nixon staff mentality. My receptionist buzzed to say the White House was on the line. I stood at attention, waiting to hear Richard Nixon's voice. After two minutes on hold, some officious little twerp from the intergovernmental affairs office asked with whom he was speaking. He then directed me to pull together an exhaustive analysis of transportation issues in the country's four hundred largest cities.

"The president wants this by the close of business tomorrow," he commanded.

Somehow, we got it done. We shipped our handiwork to the White House by 6:00 P.M. the next day. I never heard back.

Two weeks later, Monagan sent me to the annual meeting of the country's mayors in San Francisco. It was a big deal for me—going back home as the official representative of the Department of Transportation. At one of the first sessions, I noticed this young guy in a three-piece suit carrying the black book we'd prepared for the White House. I walked over and introduced myself. He was the guy who'd called me with the rush order. I asked him why the president had wanted the analysis.

"It wasn't for the president," he replied. "It was for me. If anybody asked me any questions, I'd have the answers."

"Was it satisfactory?" I asked, biting my tongue.

"I haven't looked at it yet and I probably won't need it before I fly back tomorrow."

At least I was smart enough to keep my anger in check. Two dozen people had worked literally through the night to be responsive to some twit who hadn't bothered to look at what we'd produced. From top to bottom, that was typical of that White House. Twelve years later, when I was running the same intergovernmental shop, I remembered this experience. I instructed my staff that before they ever said the White House wanted something, it damn well better be for the president.

At the conference, the transportation committee was chaired by Richard J. Daley, the legendary mayor of Chicago. Daley was one of a dying breed of big-city bosses who ran their fiefdoms with an iron fist. To me he was an authentic legend, the guy who allegedly stole Illinois for Jack Kennedy in 1960. (As a Kennedy Democrat, I considered it a great service to the nation.) The entire country had seen him in action at the Democratic National Convention in 1968, when he ordered Chicago's finest to kick the crap out of hippies, yippies, and the elite of the antiwar movement. A few delegates got beaten up along the way, but it must have been hard to tell the difference.

At one point, Daley announced the committee was going into executive session and asked outsiders to leave. An aide asked if that meant that the representative of the U.S. Department of Transportation, meaning me, also had to go. In a booming voice, Daley asked the DOT rep to step forward.

He came down from the podium and walked right up to me. He looked just like the famous guy I'd seen on television, only a lot shorter.

I put my hand out. He ignored it.

"Mr. Rollins, has your idiot department changed its policy about allowing highway trust fund money to be used for the operation of mass transits systems?"

"No, sir, we haven't."

Daley turned beet-red and got right in my face.

"You're a bunch of fools, a bunch of goddamned fools," he roared. "Throw this idiot out of here and take away his credentials."

I called Monagan to tell him I'd gotten the bum's rush and asked for instructions.

"Enjoy San Francisco for the next three days and hope you don't run into Daley in the hotel lobby," he said. It was the best federal meeting I've ever attended.

IN MARCH 1973, a special Senate committee had begun hearings on the Watergate burglaries. Like everyone else in Washington, I was engrossed in the daily intrigue. But the early mood was more one of fascination. No one expected that an effort would be mounted to impeach the president or that he'd be driven out of office. Ironically, many political appointees were quietly rooting against our side. Nixon's arrogant toughs had run roughshod for four years, and when they started falling by the wayside in 1973, there was considerable glee from all quarters.

Watching the government try to function while the president was under siege was a riveting experience. The town was in a frenzy. *The Washington Post* was devoured each morning for the latest Bob Woodward and Carl Bernstein exclusive. The Watergate hearings were televised gavel-to-gavel and were the talk of the town. Everyone in government, it seemed, knew someone who had heard something that somebody close to someone else knew to be a fact. Everyone had a theory on the identity of Deep Throat, the mysterious prime source for Woodward and Bernstein. As a political junkie, I couldn't get enough of it.

In the midst of this upheaval, I developed a friendship with Julie Nixon Eisenhower. We were introduced by Patti Matson, a friend who worked in Mrs. Nixon's press office and was very close to Julie. I picked Patti up at the White House one day for lunch, and there was Julie. My new Datsun 280Z had only two seats, but Julie wouldn't hear of pulling rank. She slithered into what passed for a back seat and we drove off to Old Town for lunch on the Potomac waterfront. It was the first of what turned out to be regular lunches the three of us had over the next several months.

Julie was an extraordinary woman—lovely, charming, and down-to-earth. She had excellent political instincts, and I was sure that if she ever wanted to go into politics there would have been no stopping her. We never talked about Watergate directly, but it was clear from the things she said that her father's progressive political decline was extremely painful to her.

In one of our conversations, she talked about her disappointment at not having graduated with her Smith college class for fear demonstrators would disrupt the ceremonies. She'd been picked up in the middle of the night from college by Secret Service agents and spirited away to a secret government hideaway in Virginia's Blue Ridge Mountains. She was frightened, but nobody would tell her anything except that the United States was not at war, and her father was safe. It was a full day before she was told that the family had been evacuated because of the Christmas bombing of North Vietnam. The level of paranoia within the government at the time is hard to fathom today.

Like most administration officials, I watched Watergate from afar. But its ugly tentacles reached into my own department. Egil ("Bud") Krogh, our undersecretary, was a White House aide to John Ehrlichman before he'd been dispatched to Transportation to get a handle on the hated bureaucracy. He and I used to lift weights and work out together in the department's gym. He was in his early thirties and was a nice guy, but, like most of the White House types, he was a little too intense and inexperienced for the real world. He'd been appointed to the job in December 1972, and was still learning the ropes when he was out the door.

On May 4, 1973, defendant E. Howard Hunt testified at the trial of the Watergate Seven burglars that Bud Krogh had headed up the "plumbers," a secret White House unit that had burglarized the Beverly Hills office of Daniel Ellsberg's psychiatrist in September 1971. Ellsberg had leaked the Pentagon Papers to the *New York Times*.

Transportation Secretary Claude Brinegar wanted Krogh out right away, and a few days later his presigned letter of resignation was pulled from the files. He resigned and eventually went to jail. Shortly before he left, I stopped by his office to wish him well. I asked him how he'd gotten tangled up in this mess.

"When you work in the White House for the most powerful man in the world and you believe in the cause," he said, "you don't see things in terms of right or wrong. You do what you think the president wants, or more likely what someone tells you the president wants." I remembered Bud's valedictory when I began my own career as a White House aide eight years later. Believing in a cause, and a man, is one thing; blind devotion is another.

Late on the Friday afternoon of July 13, I got a call from Alexander Butterfield, chairman of the Federal Aviation Administration

(FAA). Like Bud Krogh, Butterfield was one of Nixon's shock troops. Because FAA is part of Transportation, Monagan's congressional shop had been notified that Butterfield was being questioned that day by the staff of the Watergate Committee.

"I thought you should know," he told me, "that I've been asked to come back on Monday to talk about the White House taping system in open session before the full committee."

I didn't know what he was talking about, but the tone of his voice made it pretty obvious that wasn't something Butterfield was eager to do. He wanted me to inform Bill Timmons, Nixon's chief liaison with Congress.

"Alex, I think you'd better call Timmons yourself. This has nothing to do with Transportation."

Monagan was out of town, but I called him just to be sure I'd done the right thing. I had. "Stay the hell out of it," he warned me. He didn't have to say it twice.

That Monday, Butterfield told the world that Nixon had been secretly taping Oval Office conversations for years. Unless those tapes had been destroyed, it was only a matter of time before every last word—give or take eighteen and a half minutes—would be heard across the land.

The rest, as they say, is history. On August 8, 1974, I sat with my old friend Julius Hunter, who was covering the final days, and watched Nixon tell the nation that he'd resign the next day. We toasted Nixon's departure. Of course, Julius and I would always drink to anything, so it was no big deal. Later, when we were suitably lubricated, we drove down Pennsylvania Avenue. As we passed the White House, Julius flashed the Nixon "V for Victory" out the rear window.

At that point in my life, I didn't have the emotional attachment to Nixon that I would later develop. Like most other Americans, I was appalled by the arrogance of the coverup. And I couldn't believe the stupidity of all concerned. As the Clintons would learn with Whitewater a generation later, Nixon and his men learned the hard way that covering up (or seeming to) is far more lethal politically than the original event.

One of Nixon's final acts was to accept Bob Monagan's resignation. For someone of Bob's integrity, watching his longtime associate's demise as president was painful and disturbing. He just couldn't believe that intelligent people could be so dishonest and then so stupid. He wanted out. I stayed behind, and for the first time in Washington was alone without a mentor. Bob encouraged me to soldier on and continue my education in the way government really works.

I SURVIVED THE Ford years in Transportation just fine, keeping my head down and doing my thing. Over the next few years I'd meet many wonderful people, most of them Rockefeller Republicans who kept me around as their token California conservative. They'd invite me to their homes for dinner, pour a bottle of wine into me, and then encourage me to entertain their other guests with tales of great horror to their liberal bias. A typical introduction: "Now Ed will tell us how Ronald Reagan's going to be president in a few years." When I said that none of them understood the West and that Reagan was the best television communicator since Jack Kennedy, they all laughed and ridiculed Reagan as some western weirdo. But many of those guests and friends who trashed Reagan would be calling me to help them find jobs in 1981.

By 1976, as the next election cycle geared up, I was excited when Reagan decided to challenge the incumbent president. Like many others, I wanted Jerry Ford to step aside and let Ronald Reagan carry the flag into battle with the Democrats. Ford had pardoned Nixon and would never be able to cleanse himself of that act. Reagan was untainted by Watergate and had been one of the first to ask Nixon to step down.

Like Reagan, I thought Ford had compromised his conservative values. I never believed he had any vision. Unlike Reagan and Barry Goldwater, Ford and many Republicans who'd spent their adult lives in Washington weren't into leading revolutions. They wanted to run the government just like the Democrats. A little more efficiently and cheaply, perhaps, but they didn't want to dismantle it. Reagan and his followers wanted a revolution, and I cheered his crusade on from the sidelines.

After a bitter primary battle, Reagan came within a whisker of upsetting Ford. Reagan's campaign was run by John Sears, a pretty capable strategist who didn't believe in his candidate or his philosophy. Sears thought that Ford was so vulnerable that Reagan could coast to the nomination. He underestimated the power of incumbency and wasn't prepared for a long, drawn-out fight.

Even so, Reagan roared toward the convention; the situation had all the makings of an upset. But he lost his bearings when he named Senator Richard Schweiker, a Pennsylvania liberal, as his running mate. The conservatives thought he'd sold out, and the desperation ploy failed. Even so, the end was agonizingly close. Ford won the nomination by 117 delegates out of more than 2,200.

Despite his defeat, Reagan had impressed the convention with his speech and shown himself a class act by endorsing Ford. If Ford and his handlers had been smart, they would have named him as the running mate. Reagan was adamantly opposed, but nobody turns the job down when it's actually offered. Ford liked the idea about as much as Reagan. But with Reagan on the ticket, Ford would have carried key states like Mississippi, Louisiana, and Texas, which would have given him the election.

I'd joined the Republican Party because of Ronald Reagan, and I was bitterly disappointed. I was sure the Republican Party I'd joined because of Reagan was never going to be *his* party. I think Reagan could have defeated Jimmy Carter. In retrospect, it was probably better he didn't. If he'd followed Nixon and Ford, he might have become bogged down in the morass they created. Through his challenge to Ford, he gained strength and national recognition, and positioned himself as the Republican heir apparent in 1980. Carter's four years of mediocrity gave Reagan an opening to change the country's direction and reset national priorities.

One hour after Jimmy Carter's inaugural, I received a terse, hand-delivered letter from the new White House personnel office, telling me I had two weeks to vacate my office. I admired their efficiency, if not their tact. I kept that letter and framed it. To my mind, it was the equivalent of the Ph.D. in political science I never got at Washington University. And that very day, I started growing a beard—my own little protest.

Four years later, one of my first acts as a Reagan appointee was to hang that letter on my White House office wall to remind me that, as important as I might think I was at any given moment, government service as a political appointee is temporary work. In the first few days of the administration, our personnel shop asked me how Carter's holdovers in political positions should be handled. "Send them a letter and give them a week," I said with a smile. What goes around comes around. I didn't want the Democrats to think we were any less ruthless or efficient.

I DIDN'T KNOW what came next for me. I was sure Reagan was too old to run for president again in 1980, and California politics didn't look promising. Jerry Brown was governor now, and almost everyone I'd known in Sacramento was no longer there. Every Republican political appointee in Washington was scrounging for work and the pickings were slim. The lawyers always find work, unfortunately, but the rest of us were struggling.

I was thirty-four, unattached, and gainfully unemployed. For a few months I did some consulting, drank a lot, and dated a bunch of weird women. Like most bachelors, I lived from paycheck to paycheck and had next to nothing in the bank. My only possessions were a big Honda Gold Wing motorcycle, my 280Z, and two big Huskies, Ranger and Rocky. I had great confidence in my ability to earn enough to buy a couple of bags of dog food every month.

Out of the blue, providence appeared in the form of Howard Tipton. Tip and I had worked together at Transportation and become good friends. Another transplanted Californian, he'd been an All-American quarterback at the University of Redlands, and at age twenty-one, the country's youngest city manager. After heading the national commission on fire prevention, he'd been named the first administrator of the new National Fire Administration. One of the agency's main chores was to create a National Fire Academy, an elite training and educational operation that would be the FBI academy of firefighting. Tip was so highly regarded that he'd been reappointed by President Carter.

In the summer of 1977, I accepted Tip's offer to become the academy's deputy superintendent and dean of the faculty. Other than helping the firemen wash their trucks as a kid, I knew zip about the fire services. What I offered was an extensive background dealing with state and local government and academic experience. I wasn't teaching so much as running the place, and it was one of the most gratifying jobs I've ever had. There are no finer folks in America than firefighters. I've never worked in a campaign that matched the dedication, enthusiasm, or esprit de corps of these professionals.

In the spring of 1979, I received an offer to be chief of staff for the Republicans in the California Assembly. It was a tough choice, but I didn't agonize for long. I loved what I was doing, but I didn't want to retire there. God help me, I still had the political virus.

To the shock of all my friends, I got married shortly before leaving for Sacramento. I'd determined that when the next nice girl came along, I'd settle down. Unfortunately for Kitty Nellor, she was the next nice girl. A divorcée, she'd been raising her two boys alone for years. When we started going out, she told me she didn't think I was the marrying kind and gave me a year to decide.

At half-time during a 1979 Super Bowl party, she announced the year was up. After very little thought and too many beers, I said I'd marry her. Five days later, I did—before a justice of the peace in Fairfax County, Virginia.

It was a mistake. Kitty had spent all her life in Washington and hated politics. Four months after the wedding, I moved her, the boys, and her father to Sacramento and returned to politics. She hated every moment of it, and I did nothing to make it any better.

I was away a great deal. Much of the business of the legislature gets done at fund-raising receptions or dinners and in the bars afterwards during the week. Most weekends I was traveling the state, going to meetings in Southern California or recruiting candidates. In the election year, it was even worse. I was responsible for all eighty assembly races in addition to my legislative duties. I was supervising more than fifty staff people on the legislative payroll and several others who were running the campaigns.

Kitty had no interest in what I was doing and didn't want any part of the political world. I was a terrible husband and not much of a stepfather, either. She and the boys deserved a lot better. I failed her and I felt guilty that it didn't work. She was a wonderful person who deserved a lot more than I could give her. If I had had a normal nine-to-five job and been home every night, Kitty might have been happy. I know myself, though, and I wouldn't have been. I take full blame for the breakup and will always feel guilty about what I did to her unintentionally.

The disintegration of my personal life was juxtaposed with another opportunity to trade up to the Majors, and it proved one of the most fascinating interludes in my life. In August 1979, Julie Nixon Eisenhower called to say her father was moving back to New York after his self-imposed exile at San Clemente and was looking for a new chief of staff. She thought I'd be perfect for the job and had taken the liberty of telling him about me. He'd asked her to arrange a visit, which she'd done. I'll remember that first visit until my dying day.

He was speaking to the Young Presidents Organization at the Silverado Country Club in Napa. I was shown to his bungalow by a Secret Service agent, who said Nixon was finishing his speech and would be there momentarily. About two minutes later, the door opened and there he was.

He was smaller than I'd expected. And I couldn't believe what he was wearing. The former President of the United States, who always looked like he slept in a suit, dress shirt, and tie, was decked out in powder blue golf pants, an open-collar shirt, and a peacock blue sports jacket. Standing there in that idiotic getup, he looked like any other club member you'd find in the bar after eighteen holes.

"Julie sends her best," he said, shaking my hand. "Now, I've got to take a piss." He excused himself, but thoughtfully left the door open so we could talk.

There I was, the son of a shipyard worker from Vallejo, standing outside Richard Nixon's bathroom door while he took a leak, attempting nonchalantly to carry on a conversation with the former leader of the free world.

He reemerged, shed his jacket, and announced, "This is not an interview. If you want the job, it's yours. Julie knows what I need, and she wouldn't have mentioned you if you weren't up to it.

"You've worked for good people and come highly recommended by the Nixon with the best political judgment in the family. If you're good enough for Julie, you're good enough for me. Now, with that out of the way, let's talk. You know Reagan. Tell me about Reagan. What's he really like?"

Over the next three hours, I sat through the most stimulating tutorial I've ever been given in my life. Nixon used about three obscenities in his first sentence, which put me at ease. I've been physically beaten but never outcussed, so we both let it rip.

We were like long-lost pals, chewing the fat about politics and world affairs. I could hold my own with the former, but fell mute as he delivered a compelling overview of the geopolitical landscape.

"Mr. President," I interjected at one point, "everything I hear is that you're still highly respected as a foreign leader in Europe and by the Soviets."

"Respected?" He smiled. "I think 'feared' is a better word. If they fear you, they will respect you. If they love you, they *might* respect you. But if they don't fear you, they'll never love you or respect you and they don't have to!" It was the single best lesson I've ever gotten about politics.

If my dad had seen me sitting there with the disgraced former President of the United States—the man he called "Tricky Dick"—he would have said my damnation was assured. I was pretty amazed myself, after my negative experiences both as a Nixon campaign operative and a member of his second administration. But there was no denying the man's power; his perceptions were acute, and he really knew his politics and particularly his geopolitics. It was the chance to forge a working alliance with the man behind the tarnished image that was so seductive.

At the end of our session, Nixon asked me to give him an answer in a week. I didn't need it. He'd sold me; I couldn't wait to start, and told him so. He asked me why I was so sure. I replied that I knew I could learn a lot from him. Furthermore, he was beginning his comeback as an elder statesman and I wanted to be a part of that.

"I doubt I'll ever be accepted as an elder statesman," he mused. "The media won't allow it to happen." Then he said something that surprised me. "It isn't in my best interests because I like you and would like to have you work for me, but if I were your age and had your connections with Reagan, I'd sign up with the Reagan team in a heartbeat."

He paused to let it sink in. "Make history, Ed," he advised. "Don't relive someone else's."

A few days later, after playing his words back in my head a few dozen times, I called him to say I was taking his advice.

"You've made the right choice," he replied. "Reagan's going to be president, and you'll be a great part of his team. Call me anytime, and stay in touch."

And we did. Over the next several years, we talked regularly on the phone. One of my favorite tasks as White House political director was briefing Nixon periodically on political affairs.

AROUND THE SAME time, I lucked into a reunion with Lyn Nofziger. Since 1977, Lyn had been running Citizens for the Republic, Reagan's political action committee. He'd lost a power struggle with John Sears, who was managing Reagan's 1980 presidential campaign, and was forced out in August 1979. I immediately hired him as a consultant. He worked for me a couple of days a week and helped me maintain my sanity.

Sears himself was purged in 1980. Meanwhile, he'd alienated just about everyone with his attitude, which was: I'm so smart I can even get that dumbshit Reagan elected president. With the coast clear, Nofziger went back to the campaign in June. I didn't begrudge him, but I hated to see him go. Shortly after his departure, one prominent Sacramento lobbyist sought me out to offer condolences.

"You've gotta be really sorry to see Nofziger go back to Reagan," he said. I agreed that it was a serious blow in the middle of a campaign.

"Screw that shit, Rollins," he chortled. "Now *you're* the worst-dressed man in Sacramento again."

A couple of weeks later, Lyn returned the favor, asking me to be his deputy communications director at the Detroit convention. It was only a temporary assignment for no pay, but it was a chance to be at ringside. Not believing my good fortune, I took some vacation and headed for Detroit.

On the hot, humid evening of July 16, 1980, I was in the command trailer outside Joe Louis Arena monitoring the feeding frenzy over one of the dumber ideas in modern political history—a Reagan-Ford ticket.

A little after 7:00 P.M., somebody yelled, "Ford's on with Cronkite." The familiar nasal voice of the first man appointed president was saying, "I would not go to Washington and be a figurehead vice president." Walter Cronkite asked if that meant an arrangement something like a "co-presidency." Ford intimated that such an arrangement was a legitimate topic for discussion. As the interview trailed off, people were shaking their heads in disbelief.

"He's going to do it, Ford's going to do it," someone yelled across the trailer. I sat silently near the back and thought to myself, What are these idiots thinking? This is a disaster in the making. I'd been talking to reporters all day. Almost to a person they thought it was a stupid idea that made Reagan look weak.

"This is the ticket that should have come together four years ago," I whispered to no one in particular. If Ford had made Reagan his running mate in 1976, he'd be finishing his second term.

Far above the action—and fatally removed from it—Reagan's inner circle was huddled in a huge double suite on the sixty-ninth floor of the Renaissance Plaza Hotel. The campaign was being run by four men, not one of whom had the qualifications or the experience of us guys in the control trailer. Ed Meese was Reagan's chief of staff and a fine man, but he'd never been in a campaign. Bill Casey had been a successful Wall Street lawyer and chairman of the Securities and Exchange Commission (SEC), but was another campaign neophyte. Mike Deaver had briefly been a field man for the California Republican Party. The only campaign he'd managed was a 1971 statewide initiative to lower taxes that was badly defeated. How do you get creamed proposing to lower taxes?

In the land of the blind, the one-eyed man is king, and the guy with the eyepatch was Dick Wirthlin. He was one of the country's better pollsters. But pollsters are whores for numbers and generally have poor political instincts. They only push the decisions their numbers guide them to make. Dick has no political gut and is a very cautious man, but the others let his numbers drive their decisions.

For two days, this less than dazzling team had been presiding over a bizarre mating ritual. The short list for VP was down to Paul Laxalt, Jack Kemp, George Bush, Howard Baker, and—heaven help us—Jerry Ford. Reagan's personal A-list included just Laxalt and Kemp. His preference was Laxalt, senior senator from Nevada and once its governor. The two governors shared both ideology and style. Unlike so many other political animals, both were very secure men. They didn't need to be surrounded by crowds of adoring groupies.

The wise men around Reagan argued against Laxalt because the unwritten rule of American politics says you can't have two guys from the same region. Besides, they argued, as an ex-governor of a state with legalized gambling and prostitution, Laxalt would cause trouble in the Bible Belt.

I was just a volunteer staffer and nobody was asking my opinion, but anyone who's been around this game knows voters don't vote for vice president. Jimmy Carter wasn't going to be reelected simply because Nevada had gambling and prostitution. Besides, the religious right loved Laxalt.

Reagan's backup choice was New York Congressman Jack Kemp. The former pro football star was popular and dynamic. He was close to Reagan and many of his people, having worked as a special assistant in the governor's office during the off-season. The wise men argued against Kemp because you supposedly couldn't have an ex-movie star running with an ex-football star. I asked myself, Who the fuck made these guys the wise men? The truth of the matter was, they weren't.

Either Laxalt or Kemp would have made a superb vice president, and both would have surrounded themselves with Reagan people. Laxalt would have been his closest confidant and counsellor. He would also have been a critical bridge to Congress, where he was very well respected. Kemp would have been a bridge to the next generation of conservatives. He also could have been the principal architect for a sweeping new conservative agenda. Having been a member of the House leadership, he could have been an effective liaison there as well.

As usual, Reagan's instincts were better than anyone else's. I'd later learn from personal experience that he didn't always rely on those instincts. He'd fight like hell for the big things, but give in on the little ones. What he didn't realize that night at the convention was that nothing was bigger than the choice he'd make in the next few hours. He let his handlers roll him on Laxalt and Kemp.

Which brought them to George Bush and Howard Baker. Neither had ever supported Reagan and both had fought him on issues he felt strongly about. Bush was a very nice man who'd made a career out of being a good follower. Aside from an impressive résumé and a couple of terms in Congress, his main talent lay in cultivating friend-ships—no man ever did that to greater advantage. But while running hard for the nomination himself, he'd raised the hackles of conserva-tives by branding Reagan's tax-cut plan "Voodoo economics," which showed he didn't believe in the Reagan economic plan. Nothing was more important to the Reagan domestic agenda than the tax cut.

To those who'd worked for Reagan against Ford and the Republi-can establishment in 1976, George Bush personified everything they'd battled all their lives. Picking him would be seen as a particu-lar betrayal by the true believers. On a personal level, Reagan thought Bush was weak, particularly after the debate controversy in Nashua, New Hampshire, when Bush had pouted and opposed changing the rules to allow a freer discussion of the issues.

Senator Howard Baker was a slightly different story. Although well liked by most of Reagan's inner circle, he'd carried the water for President Carter in the floor fight that gave away the Panama Canal. As a result, he was seen as a liability and there was no support for him as the running mate.

That left Jerry Ford.

Back in the trailer, pandemonium was breaking out. The networks were paying no attention to the proceedings or the speakers. The Reagan-Ford dream team was the talk of the hour. Most of the press thought it was pretty stupid at best, and the Reaganites thought it was a nightmare. Reagan was waiting anxiously to hear from Ford one way or the other and get on with it. He clearly understood the impact of the Cronkite interview. The networks were declaring this a done deal, and he didn't like getting boxed in. He was going through this drill only because his advisers thought it would guarantee a fall victory.

The negotiations with the Ford people were positively bizarre. According to the deal reportedly being considered, Ford would serve as chief operating officer and Reagan would be the chief executive. The White House staff would report through Ford, who would choose the Secretaries of State and Treasury—presumably Henry Kissinger and Alan Greenspan, who were negotiating for Ford. Ford could also veto other cabinet choices. One jokester quipped that Ford would be president between 5:00 P.M. and 9:00 A.M. and week-ends, and Reagan would be president the other forty hours of the week.

Finally, Reagan had enough. It wasn't going to work, and Ford, who'd never been that interested anyway, agreed with him. The two old enemies met in Reagan's suite and called a halt to the lunacy. The process of elimination had played itself out. Soon after Ford left,

Reagan walked into an adjoining conference room and said to his brain trust: "I guess it's Bush."

In less than five minutes, without anyone raising a protest, it was a done deal. Neither Reagan nor anyone on his staff ever sat down with George Bush and asked him even the most basic questions about how the two of them might work together. As a guy who's spent his entire career as a staff person, I can say with some authority that this was piss-poor staffwork.

Nofziger, who'd been in the suite all evening and had listened to the discussions with amazement and alarm, called me on the hot line. He said the governor wanted to speak to Paul Laxalt, who had just delivered Reagan's nominating speech.

"Lyn," I pleaded, "please tell me it's not Bush."

"You guessed it," he chuckled. He filled me in on what had happened on the sixty-ninth floor.

Then Laxalt got on the phone and urged Reagan not to rush the judgment; they had another day to make the choice. "As campaign chairman, I have a right to be in on the decision, Ron. You promised me you weren't going to pick Bush," he said, irritation creeping into his voice.

Reagan confessed he'd already called Bush. He'd heard the convention hall had been going crazy, he added, and a quick decision was critical.

"Fine, Ron," Laxalt raged. "It's your choice to make." He slammed the phone against the wall and stormed out of the trailer. I couldn't blame him for being furious. Paul had been screwed over. I don't think he was mad about not being chosen; it was being left out of what he believed was a horrible decision.

Lyn called back and said they were on the way over to the arena. On a television monitor, I could see the motorcade leaving the hotel. Then the camera flashed a shot of Lyn chasing after it, running down the street waving his arms. A few minutes later, the motorcade arrived and we all were swept into the holding room. Lyn followed a short while later, badly out of breath. He'd stopped to tell Reagan's traveling press that the nominee was heading to the convention hall. The motorcade had left without him and he had to flag a cab.

"Come on," Nofziger said to me, "let's be a part of history."

As I stood at the back of the stage, twenty feet from the next President of the United States, Reagan announced Bush as his running mate. Soon Ford and a swarm of other dignitaries joined them onstage. I'd never experienced a more exciting moment in my life.

What I didn't realize at the time was that we'd just cut the fuse on our own revolution. The conservatives had won, but then surrendered the future back to the eastern establishment moderates.

The day after the convention, Lyn invited me to fly back to California on the charter with Reagan and Bush. I was thrilled beyond words, a kid in a candy store. We stopped in Houston to drop off the Bushes. They hosted the Reagans at a lunch at their home, then we all went off to a hastily arranged rally at the glitzy Galleria shopping mall.

En route to Los Angeles, I was exhausted, but couldn't sleep. Even three weeks of twenty-hour work days couldn't begin to overcome my adrenaline. My mind was racing. Even though the Reagans and Bushes were getting along and the press had reacted well to the choice, I was uncomfortable with the shotgun marriage. On this flight, a phrase popped into my mind for the first time to describe my feelings about George Bush: Trojan Horse. The enemy was in our camp.

I could not have dreamed in my wildest fantasies that at the next convention, I'd be the boss of the men in the trailer and everyone else in the reelection campaign.

In the end, Ronald Reagan had won the battle and handed his sword to the losers. Eight years later, the two men Reagan had wanted for his vice president, Laxalt and Kemp, either of whom would have carried on and expanded his revolution, couldn't get traction to become serious candidates to succeed him. By then, the Reagan mantle had passed to Vice President Bush. At the very outset of the revolution, the seeds had been sown for its undoing.

I WENT HOME to Sacramento, but was thrilled when Nofziger called three weeks later, in early August, and asked me to be his deputy at Washington headquarters. Carol Hallett, the Republican assembly leader, went berserk and persuaded Lieutenant Governor Mike Curb to back her up. They got every Republican fat cat in the state to bitch to Reagan's people that I was abandoning them in the middle of the assembly races. After a few days of warfare, Lyn decided it was too high a price to pay in our home state. He'd use me as a troubleshooter, but the deputy's job was gone. I was bitterly disappointed. I did a few odd jobs for Lyn, but the state races were my main focus. On election day, as Reagan won the presidency, assembly Republicans managed a net gain of three seats, but they were still in the back benches.

At this moment, I became living proof that politics makes strange bedfellows by helping get a liberal Democrat installed as Speaker of the state assembly. The Democratic majority was divided into two camps and neither could muster the votes to elect a new Speaker. Fierce jockeying erupted on both sides of the aisle to put together a coalition candidate. A few days after the election, Assemblyman Ross Johnson of Orange County, one of my closest allies, suggested over drinks that Willie Brown might make a good candidate. It was party heresy, of course; Willie was the flamboyant member from San Francisco, a card-carrying liberal Democrat. Willie had always wanted to be Speaker, and had tried to put together a coalition to elect him a few years earlier. I knew he'd deal. If I could deliver enough votes, he might be persuaded to swallow on terms favorable to the Republicans.

Terrified our scheme would be torpedoed by a premature leak, Johnson and I quickly tried to line up the votes. Once it looked like we had them, I dropped a hypothetical hint over lunch with Marty Smith, political editor of the *Sacramento Bee.* He gave it a small mention in his Sunday column. Ten minutes after I showed up for work on Monday, Willie was on the horn from San Francisco.

"Rollins, is this for real, or is it bullshit?"

"Well, Willie, I think it's at least worth talking about."

"I'll be there in a little over an hour."

"Willie, you're ninety miles away. It'll take you longer than that."

"Rollins, I'll meet you in my office in one hour and fifteen minutes."

Sixty-five minutes later, Willie's sleek black Porsche came roaring in—a new land speed record between San Francisco and Sacramento.

The terms of the compact had great short-term benefits to the Republicans. The legislature would be redistricted before the 1982 election, and Willie promised us equal access to state funds for reapportionment planning. Moreover, a Republican would be vice chairman of every committee with their own staff.

I warned my leaders that this was only a temporary arrangement. Willie would surely turn on us once he consolidated his power. But it gave us a high-risk chance to make gains in the next election. And Willie would make a wonderful target, which he fully understood.

"Rollins," he told me during one of our deliberations, "you're going to run up and down the San Joaquin Valley and tell all those redneck farmers, 'Willie's coming, Willie's coming.'" We both laughed, knowing that's exactly what I'd do.

On December 1, 1980, a sharecropper's son was installed as the assembly's first African-American Speaker. I'd brokered the deal, and it proved to be one of my dumber moves. Fourteen years later,

Willie was still Speaker, and still a thorn in the side of California Republicans. The only thing that stopped him was term limits. Now Willie and his $2,000 Brioni suits call the mayor's office in San Francisco home.

I knew the deal with Willie would make me a more significant player in Sacramento. But my first taste of the big time had been intoxicating. I was a certified political junkie now, desperate for my next fix. As it became more apparent Reagan would win the election, I'd begun to harbor ambitions about going back east again. Those dreams were dashed a couple of weeks before the election, when we had dinner in Los Angeles. Lyn said he didn't want the press secretary's job and didn't think he'd stay in Washington after the election. "But I'll do everything I can to get you a job if you want to go back," he volunteered. I knew what Washington was like without a mentor; if Lyn wasn't going, I wanted no part of it. I'd rather be a big fish in the small Sacramento pond.

A few weeks after the Willie Brown deal, Lyn called unexpectedly. He had skipped the Reagan transition and driven home from Washington, figuring the revolution had passed him by. Then Jim Baker had telephoned with an offer to run the White House political shop. Lyn was as stunned by this turn of events as I.

Then he said the magic words:

"I want you to be my deputy."

I carefully considered this offer for approximately one-billionth of a second.

"Absolutely," I replied.

"I don't know what it pays or anything else except it's the only slot I have."

"Lyn, if I can pass the goddamn FBI check, I'll take it."

"If *I* can pass it, *you* can pass it."

I'd lucked into a ticket to the Holy Grail of American politics— the White House staff! Better still, I'd be working for a president whose commitment to revolutionary change mirrored my own values. For the first time, I was excited to call myself a Republican—a Reagan Republican.

ROUND 4

THE REVOLUTION COMES TO WASHINGTON

IT WAS A few hours past midnight on January 26, 1981, when I pulled into the parking lot of an old friend's apartment building in the Maryland suburbs. Totally exhausted, I unhooked my battered Datsun 280Z from the rear of the U-Haul truck I'd been driving and living in for the last five days and three thousand miles.

I pulled a rumpled suit and change of clothes out of the back of the truck and locked it up. I was desperate for a few hours of sleep. Once I was inside and horizontal, however, I discovered that my adrenaline was pumping too hard for sleep. I got up at sunrise, showered, steamed out my suit as best I could, and headed off for the biggest adventure of my life.

Thirty minutes later, I pulled up to the southwest gate of the White House and reported for duty with the Reagan Revolution.

I was directed to a temporary parking spot fifty feet from the White House basement, passed through security with a minimum of hassle, and cleared into the Old Executive Office Building (OEOB), that wonderful gray battleship guarding the west flank of the White House. I was awestruck. I hadn't felt fear like this since I'd sparred with Joe Frazier when he was training for the 1964 Olympics. I hoped the results would be different. Frazier had knocked the crap out of me.

I made my way to the Office of Political Affairs, housed in Room 175, a first-floor suite of offices Richard Nixon had used as a hide-away, one floor below the vice president's suite.

I was shown to my office by Rosemarie Monk, Lyn Nofziger's longtime assistant. Someone had obviously made a huge mistake. It was bigger than any apartment I'd ever lived in: fifteen-foot ceilings, three telephones, a working fireplace, even a balcony overlooking the White House to the east.

Rosemarie took me in to see Lyn. "It's about time you got your ass to work," he greeted me. "We've got a government to dismantle." We chatted for half an hour, then I went back to my office.

The next couple of hours were consumed by paperwork. There were personnel forms for everything—temporary and permanent building passes, White House Mess privileges, parking space, security clearances. Lyn wandered into my office in his stocking feet and asked if I liked the color blue. I said yes.

"A good fucking thing, because I just ordered them to paint your office blue."

He looked at the pile of forms on my desk and remarked that filling out government paperwork was harder than the actual job. Nobody hated bureaucratic crap more than Lyn. When he saw that his security clearance required him to list every place he'd lived in his adult life, he filled in his current address, then wrote beneath it: "If the FBI's as good as they think they are, they can find all the others."

I finished the forms and walked them around the building. Finally, I was made official as a deputy assistant to the president by a GS-3 clerk in the personnel office who said she'd never sworn in anybody so high-ranked. I laughed to myself, feeling like a total impostor.

The previous Wednesday, I'd pulled into a Nebraska truck stop for breakfast. I read in the local paper that the president had sworn in the twenty-five members of the White House senior staff, me among them, the day before. Obviously, I wasn't there. I couldn't have known it would be one of the few times in my White House years I was happy to see my name in print—or that it wouldn't be the last time the press would get it wrong about me.

Now that I was official, Rosemarie gave my rumpled suit the once-over and suggested I might want to take the rest of the day off. I was too excited for sleep, so I walked over to the South Lawn and attended my first presidential event: a ceremony honoring the Americans held hostage in Teheran by the revolutionary mullahs for 444 days. They'd been freed on January 20, the day Reagan was inaugurated.

A great roar of welcome rang out as buses carrying the former hostages and their families drove through the gates and up to the south entrance of the White House.

Standing on the fringe of the crowd, I remember thinking there was a fitting symmetry to it all. It was a metaphor of hope, a clean break from the gloom and uncertainty of the Carter years, an omen of promise for the fledgling government I was lucky enough to be joining. As the new president spoke amid the flags and military bands and tears of joy, I was swept up in the high drama of the moment. And I don't cry easily.

As I walked back to the OEOB, I told myself that if someone grabbed my arm, said it had all been a terrible mistake, and sent me packing back to California with my U-Haul, after this one experience, I'd still think I was a lucky guy. Fifteen years later, I still do.

Sitting in my office when I got back was a scrawny, baby-faced kid. He stood up as I walked in and eyeballed me from my toes to the top of my bald head. He had the most intense eyes I'd ever seen outside a boxing ring. He stuck out his hand.

"You must be Mr. Rollins, Mr. Nofziger's deputy," he drawled in a South Carolina accent as thick as molasses. "Hi, I'm Lee Atwater, and I want to be part of your team."

Who the hell is this kid? I thought. I figure Billy the Kid's victims must have asked the same question just before he shot them down in cold blood. Over the next ten years, Lee Atwater's life and mine would be so complicatedly intertwined it would be hard to remember how innocently it had all begun.

At the end of my first week, Lyn walked me across the street to see the president. I'd met Ronald Reagan several times in California, and in the Nixon years I'd been given a thirty-second peek at the Oval Office while the president was out of town. But this was for real. I'd always been an American history buff and had read a lot about our presidents. As I sat there, my mind wandered off, thinking of what went on in this room and the great men who changed history by decisions made within those round walls. I thought of my heroes—Kennedy, Teddy Roosevelt, Lincoln. I really couldn't believe I was in the Oval Office actually meeting with the President of the United States—my new boss.

"It's great to have you on board, Ed," the president said. The three of us chatted for a couple of minutes, just small talk. It was only a courtesy call, but Reagan never seemed larger than life to me than at that moment.

PEOPLE WOULD ASK if I felt powerful working in the big time. What I mostly felt was tired and poor. As a deputy assistant to the president, I was making $49,000 a year, an $8,000 pay cut from what I'd been paid in Sacramento. Under normal circumstances, the slightly more than $2,000 monthly take-home pay would have been more than adequate to support my life-style. But when Kitty and I separated in 1980, I'd continued to pay the rent and part of her living expenses. I promised to send her $1,250 a month from Washington. That didn't leave much to survive on. I lived in an apartment hotel down Shirley Highway in northern Virginia the first month. Then I rented an unfurnished efficiency apartment for $500 a month from a Secret Service agent. It was in Foggy Bottom, about six blocks from the White House.

I've seen larger jail cells. My furniture consisted of a stereo, TV, a weight machine, and a mattress. I slept and showered in the apartment, and lived in my office. I left the Datsun in my White House parking space to save gas money, and walked to work. I ate all my meals in the White House Mess—the food was decent and the subsidized prices were cheaper than the outside world. For that first year, I managed to live on $300 a month after rent. Needless to say, I didn't have a clothes budget. In 1982, *Washingtonian* magazine named me the worst-dressed man in the administration—something Nancy Reagan quickly noted, I'm sure.

I also felt intimidated. I was a blue-collar guy in a white-collar world, populated for the most part by colleagues with trust funds and impressive net worths. Moreover, the Reagan White House was never a user-friendly kind of place. The intramural friction among the troika that supposedly ran the White House—Jim Baker, Ed Meese, and Mike Deaver—meant there were always plenty of flying elbows everywhere. Outside of our office, there wasn't any sense of camaraderie. And because Lyn was considered an outsider by the ever-increasing number of non-Reaganites, we all felt a little paranoid.

The first few weeks on the job were absolute chaos. Lyn was more accessible than his senior staff colleagues in the West Wing, and everyone knew the political shop had a big say in signing off on personnel appointments. So our office quickly became the Wailing Wall for jobseekers. Mike Deaver once observed that our anteroom looked like the bar scene from *Star Wars*.

Aside from political clearances on jobseekers, the responsibilities of our political office were ill-defined. After all, everything in the White House is political. We used to say that there were no fences; anyone could wander into anyone else's turf or business at will. So

Lyn and I wrote our own mission statement, and improvised as we went along. We had an advantage over many of the other new Reagan troops: We'd been here before. Lyn had been in the Nixon White House, and while my experience at Transportation and Commerce wasn't in the same league, I knew how the town and the government operated.

Our chores were a mixture of high policy and low patronage. We acted as the liaison office for the old Reagan political operation, the Republican Party at every organizational level, and all good Republicans wherever they were. It was also our job to make everyone else aware of the political impact of policy decisions the president or cabinet would make. It didn't mean decisions were made solely on their political merits, but at least everyone needed to understand the political consequences of their actions.

We also figured out what political events the president should attend. Building political support for the president's legislative initiatives was a major piece of the job as well. If the vote of a key member was needed, the congressional shop would stroke him, and we'd apply the pressure. If members weren't with us on key votes, we'd crank up a little not-so-friendly persuasion from their constituents and financial backers. It wasn't brain surgery: Our mandate, from day one, was to help the president get reelected four years down the road and in the meantime get his legislative agenda through Congress.

I soon learned that some jobs that came our way weren't in the operator's manual. In February, Nofziger introduced Atwater and me to a very nervous Washington lobbyist. He began spilling out a story about a golfing junket he'd put together for several members of Congress and other lobbyists. On the trip, a ravishingly beautiful female lobbyist had allegedly slept with several of the congressmen. As it turned out, he said, she'd also had affairs with several other members. So what? I thought; welcome to the National Football League.

"But she's threatening to go public," the lobbyist said, "and she's got pictures—tapes."

I'm thinking to myself that the sexual activities of Republican congressmen aren't part of my job description and that the White House needs to stay out of this.

"I'm not going to deal with this," Nofziger chuckled. "Rollins is going to take this on. It's your problem, Ed. Lee will help you."

Thanks a hell of a lot, boss, I thought to myself. Three weeks into the job, and I'm having to deal with a goddamn Republican sex scandal.

Atwater and I took the lobbyist back to my office to hash out a strategy. "Instead of a lot of different meetings," I suggested, "let's get everybody down here at once and talk about what to do." The lobbyist said he'd put together a meeting.

Two hours later, I got a call from Ken Duberstein, the congressional liaison officer for the House.

"What the hell are you doing?" he asked. "Are you having a Hill meeting I don't know about? I just got a call from the front gate. A couple of dozen House members are coming to see you." Turf is always an issue at the White House, and Ken thought I was encroaching on his. I quickly explained the situation and asked if he'd like to get involved.

"Fuck, no," he wisely decided.

In short order, more than twenty very nervous members of Congress were sitting in my office. I looked around the room in disbelief. It was a cross section of House Republicans, ranging in age from mid-thirties to mid-sixties. There were a dozen very prominent members, including some in the leadership.

Several of them claimed they'd shown up merely as interested observers or to lend moral support to troubled colleagues. They must have figured I was born yesterday on another planet. As the dialogue progressed, it was obvious as hell that damn near every last one of them had nailed her.

"What do we do about the tapes?" somebody asked.

"You can't really believe she's got tapes," I said. "Has she shown you tapes of you and her?"

"No, but I've seen tapes of her and ——," mentioning a very prominent House Republican who wasn't in the room.

I saw myself as the point man from hell. The revolution is about to go down the tubes because a couple dozen guys couldn't keep their pants zipped. There was only thing to do: stonewall.

"Here's my counsel," I said. "Obviously, this girl got around, so she's gonna have some credibility problems. There's no way to stop her from going public, and it's a big story. The way to make it a *bigger* story is for any one of you guys to walk out of here and confess." I let my eyes sweep the entire room.

"If you admit anything, the focus shifts from her to you. If you're named or confronted, shut up and say nothing. If you confess, you're finished."

Most of them took my advice, and it blew over. In the 1982 elections, only one of them was defeated because of his liaison. Congressman Tom Evans of Delaware ignored everything I told him. He walked out of the meeting, confessed to his wife, and then went public the next day. He was a very good guy and one of the president's most loyal supporters. For his honesty, the voters threw him out of office the next election.

THE WORKLOAD WAS phenomenal. Lyn would get in by 6:30 A.M., and would go off to the 8:00 A.M. senior staff meeting over at the White House. I rolled in at 7:00 A.M. so I could read the papers and be ready when he returned with marching orders for the day. Lyn usually stayed until 8:00 P.M; I'd rarely be out the door before ten o'clock. More often than not, I'd watch the eleven o'clock local news in my office. In an average day, my phone log would have over one hundred calls to return. And it went on like that seven days a week.

Lyn never met a meeting he wouldn't rather skip—and the White House is a place that meets all day long on matters big and small. He showed up for the important meetings of the cabinet and senior staff, and delegated most everything else to me. I attended budget sessions, personnel meetings, and sat in on deliberations of the judicial selection panel. There's no doubt I attended more high-level meetings than most of my peers. As a result, I got an education in how the federal government really works a lot sooner than they did. One of the first things I figured out was that the so-called troika that ran the Reagan White House was pretty much a myth.

On paper, there were three principal players and they were viewed as co-equals: Jim Baker, Mike Deaver, and Ed Meese. Almost immediately, however, the power dynamics shifted. Helped by a strategic alliance with Mike Deaver and abetted by Nancy Reagan's magic wand, Jim Baker and his brand of pragmatism had won out over Ed Meese and the California ideologues.

James A. Baker III may be viewed by his friends in the media as the most extraordinarily capable political operative of this century. That's saying a lot for a guy who's lost three presidential campaigns and boasts a two-and-four overall record, including losing his own race for Texas attorney general in 1978. The *New York Times* was right in 1995 when it called him "one of Washington's silkiest operators, a master at cultivating the press, working the Congress and outflanking bureaucratic rivals." He's all of that. Baker's a good negotiator, a capable manager, and for much of his career he's led a charmed public life, largely the result of courting the media assiduously. He's smooth, polished, can be utterly charming, and has savvy political instincts.

He's also extraordinarily cunning and manipulative—a man for whom making the deal is more important than what's in it. A staff person is supposed to take the bullets for the president. I know of at least two occasions when Baker pushed Reagan out to defend him. But Baker's compulsively cautious, extremely thin-skinned, and unusually concerned with his own image. Quick to take credit when things go well, he'll distance himself when trouble appears—which helps explain why he was invisible when he went back to the White House reluctantly in 1992 after George Bush looked like a goner.

Baker's also too cautious for the rough-and-tumble world of modern-day campaigning. James III would be good in an ambush with a rifle and scope, but he's not cut out for the hand-to-hand combat with knives and brass knuckles. Campaigns aren't the place for the timid or for those worried about their reputations.

It was his managerial skills—and his connections—that landed him the job of White House chief of staff. The deal was brokered by Stuart Spencer, the veteran California political operative who co-managed Reagan's first gubernatorial campaign.

Ed Meese was the favorite for the spot, but Spencer did a job on him and convinced the Reagans that because he'd never worked in Washington and was a poor manager, Meese would be a disaster as chief of staff. It might have had a lot more to do with Spencer being close to Baker, and that he wasn't trusted by Meese or most of the other Californians in the Reagan camp.

Spencer's view was shared by Nancy Reagan and Mike Deaver. The three of them lobbied the president-elect, and before long Meese was out of the running. Spencer then advanced Baker. It didn't hurt that Jim Baker's closest political friend was the vice president-elect, who would obviously benefit from his presence in the corner office of the West Wing. Bush lobbied aggressively for Baker's appointment, but the most important advocate was the new First Lady, who put a lot of stock in physical appearances. Baker met her image of the man Hollywood would cast for the role.

As chief of staff, Jim Baker was an effective broker and a good manager. I don't think he had an agenda initially. He saw himself as the guy who could make the trains run on time—a reputation he'd gained as Gerald Ford's delegate hunter in the 1976 primaries and later as Ford's campaign manager. He surrounded himself with strong subordinates and never forgot that he was a staff guy. He cultivated Congress and the press like nobody before or since.

Even though I wasn't his first choice, I wouldn't have gotten the top political job in the White House without his sign-off. He was good to me and usually backed up my political judgments, and he saved my ass a couple of times. I respected him, and still do, but I never trusted him. Did he use me? Sure—he used everybody.

Ed Meese was probably the most selfless of all Reagan's aides. He came to serve the president and had no other agenda. He'd been Reagan's last chief of staff in California, and was used to being leader of a team that worked together with shared goals. Moreover, he knew more about what the president stood for than any man alive, and had the closest substantive relationship with the president of all the Californians. Nobody else had the stature or the institutional memory to engage Reagan from a philosophical perspective, and nobody understood the man and his ideology better than Meese. He was an extraordinarily decent person, but he didn't adjust quickly enough to the palace intrigues. At the outset, he was the most powerful person in the White House. The national security and domestic policy operations reported to him, so he had the apparatus in place to drive policy. But from the moment he arrived, Jim Baker with Deaver's help chipped away at his power until there was little left.

Ed kept a schedule that would kill a dentist, with meetings penciled in every fifteen minutes all day long. "You're seeing people I turned down three weeks ago," I teased him once, but Ed was such a nice guy, he couldn't say no. In the end, that sapped his effectiveness. I believe that if Ed had been limited to a small staff and functioned as a true counsellor to the president without line authority, he would have been a powerhouse. In the end, he wasn't, but he deserved far better treatment than he got from the media and his troika teammates. Ed paid a heavy price for his service to the president. He lost a son in a car crash early in the administration, he lost a grandchild, and he lost his Sacramento reputation as Mister Good Government.

Mike Deaver was the deputy chief of staff, but he wasn't a manager and didn't want to be. He didn't care much about policy, either. He was the guardian of the Reagan image, and was brilliant at it. A favorite of Nancy Reagan, he'd begun as a baggage handler in Sacramento and had ingratiated himself with the Reagans ever since, rising steadily through the ranks to become a confidant without peer. On a personal level, Deaver knew the Reagans better than anyone. He had the toughest job in the White House—handling Nancy and the family. Nobody had as much capacity for punishment as Mike. And with the help of some very talented subordinates, he was extremely effective as the keeper of Reagan's image.

It's hard for me to give Mike Deaver the credit he deserves because we never got along. Deaver, Nofziger, and I had all attended San Jose State, which in those days was pretty much a poor boys' school. Mike came from a blue-collar background in Bakersfield, and his humble pedigree seemed to eat at him. We clashed once on a presidential helicopter after he made a crack about Vallejo. I told him that a guy from Bakersfield had no right to talk down my hometown. "The difference between us," I said, "is that I'm proud of my background, and you're ashamed of yours." "Life didn't begin for me at my first Georgetown party," I remember saying. But Mike loved the limelight and the glitter. His office looked like a museum, with a Childe Hassam flag painting behind the desk and autographed pictures of world leaders in sterling silver frames more expensive than my suits conspicuously scattered around the premises.

After he left the White House, Mike got mugged by enemies he'd spent a career making. He was indicted for lying to Congress when they were investigating his lobbying business, and went through a public humiliation about his alcohol problem. He's a better man today, and even though we aren't close, I admire the way he's handled his troubles. I'll never forget that he was one of the first people to reach out to me in 1993 when I blew myself up in New Jersey.

Like most shotgun marriages, the troika quickly fell apart in a flurry of elbows over people, power, and policy. It was the pragmatists and insiders—led by Baker and Deaver—versus the true believers and outsiders—led by Meese and Nofziger. Before long, the balance of power had shifted to players who'd been in Washington long before the Reagan Revolution arrived.

Predictably, the first squabble was about personnel. The Nixon-Ford alumni knew the jobs they wanted and who to lobby for them. The Reaganites just wanted to serve the president and didn't have a clue how to get placed. Meese ally Pendleton James, the White House personnel chief, thought prior government service was an important qualification. But since Reagan had opposed both Nixon and Ford, most of his people had never been in their governments.

I knew from my Nixon experience that the best shot you have to work your will is to populate the government with true believers. Nofziger and I set about trying to stack subcabinet positions with Reaganauts. Ironically, the guy who broke the back of our scheme was one of our own—Cap Weinberger, Reagan's close friend and Secretary of Defense-designate.

Cap wanted Frank Carlucci as his deputy at Defense. We countered that Carlucci was a professional bureaucrat, a Nixon-Carter alumnus—anything but a Reagan loyalist. Weinberger let it be known that unless he got Carlucci, he wouldn't go to the Pentagon.

Weinberger was one of the president's closest confidants. He had been Governor Reagan's budget director and had enormous credibility with the Boss. Cap won the argument—and the next thing we knew every cabinet officer was demanding to name his own top assistants. At Transportation, for example, Secretary Drew Lewis wanted to hire Linda Gosden as his press aide. Having grown up around the entertainment industry, she'd been a longtime friend of the Reagans. Linda had been caught in the crossfire that ended with John Sears's exit from the 1980 campaign. She could have survived it despite her alliance with Sears. But when Nancy Reagan asked her to stay, Linda literally told Nancy to go fuck herself. Lewis had to appeal to Nancy directly, and Linda was forced to apologize in person, but she got the job.

The same thing happened with Bob Packwood, chairman of the Senate Commerce Committee. He wanted Mimi Dawson, his administrative assistant, to get named to a regulatory commission, the Federal Communications Commission. She had no Reagan credentials, but Packwood said if she didn't get the job, the president could forget about any appointees who had to get confirmed by his committee. Nofziger and I fought against it, but she got the job. In fairness, it turned out to be a good appointment.

The end result was that dozens of people came into the government at senior policy levels with no real loyalty to Ronald Reagan or his philosophy. The revolution was off to a shaky start.

The same dynamic was occurring in the West Wing. Baker, whose loyalties were at best divided, started at a competitive disadvantage to Meese. Baker controlled the administrative office, press office, public liaison, and intergovernmental, political, and congressional affairs; but the policy staffs reported to Meese. To stay in the game, Baker forged a strategic alliance with David Stockman, the brainy but disloyal head of the Office of Management and Budget (OMB). In fairly short order, Baker had the analytical resources of OMB to deploy against Meese's policy wonks. When it came time to butt heads on the budget, taxes, and defense, a chief of staff who cared little for policy but plenty for power played some powerful trump cards of his own. From day one, Baker was effective because he had assembled a staff who were masters at the Washington game.

Similarly, Baker understood that a president's agenda is driven less by the force of his ideas than their implementation. With only 192 Republicans in the House, we needed 30 to 50 Democratic votes to pass any bill. To corral those votes, Baker created the Legislative Strategy Group (LSG). Under the shrewd management of Richard Darman, a protégé of Elliot Richardson and a man whose talents were as prodigious as his ego, the LSG became Baker's tactical control center. It built coalitions and hammered out policy compromises to win the votes of the Democratic boll weevils. Meese's troops were neophytes at this game; as the agenda moved from formulation to execution, they lost control to Baker.

In a matter of weeks, the turf skirmish erupted into full-scale war. It was Baker and Deaver versus Meese and national security adviser Dick Allen, and all of them against Al Haig, the Secretary of State everybody thought was out for himself. The trench warfare got so intense that an unspoken motto soon developed: You Leak or You Die.

Giving reporters inside information or gossip to influence policy or damage a rival is a way of life in Washington. I've done my share. Everyone of importance leaks in a White House, but Baker was the undisputed master of the game. He not only saw more reporters in a week than Meese did in a month, but his people were skilled Washington infighters and knew how and where to leak. When Baker wasn't doing the leaking in person, his personal assistant Margaret Tutwiler was talking to reporters.

After a few months of anonymous battering, Meese was finally persuaded to get into the game, but his guys never got the hang of it. Baker and his partisans were all over the *New York Times, The Washington Post, Wall Street Journal,* and *Los Angeles Times.* Meese's guys would plant something with the *Washington Times,* where it was totally ignored by movers and shakers.

At the height of the infighting, one of Meese's allies had the Secret Service examine appointment logs to see who was talking to the press. The winners were Jim Baker and two of his top aides—Rich Williamson and Dave Gergen. The only reason Darman and Tutwiler didn't make the winner's circle was because they shrewdly did most of their leaking by phone.

The Baker team were masters of the black art of using someone else's phrases with reporters so somebody else got fingered for their leaks. Ingenious. Baker was always blaming Nofziger and the political office for the leaks. When I succeeded Lyn, he blamed me. Lyn was totally innocent of most; me, a little less so. But Baker and his team were the real culprits of the most damaging stuff. At a senior staff meeting in 1982, CIA director William Casey complained about critical foreign policy information being leaked. Few people in the White House had access to such sensitive information. One of them was a close Baker aide, who used to read information from the president's daily intelligence summary to a favorite reporter. Several people in that meeting promptly leaked word of Casey's remarks to *The Washington Post.*

Eventually, when the flames started getting close to Baker's doors and everyone knew he was the biggest offender, he shifted the blame and threw his own confidant Dave Gergen overboard.

Baker's shop not only had the firepower to prevail in most policy battles, but their skilled media manipulation lent credibility to their views in the press and with Congress. It's no accident that the cornerstone of the remodeled National Press Club Building was dedicated in 1985 by Secretary of the Treasury James A. Baker III.

ON THE AFTERNOON of March 30, 1981, Lyn and I were returning from lunch in the mess when Rosemarie Monk told us the president had been shot. We sprinted back over to Jim Baker's office. Baker was on the phone with Mike Deaver from George Washington University Hospital. Deaver had been with the president and narrowly escaped being shot himself. Within five minutes, the entire senior staff had assembled. It felt like we'd all hit a cement wall at 180 miles per hour and somehow survived. We were all in a state of shock. It was the greatest crisis of Ronald Reagan's presidency, and there wasn't a damn thing any of us could do but pray for the skill of the doctors.

Baker, Meese, and Lyn left for the hospital. I stayed in Baker's office with the rest of the senior staff watching television bulletins.

Half an hour later, Lyn called me from the hospital. "The guy's really in bad shape," he told me. "They don't know if he's gonna make it or not." I decided not to pass on that part of the conversation to my colleagues. If Reagan were dead, we'd know about it soon enough.

By day's end, we knew the president had pulled through several grueling hours of surgery and would in all likelihood survive. Lyn's press briefings from the hospital, complete with Reagan's reassuring one-liners, were a textbook example of how to calm a nervous press and public. It was Lyn's finest hour.

As it turned out, it was also the beginning of the end for Nofziger. Press secretary Jim Brady had also been shot; he suffered severe brain damage and would never function in the job again. Neither of Brady's two deputies, Karna Small and Larry Speakes, was up to the job. So Nofziger volunteered to take over as acting press secretary until the president came back from the hospital and a replacement for Brady could be found. Baker summarily and stupidly rejected what I thought was a magnanimous offer. Baker is an unbelievable control freak, and he knew he couldn't control Lyn. So he passed Lyn over for the inexperienced Speakes, who was only too willing to be controlled.

From that moment, Lyn's heart was no longer in the job. Lyn and Baker had always been like oil and water. Their neckwear said it all: Baker wore elegant Hermès ties; Nofziger's favorite featured Mickey Mouse. After being cut out of much of the inside decision making, Nofziger made no effort to conceal his disdain. He used to say that when Jim went off to Texas to hunt turkeys, he was committing fratricide. It was only a matter of time. Even if he hadn't been my patron, I would have been saddened by the shabby treatment of a guy who believed in Ronald Reagan heart and soul and had dedicated his life to getting him elected president. And he was done in by a guy who'd done everything he could to defeat Ronald Reagan twice.

In July, Lyn told me he'd leave a year to the day he'd arrived and planned to recommend me as his successor. He also told me not to hold my breath. I didn't. Baker had created the political office and put Lyn in the job to buy the loyalty of the Reaganites. It hadn't worked. The conservatives concluded that Baker was more devoted to George Bush than Ronald Reagan. To this day, they're still suspicious of Jimmy's allegedly conservative credentials. I was sure there was no way Baker would promote me.

In August 1981, California Lieutenant Governor Mike Curb asked me to run his 1982 campaign for governor. I told Baker I'd tentatively decided to accept and would leave before the end of the year. He didn't seem heartbroken.

Baker wanted Stu Spencer for Lyn's job, but Spencer was raking in big bucks as a consultant with direct entree to the Reagans. Rich Williamson lobbied like crazy for the job, but Baker had found out he was telling Laxalt about everything that happened and so didn't trust him. Haley Barbour, now chairman of the Republican National Committee, was also interested in the job. But Lee Atwater killed that idea by reminding one and all that Haley had been Jerry Ford's guy in the South in the 1976 campaign. The truth of the matter is that Haley was a staunch Reaganite who as executive director of the Mississippi GOP in 1976 had voted for Reagan at the convention when his chairman, Clarke Reed, broke his word and defected to Ford. (In 1985, I would bring Haley into the White House as one of my principal deputies.)

Baker's inability to come up with the ideal replacement for Lyn coincided with my having serious reservations about the direction of Curb's campaign. I was offered $300,000 to run it, but wasn't motivated by money. I told Baker shortly after Labor Day that I'd changed my plans and might like to remain as the deputy to whoever got Lyn's job. Jim was very gracious about letting me stay on.

A month later, I was the most surprised guy in Washington when Baker offered me Lyn's job. It took me about three seconds to accept. I moved into Lyn's office on January 20, 1982, the first anniversary of Ronald Reagan's inauguration.

BETWEEN 1969 AND 1974, Room 175 of the Old EOB was Richard Nixon's hideaway office. During his eight years as Eisenhower's vice president, Nixon had grown fond of the building's marble floors, high ceilings, and ornate baroque architecture. When faced with difficult decisions, Nixon would leave the Oval Office, cross West Executive Avenue, and climb the granite steps to work in seclusion in his hideaway.

It was there, Nixon later told me, that he made the decision to mine Haiphong Harbor and to order the controversial Christmas bombing of North Vietnam in 1972. He didn't tell me that many of the incriminating Watergate conversations that led to his downfall took place there, too. It was also there that he reached the first reluctant conclusion to resign the presidency.

Now the kid from Vallejo occupied that office—ghosts and all. I had an awesome new responsibility: Tending to the political health of another president.

Ronald Reagan was always being underestimated—even by those of us who loved him and were privileged to serve him. And he was simply the nicest man you'd ever want to meet. He was the most unpretentious politician I've ever known, and certainly the best human being. He had a big heart and a kind soul, and he preferred to believe the best about everyone. The only time I saw him angry in the five years I worked closely with him was after Menachem Begin went back on his word and bombed Beirut in 1982, killing hundreds of innocent people. For the most part, Reagan was a forgiving person. If he'd held grudges, George Bush would never have been his vice president. And Howard Baker, a strong supporter of the Panama Canal Treaty Reagan detested, would never have become his White House chief of staff.

In 1982, I wanted him to do a fundraiser for San Diego mayor Pete Wilson, who was running for the Senate. We were meeting in the family quarters with Nancy and Maureen present. The Reagan women had never forgiven Wilson for supporting Jerry Ford in 1976 and showing up in New Hampshire as a member of the anti-Reagan truth squad before the primary. To top it off, Maureen had just lost badly to Wilson in the Senate primary. The two of them were furious with me for even suggesting it.

"Isn't Pete Wilson mad at us for some reason?" the president asked.

"Mad at us?" Maureen bellowed. "We're furious at *him*." She and Nancy then reminded the president of Wilson's 1976 betrayal.

The president sort of sheepishly said, "I thought he was mad at *us*. I didn't realize we were mad at *him*. We'll go do the fundraiser." It was vintage Reagan.

His ego needs had been taken care of in Hollywood, or maybe even earlier as a lifeguard in Lowell Park, Illinois. A supremely secure man, he was probably the most emotionally comfortable president in modern times. We were returning from a trip one day, and as Marine One hovered above the South Lawn, he pointed to a color picture of his beloved ranch on the bulkhead above his seat. "I wish we were landing at the ranch instead of here," he said wistfully.

Not knowing what to say to a leader of the free world who didn't want to go back to work, I just said, "Some day it will all be worth it, Mr. President. History will be very kind to you." He looked at me and chuckled.

"I don't care what history says about me," he said. "They'll distort the truth, and I'll be dead and gone anyway, so it doesn't much matter. What I *do* care about is leaving this country in better shape than I found it, and creating opportunities for all those young people we saw on our travels today."

He turned to Senator Paul Laxalt, who was sitting across from him. "Just think what a wonderful land of opportunity we live in," he went on. "My father was a traveling shoe salesman. Paul's father was an immigrant Basque sheepherder. Your dad was a shipyard worker, and here we are. I don't know why I was chosen for this job, but as long as I have it, I have a sacred trust to give those young people the same opportunities we all had." Then we landed, and he hopped off the helicopter and went back to work.

Ronald Reagan always had a keen sense of who he was, and never lost his bearings. On one occasion, I was riding in the presidential limousine in midtown Manhattan. The streets were packed with thousands of onlookers, most of them cheering his presence. I was astonished by the warmth of the crowd. "Mr. President," I said, "don't you find this outpouring overwhelming?" He looked at me with that infectious Reagan grin. "Just wait about half a block," he said. "Some guy will be flipping me the finger and yelling, 'Fuck you, Ron, you prick.' That's the guy who always puts it in perspective for me."

For all his fantastic people skills, Reagan was at heart a loner. He didn't have many real friends—and really didn't need them. Their friends were in actuality *her* friends. Left to his own devices, he'd rather be chopping wood at his ranch in the Santa Ynez Mountains than just about anything else.

You could walk away from a dinner with Ronald Reagan believing he was your new friend for life—and you'd never hear from him again. I once asked Paul Laxalt, one of his closest friends, how often they spoke. He told me every three or four weeks. "He never calls me," Laxalt said, "and if he does, I'm on a call list Baker or Duberstein put together." It just wasn't a natural thing for Reagan to make a lot of calls. Unlike his wife, who was on the phone constantly.

The press loved to write that Reagan was out of it because he didn't pay attention to substance and policy. It's true that he wasn't a details man, but the criticism was grossly unfair. What he had was great common sense. After the U.S. Navy shot down two Libyan jets over the Gulf of Sidra in the summer of 1981, the press caused a flap because Ed Meese hadn't awakened the president. When asked about it, Reagan quipped, "I told Meese, 'If we shoot down their jets, let me sleep. If they shoot down ours, wake me up.'" That proved to me Reagan asleep was better than Jimmy Carter awake.

He also wasn't into politics in the traditional way. George Bush was a former chairman of the Republican National Committee (RNC) and personally knew all fifty of his state chairman and all one hundred members of the national committee. Richard Nixon was a political junkie; in some states, he could tell you who was doing what at the precinct level. But Ronald Reagan didn't pay attention to those sorts of details.

We were flying out to Kansas for a gubernatorial fundraiser in the first term when the president asked me if there was anyone he should mention in his remarks who wasn't in his advance text. I told him he should include Dick Richards, one of his longtime supporters.

"Who's Dick Richards?" the president asked me. "He's the national chairman," I replied, "the guy sitting right over there." He dutifully nodded and added Dick's name to the text.

My point is that this was one aspect of politics Reagan didn't care about. He knew Dick Richards and assumed the RNC would be run by people loyal to him, so he didn't worry about it. He didn't bother himself with minutiae, and he was a better president because of it.

Ronald Reagan never saw himself as the country's manager; he viewed himself instead as its inspirational leader, the cheerleader-in-chief who could pull the country out of its sense of self-doubt.

The day he was sworn in, American hostages had been held for 444 days by a third-rate revolutionary government in Iran. Our military had planes that couldn't fly and ships that couldn't sail. The economy was in dreadful shape. Reagan thought it was his destiny to make the country believe in itself again, and he did. The theme song of his 1984 reelection campaign said it all: "Proud to be an American."

Ronald Reagan was the last American Hero. He may have forgotten your name, but he never forgot who he was or what he believed in—and that was his magic.

He would never have been president, however, without his wife. Tough, shrewd, and fanatically loyal to her beloved Ronnie, Nancy Reagan made short work of anyone in her way—just ask Don Regan, Jim Watt, or David Gergen, among many others. Paranoid, highstrung, and neurotic, she could make life miserable for everyone who had to deal with her—including me. But Ronald Reagan could never have asked for a more supportive spouse or better friend and adviser.

Nancy had good political instincts and a great feel for public relations. She knew which brush fires could turn into firestorms. But unlike her husband, she was terribly insecure. He trusted everyone— even those who abused his trust. She didn't trust *anyone.* It took very little to get her worked up; when she thought somebody on the staff was becoming a political liability for her husband, his or her days were numbered. She wasn't known for taking many prisoners.

I was surprised to learn she didn't have much use for any of the Reagan loyalists. Ed Meese, Cap Weinberger, Bill Clark, Marty Anderson, Dick Allen, and Lyn were never in her favor—mostly because she was more interested in results than philosophy. In fact, her decision to cast her lot with the pragmatist wing of the White House early on helped doom the influence of the Californians who'd gotten her husband to the White House.

Many of her critics have described her as ruthless. I think *relentless* fits her better. She could be small and petty. Because of her persistence, she was the most feared person in the White House. She was easily swayed by personal appearance, for example, which is a big reason why she never cared much for Lyn Nofziger or me but was charmed by Jim Baker and Mike Deaver. Your chances for survival were always better if Nancy Reagan didn't know who you were. Once you were in her sights and she decided you'd made a misstep, you were finished. She could really make your life miserable—and frequently did. If I'd had any idea just how much grief she'd give me over the next four years, I'd have traded in one of my two suits for body armor.

Ronald Reagan adored his Nancy, even if they were as different as night and day, and never understood why reporters would write all those mean things about her. I remember another conversation we had on the helicopter in the summer of 1981. The day had begun with a visit to the aircraft carrier *Constellation* off the California coast and was followed by a fund-raising reception with the faithful in Orange County. Both had been great events, and he was really up. As we were helicoptering back to his suite at the Century Plaza Hotel, the president noticed we were over Beverly Hills. He asked if I'd heard of a restaurant called Chasen's, one of Nancy's favorite hangouts. I said I knew the place.

"Well," he mused, "I've got to go back to the hotel, change into black tie, and go downtown and have dinner at Chasen's with the same group of people I'm going to have dinner with every other night this week." It was clear that he didn't relish the prospect. But Nancy always got one week of Beverly Hills glitter for every two weeks at the ranch.

"You know what the end to a perfect day would be? If I could just go back to the hotel, get in my pajamas, order room service, and watch TV."

I smiled but said nothing.

"What are *you* going to do tonight?" he asked me.

"Mr. President," I said, "I think I'm going to do what you want to do."

"Lucky man," he said with a mixture of envy and wistfulness, and it was impossible not to feel sorry for the most powerful nice guy on earth.

He was clearly the right man at the right time. After Jimmy Carter, the country was desperate for someone who could reassure them that their kids would have a better life than their grandparents had. Reagan was able to make the country feel better about itself. People liked him even if they hated his policies, and they gave him the benefit of the doubt because they liked him and trusted him.

JUST BEFORE I took over the political office, a couple of grenades went off in my pockets. Actually, I inadvertently pulled their pins. The upshot was that I almost was out of my new job before I had Richard Nixon's old desk even warmed up.

I'm very honest about myself—always have been. I pride myself on not being a yes-man. I've told everyone what I think, including a lot of bosses over the years who didn't want to hear it. And one of the reasons why I've been described as every political journalist's favorite source is because reporters know I'm honest—even as they sometimes take advantage of it.

In my line of work, there's a downside to candor. You can be *too* honest for your own good. God knows, I learned that the hard way. In the space of four months, these two controversial incidents cemented my reputation forever as a guy who tells too much truth. Or, as my detractors prefer to describe it, I'm a guy with a terminal case of foot-in-mouth disease.

In August 1981, Maureen Reagan had asked me to dinner at Harry's Bar and Grill in Century City, across the street from the Century Plaza Hotel. She told me she planned to run in the Senate primary in 1982 and wanted me to manage her campaign.

"Maureen," I said, "I just don't think you're a viable candidate." I diplomatically refrained from adding that even though she was energetic and an excellent speaker, her campaign skills were negligible, and she had scores of enemies in the party. More to the point, her father's finance guys didn't want her in the race, so she'd never be able to raise enough money. Her greatest asset—being the president's daughter—would backfire on her. She'd be a disaster, I knew, and a bitter primary slugfest would make it that much easier for Jerry Brown, God forbid, to be the next senator from California.

Her better strategic option, I counseled, was to run in a safe Republican congressional district created by reapportionment. The Reagan name alone was enough to win that seat, and after two terms in the House, she'd have the credibility to challenge Alan Cranston in 1986. She dismissed my advice. "I'm running now," she insisted.

For the next several months, the White House and California party leaders mounted a concerted campaign to persuade Maureen to stay out. When reporters asked her father if she were running, the president forthrightly blurted out, "I hope not."

On the afternoon of January 8, 1982, I was interviewed in my office by Leo Rennert of the McClatchy papers. I didn't know him, but he was doing a profile of the new White House political director for the *Sacramento Bee*. In the course of that conversation, he said he'd heard Maureen had asked me to run her campaign. I told him I was absolutely not interested. When he pressed for an explanation, I said I was reluctant to talk about it.

Then Leo did what Connie Chung would do to Newt Gingrich's

mother thirteen years later. "This is just between you and me," he said, closing his notebook and sticking it back into a pocket of his coat jacket.

To me, that meant off the record. So I told Leo the truth. Maureen was too strident and too inexperienced to be a good candidate, I said. Reagan's Kitchen Cabinet didn't want her in the race, and if her last name wasn't Reagan, we wouldn't even be having this conversation. "She has the highest negatives of any candidate I've seen," I admitted.

The next morning, a Saturday, a White House operator rang my apartment just as I was leaving for the office.

"Mr. Rollins," she said, "Maureen Reagan wants to talk to you—and she is *really* mad." I did what I had to do: I ducked.

"Tell her I'm on the way to the office," I said. I couldn't imagine why Maureen would be on my case.

By the time I got to the office, Maureen had called again, demanding to know, "Where *is* that little bastard?"

"What did you say to the *Sacramento Bee* about Maureen?" a distraught Atwater asked me. As my new deputy, he knew that if I'd screwed up, he'd be out the door thirty seconds after me. The light bulb went off. Did that motherfucker Rennert screw me on this? I couldn't believe he would take off-the-record remarks and blow me up with them. We started waking up old friends in Sacramento, hoping one of them had gotten the paper and could read the story to us. We'd had no luck by ten-thirty, when I got a call from Margaret Tutwiler.

"Mr. Baker wants to see you," Margaret drawled in her sweetest Alabama accent. "Has Maureen Reagan talked to you? She's talked to everybody *else* in the White House."

When I walked into the chief of staff's elegant West Wing corner office, Baker was sitting at the conference table. Mike Deaver was in a Queen Anne chair in front of the fireplace. They weren't interested in small talk.

"Have you talked to Maureen yet?" Baker asked. I said I wanted to know what had set her off before I called her back.

Deaver waved a piece of wire service copy in my direction. "Are you the Ed Rollins mentioned in this Leo Rennert story?" he asked. I lamely said I hadn't seen it. "Well, the *president* has seen the story," he said. "The First *Lady* has seen the story. And they're not happy. Let me just read you a few of the quotes."

He sat there like a schoolmarm, gleefully reading off the offending passages without giving me the courtesy of seeing the piece. The little prick is enjoying this too much, I said to myself.

"Is that your quote?" he asked.

"Yes, it is," I admitted. My gut was churning in overdrive. "Obviously, this is serious," I said. "I just got burned." I knew it was futile to try to explain what had happened.

"I don't understand why the fuck you'd even talk to an asshole like that," Deaver exploded. "You know the guy hates our guts. He's never done anything but screw us. I can't believe you'd be so stupid."

I said to myself, Fuck, it's over. And Mike was right—I *had* been stupid. I was too honest and too trusting for my own good, and I was about to pay with my job.

"If you want my resignation," I said, "you have it."

"Well, clearly that's an option that has to be considered," Deaver replied icily.

"Fine. But can I read the story?"

"You don't need to read it. You've heard the high points. I can't believe you'd say something that stupid about the President's daughter."

Up to that point, Jim Baker hadn't uttered one word. "Ed," he said finally, "we'll talk about it on Monday."

The sixty-second trip across Old Executive Avenue to my office was the longest walk I'd ever taken. I was sick to my stomach and totally disgusted with myself. I'd been shafted by Rennert, but I knew it was my own goddamn fault. Baker and Deaver had doubted I was up to the job; now I'd shown them I wasn't. By Monday, I'd be the laughingstock of the White House. My colleagues would be looking at me like I had leprosy—even if I wasn't fired. Once again, shooting off my goddamn mouth had finished me. I spent a long and lonely weekend kicking myself for being such a dumbshit. By Sunday night, I knew they couldn't fire me without blowing it into a gigantic embarrassment, but I also knew I'd dug a very deep hole for myself.

On Monday morning, Baker called me aside after the senior staff meeting and said I wouldn't be fired. But I had to apologize personally to the president.

"You've gotta go to the woodshed," he said, "and he'll kick your ass good, but I saved your ass." Baker walked me down the hall to the Oval Office, then shut the door.

I felt like I was about to get a root canal without Novocain. The president was sitting at his desk and motioned me to sit down. I stammered my apologies as best I could.

"Mr. President, I can't tell you how badly I feel about this. I'm especially sorry about ruining your weekend at Camp David, because I know how important that down time is to you." I was stalling, scared shitless what he'd say when I finally stopped talking.

"Well," he chuckled, "Maureen *was* a little worked up about this. But, hell, Ed, don't worry about it. I know she shouldn't be in this race. There's nothing you said that I haven't thought to myself. I wish she weren't running, too, but we've both got to be careful. I've said something I shouldn't have said, too."

He paused for a moment and looked me in the eye. "I'll make you a deal," he offered. "We both have a lot of friends in this race. If you don't say anything about the candidates, I won't, either."

As he walked me to the door, he put his arm around my shoulder, smiled, and said, "Just be real careful."

I was giddy with relief. I walked out of there saying to myself that I would kill for this guy if he asked—and believing that Baker had tried to take credit for something he hadn't done. I later learned the president *had* originally thought I should walk the plank, but changed his mind after deciding that might create more problems than it solved. At any rate, it was vintage good-cop Ronald Reagan, and I loved him for it. I felt like a million bucks. It was true what they said about Reagan: His heart was big as the West he loved.

I reported back to Baker as instructed. My relief and exhilaration at surviving seemed to set him off. Obviously, I hadn't been chastened sufficiently by the Boss for his tastes.

"Now, goddamnit," he said, "you walk out of here like a guy who's been to the woodshed. I don't care how good you feel. You're a mighty lucky man." He was definitely right about that.

"And just remember who your friend was."

As if one near-death experience wasn't enough, I was back in the Dumpster a month later. This time my antagonist was Roger Jepsen, the Republican senator from Iowa. Some senators are gone but not forgotten. Jepsen, appropriately, is gone *and* forgotten. But he nearly got me fired.

The previous October, the Senate had agreed by a four-vote margin to approve the president's request to sell five AWACS radar planes to Saudi Arabia. The sale was bitterly opposed by American friends of Israel. Only a furious arm-twisting campaign by the White House saved the day. The outcome was in doubt until the very end. It wasn't a done deal, in fact, until the day before the vote, when Jepsen, a staunch opponent, announced he'd reluctantly changed his mind and would vote with the president. He didn't say that the White House had orchestrated a massive pressure campaign against Jepsen, who was up for reelection in 1984.

That very evening, October 28, 1981, I taught a class on the media for a friend of mine at Georgetown University. As I walked into the classroom, one of her students asked me, "How did you get Roger Jepsen's vote?"

I offhandedly replied, "We just beat his brains in." I thought nothing of my comment and proceeded to do the seminar. I'd been assured everything was off the record.

What I didn't know was that the guy who asked the question was a reporter for the *Des Moines Register and Tribune* named John Hyde. His girlfriend had smuggled him into the class. A couple of days later, Hyde wrote a front-page piece using my comment about Jepsen. To protect himself, he referred to me only as a senior White House official and made no mention of the circumstances in which my statement was made. I didn't see the story until much later.

Jepsen blew a gasket. He contacted the White House in a rage and soon had the entire place shook up. Baker fingered Lyn, who already had one foot out the door. The president circulated the remarks in a letter to the senior staff and said he'd fire the culprit. Lyn asked me about it.

"Lyn, it sure as hell *sounds* like me, but I've never talked to this guy John Hyde or any other reporter about Jepsen."

"One of those motherfuckers over in the West Wing has got your language down to a tee," he laughed. "You better watch out."

Over the next two months, Jepsen went on a witch-hunt to track down the anonymous White House official who'd dissed him. He had his press secretary put together a goon squad, which, among other things, found out about the class and demanded that the Georgetown registrar provide a list of students taking the course. The university refused, but Jepsen was relentless. Finally, one of his storm troopers tracked down a student who said I'd taught the class.

On February 6, 1982—a mere fifteen days after I'd officially succeeded Lyn as assistant to the president for political affairs—Jepsen demanded to see Jim Baker, Ed Meese, Mike Deaver, and me.

In Baker's office, the senator presented us with a thirty-three-page memorandum naming me as the source and demanding that the president fire me. When I saw a reference to the seminar, I finally realized I was the culprit. I apologized profusely, and explained the circumstances. Jepsen wasn't mollified. I walked out figuring I was going to set a new record for the shortest White House job tenure.

As luck would have it, the president was due to visit Iowa the following week to campaign for his New Federalism program. Jepsen's ultimatum was leaked to the *Register and Tribune* the day before the president was to arrive in Iowa. I felt like a condemned man the entire time we spent there. When the senior White House staff was introduced at a fund-raising breakfast, there was dead silence at the mention of my name. I wanted to die. I felt better, however, when the president referred to his good friend "*Robert* Jepsen." And my spirits revived totally when former governor Bob Ray flung an arm around me and said I shouldn't worry about Jepsen.

"Anyone who knows the dumbshit knows he doesn't have any brains to beat out," Ray deadpanned.

I figured I was history. I also was beginning to think I was either the dumbest or unluckiest guy ever to serve in the White House, or that maybe I couldn't handle the big time. But I wasn't going down without a fight. Lee Atwater and my executive assistant Michele Davis leaked the details of Jepsen's investigatory excesses to columnist Rollie Evans, who made the senator look like a total jerk. When the column broke the day after the Iowa trip, I now looked like the victim, at least in the eyes of my colleagues and especially my supervisors. The pressure eased for my scalp.

After the trip, the president called me in. It seemed like I was beginning to wear my very own footpath to the woodshed.

"Ed, I can't have my political director at war with a Republican senator," he told me. "Go make peace." I wanted to punch Jepsen out, but I did what I was told. I groveled. I issued a public apology. I sent a letter to the *Register and Tribune* saying I'd done the senator a terrible injustice. And I went to see Jepsen in the office of Senate Majority Leader Howard Baker.

"Senator, I can't apologize more profusely," I said. "I didn't mean to hurt you, and I can promise you it will never happen again. We've had a good relationship until this, and I think we should put it behind us."

Jepsen wasn't satisfied. He kept ranting and raving about it. "I think it was terribly irresponsible," he said. Finally, I lost it. "Senator, if you want my ass, you'll get it. Keep screaming about this, and I have no doubt I'll be forced to resign. But I want you to know that if I'm fired, I'm going to Iowa. I'll find a candidate to run against you in the primary, and I'm going to beat your motherfucking ass right into the ground. You've never had someone like me in Iowa running campaigns. I'll bomb your ass back to the Stone Age."

Jepsen couldn't believe my impertinence. "You can't do that," he shouted.

"Just watch," I shouted back. "We can walk out of here in peace, or we can go to war. The choice is yours." He decided to declare a truce.

Much to my relief, I'd survived. But from that day on, I was a marked man. I'd come east with two suits, one patron, and no pedigree. Now my patron was gone, and I'd screwed up royally—twice. Overnight, I'd been tagged as the most accident-prone guy in the White House since Jerry Ford. Foot-in-mouth Ed, just resting between screwups. I had such a reputation for talking out of school that I was automatically the prime suspect for any leak.

I felt totally snakebit. My margin for error was now below zero. For the rest of my career, I'd walk around with a bull's-eye taped to my forehead. My heart said I'd been screwed, but my head reminded me that both these episodes were self-inflicted.

I also decided I wasn't going to roll over and play dead. I had a job to do and I was going to do it. I owed that much to myself. I owed that much to Lyn for bringing me to the White House. I owed that much to Ronald Reagan for letting me stay.

REAGAN BELIEVED THE 1970s had been a period of psychic trauma for the country. He had great confidence that if he could cut taxes, stimulate the economy, and rebuild the nation's defenses, he could get America moving again. That was the driving force behind the Reagan Revolution, and he pushed it with a quiet conviction and single-mindedness that made it even more powerful.

The core of his agenda was defense. Reagan was a product of the cold war. He was convinced that left unchecked, the Soviet Union would prove itself the evil empire. He was determined to stem the decline in America's military readiness, and he picked the right lieutenant for the task.

Cap Weinberger was the most indomitable infighter I ever saw— the only member of the inner circle Nancy Reagan couldn't trump. Ronald Reagan had sent him to the Pentagon to rearm America, and he meant to do it, without taking any prisoners. Not even David Stockman's analytical brilliance could tame Cap's missionary zeal. I was witness to a confrontation at a budget review meeting one day where Stockman pleaded with Weinberger to make a modest concession on a defense manpower issue.

"I've made a concession just by sitting here, and I'll make no more," Cap said. "If you want to walk across the hall to the Oval Office, we can do that, but I'll remind you that you've not had great success in appealing anything against me to the man across the hall." Stockman folded his tent.

For all practical purposes, so did the president's congressional critics. By the end of 1981, most of Reagan's agenda had been accomplished. Even though he didn't get everything he wanted, Congress had cut income taxes and passed a budget significantly reducing federal spending. The defense budget was given a major boost, and government deregulation was finally on its way. The administration was standing up to the Soviets, helping keep the peace in Lebanon, and supporting democracy in Central America. Psychologically, Americans were beginning to feel better about the future. It was a great freshman year, the strongest since FDR's first in 1933.

Reagan had accomplished this against very long odds, but the pundits hadn't reckoned with his personal popularity. Time and again in 1981, members of Congress would tell me they opposed his legislative agenda but couldn't risk voting against a president who was six to ten points more popular in their districts than they were.

I've always believed that the way the president comported himself after the March assassination attempt was a powerful hidden weapon for his legislative program. He came closer to dying than most people realize, but he never seemed larger than life than when he laughed in the face of death, cracking jokes about the political affiliation of his surgeons and telling his wife he forgot to duck. In those tense days, he formed a bond with his countrymen that earned him a powerful reservoir of goodwill and affection for the rest of his term and that ultimately was transformed into political support. Until the day he left office, Reagan was given the benefit of the doubt by many people who liked and trusted him even if they hadn't voted for him.

In an election year, the task of the White House political office is fairly obvious: Get the president reelected. If it's an off-year election, you do everything in your power to hold down the losses to your party. You do that by working closely with campaign committees on Capitol Hill and deciding where to send the president stumping for his troops. That's if he's popular. As Bill Clinton learned in 1994, sometimes your own troops want you to stay the hell away from their state or district.

Reagan was personally very popular and had made a strong showing in 1981, but I knew our prospects for the 1982 mid-term elections were mediocre. The Reagan landslide hadn't changed control of many state legislatures, and the party fared poorly from reapportionment plans mandated by the 1980 census. We were especially hard hit in California, where a brilliantly ruthless scheme crafted by the late Congressman Phil Burton and signed in the closing hours of his term by Governor Jerry Brown effectively redistricted several Republican incumbents into Democratic enclaves. By redrawing the lines, they took back every seat we'd won in the seventies.

The economy was also heading toward recession, and Americans almost always vote their pocketbooks. People still loved Ronald Reagan, but that probably wasn't going to be enough for the fall. In the summer, I predicted in a memo to the president that we'd lose a minimum of twenty seats in the House. I didn't realize it at the time, but I'd taken over the political shop at the high-water mark of the Reagan presidency.

In late 1981, after I'd been named to succeed Nofziger, Lyn and I flew up to New York to talk with Richard Nixon about 1982 congressional elections. As usual, Nixon dispensed some trenchant political advice.

"There's no disciplinarian in this White House," he complained. "There needs to be a nutcutter to keep the troops in line. There's no Colson. There's no Haldeman. Jim Baker's too cautious to play the role. George Bush is a wimp and can't play the role; hasn't got the guts. And Reagan's too *nice* to play the role." This line was delivered with a whiff of disgust. I knew that Nixon had grudging respect for Reagan's skills at communicating and envied his charismatic gifts, but was offended by what he considered the president's lack of substance and modest grasp of the issues.

I decided that Nixon was right, and I was the best candidate for the job. If nobody else was interested, I'd nominate myself as the White House nutcutter. I had no idea just how miserable a job that would turn out to be, or that I'd spend most of my energy over the next year fighting fires created by the president's friends, not his enemies.

The need for a hardass became painfully obvious in the early spring of 1982, when I had nasty encounters with two Republican senators who lost sight of the Reagan agenda in their eagerness to promote their own.

The National Republican Senatorial Committee had recently sent out millions of copies of a fund-raising letter above the president's signature. The language, which in a breach of protocol had never been shown to the White House, was anything but vintage Reagan. It was shrill, nasty, and very un-presidential. The president and Mrs. Reagan were understandably upset when their friends started sending them copies of the letter. I sent a message to Senator Bob Packwood of Oregon, the committee chairman, telling him that the president wanted the letter pulled. Packwood refused, so I asked for a meeting. On March 30, I met with Packwood and other members of the campaign committee in a Senate caucus room.

I repeated that the letter hadn't been cleared with the White House, and the president wanted it withdrawn.

"You are a liar," Packwood told me. "We *did* have permission."

The hair on the back of my neck stood up. "Senator," I said, "you've got one minute to take that back."

Everyone else was looking at their shoes, but I wasn't finished. "There was a time in my life when I would have knocked the teeth out of anyone who called me a liar. Now, I'll just promise you that if you don't take back what you said, you'll never have any cooperation from the White House as long as I'm the political director."

The silence was deafening. Finally, Paul Laxalt shattered the unwritten code of the Senate club. "Goddamnit, Bob," Laxalt said, "I don't know why you're in this job. You hate Reagan. You hate everything he's all about. Why don't you just quit?"

Packwood could ill afford to cross Ronald Reagan's closest friend in the Senate.

"I take it back," he said, without a hint of apology. "I should not have called you a liar. But *somebody* over there is a liar. We had permission."

"Show me the permission," I replied.

Packwood had no comeback, and the letter was pulled. I knew *he* was the liar, and I was right. Months later, one of his top staffers told me that Packwood had ordered him to put the letter out without clearing it with the White House.

Just as Packwood and I reached an uneasy truce, another nasty squabble with the late Senator John Heinz of Pennsylvania was heading for the Oval Office.

Packwood and the White House had previously signed off on a deal for the president to make ten appearances in the fall of 1982 for senators up for reelection. Packwood would choose the beneficiaries of a Reagan visit, but agreed that I could overrule him on any race we thought was either hopeless or a runaway. There's no use wasting a president's time and political capital stumping for sure losers—or winners.

When I got Packwood's list, Heinz's name was on it. I rolled my eyes; he was a lock for reelection. More important, he'd kicked the living crap out of the president every day since the inaugural. Heinz was always complaining that the president's budget cuts were heartless and mean-spirited. He didn't need our help, and he sure as hell didn't deserve it. I told Packwood that the president would be delighted to campaign for Dick Thornburgh, who was running for reelection as governor and had supported the president faithfully. But John Heinz wouldn't be making the cut.

Heinz immediately bitched to Jim Baker, who ordered me to take care of Heinz.

"He'll win with seventy percent of the vote," I argued. "And if he rolls us, I won't have any credibility left as an enforcer." Baker was insistent. The president would do an event for Heinz and another for Thornburgh. I was so ripped with Heinz that I gave Thornburgh first choice—lunch or an afternoon reception. Ever gracious, he said it made no difference to him. Heinz grabbed the reception.

A few days later, Heinz changed his mind. He was afraid the fat cats would go to lunch and skip his reception. Now he wanted the lunch slot back. But Thornburgh had printed up invitations and was determined to keep to the original plan. Heinz didn't care. Rich guys always think they can make their own rules.

The trench warfare was getting out of hand. I called representatives from both sides into my office and flipped a coin. Thornburgh won, and kept the lunch.

An hour later, Heinz called to accuse me of disrespectful behavior. "This is no way to treat a United States senator," he fumed, "flipping a coin."

I let him rant and rave for a while. Then I pulled a quarter from my pocket.

"Senator, I just flipped another coin, and Dick Thornburgh won again. And if I flip it again, Dick Thornburgh will win again." He hung up and called Jim Baker, demanding to see the president.

Preparing background memorandums for presidential meetings is usually a tedious chore. This one was a labor of love. I attached copies of every last cheap shot Heinz had taken at Ronald Reagan over the last fourteen months. When he read the memo, the president called me in disbelief.

"Why are we doing *anything* for this guy?" he asked. My sentiments exactly.

When Heinz came in for his appeal, the president deferred to me. I made some crack about his financial situation.

"There you go," Heinz complained. "You think I'm rich. I'm not rich. I only have thirty or forty million dollars. It's my aunts and uncles who are rich." He then asserted that the president's economic policies had cost him more interest on a $300,000 personal loan he'd taken out to help pay for his last campaign.

By now Jim Baker must have wanted to go hide somewhere, and the president was astonished.

"Senator," he said, "I don't get into these things. This is Ed's call."

"Mr. President, we flipped a coin, and Dick Thornburgh got the lunch."

"Well, that sounds fair to me." An heir to the Heinz pickle fortune had overplayed his hand with a poor kid from Dixon, Illinois.

Just to make sure everyone got the message that loyalty would be enforced when necessary, I delivered it through the media. On April 13, 1982, I met with a group of reporters over breakfast at the Sheraton-Carlton Hotel. I said that I was toting up the score before deciding where to recommend the president make campaign calls in the fall. Republicans who'd been trashing Ronald Reagan better not hold their breath. When Ann Devroy of *USA Today,* now of *The Washington Post,* asked how I intended to do that, I gave her a smart-ass reply.

"If Teddy Roosevelt carried a big stick," I said, "Ronald Reagan needs only a small bat." That obviously became the lead of her story: Reagan planned to use a baseball bat on disloyal Republicans.

Within minutes, word spread on the Hill that the White House had an enemies list. This time it was no slip on my part. I knew exactly what I was saying, and precisely what the reaction would be. The congressional relations office was bombarded with complaints, and before I walked the two blocks back to the White House, Jim Baker had persuaded the president to disown my comments. There would be no litmus test. Perish the thought. Privately, many of the president's supporters applauded my remarks and felt we were finally going to get tough in the bruising battles that lay ahead.

I actually managed to stay out of trouble for several months. Then, in July, I got another reminder that my reputation for talking too much had made me an easy target for other leakers.

Margaret Tutwiler called me one morning to say that Baker wanted me to talk with Maureen Santini of the Associated Press. I ignored the request for several days, until Margaret called back to say that Santini was bitching I hadn't returned her phone calls.

"Let me make it clear," Margaret said. "Mr. Baker wants you to talk to Maureen Santini." So I gave her an appointment that afternoon.

She was doing a story on the White House strategy for the 1982 congressional elections.

"I hear you've got it all laid out," Maureen said. She was right. A week before, I'd done a memo to Baker and Deaver recommending a heavy schedule of presidential campaigning for Senate and House candidates beginning around Labor Day. I didn't want to lie, and I didn't want to confirm the story. So I used the time-honored Washington device of saying that all the final decisions hadn't been made. That was literally true.

Maureen then whipped out a copy of my memo and handed it to me. I checked the routing hieroglyphics and quickly saw that it was a copy of Jim Baker's original.

I told Maureen that since she had the memo, it was a waste of our time to talk about it. That was fine by her; she just wanted me to confirm the memo was indeed genuine. I would have looked like a fool not commenting, so I confirmed the obvious.

When she wrote her story laying out the president's fall schedule of travel, Deaver went crazy and thought my office had leaked the memo. Deaver was in charge of the schedule, and knew he'd get a load of crap from candidates who hadn't made the president's dance card. The afternoon the AP story ran, Baker summoned the entire political crew to his office for a tongue-lashing. He began the meeting by demanding to know why Morgan Mason, one of my assistants, was absent. Then he looked straight at me and flew into a rage.

"You guys are the biggest goddamn leakers in the White House," he roared as Deaver looked on. "We don't need a political office. If you keep leaking, we're gonna abolish your goddamn office!" I sat there astonished but silent. I hadn't been chewed out like that since Marv Comstock, my high school football coach, devoted a halftime to kicking my ass from locker to locker for throwing a punch during the game. We were specifically ordered to stop talking with reporters. I couldn't exactly say in front of a dozen people that my staff had been set up by my boss, so I just took the bullet.

When I got back to my office, my hot line to the chief of staff was ringing.

"Ed, I know you understand what I had to do," Baker soothed. "Deaver's upset about this scheduling stuff getting out, and he got the President all worked up this morning. I had to go through the motions to calm them down." I was doing a slow burn, but said nothing.

Fifteen minutes later, my hot line jumped off the hook. Baker was in a new fury. "I want that little shit Morgan Mason fired," he bellowed. "I don't care who the hell he is or who the hell he knows. I want him out of here."

Morgan Mason was like a son to Nancy Reagan. He was the offspring of actor James Mason and his wife Pamela, and the culture and refinement so loved by Nancy and Mike Deaver oozed from every handsome pore. Morgan was charming, well mannered, and had impeccable Hollywood connections. He dated a stable of starlets and was always up on the Beverly Hills gossip. In no time, he became Nancy's favorite staffer and Mike Deaver's pet. A week seldom went by without Morgan having lunch with the First Lady in the residence to exchange Tinsel Town gossip or playing tennis with Deaver on the White House courts.

Morgan had started out as deputy to chief of protocol Lee Annenberg. Then they had a run-in, and both of them sprinted for Mrs. Reagan. Nancy had to side with Lee, the wife of Walter Annenberg, a longtime friend and former ambassador to Great Britain, but she told Morgan he could work anywhere in the White House he wanted. Much to her and our chagrin, he said he wanted to work for Lyn Nofziger. We didn't have a slot, so one was created by order of the First Lady. He worked half-time for me, half-time for Deaver. Unlike Mike, Jim Baker has no use for pretty boys, so Morgan wasn't one of the chief of staff's favorites, to put it mildly. But I loved Morgan, against all odds. The kid brought humor and irreverence to our office and was a delight to have around. He served as sort of my personal ambassador to the West Wing, where he had much better entree than I did.

I called Morgan in and got the rest of the story. He was AWOL from our tongue-lashing session because he'd been with the president and First Lady at an event. He showed up ten minutes after we'd left Baker's office. According to Morgan and Margaret Tutwiler, Baker asked Morgan where the hell he'd been. "I was with the Boss," he explained.

"Well, goddamn it, *I'm* your boss," Baker reminded him, "and when I call a meeting, I expect you to be here."

"Well, yes, Jim, but the president is *your* boss." Baker was ripshit—nobody talked to him like that.

The next day, Margaret asked me if I'd taken care of "that problem."

"Margaret, I'll be happy to fire Morgan Mason when it's been cleared with Mrs. Reagan and Mike Deaver." I knew Baker was too gutless to go up *that* mountain, so I thought Morgan was safe. Every day for the next three weeks, Margaret would call and ask whether I'd taken care of the problem. I'd say no, and ask whether Mrs. Reagan and Deaver had signed off. Baker didn't want to have Nancy on his ass any more than I did, so he punted.

Morgan stayed on—until somebody leaked that he'd met with divorce attorney Marvin Mitchelson and allegedly talked out of school about the First Lady's best friend Betsy Bloomingdale, whose husband Alfred had caused a deathbed scandal when his model mistress visited him in the hospital dressed as a nurse. Morgan decided it was time to leave. I was really sorry to see him go. He'd become about the only guy in my office I could really trust.

A couple of weeks later, I accompanied the president on his August vacation to California. The morning of the flight, I picked up a copy of the staff manifest and found that my regular seat assignment on Air Force One had been changed. There's a long-established pecking order on the presidential aircraft: The president's quarters are up front; then comes a line of compartments for the chief of staff, senior staff, other staff, guests, and the Secret Service. The press pool sits in the back of the bus.

I checked with one of Deaver's aides, who told me I'd been moved from the senior staff area to the guest section on Jim Baker's order. But it was only for one leg, I was assured.

I couldn't figure out why I'd been moved until Doug Brew of *Time* magazine sat down next to me. I asked why he wasn't in the back of the plane with the press pool. He told me *Time* was doing a cover story on the 1982 elections, and he had an interview with Baker en route to California. Half an hour after takeoff, Margaret Tutwiler came back and escorted Doug to Baker's cabin, where he spent much of the trip. The light bulb went off in my head: Goddamn, I'm being set up. If there's anything in Brew's piece that isn't flattering or is too revealing, Baker has the perfect alibi: What do you expect? The guy sat next to Rollins on Air Force One.

When we landed in California, I was steaming. As we deplaned, I couldn't resist needling Baker on the square. "Baker, you bastard, I hope you made me sound brilliant." I smiled.

"Rollins, you never sounded so brilliant." Jimmy said, grinning.

In the end, the elections turned out pretty much the way I'd expected—lousy. We'd compounded our problems by throwing in with congressional leaders, including Republicans like Howard Baker, Bob Dole, and Pete Domenici, who'd been looking for an excuse to raise revenues almost from the day the 1981 tax cut passed. In the summer of 1982, Congress passed the Tax Equity and Fiscal Responsibility Act (TEFRA), which was really neither. Only a year after the president had cut taxes, TEFRA *raised* them by $100 billion over three years. Baker, Darman, and Stockman had persuaded the president he'd actually get three dollars in spending cuts for every dollar raised in new taxes, so he was able to come to terms with a bill he didn't really want to sign. They totally bullshitted him and got him to sign off on something that violated his core beliefs. The voters weren't fooled; they felt he'd compromised his principles. When unemployment hit 9.8 percent in July, the highest in forty years, public sentiment turned against us dramatically. We lost twenty-six House seats in November, robbing the president of the working majority he'd used so well in the first year. It was clear to me that Reagan's revolution was being derailed by his own people.

AS IT HAPPENED, I spent election night in a hospital bed. For much of the fall, I'd been traveling everywhere with the president and still trying to take care of all the other campaign activity. I also was focusing heavily on California, helping out where I could with the Wilson and George Deukmejian campaigns. I was running myself ragged, and three transcontinental red-eye flights in ten days in October had left me exhausted.

It was about six-thirty on the evening of October 25. I was supposed to play racquetball in an hour with Rich Bond, deputy chairman of the RNC. I was going over some fresh polling data, trying to figure out where best to send the president over the next seven days. All of a sudden, I felt extremely hot. I stood up to pull off my sweater, and an explosion went off in my head. All I could see was white. I staggered into my chair and tried to talk, but couldn't. By the time two competing ambulance crews decided which would take me the six blocks to George Washington University Hospital, I couldn't move. I thought I was dying at the age of thirty-nine. All I remember is Dr. Arthur Kobrine, the neurosurgeon who saved Jim Brady's life, feeling my neck and saying, "It's a stroke, it's not a heart attack."

I was extremely lucky. In a couple of days I was able to talk, and by the end of the week I was moving my limbs. It turned out the stroke had been in the making for fifteen years. During the brutal drubbing I'd gotten in my last fight in 1967, my neck had been caught on the ropes. The huge welt on my neck had healed, but my carotid artery had been damaged and had narrowed over time. At some point, a blood clot had formed. A piece of it had broken off and caused swelling in my brain on that October evening. The doctors told me that if I'd kept my racquetball date, I would have died on the court.

One of the first calls I got when I came to was from the president.

"I want you to know I'm not letting you off the hook this easily," he said. "When you've recovered, I want you back on the job." I came very close to telling him I wasn't sure I wanted back into the White House pressure cooker.

On election day, my mother ordered me to put a bathrobe over my hospital gown. I should have realized she knew something I didn't. An hour later, the president and Jim Baker showed up for a visit. It was one of the kindest things anyone has ever done for me.

"Mr. President," I said, introducing him to Ed and Mary Rollins, "the three of you have a lot in common. My parents used to be Democrats, too."

That launched the president into one of his favorite yarns about how he'd been a lifelong Democrat until the party had left *him*. Here was the President of the United States charming them out of their shoes. If they hadn't changed their registration to Republican six months earlier, they'd have done it on the spot.

When the president walked outside, he told reporters I'd said we'd do very well in the elections. What I actually told him was a little different.

"Mr. President," I'd said, "I think we're gonna get our butts kicked."

The following day, I was told that Rich Williamson, one of Baker's top aides, was making a move to take my job. Dancing on the grave already, I thought. At that point I didn't care, but Lee Atwater did, and launched a ferocious counterattack.

A couple of weeks later, on November 16, surgery was ordered to repair my carotid artery. During that operation, I had a second, more severe stroke and nearly died on the table. Fortunately, neither Williamson nor the press ever learned about it. When I came to, my left side was totally paralyzed. Leg movement returned quickly, but my left arm was useless for days. I was in the hospital a few more days and spent another month at home doing very little but sleeping.

In the few hours I was awake, I chewed myself out about how royally I'd screwed up the priorities in my life. The day after my first stroke, the president had flown off campaigning without me. It was a stark reminder that nobody's indispensable. At first, I'd assumed that my White House days were over, and for the time being so was my political career. That was fine by me; for the first time in my life, I understood that living was more important than all the other crap I'd been doing.

But I owed the president, and I wasn't about to let that snake Williamson get my job by default. I returned in mid-December, working a few hours a day and swearing I'd never pull another seven-day week again. I'd survived the toughest year of my life, and was a better man for it. I didn't know where the future led, but I knew if I chose to stay in this arena, I could battle with the best of them. Yet I wasn't sure staying in the game made any sense. I now knew I wasn't indestructible, and the sooner I got out of there, the better it would be for me physically and mentally.

I'm sure I was influenced by my own sense of fragility, but I couldn't help noticing a troubling mood shift at the White House. The mood had been euphoric at the 1981 Christmas party, but it was far more subdued in 1982. The internal bickering and the mid-term elections had taken their toll on the collective psyche.

On my first day back a few days before Christmas, Jim Baker took me in to see the president, who was receiving an update from White House counsel Fred Fielding about Anne Burford. The embattled head of the Environmental Protection Agency (EPA) was being forced out. Anne was a protégée of Joe Coors and Jim Watt, but her tenure at EPA had been controversial, and she'd been ground up by the Washington crowd. She was a loyal ally, and I'd tried to help her. At the midpoint of the president's first term, another of his loyalists was walking the plank. By now a pattern was developing: Nofziger, domestic adviser Marty Anderson, and national security adviser Dick Allen were already gone; Bill Clark was under assault; and Meese was losing more ground daily. These were Reagan's principal campaign advisers, the guys who helped get him here. In my gut, I had the queasy sense that the revolution was in the process of being consigned to a premature grave.

As my courtesy visit came to a close, the president invited me to join him while he lit the national Christmas tree by remote control. As I stood there on the portico outside the Oval Office, I felt great joy in my heart when the giant tree lit up on the Ellipse. Christmas was always my favorite season, and this one was very special. The mere fact that I was alive, and could still walk and talk, was the best gift ever under my tree. I would never take life or good health for granted again. Even though I hadn't been to church in many years, I then and there said a prayer of thanks—a prayer for myself, and one for our nation that this great man still had to lead.

ROUND 5

MORNING IN AMERICA

I RETURNED TO the White House in December 1982 with a whole new outlook on life. Every morning, I'd stare at a six-inch scar in the bathroom mirror, a souvenir of the surgery on my carotid artery. I had my throat cut in the White House, I'd tell myself—and survived. The stroke damn near killed me, but if I hadn't been stricken, I probably would have died from the stress of my job. I was determined to learn from my scrape with death.

I found myself more reflective and less driven. I'd completed my obligations to my former wife and gotten a nice raise with my promotion to a presidential assistant, so my financial burdens were eased. I'd moved to an eleventh-floor Virginia duplex overlooking the Iwo Jima Memorial, with a majestic view of the city across the river.

I found my job less of a hassle, and not just because I was working fewer hours. If I hadn't had the stroke, I'd have been floating in limbo, and more than a few colleagues would have scapegoated me for the mid-term election losses. Instead, the president had welcomed me back with open arms, and even my enemies seemed to be treading gingerly. I guess nobody wanted to be responsible for killing me. My plan was to stay until 1983, then stake a claim to be the western regional coordinator for the president's reelection campaign. Then I'd leave Washington forever and go home to California.

I pronounced myself a changed person. But it wasn't long before I was reminded that the more things change sometimes, the more they stay the same.

In early January 1983, I received a call from Richard Nixon. After inquiring about my health and welcoming me back, he urged me to make sure that the twenty-six House Republicans defeated for re-election in November were given jobs in the administration if they wanted them.

"You've gotta take care of those who lost," Nixon told me. "That's what I did in 1970. Reagan has to do this. They walked the line for him. Now he has to do the right thing for them. Get Bush to help you. Remind him I saved his ass after he lost in '70."

I called Helene von Damm, the president's longtime personal secretary, who was now running the White House personnel shop, and relayed Nixon's pitch along with my concurrence. She understood the need to take care of our own, and said she'd do what she could. A few weeks later, Helene called me back.

"Are you still insisting on us appointing *all* these ex-congress-men?" she asked. Ten of them had asked for jobs, and Helene had found homes for most. "I'm having trouble with two of them—Millicent Fenwick and Margaret Heckler."

I wasn't surprised. Fenwick and Heckler represented liberal districts in New Jersey and Massachusetts, respectively, and neither had ever been an enthusiastic supporter of the president. But they were high-profile women, and it was important to take care of them. To my taste, Peggy Heckler was far the less deserving. Reapportionment had thrown her and Democrat Barney Frank into the same district, and their race had been a donnybrook. She was trying to come across as liberal as Frank, and had spent more time bad-mouthing the Boss than a lot of Democratic members. There weren't many tears shed when she lost. We needed to find something for her, but not much.

Helene had scrounged around in her bag of goodies and come up with a position for Fenwick as ambassador to some United Nations do-good agency headquartered in Rome. It was a perfect fit for the aristocratic, pipe-smoking liberal.

"What do you have in mind for Heckler?" I asked.

"Associate administrator of NASA for congressional affairs."

"That's perfect," I said. "Even Peggy Heckler can't screw up NASA." It was an appropriate comedown, considering how little she'd supported the president.

That was the end of it, until my red White House phone rang at home late one January evening, and someone told me that Peggy Heckler was about to be named Secretary of Health and Human

Services, replacing Richard Schweiker, who'd resigned unexpectedly earlier in the day. I started cussing into the phone.

I couldn't believe it. Giving her a job was one thing—but a cabinet appointment, and an important one at that? Peggy had a reputation as a complete organizational ditz. She couldn't even run her congressional office. She'd be a disaster. And she damn well didn't deserve such a lofty position.

I arrived at the senior staff meeting the next morning in a foul frame of mind. As soon as Jim Baker opened the meeting to questions, I raised the Heckler nomination. I was surprised to find myself the fly in this punch bowl.

"This is just nuts," I argued. "It sets a terrible precedent."

"But you signed off on her," Helene objected.

"As an underling at NASA," I reminded her. "Not the secretary of the biggest cabinet department in the government."

Ed Meese sided with Helene. "I'm really surprised by this," he said. "Helene said you had no objections." I repeated that she was fine as a NASA bureaucrat, but not as a cabinet officer.

With the tone of a schoolmarm, Jim Baker broke in.

"Ed, I think you want to keep your opinions to yourself."

I knew something was up; Baker had always been scrupulous about allowing everyone a say at senior staff meetings. "The president is announcing her appointment in two hours," he went on.

"You're going to live to regret this decision," I said to nobody in particular. "This will come back to haunt us."

I left the meeting muttering to myself that the black hats were up to no good again. I was determined to find out who was behind this idiotic decision. It turned out to be Dick Darman.

Darman was one of Baker's closest allies. He was the staff secretary who regulated all the paper flow in the White House. He controlled what the president saw or didn't see. He knew who called the president and what was said. Darman had more experience in government than anyone in the White House. He had been Elliot Richardson's policy person and served with him at Defense, Justice, HEW, and Commerce, in both the Nixon and Ford presidencies. He was brilliant, well educated, well married, and one of the richest men in government. He was also one of the most liberal members of the staff, a guy who made George Bush look like a right-winger. And he was dangerous because he understood power as well as the best.

When Lyn once sent a memo to President Reagan complaining about the 1982 bill that was going to raise taxes, Darman wrote in large bold script across the first page: "Mr. President, I need not remind you that Mr. Nofziger knows nothing about tax policy."

Nofziger ripped Darman a new one when he was tipped off by one of the president's secretaries. As director of the budget office, Darman later proved that he knew plenty about tax policy but nothing about politics when he convinced President Bush to break his pledge and raise taxes in 1990.

Dick's father, a wealthy Massachusetts industrialist, had been a big financial backer of Heckler. When Helene had offered her the NASA job, Heckler went batshit. She claimed that as dean of Republican women in the House, she deserved at least a cabinet post. Darman had sold Baker, who sold Meese and then the president. The president had been widely applauded for recently appointing Elizabeth Dole Secretary of Transportation. Their rationale was that another woman in the cabinet would be a real plus. I agreed, but we should have found a competent one who was loyal. Suddenly it all made sense—sick, stupid sense. Like me, Meese had objected to Heckler's lack of loyalty. But Baker had quieted his qualms, using his old California comrade Helene as the evidence that the conservatives had signed off.

The president's third year had begun like the second had ended. If this was the future, I suddenly couldn't wait to get the hell out of there. More than once, I caught myself dreaming of California—until the afternoon of April 8, when Jim Baker telephoned me.

"Rollins, get your ass over here right now," he barked, "I want to talk to you." As I hurried over to Baker's elegant West Wing corner office, I racked my brain to remember what I might have done to land me in hot water again. I still hadn't come up with anything by the time I was sitting in his office.

For all his charm and sophistication, in private Jim Baker prefers the salty language of an ex-Marine. "Rollins," he said, "I want you to know that I'm going to give you a place in history, and you damn well better remember who did it for you.

"I've been in there fighting for the last two hours to make you Reagan's campaign manager. It's not a done deal, but if you get it, it's because of me."

I almost fell out of my wing chair. Twenty months before the 1984 elections, I had no idea the president was even thinking about a reelection campaign, much less considering me to run it.

I knew Baker's modus operandi well enough by then to suspect that despite his caveats, it *was* a done deal, but I was so stunned I barely managed to stammer out my thanks. I hurried back to my office and informed Atwater and Michele Davis. Lee's adrenaline was pumping as high as mine. He hated the daily White House bullshit and was anxious for the combat of the campaign.

About an hour later, Baker called to confirm that the president had signed off on the plan. If Reagan decided to stand for reelection, he said, I'd run the campaign and Senator Paul Laxalt would be the chairman.

Later that afternoon, Laxalt called to congratulate me. I told him I guessed I really owed Jim Baker for backing me. Paul laughed and asked where I'd gotten that idea. I told him about my meeting with Baker.

"So *that's* where he went when he snuck out of the meeting," he chuckled. "Ed, you need to know Jim was fighting against you all the way. He and Spencer wanted Paul Manafort."

Manafort was Baker's closest political aide in the 1976 Ford campaign. He was a convention whiz and had taught Baker everything he knew about delegate selection. But Manafort was vetoed for being too close to Baker, Laxalt added, so I became the acceptable alternative.

I was too excited to worry about the infighting. All I knew was at the age of forty, a poor kid from Vallejo was about to run the reelection campaign of the President of the United States.

I STILL HAD a tough road ahead. The first manager picked usually doesn't last. Laxalt warned me that Baker's closing words had been, "He'll never survive, and then I get my pick." But at least I now controlled my own destiny; if I failed, it was my fault, nobody else's.

Almost immediately, I got a new reminder that I was still a marked man despite my elevation. In May, the president was preparing to fly to Ohio to dedicate a new school of politics at Ashland College that was being named after John Ashbrook, the late conservative congressman. Every right-wing kook in the country would be there. I'd persuaded the president to do the event over the objections of Baker and Deaver. I was manifested to fly with him on Marine One to Andrews Air Force Base. As I waited in the reception area of the East Wing for the Reagans to emerge from the family quarters, Jim Baker summoned me to join him in the corner.

"I got bad news for you, Rollins," he said. "Mommy's running late and wants to bring her hairdresser—Julius." I asked him why I should gave a damn.

"Because the hairdresser gets your seat on Marine One," he said. I couldn't believe what was happening.

"What are you talking about, Jim? I'm the goddamn political director, and you think I should give up my seat for some fucking *hairdresser*?"

"Not *some* fucking hairdresser, Rollins—Mrs. Reagan's hairdresser. And unless you think you can do her hair better than Julius, you had better get your ass in gear and get a car or you'll miss the plane."

We both knew what he was saying. Driving to Andrews takes a good half hour. Marine One does it in about seven minutes. Air Force One leaves the instant the president is aboard. There was no way I could make it in time.

"Well, you better try," he said. "Every event on the schedule is one of your right-wing kook events, so you better hustle."

I tore ass out of the White House, sprinting like a fool across the South Lawn yelling obscenities at no one in particular. As a blue Chrysler from the motor pool pulled up at the basement entrance of the White House on West Executive Avenue, I could hear the roaring engines of Marine One lifting off.

I was sweating like a plow horse, and my overweight body wanted to lie down in the back seat and die. I'd never hear the end of this one—keeping a president waiting is simply never done.

As Marine One disappeared into the distance, my driver, an Army master sergeant, tore down the Suitland Parkway with red lights flashing and set a new land speed record of twenty minutes. I'd been cleared right onto the runway. The driver pulled up to the front steps of the presidential aircraft.

I flew out of the car and dashed up the steps, totally out of breath, my suit soaked with perspiration. Baker stood at the top of the steps with an ear-to-ear shit-eating grin. "Rollins," he barked in a voice loud enough for most of the passengers to hear, "how many times do I have to tell you to be on time?"

"Fuck you, Baker," I gasped, "and your hairdresser pal, too."

As I passed the president's cabin, I heard Mrs. Reagan say: "It figures *he* would be the one making us late, Ronnie."

Despite this unnerving encounter, I knew I'd lucked into the best political job in the universe—on paper. The reality was considerably more tentative. While I always assumed the president would run for reelection, he made a point of telling everyone, including me, that he hadn't made up his mind. That meant I had to gear up a campaign in a vacuum. And the electoral terrain was a lot more uncertain than it appears in retrospect. In fact, it looked damn daunting at the time. A majority of Americans still loved Ronald Reagan, but all the polls in 1983 had him consistently trailing Walter Mondale, the likeliest Democratic opponent.

The truth is that for all practical purposes, the Reagan adminis-tration was out of gas by the spring of 1983. The 1982 mid-term losses had robbed us of our operating margins in the House. We no longer had the votes to put together a working coalition, so the chances for legislative accomplishments to tout in 1984 dropped to zero. Foreign policy was a mixed bag. Reagan embellished his cre-dentials as a statesman by a strong performance at the May 1983 economic summit in Williamsburg, Virginia, but his deployment of Marines into the Lebanon civil war in September 1982 was a political loser. Unemployment finally dropped for the first time in two years, and our economic gurus insisted the economy was on a course for recovery. But all the polls showed that people still worried about inflation and their jobs.

Actually, they were just plain worried about *everything*. Not long after my appointment as campaign manager, I asked the Republican National Committee to commission a poll by Bob Teeter aimed at helping me learn the answer to a single question: Aside from the economy, what's really bothering Americans? Teeter's findings showed that people were worried about the future and were particu-larly concerned about their kids. When voters decide that their chil-dren may have a less comfortable life than they did, it's bad news for any incumbent. In response, we threw together some educational reform proposals, which sounded nice but sure weren't going to win us votes. That was my job, and there were moments it scared the hell out of me.

I kept my day job as assistant to the president for political affairs, but focused on the reelection. From the day my appointment was formally announced in June until I moved into Reagan-Bush '84 headquarters on Capitol Hill in October, I devoted myself to assem-bling a team and developing a strategic campaign plan.

More often than not, it makes perfect sense for an incumbent president to run on his accomplishments and ask for four more years to finish the job. I didn't think a more-of-the-same strategy was good enough for 1984. I figured we'd pick up some House seats, but not nearly enough to resurrect our 1981–82 coalition, much less control the House. And the Senate would remain roughly evenly divided even if we managed to retain control.

In other words, Tip O'Neill and the House Democrats would be setting the legislative agenda for the next four years—unless we cam-paigned on an activist agenda of our own and asked for a mandate to enact it. I wanted the president to emphasize a strong national de-fense, more tax cuts, and major education initiatives.

I got absolutely nowhere with this rationale. Ed Meese was the only guy at the White House with the clout to press the argument, but he'd been nominated Attorney General and taken himself out of the campaign. The domestic policy staff was outmatched by Darman and Stockman's maneuverings, and the powers-that-be weren't interested in seeking a mandate. Baker, Darman, and Stockman all believed the economy would crater in a second term, and an agenda grounded in more defense spending and no additional taxes would send the deficit sky-high. Deaver and Nancy Reagan were opposed as well. They wanted the candidate to be perceived as the world's peacemaker. In their view, emphasizing defense would damage those credentials.

"It's a helluva lot easier to campaign than it is to govern," Stockman needled me one day.

"It's a helluva lot easier to govern if you get a mandate for what you campaigned on," I shot back.

Every time I peddled my agenda, it disappeared in the great gauze machine. Any hope I had for an issues-driven campaign drifted away.

At the start of every campaign, I always try to zero in on the three or four words I want voters to associate with my candidate. You have to know what they are—or what voters want them to be—in order to drive your message. If they already connect him with those words, you're halfway home. If not, he's got a perception problem to fix.

As the election year approached, public opinion began to crystallize. Every poll I saw in 1983 found that people wanted a leader they could trust. More to the point, they already believed Ronald Reagan was the political rarity who lived up to that billing. That's why we developed a simple campaign theme and made it our driving slogan: Leadership You Can Trust. It proved remarkably successful; when we asked Reagan voters after the election why they'd voted for him, 85 percent said it was because he was a leader they trusted to do the right thing.

The tone of the campaign emerged as a traditional, feel-good campaign, short on specifics and long on fuzzy thematics. As our "Morning in America" spots would memorably argue, people were feeling better about themselves and their country these days, so why in the world would they ever think of turning back?

By Labor Day 1983, we'd essentially picked the team and settled on a strategy. We still had no candidate. On October 17, when I left the White House to set up the campaign headquarters, the president was still playing hard to get—even though he'd just signed the legal documents authorizing the creation of his reelection committee and given me a $21 million budget through the 1984 primary season.

"You're not going to hang me out here, are you, Mr. President?" I asked in my exit interview.

"Well, Ed, I've not quite made up my mind yet."

"That's not very reassuring," I said, laughing.

"Well, I'm thinking about it."

Not until much later did I realize that Nancy Reagan and her ditzy astrologer were unindicted co-conspirators in the president's little Hamlet act.

I moved into campaign headquarters at 440 First Street N.W. the next day. Five days later, on October 23, a suicide bomber blew up a Marine barracks in Beirut, killing 241 U.S. servicemen. It was the culmination of a disastrous deployment that had given the American psyche a bad case of Vietnam sweats. Shortly after his 1980 election, a Gallup Poll placed the president's approval-disapproval rating at a gaudy 70–14 percent. A week after the Lebanon tragedy, his approval rating had dropped to 49 percent. But his disapproval number—always the greater threat to a candidate—had ballooned to the same 49 percent. I had little more than a year to turn those numbers around.

IF THE PUBLIC face of a campaign is about image, the back room is about turf. My first job was to line up my troops and stake out our territory. For the most part, I was dealing with the same cast of characters—and the same factions—as the past three years. But there were a few new faces and some welcome returnees.

I brought Lee Atwater along to serve as my deputy. And I called back our old boss, Lyn Nofziger, to be my chief troubleshooter. I trusted Lyn absolutely. Counsellor, consigliere, father confessor, enforcer, you name it—Lyn wore all those hats for me. Lee, on the other hand, was like my mischievous kid brother, a guy I needed but couldn't trust.

Lee Atwater had superb political skills, as good as anyone I've ever met in this crazy game. He wasn't a strategist, but he had great tactical gifts and enormous nervous energy. He simply couldn't be outworked, and he'd do anything to win. There were no rules or standards in Lee's operating manual; winning was all that mattered. He was Oliver North in civilian clothes: Tell me what you want done, but let me worry about how to do it.

In our first White House incarnation, we'd worked side by side fourteen hours a day, six days a week. Lee probably spent four of those hours camped in my office every day. I was his big brother, counseling him on his marriage, relationships, problems, insecurities, and everything else. I listened to him pour out his life story.

Lee had started in South Carolina politics as an intern for Senator Strom Thurmond and later worked in Thurmond's 1978 reelection campaign. After Reagan's election, Thurmond drove Jim Baker crazy trying to get Lee hired at the White House. In desperation, Baker gave Lyn Nofziger an extra slot in the political office if he'd take Atwater and get Old Strom off his ass.

Lee started at the bottom of the heap. He had no title, no rank, no mess privileges, no presidential commission, and no real office. Within days he'd commandeered a staff, confiscated an office, stolen some furniture, and taken a bead on the two guys directly above him. Fortunately for me, I was three guys up.

When I succeeded Lyn at the end of 1981, Lee got the job of my deputy by default. There was nobody else in the shop who could do what he did any better.

Lee was a real character, with incredible vitality and a singlemindedness of purpose so powerful that at times it seemed it would burst out of him. He had an attention span of fifteen seconds on his best day, and couldn't sit still for more than a minute or two. In meetings, he'd shake with a nervous energy that could light a city block. He was also a complete bullshit artist who always had his own agenda. He had absolutely no interest in public policy unless it affected South Carolina. His passions were politics and music. Lee worked relentlessly and courted the press constantly. He was the biggest leaker in our office, but he only allowed himself to be quoted by name in his home state newspapers. He was a superb ass-kisser, and was particularly successful in stroking George Bush, Jim Baker, and Mike Deaver. He was very insecure at first, but in time he started believing his own press clippings—many of which he'd embellished with outright falsehoods about races he'd never managed, much less won. Even then, in the words of one of his favorite blues ballads, Lee Atwater was in every respect "a bad, bad boy, a long way from home."

We had many common bonds. Both of us were in the White House because of dumb luck and powerful mentors. We'd both been superimposed on the Washington political power structure, and they didn't like it. Lee was a southerner and understood the changes going on in the South like no one else in the party. I was a westerner and knew the protest movement that was building out there. I was blue-collar and a former Democrat. Lee was from the middle class, not the southern country club Republican set. We both had graduated from state colleges magna cum lucky. I played sports; he played the guitar.

There were differences as well. He was ruthless and manipulative with people. He treated his staff like slaves and showed them no respect. Yet for some reason they all would kill for him. I'm a bit of a soft touch, sometimes too soft for my own good. He couldn't stand to be alone and always had a group around him. I loved my moments alone and can't stand being surrounded by crowds. I think I'm a pretty secure individual and don't intimidate easily. Lee was terribly insecure and would run at the first shot. He was afraid of physical confrontation, and it never bothered me at all. We were so different yet so much alike—especially in our love of the game. We were ferocious about winning at all costs. But now we were a team, and we needed each other to survive in a jungle where no one cared if we made it or failed.

In many ways, he was the perfect deputy for me, a classic case of opposites compensating for each other's weaknesses. I like developing the strategy and a message, and figuring out how to drive it. But I'm terrible at details. Lee could cut through the details and get things done whatever the price. All in all, we were a strong tag team. We were always better working together than either of us was going it alone.

Lee loved to impress people with his smarts. He told everyone he was working on his Ph.D., but his academic record was about as unimpressive as mine. His staff would summarize best-sellers and political tomes so Lee could throw out quotes at meetings and parties of books he'd never read. He was always bringing me thirty-page memoranda he'd just whipped up, but he couldn't write a sentence. Most of his memos were written by his in-house guru, Jim Pinkerton. In fact, some of Lee's memos were produced *after* an event, and backdated. Some were even produced after the election to make him look more brilliant. The truth is that a lot of political operatives have learned to postdate memos and hand them out to unsuspecting reporters and academics doing campaign books. But nobody did it better than Lee.

Before long, I began hearing from friends in the White House and outside the campaign that Atwater was backchanneling with the Baker staff and taking credit for things he hadn't done. This became such a pattern that Michele Davis began privately referring to him as my Iago. When I confronted him, Lee would go into full denial, saying he loved me like a brother and would never treat me ill. I was his mentor; how could he possibly turn on me? In time I learned that most of what I heard was true: My trusted deputy couldn't be trusted. Despite all this, I really liked the guy. There was something endearing about him.

In those days, Lee wasn't taken seriously. He simply wasn't considered an adult. He was awkward in social settings, and his nervous energy made him seem like a high-strung flake. In other words, he couldn't succeed unless I did, and we both knew it. Lee's agenda was the future: He wanted to run Bush's 1988 campaign. Mine was the present. My two motivations were survival and getting Reagan re-elected.

"Just remember," I reminded him just before we left the White House, "if I go out the door, *you* go out the door thirty seconds later."

"Boss," he protested, "I'd never do anything to screw you." I think he knew I knew better. I needed Lee, but I'd have to watch him like a hawk.

THE REST OF my team was a mixed bag. Half of them were all-stars, some were guys I wouldn't have chosen but were assigned to me, and I had my share of troublemakers and minor league players.

Bob Teeter was one of the best pollsters and theoreticians in the business, a serious player in every Republican campaign since 1972, and a very good guy. But like most pollsters, he wasn't much of a decision maker.

Dick Wirthlin had been Reagan's numbers-cruncher since the 1966 California gubernatorial race and the major player in 1980. Wirthlin was respected for the integrity of his data and his analysis of his numbers. But he also thought he was a superb political strategist. In fact, he wasn't. Wirthlin wanted to concoct campaign strategy, create themes, and devise television commercials. He wanted to control the president's speeches and structure his schedule. In other words, he wanted my job.

Jim Lake was a superb press secretary, mainly because he didn't give reporters too much information. He kept me out of trouble for an entire election cycle, in itself a major accomplishment. Sig Rogich, a Las Vegas ad executive and Laxalt ally, managed the Tuesday Team, which produced our superb campaign spots. Ken Khachigian, a confidant of Richard Nixon and a full-fledged Reaganite, ran the opposition research team and was a first-rate speechwriter. He also despised, and was despised by, Dick Darman, which didn't hurt his reputation much around campaign headquarters. I had total control over how our $80 million campaign budget was spent; every money decision was made by me. Campaign treasurer

Bay Buchanan, Pat's sister, did a spectacular job of strategically allocating those resources. She terrified Lee Atwater by the ferocity with
which she nailed his expense account extravagances. Joe Rogers, the
finance chairman, raised funds quicker and more efficiently than it's
ever been done.

And then there was Stu Spencer. To Jim Baker and the Reagans,
Spencer was first among equals. Stu could have been the campaign
manager, but he didn't want it. Too much work and risk; Stu wasn't
into heavy lifting. He'd ride Air Force One and then either play golf
or bet the ponies when he was home. His day job was troubleshoot-
ing for me. His real job was handling the candidate and his wife, no
small task. Not even Mike Deaver did it as well.

Even in my role as campaign commander in chief, I knew I'd
never be a Reagan insider. Deaver and Nancy didn't like me and
were counting on Spencer and Teeter to report back regularly if I was
screwing up. Baker, I learned through the grapevine, had not only
predicted my demise but had picked my successor: Drew Lewis, the
former Secretary of Transportation.

My best chance of survival in this den of vipers was to forge a
relationship with Paul Laxalt, the campaign's general chairman. Laxalt was an extremely trustworthy man and his only agenda, like mine,
was to reelect his friend. He had the president's ear and was the only
player I felt could protect me from Nancy Reagan. So I made a
conscious decision to locate the campaign headquarters on Capitol
Hill, a couple of blocks from Laxalt's Senate office. It was my way of
signaling that I wanted and needed his help. A campaign is a constant series of brush fires; Paul was a great colleague to have at the
pump. Our collaboration developed into a strong friendship, and in
the spring of 1984, when at his urging I bought a country cabin in
Front Royal, Virginia, Paul and I would become weekend neighbors.

Jim Baker had instructed me to report to him, not Laxalt. I met
with Paul one day in November in his Capitol hideaway office.

"I don't want to get at cross purposes here," I said, explaining
Baker's edict.

Laxalt was furious. He rang up Baker and asked to see the president. Baker asked him what he wanted to talk about.

"I've known Ronald Reagan a lot longer than you," Laxalt replied, barely keeping his anger in check. "I don't have to tell you
what I want to see him about."

According to Laxalt, it was a short meeting in the Oval Office.

"Mr. President, I just want to know who's running your campaign,
me or Jim."

"You are," Baker interjected.

"I didn't ask you, Jim," Laxalt retorted.

Predictably, the president gave Laxalt the grant of authority he wanted. Laxalt closed the meeting with a warning.

"Jim," he said to Baker, "leave Rollins alone. He reports to me; I'll report to the president and keep you informed."

Baker was beside himself. He called me and reamed my butt royally.

"Why the hell are you sandbagging me?" he demanded to know.

"I'm not sandbagging you, Jim," I said. "I'm just trying to get the pecking order straight." I reassured him I wouldn't be making decisions he hadn't okayed and that we'd continue to have a smooth working arrangement. "You still control the president and the policy," I said. "I just want to run the campaign."

In the end, Laxalt had cleared the lines of authority—and the foul air. For the rest of the way, relations between the campaign and the White House were exceptionally smooth.

In late November 1983, the campaign high command assembled at the Airport Marriott in Los Angeles for a strategy session. We didn't make any major decisions. The aim was to make sure everyone was reading from the same sheet of music as we headed into the campaign.

The major accomplishment of this meeting, however, was to call a truce between Lyn Nofziger and Stu Spencer. These two California warhorses had loathed each other for what seemed centuries. They'd been political adversaries in 1964, when Spencer worked for Nelson Rockefeller and Nofziger backed Barry Goldwater. Nofziger was still furious that Spencer had abandoned Reagan, the guy who'd made him famous as a political guru, and worked for Jerry Ford in 1976. Lyn valued loyalty above everything else, and loyalty wasn't a word in Spencer's vocabulary.

Now, they were on the same side of the barricades, and they still couldn't stand the sight of the other.

After several hours of shop talk, we'd decided to break for a while and continue our deliberations over dinner. But Lyn and Stu needed to take care of unfinished business, so I ordered them to adjourn to the bar and hash out their ancient enmities first.

"I can't have two guys working for me who can't stand each other," I said. "Go do whatever you have to do, but try to get this thing worked through."

Two hours later, they were still at it in the bar. They looked like they'd had ten pops each at a minimum.

"It's still not settled?" I asked. "Are you up to 1976 yet?"

"Hell," Lyn growled, "we're fighting about an assembly race in the sixties." I knew it would be a long night, and told them to catch up with us later.

They never showed. When we got back to the hotel around 2:00 A.M., they were still going at it, even though they both were as shit-faced as any mortals could be while remaining vertical.

"We've decided we don't like each other and we probably never will," Nofziger reported, "but we're not gonna bad-mouth each other for the next eleven months." That was as decent a standoff as I could hope from these two political mavericks. It was critical for me, because Lyn was the only guy in the high command who would protect my backside. With Laxalt and Lyn in my corner, I had a shot at making it to the finish.

The next order of business was hosing down Wirthlin. I didn't want to confront him head-on. He was a tenacious infighter and had many important allies, including Nancy Reagan and Ed Meese. He handed me an opening by submitting the biggest polling budget in presidential campaign history.

Polling is a lucrative business, and it had made Wirthlin rich. Even after tithing 10 percent of his earnings to the Mormon Church, the former economics professor was driving a Porsche and living in an expensive home in suburban McLean, Virginia. When I saw his budget, two words leaped to mind: "ridiculous" and "profiteering."

For a president running unopposed in his own party, the volume of polling Wirthlin proposed to do in the primaries was absurd. He wanted to start nightly tracking on January 1, 1984. It made no sense—except that the data he'd be collecting would be very useful to some of his other clients.

Jim Baker's nickname for Wirthlin was "Numbers"; after reading this proposal, Baker should have changed it to "Dollars." I went to Baker, who backed me up completely. Wirthlin's budgets took a major hit.

The first real threat to my authority had been squelched. I could stop worrying about turf for the moment and turn my attention to strategy.

From day one, we all knew the greatest potential threat to Reagan's reelection was the age issue. At seventy-three he was the oldest elected president in history, and there was no question the assassination attempt had slowed him down a bit. We all recognized the need to neutralize the age issue early and often.

A terrific opportunity arose one day while I was having lunch with Roy Cohn at The Palm in New York. The legendary attorney was a big fan of the president and an old friend of Mike McManus, the superb presidential assistant who oversaw scheduling and advance operations. He was also very close to publishing magnate Si Newhouse.

"I can give you anything the Newhouse papers have," Roy promised. He mentioned that the Newhouse family owned *Parade* magazine, with its astronomical Sunday circulation.

"If you had your druthers," he asked, "what would you like to see on *Parade*'s cover?" I didn't have to think about my answer.

"Ronald Reagan working out," I said.

My mind flashed back to the spring of 1982, when I found myself in the presidential limousine alone except for two Secret Service agents. These solos occurred only rarely, and were occasions for extreme caution. I never tried to talk shop with the president when we were alone. If I were stupid enough to lobby him, he'd mention it to Baker and Deaver, and I'd soon be back in the doghouse for talking out of channels. So I always kept the conversations casual—movies, family, weather, and just a little politics.

In this conversation, I asked him what he considered his proudest achievement in his first year as president. He thought for a while, then replied, "I think my proudest achievement is my workout program. You know, I've always been healthy and swam a lot. But I've never lifted weights. After I got shot, the docs put me on a workout program, and it's working. I've put an inch of muscle on my chest and a quarter-inch on each arm." He was as proud as a fifteen-year-old kid.

I told Cohn about the conversation, and he picked up on it immediately. It took a few weeks for everything to fall in place, but on December 4, 1983, *Parade* ran a cover story on the president's workout program: "How to Stay Fit," by Ronald Reagan. The cover image was a blockbuster: The president as Arnold Schwarzenegger, pumping iron. Until the first debate the following October, the age issue disappeared.

When the president formally announced for reelection on January 29, 1984, his political health appeared equally robust. Our first private poll after his announcement found that the president would beat Walter Mondale by 54 to 42 percent, with only 8 percent undecided. Barring political reversal, a tougher opponent than Mondale, or me screwing up, the odds were fairly comfortable the president would be reelected.

I ALWAYS KNEW they were looking over my shoulder, of course, but for the most part the White House gave me what I needed—not always the case when an incumbent president is running—or left me alone. To guard against freelancing, Baker established clear lines of authority with the campaign, and his deputy Margaret Tutwiler proved to be an effective and reliable liaison. I'd brief Baker every day by phone or in person, and his team every Tuesday afternoon at the White House. They were almost always agreeable.

Except when he was traveling, I didn't have much face time with the president in the campaign. I saw him maybe every two weeks in a group, but these were always cut-and-dried sessions, mainly show and tell. Occasionally, Laxalt, Baker, and I would see him alone. He telephoned me only a handful of times all year. He ran the last race of his career the same way he governed—with a minimum of personal involvement. Just like in the movies, he was content to take direction, and he did it very well. He knew what his job was, and he went out and did it superbly every day. He was always confident the boys over at the campaign knew what they were doing, and it all seemed to be working fine.

The worst time for an incumbent's campaign is the first half of the year, because you're essentially out of the game while the other side decides who you'll run against in November. The media is focused on the horse race and couldn't care less what you're up to. All things considered, that's a far better deal than having a primary opponent. Just ask Jerry Ford, Jimmy Carter, George Bush, or Bill Clinton. You can save your money and hold your fire. But you're treading water, and if you're not careful, your campaign can get complacent out of inactivity.

Luckily for us, the Democrats had much bigger problems on their plate—like finding a viable candidate. The guy I'd always worried about was John Glenn, who for most of 1983 had run consistently ahead of the president in the polls. A Marine fighter pilot and astronaut hero, Glenn was chipping away at our Americana base. It would be hard to paint him as a left-wing liberal or tie him closely to Jimmy Carter. That would be child's play with Walter Mondale, our candidate of choice. Mondale was a card-carrying liberal of the old school in a country growing more conservative by the minute. Better yet, he had the albatross of Jimmy Carter's failed presidency hanging securely from his neck. I'd always assumed Fritz would be the nominee; but Glenn made me very nervous on paper. Then he followed up a fifth-place finish in the Iowa caucuses by placing third in New Hampshire, and he was toast.

When Gary Hart burst from the pack in the New Hampshire primary, my preconceptions were scrambled. I wasn't alone. The morning after Hart's upset win, I got a call from Nancy Reagan.

"What do we have on Hart?" she wanted to know.

"He's an attractive alternative to Mondale," I replied, "but I don't think he's gonna make it."

"Well, you better look into this. I'm getting calls from my friends that we better take him seriously."

Hart would have been a very formidable opponent, not just because of his Kennedyesque overtones. It was his youthfulness that scared me. Reagan had an extraordinary appeal to young voters, but Hart would cut into that support. He would also be competitive in the West, Reagan's bailiwick. And he had new ideas, while we were essentially into subsistence. I tracked Hart in our polling long after he was out of the race, and wasn't surprised to learn he would have been a far stronger candidate than Mondale. Once Hart self-destructed, I breathed much easier as Mondale's inevitability took hold.

The time would come to remind voters just who Fritz was and from whence he came. For now, my strategy was to remain presidential as long as possible. In the president's speeches, we tried to avoid referring to Mondale by name. We simply called him "our opponent." I didn't want to elevate his standing. I got some help from the calendar in this regard. On June 6, the day Mondale announced he had enough delegates to win the nomination even though he'd just lost the California primary to Hart, Ronald Reagan stood on the cliffs of Normandy at Pointe du Hoc, commemorating the fortieth anniversary of the D-Day landings with one of the greatest speeches of his career. My candidate was no mere politician—he was president of the free world.

On the other hand, we'd been sitting on our butts for six months while the Democrats captured the headlines. The strengths and weaknesses of our organization hadn't been battle-tested in the primaries. And our convention was late. We needed to come roaring out of Dallas on August 24 if we were going to build momentum for the fall. And we did. I was the grateful beneficiary of the best-run national convention in my lifetime—directed by Ron Walker and Mike McManus—and Reagan's lead jumped another ten points. If Ronald Reagan couldn't beat Fritz Mondale, I deserved to be keel-hauled.

But you can't take anything for granted in this business. Political supporters need constant tending, and one of the president's biggest backers, the powerful International Brotherhood of Teamsters, had become a little shaky. Reagan's workingman support had been eroded when he fired the air traffic controllers in 1981. Teamster president Jackie Presser was a Reagan fan, and his union had endorsed the president in 1980. But several members of his executive board were opposed to another endorsement. It was my job to keep the Teamsters inside the fold.

In August, shortly after the convention, Presser invited me to meet with him in the penthouse suite at Harrah's Hotel and Casino in Atlantic City. Accompanying me were Lyn Nofziger and Ed Allison, Paul Laxalt's eyes and ears in the campaign.

I'm a former Teamster myself from my college days and had handled the union's needs personally while working at the White House. I knew Presser well by now; he'd once shown up for an appointment with me packing a pistol in an ankle holster and had to dump it in a planter box in front of the Old EOB.

When we arrived at the suite, Jackie's 300-pound frame was draped in a XXXXL terrycloth bathrobe. He was built like a middle guard for his beloved Cleveland Browns—low to the ground and as wide as he was tall. He was balding, had the face of a bulldog, and was every bit as mean. He'd survived the Cleveland mob wars, and having risen to the top of one of the toughest unions on the planet was not someone to screw with lightly.

We had a couple of rounds of drinks, then Presser ordered giant porterhouse steaks for all of us. In the middle of dinner, he popped the question I'd been dreading.

"This is what I want in return for our endorsement," he said. "I want you to fire that dumb fuck who's running the National Labor Relations Board." I swallowed hard.

"Jackie, I can't do that," I said. He scowled at me and tried again.

"Well, I want another seat on the ICC."

"I can't do that, either, and besides, you've already got two of the five seats."

"All right, Rollins, what *do* you propose giving me for the endorsement of one of the largest unions in the country with more than two million members?"

"Jackie, I can't offer you anything but our goodwill," I sheepishly answered. "It's a federal offense to promise someone a government position in return for political support. After the election, we'll remember who our friends are."

He shot me a look of disdain as though I'd just pissed on his living-room rug. He turned to Paul Locigno, his longtime right arm, and said: "This guy's a real kidder, ain't he, Paul?" Locigno looked at his shoes.

"Well, I've got a couple of questions for you clowns. Rollins, are you going back in the White House?" I told him I wasn't. He asked the same question of Lyn.

"Fuck, no! I left three years ago, and what kind of fool do you think I am?" Allison answered similarly.

By now, Jackie's blood pressure was probably around 240 over 180. "Let me get this straight," he said. "You're offering me in return for the endorsement of the Teamsters Union the goodwill of three dumb fucks who aren't even going to be in government?"

I nodded yes, and began to wonder if I could survive a twelve-floor drop when his goons tossed us out the windows. After a few seconds of silence that seemed to go on forever, he grunted out his benediction.

"Listen, you motherfuckers. I'm gonna give you the fuckin' en-dorsement. But if you ever tell anyone that all I got was your god-damn goodwill, I'll hunt you down and make you a part of the Inter-state Highway system. They'll find Jimmy Hoffa before they find youse guys. Do we understand each other here? I'd be the laughing-stock of the labor movement. I'll take care of the executive board, but it's only 'cause I like Reagan.

"And *you*, Rollins, I thoughts you was my friend. For you to come up here and drink my booze and eat my steak and make that bullshit offer shows you got one hell of a pair of balls or you're fuckin' nuts."

Nuts, I thought to myself, because by now my balls were shriveled in fear to the size of BBs.

Jackie Presser's reward for endorsing the president? The Reagan Justice Department indicted him in the second term.

WINNING THE ELECTION is merely the most important part of a campaign manager's job description. An unbelievable amount of time is also spent managing the tensions and jealousies bubbling beneath the surface in every campaign. I found myself mediating everything from office space and expense accounts to job titles and presidential access—even shared girlfriends. Two of my top assistants turned out, much to their mutual distress, to be involved with the same woman.

The long hours and pressure-cooker environment inevitably result in a slew of such romances. Most of it was reasonably discreet in the Reagan campaign, but there were exceptions. One of my senior aides was notorious, for example, for packing his bags and telling his wife he was off to the hinterlands for the week. Then he'd be chauffeured to his girlfriend's apartment. He finally got caught when his wife noticed dozens of long-distance calls on his credit card from the same local number while he was supposedly out of town. He wiggled off the hook by claiming he'd let his young driver use the phone card.

The very uncomfortable driver was ordered to show up at the suspicious wife's door with a check and an apology for making personal calls from *his* girlfriend's apartment.

Of all such intramural headaches, my most labor-intensive was managing the candidate's wife. It wasn't just that Nancy Reagan was extremely demanding, or that she was always suspicious of my reassurances. Part of it was chemical. I'll admit it: Nobody could unnerve me like Nancy—and I don't intimidate easily.

Just before the convention, Baker, Spencer, and I had been summoned to the family quarters to brief Nancy on the game plan. I sat down, crossed my legs, and noticed to my horror a huge hole in the sole of my right shoe. Nancy's eyes focused like lasers on my shoe, then shot back to my face. She didn't utter a word, but I was totally rattled by her white-hot gaze. To this day I can't remember a single word I told her.

I do remember that she made it very clear she didn't like the way the campaign was going. She just hammered the crap out of me—everything from why didn't we have a campaign office in Beverly Hills where her rich friends could send money and volunteer to how much she didn't like the convention documentary about her. Not one of the chickenshit bastards in the room came to my defense, even though they all knew she was off the wall.

"She could smell fear all over you, Rollins," Spencer wisecracked as we were leaving. "You're doomed."

No issue was too trivial for Mrs. Reagan to drive me crazy over. Like the day she called to ask where one of her California friends could send a campaign contribution. I told her I'd call her back with the address.

"Shouldn't you know the address in California where people can send checks? You're the campaign manager. This is embarrassing."

I promised to get back promptly. In no time, my phone rang again.

"Well, did you get that number? I promised to call her right back, and it's been three minutes." I was beginning to understand why some White House aides called her "Mommie Dearest."

Close as he was to the Reagans personally, even Stu Spencer got burned out on the Nancy Watch. He called me one day from Air Force One, in agony.

"Christ," he moaned, "I've been on the plane for forty-five minutes with Mommy, and it hasn't stopped."

She drove Stu so crazy that for a while he left standing orders with his secretary to say he was in a meeting whenever she called and to refer her to Rollins. Then she'd call me. When I learned what was happening, I left standing orders of my own: "Tell her I'm in the same meeting with Stu."

She always thought I was too cocky about the race, especially in my comments to the press. As election day drew closer, she became more neurotic. Every time she'd read that I'd said we were ahead in forty-four or forty-seven or forty-eight states, I'd hear about it.

"You're jinxing the campaign," she complained in one of her phone calls. I tried to explain that a campaign manager has to be the head cheerleader as well as the chief operating officer.

"Do you want me to go out and bad-mouth us?" I countered. "Should I say the campaign is doing well today but we'll probably stumble in the closing weeks?"

In spite of her ferocious devotion to her husband, Nancy was bad for him in a campaign environment. I noticed early on that the president didn't seem to enjoy himself as much when she was along for the ride. When she wasn't there, he'd sometimes slip into sweatpants and mingle with the staff on Air Force One. With Nancy on board, we almost never saw him for the duration of the flight. It was clear to everyone that he was just more relaxed without her, not to mention better on the stump. It became so obvious after the campaign kickoff on Labor Day weekend that we cooked up a plan to keep her away from him, and us: Her very own campaign schedule.

Her shenanigans that weekend convinced us all that if Nancy were on the trail with the candidate, none of us would survive. At a huge kickoff rally in Orange County, California, more than fifty thousand people turned out to see the president at Mile Square Park. It started at ten in the morning, and even at that hour it was quite warm. Mrs. Reagan was miserable and couldn't understand why we'd take her husband anywhere where *she* would be so hot. Aides brought her ice-cooled cloths in relays and rigged up some fans to cool her from beneath the stage.

Sitting eight seats down from her, I knew I was in trouble when one of the advance men said she wanted to talk with me. She wanted to know why Gene Autry and Roy Rogers were among the few dozen people on stage. Why didn't I know, she asked, that they weren't personal friends of the president.

Trying to fake surprise while coming up with an answer I knew would be either wrong or dead wrong, I lied. I said we had to include Gene Autry because he owned the park (not true), and he'd insisted on bringing Roy, who hadn't seen his old pal Ron in years. I promised to kick them off after this stop, which was their sole appearance anyway.

Nancy's only role was to gaze up lovingly at her husband, as if he were proposing marriage. It always amazed me how she did it, but as Lyn Nofziger liked to tell me, "Remember, they're both actors."

Afterwards, Mrs. Reagan went over to her dear friends Roy and Gene to thank them for coming and to say how fabulous they looked. "Please give our best to Dale and Trigger," she told Roy. I guess she didn't know Trigger had been dead and stuffed for about twenty years. Definitely an Academy Award performance.

As I waited for a departure, Jim Baker popped out of the presidential limousine and hopped into Staff Car One. "You get up front in the limo with them, Rollins," he ordered. "I've had enough of her shit." I respectfully declined the offer, so he ordered Stu Spencer to get up front.

"Fuck you, Baker," I believe were Stu's exact words as he scrambled out the other side of the staff car, scurrying as fast as his little legs could carry him out of harm's way.

"You've *got* to go up there with them," Baker pleaded. I may have echoed Spencer's curt response. He then tried to get Mike Deaver, who was in the lead car, to join the First Couple. I don't know how Deaver got out of it, but neither he nor Spencer were seen for the next two days.

On the way to the airport, Jim begged me to do something about Nancy. There was no way we could spend an entire campaign listening to her bitch. He said it was up to me to convince her not to ride in the plane with us.

"What's this 'us' shit?" I replied. I reminded him that my job was back in Washington running the campaign and I wasn't chief of staff, but I'd be happy to back up the guy who was. Baker countered that since she already hated me, I had nothing to lose. After this trip, I sat down with Mrs. Reagan and told her that the campaign wanted to take full advantage of her spectacular work with drug prevention. We needed her to travel the country with her "Just Say No" program. She knew I was bullshitting her, and I figured she'd just say no to me. Much to my astonishment, she bought it.

BY MID-SEPTEMBER, I was feeling fairly confident—and had been since the Democratic Convention in July, when Mondale's coronation was overshadowed by a dumb self-inflicted wound. He shot both feet off during his acceptance speech by promising to do what liberals love more than anything, raise taxes so they can spend more money on social programs. We might as well have written that part of his speech ourselves.

Watching it on television, I knew my friend Bob Beckel, Mondale's manager, was having a coronary somewhere. "We've got you now, you liberal son of a bitch," I chortled into the screen.

Mondale was also hurt by the media frenzy over his historic selection of New York Congresswoman Geraldine Ferraro as the first female vice-presidential nominee of a major party. Ferraro was feisty, turned out to be a creditable campaigner, and did a good job in the debate against George Bush. Her nomination was a bold move by a guy not known for his boldness, and her novelty value resulted in heavier media attention than usual. But the Democrats could never convince anyone except true believers that she was qualified to be vice president. The notion of President Ferraro was absurd, and the voters knew it. It was a long-shot play that backfired—in large measure because of a clandestine operation to discredit Ferraro run by two of my subordinates without my knowledge.

Our strategy was to treat Ferraro very gingerly. To avoid a sympathy backlash, we ruled out direct attacks on her meager qualifications to be a heartbeat away from the presidency. Instead, we would make fair note of the extreme disparities between her résumé and Vice President Bush's.

"*Do not* raise and discuss her gender," we instructed in a July 12 computer message to all outposts. "The issue for the campaign will be her experience and qualifications, and those alone."

Taking the high road was the smart tactical call, but not everybody agreed with it. Nancy Reagan, for instance, flew into a rage when she read what Ferraro had said about her Ronnie at her first press conference: "He walks around calling himself a good Christian," Ferraro said, claiming that his policies hurt poor people. "I don't for one minute believe it."

Mommy, as her husband called her, went berserk. Ferraro couldn't be allowed to get away with such slander. It was time for the gloves to come off, she told Stu Spencer. She wanted us to scrutinize the hell out of Ferraro's past. If anything turned up that was useful, we shouldn't be squeamish. She repeated the same thing to me in one of her daily phone calls.

Like any campaign manager, I wanted to know everything I could about Ferraro that might help the president win. The only Ferraro "operation" authorized by me, however, was a routine opposition research effort, run by one of my assistants, John Roberts, and Art Teele, an assistant to Spencer. Such "Oppo" research is a standard and accepted political technique. Every campaign devotes considerable time and money to finding out everything about an opponent that might be politically useful.

Roberts and Teele learned plenty about Ferraro, but the most promising avenue of legitimate inquiry involved her husband's tax returns. On August 12, Ferraro said she'd release her returns, but not her husband's. I smelled blood. We passed word for Reagan surrogates to start asking what Ferraro had to hide. Just before our convention opened in Dallas on August 20, Spencer proposed that Teele and Roberts be put in charge of sleuthing out John Zaccaro's tax returns. I okayed the idea in a meeting with the three in my office.

"But I want three things understood," I said. "This could look wrong. If you screw up, you're out. Second, don't get carried away. If you think you're getting into an area that's unethical, stop. I don't want this campaign in trouble, because we're going to win anyway. Third, keep it secret. No one besides Stu and I need know what you're doing."

Stu reported back to the First Lady, who was pleased to learn that the gloves were coming off. What she—and I—didn't know was that we'd already pulled out the brass knuckles.

One morning in early September, Lee Atwater walked into my office and asked for what he called "a small favor." Jamie Gangel, who was covering the Ferraro campaign for NBC, wanted to interview me. I knew that Lee and Jamie's producer, Leslie Sewell, were very close personal friends, so I knew why Lee was pushing the interview. He told me Gangel just wanted to get some background on what the campaign thought of Ferraro. I asked Lee to make sure Jim Lake, Director of Communications, signed off, which he didn't do.

It was an ambush worthy of *60 Minutes*. Jamie cut right to the chase: Was the Reagan campaign running a dirty tricks operation to smear Ferraro? I said we were doing nothing of the sort.

NBC led with the story that evening, asserting that sources inside the campaign had confirmed that Lyn Nofziger and I were personally directing a covert operation to defame Ferraro and were responsible for anti-abortion protests, negative news reports, campus heckling, and attacks on Ferraro by Catholic clergy. I knew right away what was going on. Lee had planted the story with Leslie, knowing I'd be blamed whether it was true or not. It was a premeditated effort to take me out. I stormed into his office and started screaming. I was angrier with him than I'd ever been.

"How could you do this to Lyn and me?" I yelled. "We've been your fucking godfathers and you're trying to take us out with six weeks to go." I know he thought I was going to deck him.

He was sheepish and apologetic, but never actually denied he'd done it. "I'd never do anything to hurt you," he said. In the press business, that's known as a nondenial denial.

"Fuck you, Lee. If you ever fuck me again, I'm gonna pound your ass into the ground," I said, and stormed out.

Seconds later, a worried Jim Baker was on the phone. "Rollins, what the hell is going on over there? These are not the kind of things we want to do in this campaign."

I went ballistic.

"Thanks a helluva lot for the vote of confidence, Jim, but the story is pure horseshit and flat-out wrong." Baker accepted my explanation and quickly backed off, but reiterated what we both already understood. "This is the only way we can lose this election. If anything is gonna screw it up, it's this."

The story spun out of control for twenty-four hours. The Democrats condemned us; we denounced the report and demanded an apology. With Atwater as their Deep Throat, NBC hung tough. I figured I was finished. Then, as quickly as it had erupted, the thing sputtered out. Washington political reporters simply didn't buy the story. Their attitude was that if it *were* true, they'd have all heard from us about it. Since they hadn't been fed dirt about Ferraro, the operation probably didn't exist. I'd been saved from the treachery of my loyal deputy by the arrogance of the Washington press corps.

Long after the campaign was over, I learned that the campaign *had* been running a very elaborate dirty tricks operation in violation of my orders.

When Nancy Reagan began pressuring the campaign to punish Ferraro, Roberts and Teele were drafted to comb through every element of Ferraro's personal and professional history, and leak anything damaging they turned up. It was an all-out investigation that ultimately involved teams of attorneys, a former IRS commissioner, retired policemen, researchers, investigative reporters, organized crime experts, and a former CIA officer.

Unbeknownst to everybody, Atwater was running his own little game at the same time: a freelance opposition effort that was a rogue operation from start to finish. One of its low points was an illegal request for a search of Department of Housing and Urban Development records to see if Ferraro had intervened to get lucrative HUD contracts for her husband. That request was never acted upon because the Roberts operation stumbled onto it and shut it down for fear it would compromise *their* activities.

Roberts and Teele knew that if their operation became public, they were dead meat—along with Spencer and me. They decided not to use Washington reporters to disseminate their findings. Lee Atwater had scores of contacts in the media, and if one of them tipped him to the operation, he'd expose it, and reap the rewards while Spencer and I took it in the neck. So they decided to strike a deal with the *Philadelphia Inquirer,* which had a well-deserved reputation for the quality of its investigative reporting.

In a meeting with an *Inquirer* reporter and editor at the J. W. Marriott Hotel in Washington, Roberts and Teele offered to pass along leads on Ferraro on the condition that the *Inquirer* never identify the Reagan campaign or Republicans as the source. The *Inquirer* was to verify all leads independently and report them as its own. A second collaboration was established with the *New York Post,* whose owner Rupert Murdoch was a strong Reagan supporter.

When an anonymous source told Roberts and Teele where to find records proving that Ferraro's parents had been arrested (though never convicted) for numbers-running in the 1940s, the tip was passed to the *Inquirer* and to the *Post,* which ran it in October. Ferraro broke down in tears, canceled several appearances, and the Mondale campaign was plunged into chaos. In a matter of days, Ferraro had become a drag on the Democratic ticket.

I was appalled and furious when I found out about this operation. It was stupid, unethical, and totally unnecessary. The Mondale-Ferraro ticket was going to self-destruct without anyone's help. Some of those going after Ferraro may have done it out of fear of Nancy Reagan, but Atwater did it out of raw ambition. With Lee, it was never enough to win. He always needed to drive one more spike through somebody's heart.

ONCE MONDALE PROMISED to raise taxes in his acceptance speech in San Francisco, the die was cast. From where I was sitting, only a medical emergency could keep Reagan from being reelected. But prudent politicians always prepare for the worst while expecting the best, so we did a lot of war-gaming to bolster our advantage. One of the more successful of these gambits was the brainchild of Richard Nixon, which he proposed during a dinner in mid-September at his home in Saddle River, New Jersey.

Nixon had suggested that we pick a single state in the northern industrial crescent that Mondale *had* to win and carpet-bomb it with Reagan surrogates, direct mail, media spots, and presidential visits. In other words, Nixon argued, treat it like a governor's race. This saturation strategy was a no-lose proposition; if we won, Mondale was finished. If Mondale managed to win despite our scorched-earth assault, he would have depleted precious assets from other key states to stay in the single-state game with us.

By the time I got back to Washington late that night, I knew Ohio was the ideal battleground for this strategy. The land of Taft had always leaned Republican, and its Democratic governor, Dick Celeste, was highly unpopular after signing a $300 million tax increase. Reagan could win without Ohio, but Mondale couldn't.

The next day, I approached Roger Stone, who was running the northeastern states for me and was one of our better operatives. Stone was despised by most of the people he'd ever worked with, and was one of Atwater's closest friends. They were cut from the same mold.

"Roger, have you ever worked in Ohio before?" I asked. He said no. "Good. You're running Ohio. If they don't know you, chances are they don't hate your guts yet."

I instructed Stone to behave as though we were ten points behind in the Buckeye State. We increased the Ohio budget to nearly $4 million and flooded the state with 6 million pieces of direct mail linking Mondale's tax-and-spend philosophy to Celeste's tax increase. Every Ohio Democrat and independent got at least three mailings. We laid on the biggest radio media blitz in Ohio history, and Reagan's visits were doubled.

The Great Ohio Flood worked beautifully. By October 1, the president's lead there was an impregnable twenty points. Barring some catastrophe, Mondale was dead in the water.

There was one last hurdle preventing a Reagan landslide: the presidential debates, which would begin six days later, on October 7, in Louisville.

Historically, incumbents usually don't fare well in debates—witness Ford in 1976, Carter in 1980, and Bush in 1992. Part of the reason is they're out of practice at being treated like an equal. We were all convinced Reagan would beat those odds. After all, he was the Great Communicator. Ronald Reagan was to television what Franklin Roosevelt was to radio; Fritz Mondale was a total stiff before the cameras. I had no doubt Reagan would wipe the floor with Mondale. Unfortunately, he proved the rule, not the exception.

Reagan hadn't been on a stage in a debate format for four years, and his rustiness showed. In that first debate, he came across as old, tired, and a bit befuddled. He groped for words, lost his train of thought, and mangled his closing soliloquy. The whooping and hollering that blasted through the walls of Mondale's adjoining holding room said it all. By his performance, the president had resurrected the only issue on which he was potentially vulnerable: age. Against all odds, Mondale had an opening.

My only consolation was that at least I wouldn't be hearing from Nancy Reagan on this one. When Paul Laxalt was quoted saying his friend had been "brutalized" by the Baker-Darman-Stockman team of handlers, I knew the Missus was on the warpath. Jim Baker and Dick Darman had run this show, and the senior campaign staff had been frozen out of the debate preparations; we hadn't even been allowed to sit in on the mock debate.

One of their biggest blunders had to do with timing. Ronald Reagan liked being in bed by ten o'clock. The debate began at 8:00 P.M., central time, but that was 9:00 P.M. Reagan body time. By the second half of the debate, he was beginning to fade. I kicked myself for not pressing my earlier recommendation that the first location should be Los Angeles so the debate would be over well before Reagan's normal bedtime.

There's no question our morale went right into the toilet temporarily. It was obvious as hell that Reagan had lost the debate. For the first time since Gary Hart's flameout, I was nervous. Mondale might have a long-shot chance, I thought. Momentum is a precious campaign commodity, and now the other side had it.

Providentially, the Democrats promptly made a key tactical blunder by piling on. Congressman Tony Coelho of California did us an enormous service by saying the president was so out of it that he'd done everything but drool onstage. The remark was totally in character for a mudslinger like Tony, but it struck most fair-minded people as overly severe. The media helped out as well, the news shows overdosing on clips of Reagan falling asleep with the Pope and Nancy prompting her husband when he forgot his lines on arms control. The *Wall Street Journal* did a medical piece suggesting that Reagan might be on the verge of diminished mental faculties.

It was painful to watch, but in the end it was a classic case of overkill. There's no disputing that Reagan had had an off night, but only reporters and Democrats really believed he was unraveling. As a result, a sympathy backlash developed for the president.

More to the point, expectations had been lowered for the second debate in Kansas City on October 21. The media now assumed Reagan would lose. As a practical matter, all the president really needed to do was to stay on his feet for ninety minutes without slobbering. Instead, the Gipper rose to the occasion. He wasn't perfect—but he didn't have to be.

Mondale's handlers had screwed up the lighting: They put a piece of white cardboard on Fritz's podium at the last minute, which reflected light back into his face and made him look like a pasty-faced old man with dark pouches under his eyes. When Reagan was asked if he might be too old for another term, he brought down the house with a one-liner he'd been saving for just the right moment:

"I am not going to exploit for political purposes my opponent's youth and inexperience."

The age issue was dead—and so was Mondale.

Reagan's triumph was no thanks to his handlers, who were still trying to explain television to a guy who didn't need any tips. In a mock session before the second debate, the president insisted on looking at his interlocutors when he answered a question. Roger Ailes, one of the best in the business, insisted that he should be looking directly into the television camera.

"Don't you think," the president asked in exasperation, "that people will think I'm a phony if I don't look at the people who are talking to me?"

Ailes insisted, and Deaver sided with him. Deaver even taped a reminder card to the president's podium. For the rest of the rehearsal, the president looked squarely at the camera.

During the debate, he went with his instincts and ignored the high-priced advice. He looked reporters square in the eye as he answered their questions. He always knew an audience better than any of us.

The next fifteen days were little more than an extended victory lap. People seemed to know Reagan would win, and they clearly liked the idea. For the first time since Eisenhower, voters had a candidate who excited them, and our private polls said it would be a landslide. Reagan's politics of optimism had overwhelmed Mondale's dour Calvinist pessimism. Even a complacent campaign couldn't have blown our lead.

THE FERRARO FUROR was my biggest nightmare that fall, but in a campaign nothing is ever easy. One morning I received another call from my least favorite kibitzer. Usually, Nancy Reagan's calls were as welcome as root-canal surgery. Instinctively, I stiffened when I heard her voice. This time, however, she wasn't calling to bitch.

"I have good news, Ed," she said. "I just got off the phone with Frank Sinatra, and he's volunteered to give the campaign thirty days of his time." I lit up at the prospect of several Sinatra concerts for financial donors.

"Oh, no," she corrected me, "he doesn't want to do any performances."

Perhaps, I countered, he could mix and mingle with campaign volunteers and fat cats.

"He doesn't want to do that, either," I was told.

Maybe, I thought to myself, he wants to advise us on foreign policy.

"He just wants to travel with us and give Ronnie good counsel," Nancy said.

I saw the makings of a personal nightmare. I had a White House staff second-guessing me every day, and a dozen guys down the hall who wanted my job, including my trusted deputy. I had the president's wife breathing down my neck. The last thing I needed was Frank Sinatra on the plane "giving good counsel" to the candidate.

But there was no way out. Trying to make the most of it, we laid on a campaign stop in Hoboken, New Jersey, Sinatra's hometown. We were taking Reagan and Sinatra to a parish bazaar at Sinatra's boyhood church. It would be a political ten-strike for us in a critical northeastern swing state.

As Air Force One taxied to a stop at Newark Airport, I could see the "WELCOME HOME FRANK" signs plastered throughout an exuberant crowd. The president and First Lady were waiting to deplane triumphantly with their friend. That's when I learned the awful truth: Sinatra had decided he wasn't interested in the homecoming.

With his usual skill at delegating any chore that might cause him trouble, Jim Baker informed me that I had a big problem and I'd better fix it pronto. I walked to the guest compartment and asked Ol' Blue Eyes, who'd had a few pops, just what the problem seemed to be.

"I don't know what *your* problem is, pal," he informed me, "but this is a stupid fucking idea and I'm not getting off this fucking plane. I don't like these people and it's no accident I haven't come back in forty years. So you can take this act and shove it. This is a solo act tonight. Ron doesn't need me, for Christ's sake. He's the fucking president." Everyone else in the cabin was checking the creases in their pants.

"That's right, Mr. Sinatra," I said. "He *is* the fucking president, and as a courtesy to you he came to this shitass town for your homecoming. You signed off on this event, and if you don't get your ass up to the front of the plane and walk off with him and the First Lady, I'm going to tell the two hundred national reporters who are following this circus what a prick you are. Then I'm going to tell every New Jersey reporter I can find what you just said about the lovely folks from your hometown standing out there to greet you. When I'm finished, you won't get back to New Jersey with a pass from the Pope."

Sinatra gave me a poisonous stare, and asked his old friend Joe

Canzeri, a campaign aide and Nancy favorite, if he thought I was bluffing.

"No, Frank," Joe advised. Sinatra pondered a moment, marched to the front of the plane, and walked off as though he'd been rehearsing his triumphant return forever.

It was a huge success; Sinatra could have been John Paul II returning to Poland. An hour later, the three of them arrived back almost giddy from the experience. Sinatra told the president he'd never believe how much trouble he'd had persuading the campaign to sign onto his idea.

"Ron, if there's one thing I know, it's show biz," he crowed. "And politics is just show biz." I wanted to puke.

About a month before the election, I knew I'd be hearing from Nancy again when a *Washington Post* poll showed that Reagan's margin had narrowed to single digits in California. *Our* polls said the president's lead there was nevertheless rock-solid. Californians knew Ronald Reagan, and either loved him or hated him. He'd been on the ballot there six times and never lost. Even though Mondale had been spending a lot of time in California, there was no way he could win in Reagan's sandbox.

Sure enough, she called me on the verge of hysteria.

"You have to do something," she said. "It's extremely close." I tried to tell her there was no cause for worry.

"I don't want to hear any more of this," she shrieked. "Do you want to be responsible for the president losing his home state?"

"Mrs. Reagan, it's my home state, too. I promise you Ronald Reagan is *not* going to lose California."

"I'm sick and tired of your promises," she retorted. "You have to do something."

Which is why I ordered up another expensive Wirthlin poll, laid on more phone banks in California, and sent Lyn Nofziger home as a troubleshooter. We blew an extra million dollars in California that, if we'd poured into Minnesota instead, would have given the president the first fifty-state sweep in political history—just to placate a superstitious and neurotic First Lady.

A couple of weeks later, the *Post* ran a correction: Their numbers for California had been in error.

After the campaign, I harassed Ben Bradlee, *The Washington Post*'s executive editor, about his paper's lousy polling methodology. Ben is *never* repentant.

"Tough shit, Rollins, I'm glad it cost you plenty," he rasped. "It's my in-kind contribution to the Mondale campaign." As if the *Post* had to do anything more to help Mondale beyond their editorial endorsement and soft coverage.

On November 1, we left Andrews Air Force Base on Ronald Reagan's last campaign swing. Over five days, we would hit ten states and fifteen cities, ending at home in California. When I got to my seat on Air Force One, I found a letter from the president thanking me for my efforts.

"Working and traveling together," he'd written, "you and I have been privileged to witness firsthand the dramatic resurgence of the American spirit. . . . Four years ago, I promised America a New Beginning. Now we can say with confidence not only that America is back, but also that America's best days are yet to come."

Dick Wirthlin's polls were showing that the American people embraced that uplifting message just as fervently, which was why it was all over but the counting.

The day before the election, we headed home. As we flew west, the mood on the plane was light and jovial. Everyone was exhausted, but the usual last-day tensions were missing. We knew we were going to win, and win big. An hour before landing in Sacramento, Baker asked Wirthlin and me to give the president a status report. When we arrived in his stateroom, the president was wearing gray sweatpants and a white golf shirt. Nancy was in blue sweats and an Air Force One flight jacket.

Dick began with some of the ass-kissing for which he's notorious. "Mr. President, Nancy, I started with you in 1966. Next to my family and my church, working for you has been the most meaningful thing in my life." Almost teary-eyed with emotion, he predicted that Reagan's victory might surpass his margin over Jimmy Carter in 1980. Then, in typical fashion, he started mushing his numbers to hedge his bets.

The president interrupted him. "Ed, what do *you* think?"

It was the first time in the entire campaign that my candidate had asked me a purely political question.

"Mr. President, you're on the verge of the greatest landslide victory in the history of the country. Massachusetts and Minnesota are still in play, but I estimate you'll win forty-nine states and fifty-eight or fifty-nine percent of the vote. I think we'll win twelve to fourteen House seats and lose Jepsen and Percy in the Senate."

The president tried hard to stifle an infectious grin.

"My goodness," he said, "do you really think we're going to do that well?"

"Absolutely," I replied. "This thing is really rolling." In an informal poll we'd just run in the back of the plane, I added, even the

Secret Service was predicting forty-nine states. I didn't tell him that the two guys who predicted the lowest Reagan margin were Baker and Spencer, each calling it at 53 percent.

"I'd be happy," the president said with characteristic humility, "with fifty-one percent of the vote."

"Well, you better be right," Nancy interjected, nailing me with that steely glare. "You've been so overconfident in this race, Ed, you just better be right."

EVERY CAMPAIGN MANAGER will tell you that election day is the longest of your life. You make a few calls to the field, wait for exit polls, and reassure the candidate, but at that point you're powerless to affect the outcome. Inevitably, you start second-guessing yourself, worrying whether this tactical call or that campaign appointment was brilliant or stupid. But there's nothing you can do but wait for the voters to decide.

On this election day, however, I could have been gambling in the Bahamas. Except for the two weeks between debates, we'd never once been seriously on the defensive. We led the entire way, which gave us the luxury of running our own campaign from start to finish instead of reacting to Mondale. Our lead remained remarkably consistent at around ten to twelve points the entire year until the final weekend, when the undecideds broke our way. There's a certain segment of the electorate that wants to go with a winner. When it became clear that Mondale was cooked, the die-hard Democratic holdouts and independents gave up and threw in with us.

After the hammering I'd taken from Nancy all year, I really enjoyed being able to report to the Reagans on Tuesday afternoon that the exit polls showed I'd been right—the president *would* win with 58 percent. He couldn't have been more appreciative, but Nancy barely acknowledged my presence.

The next day, Congressman Vin Weber, our state chairman, called me from Minnesota. Despite the fact that we'd kissed off Mondale's home state, Weber had run a terrific, mostly volunteer campaign with virtually no money, and he'd come within 3,000 votes of beating one of Minnesota's most famous politicians. Vin told me they'd discovered that several thousand residents of a cemetery in northern Minnesota had proudly cast their absentee ballots for Mondale. He urged me to seek a recount. I let him talk for a couple of minutes, then told him to go home and get some rest. A clean sweep would have been nice, but there was no need to look greedy. Still, I'm convinced we'd have won that recount.

My father, Ed, is strong and tough, but his rugged exterior masks a gentle and generous nature. He started seeing my mother, Mary, when she was nineteen. With her flaming red hair and fair complexion, she was the most gorgeous woman he'd ever seen. My dad taught me two great life lessons. The first was humility. Second—and most important—always tell the truth.

My first real interest in politics was kindled in the summer of 1956, during the Democratic National Convention in Chicago. As a fellow Irish Catholic from Boston, John F. Kennedy was the candidate for me. He lost the vice presidential nomination to Estes Kefauver, but the convention hooked me on politics and my new hero—JFK.

Home has always been the shipyard town of Vallejo, California. My dad worked in New Ship Construction at Mare Island, the largest submarine base on the West Coast. Vallejo was my father's home, my home, and the place that made me who I am.

From the ages of thirteen to twenty-three, I was an amateur boxer. I won several major West Coast titles, and learned a hell of a lot about life from boxing. At Chico State College, I found myself. Willie Simmons (far left), the boxing coach, asked me (far right) to help coach the team. He became my mentor; he settled me down, focused my energies, and made me believe in myself.

Chico State had a superb internship program in the state legislature. In 1967, I worked for Jesse "Big Daddy" Unruh (to the right of Robert Kennedy), the most powerful assembly speaker in California history. He tutored me in the finer points of the political game—how it's really played and how you win at it. And he got me a job in RFK's 1968 primary campaign. Had Bobby won the presidency, I almost certainly would never have become a Republican.

In June 1969, I left California to join the faculty of Washington University in St. Louis. The violent student protests against the Vietnam War, which began shortly after I arrived on campus, would profoundly alter my personal philosophy. Two of my colleagues, John Duvall (left) and Julius Hunter (right), were my principal comrades-in-arms. When the first 1992 presidential campaign debate was held on the campus, J.D., Julius, and I had quite a reunion.

UPI / Corbis-Bettmann

In 1972, I was working for Richard Nixon's reelection campaign. In my family, this was the equivalent of the pope becoming a fourth-degree Mason. There's never been a presidential campaign like it, and there will never be another like it again. I developed a friendship with Julie Nixon Eisenhower during this period. She was an extraordinary woman—if she had ever gone into politics, there would have been no stopping her.

AP / Wide World Photos

Governor Ronald Reagan was Nixon's state chairman in 1972, and Bob Monagan (right) was a co-chairman. During this campaign, I began to discover that much of what I believed fit Reagan's brand of conservatism. And if it weren't for Monagan, my political career would have been over before it started. I got to Washington on his ticket; I'd never have made it there on my own.

To Ed Rollins
With our best wishes — Sincerely
Nancy & Ronald Reagan

When Lyn Nofziger asked me to be his deputy in Reagan's first term, I found
the Holy Grail of American politics—a job in the White House. To me,
Ronald Reagan was the last American hero, but he would never have been
president without his wife. Many critics have described her as ruthless. I
think "relentless" fits her better. And I'll admit it—nobody could unnerve
me like Nancy.

On paper, the three principal players in the Reagan White House—Jim Baker, Ed Meese, and Mike Deaver—were popularly viewed as co-equals when Reagan's first term began. Almost immediately, however, the power dynamics shifted in Baker's direction.

Jim Baker (standing) was viewed by some of his friends in the media as the most capable political operative of this century. He was also extraordinarily cunning and manipulative—a man for whom making the deal was more important than what's in it. Ed Meese was probably the most selfless of all Reagan's aides. He was an exceptionally decent man, but he didn't adjust quickly enough to the palace intrigues.

Mike Deaver was guardian of the Reagan image. Nobody had as much capacity for punishment as Mike—most of it meted out by Nancy Reagan.

It was Baker and Deaver versus Meese and national security adviser Dick Allen (right), and all of them against Al Haig, the secretary of state everybody thought was out for himself.

Secretary of the Treasury Donald Regan swapped jobs with Baker and became the new White House chief of staff at the start of Reagan's second term. Baker knew Regan would be a disaster and therefore would only make Baker look better. Regan damn near destroyed the Reagan presidency and ran off the best of the White House staff.

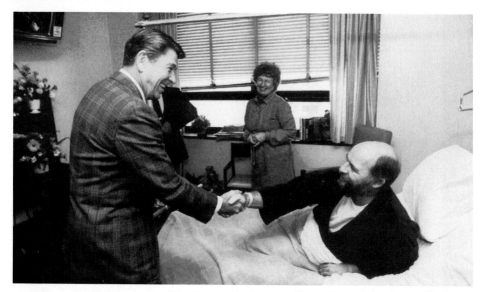

At the age of thirty-nine, I had a stroke in my office. One of the first calls I got when I came to was from the president. He later visited me in the hospital; it was a gesture that touched me deeply. "Mr. President," I said, introducing him to my parents, "the three of you have a lot in common. My parents used to be Democrats, too."

After the stroke, I assumed my White House days were over, and for the first time in my life I understood that living was more important than all the other crap I'd been doing. But I owed the president, and so when my health improved, I stayed on.

At the age of forty, a poor kid from Vallejo was running the reelection campaign of the President of the United States. Lee Atwater (center) was my deputy. There were no rules or standards in Lee's operating manual— winning was all that mattered. His agenda was the future; he wanted to run George Bush's 1988 campaign. I also brought in Lyn Nofziger (right), my old friend, as a campaign consultant. Lyn's irreverence emboldened me and taught me bad habits for life.

Ronald Reagan was always being underestimated—even by those of us who loved him and were privileged to serve him. And he was simply the nicest man you'd ever want to meet. But after his triumphant reelection, the Reagan Revolution was history, and so was I. If I'd been smart, I would have quit the business then and there.

Had Jack Kemp been Reagan's vice president, he would have been a bridge to the next generation of conservatives. He's one of the really good people in American politics today. When he decided to run for president in 1988, I was his campaign chairman. Charlie Black was the campaign manager. To this day, I believe Charlie and Lee Atwater conspired to torpedo Jack's candidacy.

Had Paul Laxalt been Reagan's vice president, he would have been a critical link to Congress, where he was very well respected. He was my friend and protector in 1984. In 1988, my loyalty to Paul got me in more hot water with George Bush.

George Bush is a very nice man who made a career out of being a good follower. He's been called many things. Revolutionary isn't one of them. Temperamentally and philosophically, he was miscast as Reagan's political heir. Soon after he was named Reagan's running mate, I began thinking of him as the Trojan Horse.

During George Bush's years as president, I sometimes felt like public enemy number one. His wife, Barbara, made their mutual feelings about me very clear at a 1989 White House reception: After I thanked her for their hospitality, she glared at me and said, "You better be grateful, because we were hospitable."

In 1992, Ross Perot definitely tapped into something in the American psyche. Except for Reagan's campaigns, I hadn't felt so excited about anything since JFK's victory at the 1960 Democratic convention. I really thought Perot could make a difference. He did—he made Americans even more cynical about our crazy political process.

I was one of Perot's four top advisers. As Jimmy Carter's chief strategist in 1976, Hamilton Jordan (center) had run the last successful outsider presidential campaign. During our collaboration, what little respect I had left for the guy went right out the window. Tom Luce (left) was one of the least equipped people for big-league politics I'd ever met. Mort Meyerson (right) was widely considered to be the brains behind Perot's business empire and was his alter ego, but he'd never even voted.

Lee Atwater was at different times my most loyal deputy and my most bitter enemy. It was the most intense relationship I've ever experienced. I loved him and I hated him, and at the end I loved him again. I can say with a clear heart that even if it took blowing me up to do it, I'm glad Lee got all his dreams. In all my life, I've never been so torn up by anything as I was by his tragic, unfair death in 1991.

New Jersey Newsphotos

After the disastrous Perot adventure, I assumed I was finished in this business. As it turned out, I was wrong—thanks to Christine Todd Whitman. I've never been prouder of a candidate, and I can't remember a more exciting rush in my life than the moment in 1993 when Jim Florio conceded the governorship of New Jersey.

James Carville had been the principal strategist for Bill Clinton's 1992 victory. In New Jersey, he and I went head-to-head. The race for the governorship would be called the battle of the super-consultants.

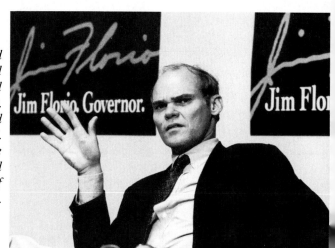

After I ignited a firestorm of controversy by suggesting that black ministers had been paid to stay silent, the Reverend Reginald Jackson (center) and other African-American leaders defended Christie Whitman's campaign against my public statements about the expenditure of "walking-around money."

AP / Wide World Photos

Soon after the controversy erupted, I answered a subpoena to appear before a federal grand jury in Newark. The thing I cared most about, my reputation, was shredded. Of all those self-inflicted wounds, nothing pained me more than being called a liar and a racist.

In three decades as a political junkie, I never worked a more miserable, depressing, or rotten race than the 1994 Huffington Senate campaign. Compared to Michael and Arianna Huffington—two of the most unprincipled political creatures I'd ever encountered—Ross Perot had been St. Francis of Assisi.

Working for George and Mary Beth Nethercutt in a Washington State congressional race in the spring of 1994 was a tonic for me. This was the way politics was supposed to be, the way it really was once upon a time. When Newt Gingrich administered the oath of office to George, it was a redemptive moment for me.

My life changed forever in the summer of 1995 when the Chinese government approved my request to adopt a little girl found abandoned on the Nanjing Bridge on Easter Sunday. We named her Lily, and in August Sherrie and I flew home from China with our beautiful baby daughter.

It irritates me no end whenever I hear some pundit say that anyone could have run the 1984 campaign. Ronald Reagan would probably have won regardless, but it could easily have been a closer race. We always had the better candidate; but we were also better organized, better financed, better targeted, and better staffed. From the opening gate to the finish line, we ran a textbook-perfect campaign. Now that Bill Clinton's strategists are telling people they're following the 1984 Reagan game plan, perhaps we'll get the credit we deserve.

THE PRESIDENT'S VICTORY party was in the grand ballroom of the Century Plaza Hotel. The Reagans had been hosting a reception for their Hollywood pals—a bunch of old movie actors long forgotten and many presumed dead. When the president and Nancy were announced onstage, my euphoria almost overwhelmed me, but in this moment of triumph, I literally came crashing back to earth. The Hollywood has-beens rushed the stage to savor the moment, knocking me off the stage. I ended up sprawled against the background curtain, hugging a loudspeaker. When President Reagan turned to thank me for my efforts, I was nowhere to be found—AWOL from my fifteen seconds of fame.

The next morning, Jim Baker told a breakfast meeting of the White House traveling press that the election results didn't amount to a mandate for the president. I was stunned when a reporter tipped me—and plenty annoyed. I went to see Baker.

"I hear you're saying we didn't get a mandate," I said.

"We *have* to play down the mandate talk," Baker replied. "We didn't get the congressional seats we needed. Tip [O'Neill] is still in charge, and we don't want to antagonize him."

"Jim, that's bullshit. The president just won forty-nine states and fifty-nine percent of the vote, and that's a mandate in anybody's book."

"The campaign is over," he said. "Now we've gotta govern."

I'd heard that Baker didn't want to hang around in a second term, but I didn't expect him to surrender to the Democrats in the full flush of victory. I left in disbelief and went off to my own press conference.

I was still fuming when one of the first questioners asked me for a reaction to Baker's earlier assessment. I said that Reagan had "an electoral mandate, probably unprecedented," and couldn't resist noting that Baker and I must have different definitions of a mandate. In my opinion, Ronald Reagan had just won one of the great victories in American politics and had been given an undeniable mandate to finish the job he'd begun in 1981.

Suddenly it was over. Overnight, I came down from the greatest high in my life. I'd spent fourteen months in a job I felt I'd been born to do. I knew I'd never get to do it again. From a political perspective, my career had crested at age forty-one and was already heading downhill. I hadn't expected such a bittersweet finale. God, I thought, I guess I've got to go find a job.

I went back to my room, packed my bags, and caught a cab to the airport. It was the first time in four years I hadn't been chauffeured by a White House or campaign car. En route home, I missed the afterglow of the evening news shows. Fortunately, I also missed the press conference where Tip O'Neill and House whip Tony Coelho embraced Jim Baker's words as their own. Of course Reagan had no mandate, Coelho argued. The House would set the agenda for the second term, and Ronald Reagan would have to deal with them. Thanks to Baker, we'd kissed off the moral authority of an overwhelming electoral victory and dissipated any chance to ride the wave into the second term.

The next morning, I drove to my office at campaign headquarters. Ten days earlier, the place had been a beehive. Now, a staff of four hundred had shrunk to a dozen or so workers, busily dismantling offices and selling off desks. It felt horrible, like the death of a loved one. I watched with a mixture of anger and dismay: We'd won a resounding reaffirmation of the Reagan Revolution and then handed the game back to the losers.

I'd felt this way only once before: in 1980, when Ronald Reagan had beaten the Republican establishment, then put George Bush on the ticket. Once again, we'd snatched defeat from the jaws of victory. I went home that night feeling as low as I'd been since the stroke. The revolution was history, and so was I. If I'd been smart, I would have quit the business then and there.

ROUND 6

TROJAN HORSES

FOR THE FIRST time since college, I needed a job. The campaign paid my salary until January 1, 1985, so I had a while to sort out my life. But the first order of business after any campaign—catching up on your sleep—never varies. Takes about a week.

I disappeared to my Virginia country cabin for four or five days, but vacations have never been my thing. I bought a new Ford Bronco four-wheel drive, and moved out of my apartment in Rosslyn to a house owned by Barry Goldwater, Jr., in the historic Old Town section of Alexandria. I'm a movie junkie, but hadn't caught a flick in over a year, so I went on a cinema binge. When I ran through all the local first runs, I rented two dozen videos and spent a string of evenings in front of my TV.

There was also a new romantic interest in my life. Early in the campaign, Jim Lake had sent me a note he thought I'd find amusing. It was a reply to a memo our lawyer had sent to all staffers advising them not to engage in any outside activities that would embarrass the campaign. One of Jim's staffers named Sherrie Sandy had written this note on the top of the document:

"Does this mean I have to give up my night job dancing at the Pink Pussycat?"

I'd never heard of Sherrie Sandy so I thought it was a fictitious name. But if she were real, I knew she had to be a knockout. Lake was notorious for having the best-looking women in the campaign on his staff.

A couple of weeks later, I found myself standing at the elevator with a gorgeous woman. She was heading off to play racquetball, which explained the athletic shorts and Nikes she was wearing. She introduced herself as Sherrie Sandy.

"So *you're* the one who dances nights," I said.

She turned a bright crimson.

"I can't believe Jim showed that note to you," she said.

It may not have been love at first sight, but it definitely was attraction. I thought she was beautiful and loved her smile. As it turned out, she was handling state and regional press for Lake, so we attended several of the same regional conferences during the spring and summer of 1984. I took her to lunch at a nearby restaurant on her birthday in June, and we seemed to click. We started dating during the fall, but there wasn't any time for a social life—just a few hurried dinners after work and late night phone calls.

With the election behind us, we had time to work on our relationship. I found myself completely smitten.

My romance with Sherrie filled a huge void in my life, but I still suffered from post-campaign letdown. It was a very strange time for me. For four years, I'd had a major piece of the action. Now, next train to Siberia.

I'd go into my office every day, but there was nothing to do. On a busy day, there may have been ten volunteers, and none of them worked for me. I couldn't even get letters typed. For a political junkie, the inactivity was unbearable. It felt just like a White House traveling staff office after Air Force One goes wheels up for the next stop. Ghost City.

My state of mind wasn't helped by the curiously deafening silence from my former employers. In 1972, I'd watched as Richard Nixon asked all senior government officials for their resignations and began systematically replacing them with loyalists, many from CREEP. I didn't expect a replay of 1972, but I *was* surprised when nobody called to ask me what I wanted to do when I grew up. I just assumed that the manager of the most successful reelection campaign in presidential history would have a choice of jobs to consider as a reward for services rendered. To the victors go the spoils, and all that crap.

It didn't happen. Neither I nor any of my senior team was offered a job in the second term. Lee Atwater and I hammered away at the White House and government agencies to help find jobs for our folks, especially the worker bees. It shouldn't have been hard, but we got zero help. I couldn't even get the White House to arrange a few hundred thank-you letters from the president to my senior HQ and field staff, not to mention our state chairmen. Reagan would have done it cheerfully, but he never thought of such things himself. And Jim Baker and Mike Deaver, who should have seen to it, were busy working out their exit strategies from the White House. When I called Margaret Tutwiler to complain about the letters, she brushed me off.

"We don't have time for that," she said. "We're busy with the inaugural." We ended up being the campaign that didn't thank anyone.

The only guy in the whole bunch who showed any class was John Herrington, the White House personnel director. Herrington was a longtime Reaganite who'd spent two years as a volunteer advance man in the 1980 campaign. In the early weeks of 1981, he camped out on my office couch returning Lyn Nofziger's phone calls. Lyn and I helped get him placed as an Assistant Secretary of the Navy, and we'd become good friends in the meantime.

John called me one day and asked what he could do for me. I told him I wasn't interested in coming back inside below the cabinet level, and I knew that would never happen.

"Why don't you think about Postmaster General?" Herrington urged. "It's one of the best jobs in government."

Actually, the Postal Service is only a quasi-official government agency, but most of its employees are Civil Service. More to the point, the president appoints the board of governors. The Postmaster General pulls down a bigger salary than a cabinet secretary, and he's got a personal jet at his disposal and a great view of Washington from a penthouse suite in L'Enfant Plaza near the Mall. I told Herrington to give it a shot.

Jim Baker signed off on the idea, and so did the president. But nobody cleared it with the board of governors, who had another candidate lined up by the time my name was floated. Nice try, blind alley.

The only job I'd really coveted was chairman of the Republican National Committee, a natural progression in my line of work. Frank Fahrenkopf, a close Laxalt ally, had enlisted in 1982 for two years only. It was the logical spot for me. But in one of our weekly breakfast meetings just before the election, Frank said he'd decided he wanted to stay on for another two years. Frank had done a super job at the RNC, and he was a dear friend and close ally. Even if I could, I wasn't about to pull a power play.

I definitely wasn't interested in my old White House job. For one thing, it had disappeared. Jim Baker never thought a separate political operation was necessary. He'd created one in 1981 because he thought Lyn Nofziger somewhere could help him with conservatives. In a presidential election year, the campaign is the de facto White House political office. It was abolished when I left to run the campaign, and Baker had no intention of resurrecting it.

For two months, I twiddled my thumbs. I had several big job offers, but nothing that turned me on. I was a hot commodity on the outside, even if forgotten on the inside. Then Stu Spencer made me an offer to join his consulting firm. Stu hated Washington, and had fled back to Southern California as soon as the campaign was over. But he wanted a greater presence in Washington. He offered me a comfortable job as his firm's vice chairman. I'd work out of his small Washington office, lobbying Congress and schmoozing corporate clients. I saw it as a holding action—a chance to catch my breath, recharge my batteries, make some serious money, and plot my next career move.

Shortly after the 1985 inaugural, I was flying back to Washington from my first meeting with corporate clients in California. As I was changing planes in Chicago, I caught a glimpse from the corner of my eye of a CNN report about a White House shakeup. I detoured closer to the television screen, and couldn't believe what I heard: Jim Baker and Donald Regan were swapping jobs. Baker was going to Treasury, and Regan would be the new White House chief of staff.

Actually, it wasn't a total bolt from the blue. Baker wanted a senior cabinet job, and Treasury was his only shot. George Shultz and Cap Weinberger weren't about to give up State or Defense. Baker played to Regan's vanity, and it worked. Regan added another choice assignment to his résumé, and Baker engineered a plum vacancy for himself.

For the next two hours, I told myself that somebody had sold the president a bad bill of goods. I wasn't surprised about Baker; it had been an open secret he didn't want to be around the White House in a second term. For weeks, his acolytes had been saying Baker thought the economy would fall apart. In four short years Jim had become legendary for his ability to smell trouble quickly and distance himself from its fallout. But Baker was also an able chief of staff. Replacing him with Regan was a disaster waiting to happen.

It was clear to me that Baker didn't want to be the most powerful man in government in a second term, and I knew why. He'd shared power in the first term, which meant he could always spread the blame if things weren't getting done. With Meese gone and Deaver going, he could blame only the president or himself. Blaming the boss is risky business, even for Jim Baker.

I'd never cared much for Don Regan. I thought he was one of the more arrogant individuals I'd encountered in Washington. More to the point, he had no political instincts whatsoever. When Lee Atwater and I went to see him at Treasury in 1982 to talk about how we wanted to use him and other cabinet officers in the mid-term elections, he told us the budget deficit could be fixed overnight if the president would simply raise the gasoline tax by fifty cents a gallon.

"People won't even notice it," he told us. With unemployment hovering near 10 percent, it was one of the dumbest ideas I'd heard.

"Don, maybe you guys with the limousines won't notice it," I said, "but I guarantee you Joe Six-pack will notice an extra ten-dollar tax every time he fills his gas tank." Regan was astonished by my answer. This conversation confirmed my view that Regan had a political tin ear.

In this same meeting, Regan said he'd be happy to campaign for Republican candidates in the fall, but only if they provided him a private jet. He claimed the Secret Service wouldn't let him fly on commercial planes, which I knew was a crock. Unlike other cabinet officers, who were content to fly first-class with a couple of hand-holders, Regan refused to rough it. Most candidates weren't able to spend $20,000 to $30,000 for a chartered jet to accommodate Regan's ego, so we ended up using him sparingly. He also asked me to stop sending him to Godforsaken places like Nebraska when he was a big draw in New York. I reminded him that the last time I'd checked, we didn't have many competitive congressional races in Manhattan.

Even after four years at Treasury, Regan didn't know diddly about Washington. I'd learned from my Nixon experience that management skills aren't enough. Without political skills, the world's best manager is naked in Washington. Baker had them, Regan didn't. In particular, he was a total novice in the two arenas that make or break you in this town: Congress and the media. Drew Lewis, the former Secretary of Transportation, was waiting in the wings and would have made a great chief of staff. Lewis would make people quickly forget JAB III—which is why Baker did everything to block him. On the other hand, Baker also knew Regan would be a disaster, which would only make Jim look better.

To inoculate himself, Baker scrambled to put together reinforcements for an unsuspecting Regan. He leaned on Max Friedersdorf, a Nixon and Ford alumnus universally admired on Capitol Hill, to return from a cushy job at Pepsico to be Regan's congressional liaison—the same job he'd had in the first year of Reagan's first term. And he floated my name as well with Regan and the president. When

Paul Laxalt called me to ask if I'd consider returning to the White House in an expanded but unspecified function, I knew that a quiet lobbying campaign was under way to save Regan from himself.

About a week after the musical chairs deal was announced, Regan's secretary called to say her boss would like to see me in his office at Treasury. I was agreeable; it's not like my dance card was full.

We met in Regan's third-floor Treasury office, an ornate corner suite with an impressive view of the Washington Monument and the South Lawn of the White House. Like Baker, Regan is an ex-Marine, but he's crustier. Maybe it's all those years working in New York. He got right to the point: He planned to surround himself with what he called "superdeputies," each of whom would have multiple responsibilities and report directly to him. He wanted me to revive the political shop. Whoever ran it would be in charge of intergovernmental relations (IGR) as well. For the time being, that person would function as one of three de facto deputy chiefs of staffs, but would get the actual title when Deaver left to set up his own lobbying and consulting firm.

It was tempting. The White House press corps kisses off intergovernmental relations as a backwater. In fact, it's the most important outreach operation in any White House. As the liaison office with state and local governments, IGR deals with the mayors and governors on a daily basis.

By this time, I knew why I might be lured back. What I couldn't understand was why a former chairman of Merrill Lynch would willingly give up the most prestigious job in the financial world, a post whose predecessors included Alexander Hamilton and Andrew Mellon, for a glorified staff job.

"Don, why would you want to do this? You're at the pinnacle of your universe."

"Well," Regan said, "I've sat over here for four years being ordered around by assholes like you at the White House. I've learned that's where the power is." I could see that Regan was salivating to be at the center of the administration universe.

"This wasn't my idea," he added. "It was Baker's idea. But the more I think about it, it's a *great* idea."

Power is the ultimate aphrodisiac, Henry Kissinger liked to say, and Don Regan could taste it. I didn't blame him. So could I.

He didn't offer me the job on the spot. We were playing out a time-honored Washington charade that's supposed to save face but fools nobody. At the loftier echelons of government, it's considered bad form to have somebody turn down your job offer, so you both dance a silly little minuet. The job isn't offered until it's clear you're prepared to accept. If you say no, the top dog can always say the job was never offered. Playing my part, I acted interested, but not too interested. We agreed I'd think about it for a couple of days. I told Stu he might lose me.

Two days later, Regan called me.

"I'm prepared to offer you this job if you want it. Do you want it?"

"Yeah," I said. "I want it."

I KNOW, I KNOW. I sound like the world's biggest hypocrite. I think my new prospective boss doesn't have a clue, and I've concluded the Reagan Revolution is all but over; yet suddenly Don Regan crooks his finger and I go rushing back for my old job and the promise of a fancier title.

The truth is that I'd thought about it a lot in the intervening forty-eight hours. I'd come to the conclusion that I was more miserable out of the game than I'd been willing to admit to myself. In government, the pay's lousy, the hours worse. You have no time for anything but your job. Every day you're at the White House, you feel your intellectual capital dripping away. After a while, you're running on empty. Deep down, you know it's not worth it. But it's like the old joke about the guy who bitches so much about his job sweeping up after the elephants that a friend tells him to quit. "And leave *show* business?" he recoils.

In plain English, I loved the game. The truth is, it's intoxicating. And after two months on the outside, I missed it like hell.

It wasn't purely vanity. Depressed as I was about the state of the revolution, I didn't want it to be over. I owed Ronald Reagan, and as one of the last Reaganites still standing, I didn't want to be watching from a distance while the wheels came off. He deserved better than to become a lame duck the day after his inauguration. Most of the true believers were going or gone. Now even the pragmatists were bailing out: Baker and Darman were leaving for Treasury, and Deaver and Stockman each had one foot out the door. The president was in the process of being abandoned by his team. I had the institutional memory, and now a bigger slice of the action, to help make a difference—or so I thought.

I accepted Regan's offer—and found myself immediately back in trouble. "Good," he said. "Now, the first thing you have to do is get rid of Lee Verstandig for me. You can bring in your own team."

Verstandig had been running the intergovernmental shop for two years. His rabbi was Mike Deaver, who'd helped him become one of Nancy Reagan's pets. Obviously, I wanted my own staff, but this would be tricky. I thought he deserved better treatment, and I don't blame him for being indignant when I gave him the boot. I knew his first call would be to Deaver, whose first call would be to me.

"Why are you getting rid of Lee?" a furious Deaver demanded.

"Mike, I didn't make the decision. It was Don Regan's call. The job's being downgraded to a deputy assistant anyway."

"He's very close to the First Lady. This is a very, very uncomfortable situation. I expect you to take care of him."

Christ, I thought. An hour into my new job, and I'm back in the soup with Deaver and Mommy. Some homecoming bouquet.

Regan wasn't interested in arranging a graceful exit. So after calling in a few chips, I persuaded Sam Pierce to take Verstandig as Undersecretary of Housing and Urban Development. Eventually, he returned as Mrs. Reagan's chief of staff and lasted about two weeks.

But I didn't let this dustup spoil my fun. I was back at the White House, with a bigger job. I'd loved operating out of Nixon's old office in the first term. But proximity is power; an office in the West Wing is preferable to a small palace in the OEOB.

There are very few offices in the West Wing, and it's always a battle royal to grab one. I drew a second-floor suite right above the Cabinet Room, and was assigned the best parking spot on West Executive Avenue, right next to the West Wing basement entrance.

There were a lot of new faces, few of them with Reagan credentials. Don Regan surrounded himself with acolytes from Treasury. A couple of them were quite capable, but as a group they weren't up to the job. They were so universally regarded as lightweights that the White House press corps called them "The Mice." One of them was so skilled at getting himself and his entire family invited to expense account meals with reporters that he was known around the West Wing as "America's Guest." Like many strong personalities, Regan had made the mistake of surrounding himself with weak subordinates to the detriment of his own reputation, and ultimately the president's.

The biggest problem with the new crowd was that most of them knew or cared little about Ronald Reagan, much less what he stood for. For the most part, the President of the United States was now being served by strangers. I had visions of him looking around the Oval Office at the end of the day and wondering, Where have all my friends gone?

The new chief of staff's operating style was definitely an acquired taste. Regan wasn't lazy, but his regimen was far more leisurely than

Baker's. A White House car picked him up at Mount Vernon at 6:30 A.M. He'd arrive at 7:15, have breakfast alone in his office, then conduct the 8:00 A.M. senior staff meeting. He'd spend the rest of the day in meetings or trying to get himself in every photo with the president. A creature of habit, Regan would flip on his computer and pore over the day's numbers from the financial markets when the president left for the residence around 5:00 P.M. He insisted on leaving by 6:15 to watch the evening news from home at 7:00 P.M. He almost never worked a Saturday.

In contrast, Baker used to be around until eight or nine o'clock on a normal day, and Saturday was a standard work day. That meant you could always get to him for a quick decision at day's end. If you were lucky, you might grab Regan for a thirty-second chat on the way to his car.

"Twelve hours a day is more than I spent managing one of the largest financial institutions in the world," he liked to say. He didn't see why the White House should be any different.

Nobody would ever accuse Don Regan of excessive modesty. He was full of himself, and he wasn't shy about letting you know, either. Early in 1985, he was complaining to me about the pounding he was taking in the press. I suggested that he needed to spend more time cultivating the media and would do well to emulate Jim Baker, whose courtship of reporters was already the stuff of legend.

"Do you expect me to spend thirty-five hours a week talking to reporters like Baker did?" Regan shot back. "I went back through his logs and that's how much time he spent with the press. I'm not about to do such a thing." He thought it was beneath him to grovel to mere scribes.

Don Regan never quite came to grips with the reality that while chief of staff is the most powerful job at the White House, you're still only "staff," not "chief." He always thought of himself as the deputy president.

My second tour of duty in the Reagan White House was both more and less than I'd hoped it would be. There's no question I was closer to the action than I'd been before, and my access to the president was far greater as well. When he was in town, he liked to have a weekly lunch with his senior aides in the Roosevelt Room. I found him more engaged than his public persona, and just as enthusiastic as I'd remembered in the glory days of 1981. But I couldn't say the same for myself.

The thrill was gone. Air Force One, the White House Mess, the Oval Office—I'd been there, done that. It wasn't the same. Six weeks after returning, however, something opened up that really piqued my interest. Ray Donovan was forced to resign on March 15 as Secretary of Labor after being indicted for alleged illegal payoffs in the construction industry. This proved one of the great miscarriages of justice, and he was later exonerated. The day after Ray resigned, I asked Regan for the job. I told him that I came from a labor background; my dad was a labor leader and shipyard worker, and I'd been a Teamster. I understood blue-collar guys better than anyone in the White House. I was a natural, I told Regan.

I could tell he thought I was crazy. He was honest enough to say he was concerned about putting too many White House assistants into the cabinet. John Herrington had been appointed Secretary of Energy after the Baker switch had been announced but before Regan took over, and he was still smarting about that. It was clearly a class thing with Regan. He thought cabinet officers should be captains of industry like himself, not staff minions.

More than once, I'd heard him announce that he was worth $30 million. "It's my fuck-you money," he liked to say. That's how he measured people—if you didn't have a comparable net worth, you weren't a peer.

"What would he do on the outside?" Regan asked me once about Bob Dole, the new Senate Republican leader. "A guy like that would starve to death on the outside."

"You don't have to worry about him on the outside," I replied. "You have to worry about him on the *inside*. The guy is key to the president's legislative strategy."

When Regan told me I'd be given serious consideration for the job, I knew from the way he said it he was bullshitting me, so I hit the phones.

In Washington, every political aspirant needs a patron, and Regan plainly wasn't going to be mine. This was the first major appointment on his watch, and it was going to have his imprint on it. So I started rounding up support for my candidacy. Paul Laxalt was enthusiastic, as were Jim Baker and several senators, including Orrin Hatch, the chairman of the Labor Committee. A majority of the major international union presidents endorsed me. I was told the president was in my corner as well. Bush also supported me, but didn't want to fight it out with Regan and Deaver.

Mike had his own candidate: Bill Brock, the special trade representative. Deaver wanted Brock out of the trade job so he and Jim Lake could get Clayton Yeutter into the slot. Knowing how things work in Washington, I assumed their motive was to have a friend and ally in that important post to help Deaver's new international clients. Brock not only turned down the job, he called me to say he thought I was the best choice, and that he loved what he was doing. When *The Washington Post* said Deaver was looking for another candidate, Mike called me to say he had no candidate and that the president hadn't made his choice.

"I didn't know you wanted to be Secretary of Labor," he assured me. Which was pure bullshit.

This conversation occurred, I later discovered, about an hour after the president had settled on Brock in a meeting attended by Deaver. An hour or so afterwards, one of Regan's secretaries tipped me to the bad news. She said Deaver and Regan had been maneuvering furiously to keep me from getting the job.

Fifteen minutes before the press conference where Brock was announced, Regan called to say the president thought I was more valuable to him at the White House and asked me not to tell anyone about Bill Brock.

"Who am I going to tell in the next fifteen minutes?" I shot back.

"Ed, you're a young man. You'll get your cabinet post someday. Go out and make some money first." I was infuriated, but Regan's brush-off inspired one of my best quotes to David Hoffman of *The Washington Post:* "I knew they'd get even with me for losing Minnesota."

I have to admit the experience took the starch out of me. It was a critical time for the Republican Party to make inroads with labor and blue-collar workers. I'd worked with all those groups in the first term and had gained their respect. Putting my own desires aside, it would have sent a clear message if the administration appointed a blue-collar, state college guy to something big—not to mention the first Reagan campaign staffer to the Cabinet. After that, my heart wasn't in the job at all. I felt guilty at the prospect of abandoning the Gipper, but I started thinking more and more about bailing out. And I started going home at eight o'clock instead of ten.

In April 1985, I took a rare three-day weekend to paint my Virginia cabin. I was up on the roof when my White House phone went off. It was Don Regan, who was at the ranch with the president.

"What do you think about Bitburg?" he wanted to know.

He was referring to a German cemetery the president was planning to visit during his trip to Europe in May. After a White House advance team had scouted the cemetery, we learned that SS troops were among the war dead buried there. Since Reagan would be participating in Allied ceremonies marking the fortieth anniversary of the war's end, it was an unfortunate choice.

I told Regan we'd probably have some problems with Jewish groups and maybe some veterans, but I'd make some calls to check out my hunch. It took me about five minutes to learn that even though the Bitburg stop hadn't been announced, Jewish leaders already knew about it and were furious. They were in the process of spreading the story to every major newspaper in the country. What's more, Bob Dole called me to say that veterans' groups were going crazy. I reported back to Regan, who asked me to put together a meeting with Jewish leaders on Monday in hopes of minimizing the political damage.

The meeting only made things worse. When the group I'd assembled sat down with Regan, they were presented with a press release saying the president would announce his Bitburg trip immediately after the meeting. The group included author Elie Wiesel, the Holocaust survivor and Nobel Prize winner. The leaders were incensed and felt they were being used for cover. Regan began by confirming that the president was committed to visiting Bitburg.

"So why have you invited us here?" one of the guests asked. "We were told by Mr. Rollins that the White House wanted our input. Are we to have input?"

"You can have your input," Regan replied, "but this is what we're going to do."

That was the high point. Pat Buchanan, our combative communications director, enraged the guests by saying at one point that maybe it was time for our guests to start thinking like Americans instead of Jews. Thank God the president wasn't up for reelection.

Later that day, the president called me for a readout.

"Mr. President, this is going to create serious political problems for us. Is there any way to make a change?"

"Ed, I totally understand. I feel very badly about this. But I've given my word to Helmut Kohl. He called me over the weekend and said it was very important that we go ahead with the visit. And when one world leader gives his word to another world leader, that's all there is to it. We'll just have to live through the firestorm."

It had been a mistake, and would prove a political disaster. But Reagan had given his word, and that was what he lived by.

We survived; but Bitburg was another sign that an era was ending. These are the kinds of things that always jump up and bite you when your political fortunes are in decline. In the first two years, when the revolution was riding tall in the saddle, Bitburg would have been a blip on the screen.

By now everybody in the place seemed to be off his game. Regan and I were at each other's throats about something or other at least once a week. I even got into a scrap with Pat Buchanan that ended up as another blowout with Don.

Pat and I were close allies in the White House and seldom disagreed on issues, with one notable exception. In mid-1985, we had two legislative fights going on the Hill at once—a strategic blunder we would never have made in the first term. In the course of a week, Congress would vote on the budget and funding for the Nicaraguan Contras. We all agreed the president had to make a speech to the nation and rally support for his program. But which one? Although I was a big Contra supporter, I felt the issue was too complicated to explain in one speech, so I argued for a budget speech. Pat argued for a Contra speech. We had a knockdown brawl over the matter for two days.

Then Don Regan called us into his office and said, "I've made the decision. It's a budget speech."

"Don, I'm glad you came down on my side," I said, "but this is a decision the president should make."

He glared at me, then repeated in his best Marine voice, "I've made the decision." By then I'd decided I was getting out of the White House before the end of the year anyway, so I didn't care.

"Don, I just ran a presidential campaign in fifty states, and I didn't see your name on a ballot in any one of them."

He exploded as I knew he would; when he was finished, the three of us went in and made our case to the president, who decided he'd give a budget speech.

If things seemed different the second time around, there was one constant: Nancy Reagan still scared the hell out of me. In the summer of 1985, the president decided to combine some California politicking with a visit to his beloved Rancho Cielo in the Santa Ynez Mountains. The usual drill was for Air Force One to fly into the naval air station at Point Mugu. Then the Reagans and the senior staff would helicopter to the ranch. Once they were safely ensconced, the staff would chopper back to Santa Barbara.

When we arrived at the ranch, the president bounded off the helicopter and walked off with his ranch foreman Barney Barnet to check on something. Just as I stepped off the backup helicopter, one of the presidential retrievers bounded up to Nancy and knocked her ass over teakettle. Her dress flew up around her shoulders. Standing at the foot of the chopper, I was the closest onlooker.

In the seconds I had to make a decision, I knew there were only two choices. I could run over, solicitously pick her up, and pull her dress down with as much aplomb as I could muster—and the First Lady would know forevermore that I'd seen her petticoats. Or, I could quickly climb back onto the helicopter and pretend I hadn't seen anything. It was a no-brainer. I scurried back up the steps and hid inside the chopper while ranch hands and Secret Service agents dusted her off.

The longer I stayed in my job, the more I realized I was going through the motions. Then financial realities made it far easier for me to decide on my next move. While I was away running the campaign, a change in the law required new White House employees to pay both federal retirement and Social Security taxes. For a bachelor with new car payments and a $1,200-a-month apartment, this was a major hit to my cash flow. Like most senior White House officials, my living expenses were considerably higher than my take-home pay. I figured that by looting my savings, I could stay in the government through the end of 1986.

Then I did a rough cut on my taxes and discovered to my horror that I hadn't set aside any money from the honoraria I'd earned for several speeches during the campaign. It turned out I owed the IRS $30,000 I didn't have.

There was no way to square *that* circle. I had to make some money—fast. After the 1984 election, an old California friend, Sal Russo, had asked if I'd be interested in opening a Washington office of his California political consulting firm. The offer was still open, so without much regret I left the White House on October 1 after only eight months on the job. Regan didn't beg me to stay when I gave him my notice, although he said he was sorry to see me go.

In one of those marvelous coincidences that spice both life and politics, I left the White House the same day Peggy Heckler was kicked out of the Department of Health and Human Services with the consolation prize of ambassador to Ireland. I'd been right from the start on this one. Peggy *had* been a disaster, and even her backers had come to realize it. Without question, she was one of the weakest senior appointments in the Reagan years. Her management style gave hapless a bad name, and she'd driven everyone crazy with her dizzy style.

Like cabinet meetings, for instance. Nobody shows up late for them. Except for deliberations of the National Security Council, cabinet meetings are the biggest deal in government. The entire senior echelon in the government gathers. Decisions don't often get made at them anymore, but they're still an institution to be taken seriously.

It was bad enough that Peggy usually arrived ten to fifteen minutes late. But no matter what the subject, she just *had* to stop and chat with the president. The entire business of government ground to a halt so Peggy Heckler could suck up to the boss with some Irish joke or small talk.

When she was paying attention, she was just as much of a joke. In one cabinet meeting, Cap Weinberger couldn't resist saying what the rest of us were thinking.

"Margaret," he said, ever the gentleman, "you've been on my side today, and George Shultz's side, and Bill Casey's side. But we're on three different sides. Whose side are you on?"

After the election, it was obvious even to the geniuses who had backed her that Heckler had to go. The Chief (as Don was addressed by his Mice) wanted her out immediately. She didn't fit his image of a cabinet secretary. He wasn't going to do the deed himself, however. Jim Baker, the man responsible for her appointment, was safely holed up across East Executive Avenue at Treasury. It was really unfair to the president, who in his movie days couldn't even fire his maid. That isn't unusual; I've never known a president who didn't sweat blood when it came time for the heave-ho. It was Regan's job to fire her, but he made the president do it.

Heckler's canning was on the president's schedule immediately before my farewell visit. Jim Kuhn, the president's personal assistant, called me to say my meeting would probably be delayed. "He doesn't want to do this," Jim told me.

Half an hour later, I called Jim for a progress report.

"It's not good," he advised. "She's been crying, and now the Old Man's starting to tear up a little bit himself." An old-fashioned Irish wake. Regan should have had his ass kicked for making the president drop the ax.

Finally, Jim ushered me into the Oval Office for my last visit as an assistant to the president as a distraught Heckler stormed out. He seemed utterly relieved to see a friendly face.

"Mr. President"—I smiled—"I'm going to make it very easy for you. I'll be happy to be your ambassador to Ireland."

"God, Ed, you could have *had* it ten minutes ago. I've spent the last forty-five minutes talking her into it. What a meeting!"

For the next few minutes he told me about what an agonizing experience it had been. Then he thanked me for all I'd done and gave me a big bear hug. I damn near had tears in my eyes, too.

The president was predictably gracious, following up with a letter praising my "consummate skill and professionalism," and thanking me for "the advice, wisdom, wit and most of all friendship you've provided to me over the last five years."

I ended the year where I'd begun it—back in the bleachers, though this time it was my choice. My first instinct had been the right one. I should never have gone back into the government. I'd gotten in with one hand, not both feet. In my desperation to find a fulfilling encore to running Reagan's reelection campaign, I'd assumed I could go home again by reenlisting in the revolution. What I realized only after signing up was that the revolution was over. Before my eyes, the torch was passing from Reagan to George Bush, and I was powerless to do anything about it.

GEORGE BUSH HAS been called many things. Revolutionary isn't one of them. Temperamentally and philosophically, he was miscast as Reagan's political heir. As I watched the rest of the Reagan second term unfold without me, I thought back to an exchange I'd had with the vice president a few months before leaving the White House that convinced me that the revolution hadn't just failed. It had also lost its leader.

The vice president had included me in a small dinner party at his residence at the Naval Observatory. At one point after the dishes were cleared, the two of us were standing alone on the front porch.

To make conversation, I asked him which of his government jobs had been his favorite. His year as director of the Central Intelligence Agency, he told me. "Most fascinating job there is," he said.

"In a place like that, how can you ever be sure you're being told everything you need to know?"

"You don't. That's why you gotta build your own system with your own checks and balances."

For five years, he'd been doing just that at the White House. While loyal to Reagan, Bush and his co-conspirator James Baker had pursued their own agenda and had been quietly planting the seeds of *their* revolution. They were building their own network of friends and allies throughout the government, and pushing policies more in tune with their own philosophy. Now, with the loyalists abandoning the president and Don Regan proving no match for them, Bush and Baker were more interested in gearing up for 1988 than blazing any trails for Reagan. The Trojan Horse scenario, as I'd come to call it.

Then our conversation turned to the tax bill working a tortured path through Congress.

"I don't think this tax thing is such a good idea," Bush confided. "What do you make of it?"

"I think it's pretty important to the president," I ducked. That was an understatement. It was essentially the only major initiative we had on our second-term agenda.

"But he's gonna pay a heavy price for all this. I think we need more revenue, not less."

It was a fleeting though telling insight into the psyche of the man who would probably be the next president. Bush was doing more than signaling that he didn't agree with Reagan's desire to lower tax rates. He was reminding me that he was too bloodless for my taste. Revolutions spill a lot of body parts, and that wasn't George Bush's style.

Richard Nixon had figured that out long before I did. When I met with him in early 1982, just after I'd been named White House political director, he made it clear that George Bush wasn't "the real nutcutter" we needed in our offensive against the Democrats. Nixon believed Bush was a poor campaigner and simply too weak to handle the bad-cop role Nixon had himself played for Eisenhower in 1954 and Spiro Agnew had performed for him with gusto in 1970. To Nixon, Bush lacked the killer instinct. Long before columnist George Will dismissed Bush as a lapdog in 1986, Nixon had reached the same conclusion.

Nixon told me he'd been mulling over a remedy to the nutcutter problem for about a week. He suggested I approach Vice President Bush and tell him that while I strenuously disagreed, some of Reagan's advisers wanted Bush dumped from the ticket in 1984. The best antidote to such dangerous talk, I should say, would be an uncharacteristically tough, gloves-off campaign performance in 1982 that would earn him Reagan's affection, keep him on the ticket in 1984, and put him in line to be the Republican nominee in 1988.

Then, Nixon added almost gleefully, I should meet individually with Jack Kemp, Bob Dole, Howard Baker, and several GOP governors, swear each to absolute secrecy, and confide that Reagan was disappointed with Bush and had reluctantly decided to find another running mate for reelection. The man who campaigned hardest for Reagan and the party in 1982 would be the president's choice to succeed Bush on the ticket in 1984.

Finally, he counseled, I should go back to the vice president and say that his enemies in the Kitchen Cabinet and within the White House were conspiring with Kemp, Dole, Baker, and others to dump him, but that I, as his loyal friend, would keep him informed of these vile maneuverings.

"Make George a little paranoid," Nixon chuckled. "Rev up his competitive juices."

This was obviously a dangerous game. What if I were caught and exposed? Nixon looked at me with a mixture of astonishment and pity.

"You just deny it," he explained. "Everyone will think you're doing it secretly on behalf of the president."

I'd always considered myself a pretty fair practitioner of the bare-knuckled style of politics, but I saw I was in the presence of Machia-vellian genius. Four years later, I also saw that Nixon had been right about the vice president.

George Bush is an extraordinarily nice and generous man, decent and courteous, a master of the small gesture. He probably has more genuine friendships than anyone in politics, and I've never known anyone who could write as many thank-you notes. The only person who comes close is my wife. She and Bush got into a Super Bowl of mash notes once, writing thank-you notes for thank-you notes. The exchanges kept going back and forth. It got so ridiculous that I finally said to her, "Sherrie, one of you has to stop. Don't send him another note, because he'll write you one back." I've got a dozen notes from him myself, and he doesn't even like me.

Despite what reads like an impressive résumé, Bush had never been seen as a major player in Republican circles. His jobs in the Nixon administration were second tier. Being UN ambassador when Henry Kissinger is the foreign policy honcho means you keep your mouth shut and the chair warm. The RNC chairman's job had always been part time. Envoy to China was a post well suited to Bush's personal diplomacy, but he was once again eclipsed by Nixon and Kissinger. The one genuinely important job he had, and that for only a few months, was CIA director.

Bush could have been more of a player. His friend Jim Baker made sure he was in the loop, and Reagan insisted that he be in-cluded in every critical meeting, but he was essentially passive. His image as a nonplayer was reinforced in the first Reagan term, where he almost never said anything in meetings. I attended hundreds of meetings with him in one capacity or another, and I don't think he ever spoke more than ten paragraphs in all of them combined. The only time I ever heard him speak passionately about anything was during the 1985 tax bill debate, when he vigorously argued the oil industry position—not only because he knew the business but also because Jim Baker had to recuse himself from the debate because he'd represented clients in the oil business as a corporate lawyer. Clearly, Bush was in a waiting game, perfectly content to bide his time for eight years.

This timidity was probably prudent. You don't make enemies when you keep your mouth shut. Over time, however, it earned him the enmity of Nancy Reagan. She'd opposed his appointment as her husband's running mate, preferring Paul Laxalt, and had never liked him much. In fact, she referred to him as "Whiny" and would mimic his speech patterns in unguarded moments. Bush finished himself forever with the First Lady in 1987, when he refused her request, delivered by Stu Spencer, to approach Don Regan and urge him to resign. Only after Bush learned that Reagan himself had decided to cut Don adrift did he go to him and suggest it was time to fall on his sword. Nancy never forgave Bush for what she considered terminal trepidation.

When Bush first announced he was running for president in 1979, I had the same thought I had when Steve Forbes announced sixteen years later—how absurd! I didn't think of him as a real conservative or as a significant player. Still, all in all he was an excellent vice president. He was loyal to Ronald Reagan, was respected by his old colleagues on Capitol Hill, and did all the grunt work expected of any Veep. And he was very good to me. I especially appreciated his graciousness in routinely inviting me to tag along whenever he traveled to California.

I had an interesting encounter with Bush in early 1982, just after I took over the political office from Lyn Nofziger. I wanted an ally to keep an eye on RNC chairman Dick Richards, and my friend Rich Bond was looking for a job. He was Bush's deputy chief of staff but had gotten into a pissing match with Jennifer Fitzgerald. Jennifer was Bush's closest confidant, much to the consternation of many of his closest friends. The only guy able to stare Bush down about Jennifer was Jim Baker, who'd threatened not to run Bush's 1980 presidential campaign unless he got rid of her. So she'd been temporarily banished, but was now back as Bush's executive assistant, more powerful than ever. Bond became so frustrated that he told Bush he'd have to leave unless she were reined in.

"Jim Baker made me make that choice once before," Bush replied, "and I made the wrong choice." Having had his bluff called by the Vice President of the United States, Bond submitted his resignation.

I went to see Bush and offered the services of my office to do for him what we did for the president. He was particularly pleased that I was willing to coordinate his heavy menu of campaigning for the 1982 mid-term elections. During this conversation, I told him about my plans to move Bond to the RNC.

"I don't know about Bond," he cautioned. "He's a hothead. I don't know if you want to put him at the RNC. But if you do, he's gotta go over under your banner, not my banner." I was surprised by his vehemence, and pointed out that since Bond was his chief political operative and deputy chief of staff, it was silly to think he could distance himself from Rich.

"Well, he can't be a Bush person," Bush insisted. "He has to be a Rollins person." For reasons I never understood, he was going out of his way to separate himself from one of the best operatives in the business and one of the most loyal Bush subordinates I've ever known.

That was my first direct insight into one of George Bush's enduring human strengths and political weaknesses: Forced to choose, he always opts for loyalty over competence. Even people who love him concede this point.

Despite all this, I did a lot of heavy lifting for him in 1982 and 1984, and we had an excellent relationship through 1985, when I left the White House. By then, I knew that although he was one of the genuine nice guys in American politics, George Bush was no revolutionary. His self-defined conservatism was in the mold of Gerald Ford, Bob Michel, and Howard Baker—moderate Republicans who wanted to run government more effectively and frugally, not change it in fundamental ways. They wanted to do everything the Democrats did for 80 percent of the cost. The more I thought about it, the more I realized that wasn't the Republican Party I'd joined.

ON MY LAST Air Force One trip before leaving the White House, the president wandered back to kibitz with the staff. He couldn't resist needling me about my pending departure.

"You know, Ed, things are going to be different for you now," he teased. "You'll have to get yourself to Dulles or National. You'll have to stand in line to buy a ticket. You'll have to carry your own bags and pick them up when you land. You'll even have to travel with money in your pocket."

"Mr. President," I asked, smiling, "how the hell would you know?"

"Well, that's what people tell me." He laughed.

I thought of that exchange many times in the next year, as I struggled once again to reconcile the trade-offs of life away from what baseball players call "The Show."

By conventional measurements, I was a howling success in my new career as a corporate fixer. I built the Washington office of Russo, Watts & Rollins into a successful lobbying and strategic communications operation, with fifty employees and a client list that included Sears, McDonnell Douglas, Norfolk Southern Railroad, and a couple dozen others. I was the rainmaker—the guy who attracts the big-bucks clients because of his access to the decision makers inside the government. I realized I was pretty good at it. But I didn't like it. It's not that interesting, really. And the role reversal can be jarring to the ego. At the White House, you're bombarded by supplicants begging for this or that. Now, I was the guy with the tin cup.

In no time at all, I got restless. I was having more fun dabbling in my old line of work. I spent about a third of my time advising senators and congressmen on campaign strategy. I never took a penny for this counsel. I didn't want to be in the situation of accepting a fee for helping elect someone, then turning around and putting the arm on them for one of my corporate clients.

I was still on the fringes of power, but it wasn't the same. It never is. Don Rumsfeld, Gerald Ford's chief of staff and Secretary of Defense, once said that in Washington you're judged by what you are, not who you are. If you doubt that, he added, just watch and see how fast those invitations stop flooding your in-box when you're out of government.

When you leave the White House, they come to your house the next day and rip out your special White House telephone. You lose your toll-free number to the White House switchboard, which can relay you to any number in the world, courtesy of the taxpayers. Reporters stop calling. Like it or not, you're not on the A-list any more. I've seen business cards that read: "Former Member of Congress." It ain't the same.

I once saw Al Haig on the old Eastern Shuttle from Washington to New York shortly after he was eased out as Secretary of State. He was wandering aimlessly up and down the aisle looking for seat number 98. When he saw me, his eyes lit up and he asked if I knew where this "bloody seat" was. I explained that the shuttle had open seating and he could sit anywhere. The number 98 only signified he was the ninety-eighth person to buy a ticket. He stumbled into a seat in front of me. I felt sorry for the bastard. Al Haig, former four-star general, White House chief of staff, NATO commander, and Secretary of State, had probably not flown in a commercial airliner by himself in twenty years, and he was befuddled. Life on the outside can be tough.

A piece of me, however, was glad to be out. I had escaped what turned into an extremely disappointing second term, crippled by internal disarray, scandal, and the loss of the Senate to the Democrats in 1986.

Reflecting from a safe distance, I realized Bill Brock's appointment as Secretary of Labor was far more than the emotional wedge that had driven me off. It was a metaphor for everything that followed in Reagan's last term. Bill is a great guy and a friend, and he did a good job at Labor, but he was never a Reagan man. In fact, as RNC chairman he'd fought Ronald Reagan all the way to the convention in 1980. There was great opposition to giving Brock anything in the new government by the Reagan people. His appointment as special trade representative was one of the last senior jobs filled in the first term. Like far too many of the Reagan appointments, he represented the old Washington order.

From start to finish, the second term was a struggle. In Congress, the Democrats rejected funding for the Contra rebels in Nicaragua and slashed funding for the Strategic Defense Initiative ("Star Wars") missile defense system. Terrorists hijacked a Trans World Airlines jet in June, murdered an American serviceman on board, and held its crew and passengers hostage for sixteen days. The president had cancer surgery in July 1985, and never fully regained his vitality. Nancy became justifiably more protective of him than ever.

An October summit meeting in Geneva with Mikhail Gorbachev, and the 1986 tax reform bill, which lowered tax rates for millions of Americans, weren't enough to jumpstart the president's political fortunes. The Democrats scored points with the argument that Reagan wanted to cut Social Security benefits for older Americans, and whispered that he was getting old. The perceived failure of the Reagan-Gorbachev Summit in Reykjavik a month before the mid-term elections damaged the president's credentials as an effective foreign policy leader.

It was a tribute to his personal standing with voters that Republican losses were well below the historical average. Nevertheless, the Democrats picked up six seats in the House and recaptured the Senate. Any chance to control the legislative agenda for the remainder of Reagan's term had evaporated—particularly since an ill-advised decision by his new handlers to give Reagan a more partisan tone on the campaign trail not only undercut his nice-guy reputation but also needlessly irritated the Democrats, who were now calling the shots on Capitol Hill. If I'd been around, I would have argued against letting Reagan say the harsh and partisan things he said during that campaign.

The Iran-Contra scandal erupted a day before the mid-term elections, and for all practical purposes the Reagan presidency was over. A majority of Americans didn't believe his explanations then, and to this day, many still suspect the president knew more about the policy of trading arms for hostages than he acknowledged.

What I believe is that subordinates, including William Casey, took advantage of the president's inattention to details to pursue their own foreign policy agenda.

I can picture the Oval Office scene: Three old men in their seventies discussing this sensitive subject. Don Regan and the president were both hard of hearing, and Bill Casey mumbled so badly you couldn't understand him a foot away. The joke at the CIA was that Casey was so hard to understand he didn't need a scrambler on his secure telephone. I figure Casey and Regan briefed the president and went off thinking they had his okay. Maybe they did—but it was the most inconsistent and stupid thing in Ronald Reagan's presidency.

The only good to come from Iran-Contra was that the controversy finally gave his enemies an opening to force the removal of Don Regan, whose imperious style had earned him the enmity of the worst enemy anyone could have: Nancy Reagan. She hated him, correctly believing he didn't give her husband the deference a president deserved.

Not to mention the deference she thought *she* deserved. A couple of months after he'd taken over, he was complaining one day about a succession of calls he'd just fielded from the First Lady.

"I'm not taking any more of her goddamn calls," Regan bellowed. "She can talk to one of my staff people. I've got more important things to do than deal with her anxieties." Which was true—but definitely not the way to deal with Nancy Reagan.

I offered a friendly warning: "We all have our crosses to bear, Don; she's yours."

"I signed on to be chief of staff to the President, not the First Lady, goddamn it, and she can go screw herself. If he's not man enough to tell her, I will." Hearing this, I knew he'd just kissed his rich ass away. She may have been able to smell fear on me, but she'd have to be blind to miss his arrogance.

Don Regan was one stubborn Irishman. He had to learn the hard way. In Nancy's eyes, he never recovered from his 1986 comment likening his efforts to correct the president's verbal missteps to the guys who sweep up after the circus animals parade by.

Regan had agreed to resign on a Monday in February 1987. Nancy was so determined to settle scores that she instructed one of her closest aides to leak word that he was being cashiered the Friday before—knowing Regan would be so furious at the insult that he'd storm out in a huff immediately. And that's exactly what happened.

Regan was the wrong man in the wrong job at the wrong time. Ronald Reagan needed people around him who could debate the issues and make sure he knew all the options. The first-term team might have done more infighting, but nobody made decisions independently. Regan once told me, "I can make eighty-five percent of the decisions better and quicker than he can, and I will." I don't doubt that he tried.

He damn near destroyed the Reagan presidency and he ran off

the best of the staff. In 1985 alone, I left in October, Bud McFarlane left in November, and Max Friedersdorf left in December. Among us we had over two decades of White House experience from three administrations.

As the end came for Regan, there's no question most of the town was cheering his demise. When the mighty fall in Washington, folks line up to kick them on the way down. And when you step on as many people as Don did on his way up the ladder, your rate of descent is triple your rate of ascent. There was a strong collective sense that Regan got what he deserved. Reagan deserved better, of course, and he got it in Regan's replacement, Howard Baker.

Not that Baker could single-handedly save an administration that was running on empty. During a dinner at the Occidental Restaurant with House Speaker Tip O'Neill and Danny Rostenkowski not long after Baker had succeeded Regan as chief of staff, he berated me in mock horror.

"I thought you were my friend," he complained. "How could you have let me go into this White House?" By the end of the conversation, it was clear Howard wasn't kidding. Things *were* a mess, he confided. The president was distracted, the staff was demoralized, and there was no strategic agenda to finish out the term. He was genuinely distressed at the wreckage Regan had left in his wake.

As a former senator, presidential candidate, and Senate majority leader, Howard Baker was obviously overqualified for the job, and had been reluctant to take it. Before long, stories leaked out of the West Wing that he didn't like being a manager at all. After a while, he started spending more and more time in the White House darkroom, pursuing his avocation as an amateur photographer. Well before he succeeded Baker in the closing months of the administration, Ken Duberstein had already become the de facto chief of staff and did a superb job when he became official. But Baker did the country and the president a great service by going into the White House. He restored confidence, dignity, and a sense of common decency to the West Wing.

By this time, I believe the president had aged dramatically and was even more distracted and disengaged than his critics alleged. The mission of Baker and Duberstein was to get the ship back into port without taking any more torpedoes. They did a remarkable job. In politics, what destroys your reputation irretrievably isn't adultery—witness Bill Clinton—but being perceived as a liar. Almost 70 percent of the American people believed Ronald Reagan was lying about Iran-Contra, yet his numbers came back. He was the first president since Eisenhower to leave office as popular as when he arrived.

It was a testament to his fundamental decency and his likability—and the political skill of his last two handlers. Baker and Duberstein had stopped the bleeding, and preserved a legacy on which George Bush could proudly campaign in 1988. Unfortunately, I knew by then that it was a case of right message, wrong messenger. It was just as well that I wouldn't be along for the ride.

A FEW WEEKS after the November 1986 mid-term elections, Charlie Black came over to see me with an offer I knew I should refuse. I'd known Charlie since the 1980 Reagan campaign, when he found himself out in the cold with John Sears and Jim Lake after the three of them were fired just before the New Hampshire primary. I'd always thought Charlie had been unfairly tarred by the Reaganites, who considered him persona non grata. I was called on the carpet by Mike Deaver one day in 1982 after someone turned me in for inviting Charlie to lunch in that ultimate Washington status symbol, the White House Mess. In 1984, I brought him back into the Reagan campaign, where he did a great job as a senior adviser and trouble-shooter. Charlie was now running an extremely well connected and prosperous political consulting firm with Paul Manafort, Roger Stone, and Lee Atwater. In his spare time he was also the principal adviser to Jack Kemp, who was known to be considering a challenge to George Bush for the 1988 Republican presidential nomination.

Charlie Black likes to play hardball. He was a founder of the National Conservative Political Action Conference, which helped write the book on negative campaigning. A North Carolinian by birth, he's a protégé of Jesse Helms, who knows a little about down-and-dirty campaigns. Like Lee Atwater, if given a choice, Charlie will always go for the jugular.

In real life, Charlie is an amiable, mild-mannered guy with a courtly disposition. He's worked for some bad hombres and has helped carve up some good people in the process, but nobody really thinks of Charlie as a bad person. It's easy to hate guys like Lee Atwater and Roger Stone. Hard as it is to believe, it's even easy for some to hate Ed Rollins. It's next to impossible to hate Charlie Black. But if the truth be known, he's as vicious as anyone who plays the game.

"Jack wants to go," Charlie said, "and he wants me to run the campaign. But I'm in the middle of a messy divorce and I can't do it. Jack wants you to be the campaign manager."

I was tempted. I was having a good enough time and making good money as a lobbyist, and the networks were taking care of my ego needs by booking me onto the talk shows regularly. But being principal strategist for the sale of Conrail to the private sector is a far cry from managing a political campaign. I missed being at the center of the action. On the other hand, I couldn't just walk away from my business. I was pulling in half of my company's revenues. I owed it to my partners not to disappear. I also needed complicated surgery to correct a doctor's error when he repositioned my stomach during back surgery years earlier. My new doctors said that if I put it off much longer, I'd get cancer of the esophagus. On top of all this, Sherrie and I were engaged. (We were married in May 1987.)

I also had a very strong commitment to Paul Laxalt. Paul and I had talked about his making the race in 1988 for over a year. I'd laid out a series of things he needed to do in the 1986 campaign season. Paul was retiring from the Senate after twelve years. He was still the most popular man in the Senate, and as Reagan's closest friend he was a big campaign attraction. My counsel that he announce for president immediately after the 1986 elections went unheeded. He hadn't made up his mind, he told me, and wouldn't for a few months. I knew he had to begin immediately to have any chance of raising money and preserving the old Reagan team before many of them went with Bush. I erroneously assumed by his delay he wasn't going to run.

I liked and admired Jack Kemp, but the timing was lousy. "I'm glad to help informally," I told Charlie, "but I can't take a year out of my life to run a campaign."

A week later, Charlie telephoned to say that he'd reluctantly agreed to be Kemp's manager, which should make it easier for me to accept the less demanding position of national chairman. I tried to separate the emotional appeal of the offer from the practical political consequences. I knew from our previous conversations that Charlie had serious disdain for George Bush's political skills. He also believed that in time, the Reagan conservatives would abandon Bush when they realized he wasn't another Gipper.

"He'll flame out, and we'll be there to pick up the pieces," he cheerfully predicted.

It seemed a safer bet that it was Bob Dole, the other leading contender, who'd flame out, not Bush. But like Charlie, I also thought the vice president didn't have the right stuff. To paraphrase Lloyd Bentsen, Ronald Reagan was a hero of mine, and Bush was no Ronald Reagan.

Something else propelled me away from Bush. For nearly two years, my former friend Lee Atwater had been doing a number on me with the vice president. After our falling out during the 1984 campaign, Lee felt threatened by me and was determined to freeze me out of the Bush operation in 1988, which he was slated to manage. Throughout 1986, I'd gotten job feelers from every Republican considering a run in 1988. Pat Robertson had asked me to manage his campaign. I never heard anything from the Bush camp. Their silence was eloquent. Atwater had poisoned the well but good.

We all have egos, and mine was bruised. If Bush and his people had taken me to their bosom out of party loyalty, I might have felt differently about walking away. But they'd left me adrift. I felt no obligation to them any longer.

I chewed it over for a week. Sherrie was a big Bush fan, and her close friendship with his youngest son Marvin dated back to their college days at the University of Virginia. But it was my decision to make. I called Charlie back and accepted. I agreed to give the campaign two to three days a week of my time. I'd sit in on strategy sessions, provide counsel to the candidate, be a principal campaign spokesman. I was in effect a senior counsellor, without pay or line responsibilities. As manager, Charlie would run the operation and have final authority for day-to-day tactical calls. It seemed I could have it both ways. I'd be back in the game for 1988, but I could keep running my business. If there was a downside, I didn't see it.

I visited Jack at his congressional office in December to seal the deal. He was excited about the prospect of working with me. Having Ronald Reagan's campaign manager as his national chairman would be a big plus for him. I told him I couldn't be a full-time adviser, but I didn't want to be a figurehead, either. He assured me that wouldn't be a problem. Little did I know that this conversation was the high-water mark of the Kemp campaign. From that moment on, we marched steadily off the cliff.

I couldn't start working for Kemp without taking care of some unfinished business with the Vice President of the United States.

A year before, in early 1986, I'd asked to see George Bush privately. Craig Fuller, his chief of staff, called back to ask if he and Lee Atwater could sit in on the meeting. That was typical; Craig had been cabinet secretary for Reagan, but his ego had gotten swollen all out of proportion. He now had delusions of adequacy, which would later be dispelled to all but himself when he was passed over as Bush's White House chief of staff. Fuller and Atwater wanted to be sure I didn't trash them with the boss. They both knew me to be candid; if asked a question, I'd give a straight answer. But I wasn't a back stabber and wouldn't bad-mouth either of them for the hell of it.

"If I feel you or Lee is doing a fucked-up job," I replied, "I'll be happy to tell him in front of you anyway. That's not the point of my meeting, but obviously it's the point of your paranoia."

In the meeting, we discussed the vice president's strategy and a lot of the things he should be doing. Bush then asked, "Can I count on you?"

I told him the only reason I *wouldn't* support him in 1988 was if Paul Laxalt decided to run. "I feel a moral obligation to Paul," I explained. "He's been my friend and protector, and I hope you'll understand." I added that I didn't think Laxalt would run so the caution was probably academic, but I didn't want him to be blindsided.

Bush didn't react well at all. He stiffened in his chair and made it clear he resented the very notion that Paul Laxalt would think about challenging him. What I considered little more than a courtesy had backfired. He was clearly as annoyed with me as with Laxalt.

Now, a year later, Laxalt had decided—or at least I thought he'd decided—not to get into the race, and I'd signed on with Jack Kemp. That flew in the face of what I'd told Bush in our previous conversation, so I felt he deserved an explanation out of common courtesy even though I dreaded it. When I asked for a meeting, Fuller asked why. After I explained, he said the Veep would rather do it with a phone call. When we connected, I could tell he'd already heard and wasn't pleased.

"Well, I understand you're going to go with someone else," he said with a jocularity I knew was feigned.

"Mr. Vice President," I replied, "I was hoping to sit down with you and talk about this."

"Well, there's no need if you're going to go with someone else." I tried to explain my rationale, but he'd tuned out. "I wish you well," he said, "but not *too* well," and that was it.

I came away feeling that he'd been a little too pissy, but he clearly had taken my defection as a personal affront. I've always thought that was one of his defects as a politician. I believe in sometimes getting mad and *always* getting even. But I don't believe in taking political decisions of this sort personally. They almost never are. Besides, nobody in his camp had been beating down my door to get me to join up.

Having cleared my conscience with the vice president, I set about to concoct a strategy to steal the nomination away from him.

For my money, Jack Kemp is one of the really good people in American politics today. A lot of folks remember him from his quarterbacking days with the San Diego Chargers and Buffalo Bills. Some may still think of him as a jock, but he's moved a long way from his days as an all-star athlete. Jack's an extremely articulate and well-read guy, a self-educated man with a passion for the power of ideas and an instinctive feel for the problems of ordinary people. He has a strong following throughout the party's grass roots and great appeal to blue-collar workers. He was the advocate of broadening the base of the party to minorities and blue-collar Democrats, a radical idea essential if the Republicans are going to hold on to their power. Newt Gingrich may have been the architect, but there's no question Jack Kemp was the spiritual godfather of the 1994 Republican landslide.

Next to the nominee, Jack is always the most popular guy at a Republican National Convention, and in my opinion is yet today the sole legitimate heir to the Reagan Revolution. That was his secret weapon—if we could stay in the race until the convention. I recognized that Kemp was a long shot, but not nearly so long as it seems in hindsight. And if he *didn't* win, he'd have gained the credibility to set the GOP agenda for years to come.

I thought it made no sense going head-to-head against a sitting vice president and the Senate Republican leader. I wanted us to run a guerrilla campaign, conserving our money and picking our shots carefully while Dole and Bush beat the hell out of each other early on. Sooner or later, one of them would fall by the wayside—Dole, I guessed. By careful targeting, we could stay competitive until the campaign shifted westward, where we could plant the flag in California. Kemp had grown up there and was still popular from his football days. If we could beat Bush in California, Jack might arrive at the convention in a position to parlay the hearts and souls of the delegates, which he commanded then and does to this day, into an upset win.

But we had to stay in the race to make a western strategy viable. To lower expectations and husband resources, I wanted Kemp to skip the Iowa caucuses, the first battleground, where he had no chance, and shoot for second or a strong third in New Hampshire. Then I thought we should pick a couple of contests in March where Bush and Dole weren't heavily invested. With one win and a couple of seconds on Super Tuesday, we could stay in until one of the others faltered. We didn't control our own destiny, but I was sure one of the front-runners would kill off the other. If we were careful, we'd be around to pick up the pieces.

Charlie wanted to replay the 1980 primary campaign, when Reagan had mounted a front-runner's campaign as though he were the party's obvious choice. But Kemp was nowhere as well positioned as Reagan had been. Charlie had built a big headquarters staff and wanted to bash heads with Bush and Dole from the start. If Kemp could finish second in either Iowa or New Hampshire, he thought, the money would begin to flow and Kemp could be competitive the rest of the way. We were in direct conflict: Front Load versus Survive and Keep Moving. His strategy was to spend big early. Mine was to live off the land and make the free press carry the story—and our press secretary, John Buckley, was brilliant at coining the kind of sharp-tongued quotes reporters love.

Since Charlie had the day-to-day portfolio, I lost the argument. But the strategy made no sense: Kemp, the third choice of party faithful in all the polls, would wage a front runner, incumbent-style campaign. Before long, I had the distinct feeling Charlie was less interested in actually winning than positioning Kemp to be Bush's vice president—which would never happen because Bush couldn't stand Kemp.

This misguided strategic call at the outset was exacerbated by what I'll euphemistically call the candidate's defects as a campaigner. Jack wasn't prepared for what goes on in a presidential campaign. He'd been in Congress for eighteen years, but only his first race had been tough.

It's hell helping run a campaign for a friend. Just ask Jim Baker, who has scars all over his backside for standing up to George Bush's temper tantrums in three presidential campaigns. It was particularly frustrating for me because, to put it bluntly, Jack was a totally un-manageable candidate. We're dear friends today, but he was a total pain in the ass in that campaign. He was impossible to discipline and simply wouldn't listen. He loved making speeches and relished the intellectual combat of candidate forums and debates. He had a magic with crowds. But he fought all of us tooth and nail over the rest of the crap a candidate has to put himself—and his family—through to get elected. He didn't want to make his fund-raising calls or practice for debates, for instance.

I call it the quarterback mentality. Quarterbacks think they can always make the big play, and resent being controlled by anyone. I tried to turn this analogy on him, without any success.

"I'm the coach, and you're the quarterback," I'd tell him.

"You're *not* the coach," he'd shoot back. "And I always called my own plays anyway."

He gave wonderfully eloquent speeches, which usually ignored the script. This inevitably meant that the sound bite we'd carefully prepared for him never passed his lips, much less made it onto the evening news. During a campaign swing to Ohio, he forgot to mention the names of the local Republican officials who'd just endorsed him.

God knows, I tried. He loved big words and he could talk at length on many complex subjects, but sometimes his remarks would go on forever or sail over the audience's heads.

"If I could remove two-thirds of your knowledge and three-fourths of your vocabulary, I could make you into a decent candidate," I teased him one day. We put him on a Word Diet and actually made him use a timer for his speeches. He usually left it on the podium, a sure sign of his disdain. Jack would nod his head obediently and behave for a speech or two. Then it was back to mumbo-jumbo like the gold standard, Malthusian theory, baskets of commodities, T-Bill rates, Hannah Arendt, and Maimonides, whoever the hell that is.

I could never make him understand that in politics, the messenger is as critical as the message. He thought the power of his ideas was so compelling that nothing else mattered. Barry Goldwater thought the same thing in 1964, and so did Newt Gingrich in 1994. The quality of the messenger *always* matters.

Meanwhile, we also had serious strategic and operational problems. As Jimmy Carter proved in 1976, presidential elections are won in the year *before* the voting, when the seed corn of organizing and fund-raising is planted. In this critical period, we were marching around in circles. The general lack of direction was painfully obvious. The headquarters staff was bloated, the field organization minuscule. The fund-raising operation couldn't raise money as fast as Charlie was spending it. If we *did* win in New Hampshire as Charlie hoped and money started rolling in, we wouldn't have an organization to capitalize on the money or the momentum. Kemp didn't know it, but he was headed for major embarrassment.

By midsummer 1987, we were still drifting, and Charlie and I weren't agreeing on much of anything. At the end of one of my frequent bitching sessions, Kemp asked me to come into headquarters every day for a month, assess the state of play, and "give me a real analysis of this campaign." He wanted an eyes-only memorandum, and encouraged me to be frank in my assessment of Charlie.

I showed up every day, talked to just about everyone on the staff, and listened quietly in staff meetings. I learned an awful lot. One thing I learned was that every time I walked into Charlie's office, he was on the phone with Lee Atwater.

The more I thought about it, the more I began to think Lee and Charlie had cut some sort of deal. I thought Charlie was simply too good an operative to run a campaign as mediocre as this. (My opinion has changed since his stewardship of Phil Gramm's disastrous 1996 campaign.) It made no sense—unless it was part of some dark bargain between Charlie and Lee to keep Bush propped up in the event he stumbled early.

On a weekend at the cabin in August, I wrote a memo explaining why I thought we were headed for disaster. The truth is I suspected it was over before I wrote my first sentence. I was competent enough at this game to know what had to be done, and realistic enough to know it wouldn't be.

"We still don't have a clearly defined message," I argued. "You've got to sit down and write out: Why should you be president? What is it that you want to run on? What do you think a Kemp presidency will try to accomplish? Why should voters trust you with the country's most important office? What is your vision of America in the future? After you've answered these questions, we have to narrow your stump speech down to six or seven topics and repeat them over and over again."

I laid much of the problem at Charlie's feet. Charlie was micromanaging the campaign, when he needed to be delegating. The real problem, I wrote, was that Charlie was an excellent tactician but a poor strategist.

I argued that Charlie had built the campaign on a series of false premises, the dumbest of which was that Bush would fold like an accordion after the first setback. "George Bush is in the race to the end," I predicted. "He will not quit; Jim Baker and others who have a vested interest in a 'Bush presidency' won't let him." Unless both the strategy and the candidate came to their senses quickly, "The odds are very high that we'll end up like Gary Hart—in debt and not nominated."

I sent the memo to Kemp, and we got together on a Friday afternoon in September to discuss it.

"God, it can't be this bad," he said after flipping through my prose.

"Jack," I replied, "it's this bad." We sparred a little longer, then Jack did what he always does in these awkward situations—he punted.

"I can't focus on this now," he said. "I've got to go to [his youngest son] Jimmy's [football] game. You and Charlie get together. You got to work this out. Make it happen."

He promised to think about my memo over the weekend, but amazingly he never got back to me. You'd think that a guy who'd just been handed a vote of no confidence by his campaign chairman might at least have told me to go screw myself. But nothing changed—except that more money went down the rathole and we were becoming less and less viable. A couple of weeks after my meeting with Jack, Sherrie and I went to France on a ten-day vacation. In a campaign headed anywhere except oblivion, that would have been a firing offense.

There's nothing harder in politics than to keep plugging away in a doomed cause. You have to pretend that all's well even though you know better. The slightest whiff of hopelessness will infect your staff like a runaway virus. Next thing you know, the press has heard about it and you're presiding over the Last Days of Pompeii. I handled it by tuning out emotionally.

I was experiencing the worst of all worlds. In my gut, I knew I was right about what had to be done to keep Jack alive. I also still believed he was the man to reignite the Reagan Revolution. But when I turned down the manager's job, I passed up the authority to impose the necessary fixes. I hated feeling so impotent—especially since I knew how this movie was going to end.

Jack was the odd man out from the start of the primary contests. Ronald Reagan was officially neutral, but everyone knew he'd put his arm around his vice president. So Republicans who liked Reagan were for George Bush, and Republicans who didn't like Reagan were for Bob Dole. Kemp started way behind, and the way we ran the campaign made sure he stayed there. By mid-January 1988, Kemp finally reached double digits in the polls, but he finished a weak fourth in Iowa and an even weaker third in New Hampshire, with 13 percent of the vote. We were out of money, momentum, and excuses.

I watched the New Hampshire returns cursing from my bed at Johns Hopkins Hospital in Baltimore, where I was recovering from my stomach surgery. I was miserable, with tubes coming out of everywhere. When I heard Bob Dole tell Bush in an interview with Tom Brokaw to "stop lying about my record," I knew it was over. Dole had self-destructed, and Kemp was broke. I called Jack and Charlie to recommend we withdraw and endorse Bush. Jack had nothing left, I told them. By being a good sport he might get to play a role later. Bush might also feel generous and help pay off the campaign debts. At this point, we hadn't met a payroll for weeks. They both resisted, arguing that anything could still happen. I thought they were both nuts.

"This thing is over," I said. "Bush has a wide-open road. He has the money, the momentum, the organization, and no one is there who can stop him."

A couple of days later, Charlie called to say that Jack had decided to make a stand in South Carolina. That was a decision beyond stupid. Through his alliance with Governor Carroll Campbell, his former boss and business partner, Lee Atwater had his home state wired for Bush, and Charlie, who still talked to Lee every day, certainly knew it. Campbell had even moved the primary to the Saturday before Super Tuesday to add momentum for Bush. We'd be slaughtered. Nevertheless, we spent approximately $400,000 we didn't have on media spots in South Carolina in a hopeless cause. Kemp got clobbered in South Carolina, destroying his last semblance of credibility.

It was time to throw in the towel. We all agreed that Kemp should withdraw and endorse Bush. In late March, two politicians who had almost no use for one another staged a joint press conference in Milwaukee to pledge their mutual respect and eternal devotion.

Afterwards, Jack, Charlie, and I joined Bush in his hotel suite for a couple of minutes of bury-the-hatchet bullshit. I was the Stealth guest. The vice president never said a word to me. I listened in amazement as Bush and Black fought to see who could kiss the other's ass more.

"We're all here to serve you, Mr. President," Charlie said, addressing Bush as though he'd already been elected.

"Well," Bush gushed, "Lee tells me all the wonderful things you're going to do for us."

Bush's remark convinced me I'd been right. Charlie killed Jack off in South Carolina to seal the nomination for Bush. His reward, arranged by his partner Lee Atwater, was to join the Bush campaign as a senior adviser. The revolving door of politics at work.

"This is fucking ridiculous," I muttered to myself as the three of us left the suite. "He's more pissed at me than Kemp or Black, and I'm the only one of us who actually has any positive feelings for the guy."

Jack was a grownup about losing, but he was deeply in debt and angry about it. In one of our very first conversations before I'd signed up, Jack had laid down a clear financial marker.

"I have no money," he'd said. "I don't want to be like John Glenn, paying off campaign bills for years. Whatever you do, don't leave me in debt." Every time I remembered that conversation, I wanted to punch Charlie out. To this day, I believe Charlie and Lee Atwater conspired to torpedo Jack's candidacy so he wouldn't be a credible threat to George Bush. There's no other rational explanation for the South Carolina debacle. My suspicions were strengthened when I learned that after Bush lost to Dole in the Iowa caucuses, Charlie and Jim Lake met secretly with Dole to talk about joining *his* campaign if Bush lost New Hampshire and faltered.

It became even clearer when I was told months later that Charlie and his partners had tried to pull off a grand scheme in which their firm would manage *all* the major Republican contenders in 1988. Atwater was all set for Bush; Black would manage Dole; and Stone would run the Kemp campaign. No matter who won the nomination, Black, Manafort, Stone, and Atwater would be wired. But Kemp wouldn't agree to Stone because like everybody else in the political world, he didn't trust him. (They're at it again in 1996. Stone managed Arlen Specter; Black ran Gramm into the ground; and Manafort is working for Dole.)

It's interesting—but not surprising—that the person with the best insight into my candidate's limitations was his wife. Back in September 1987, about a week after I'd written my Apocalypse Now memo, I showed it to Joanne Kemp during a campaign stop.

"You're absolutely right," she said after reading it. We talked a little more, then she said something that told me this was one political wife who really knew her man.

"Ed," she said, "it just may be that he's not ready to be President yet."

Joanne had put her finger on it. Jack wasn't ready to be president in 1988, but he would have been a *great* vice president. If Reagan hadn't been talked out of picking him in 1980, Jack would have been unbeatable in 1988 and 1992. The Reagan Revolution would have grown and prospered. If he'd run in 1996, he would have been the logical alternative to Bob Dole and the eventual nominee.

The Kemp experience left me feeling totally fucked over. I don't blame Jack for what happened: I blame myself. I knew what should have been done to get in the game, and I shouldn't have been so passive. Instead, I'd spent the better part of eighteen months ignoring my business and having my counsel disregarded. As campaign chairman, I never had control of the operation and turned out to be essentially a figurehead. Still, I ended up being blamed not only for running a lousy effort but for leading the charge against George Bush. My candidate, on the other hand, became one of Bush's most popular surrogates. Charlie Black found a home with the Bush campaign, thanks to his Atwater connection. And I was in the doghouse with the nominee of my party. But that's the game, and I knew the risks going in.

In April 1988, my business dissolved. It was an amicable split, a case of three partners deciding they all wanted to do different things in different locations. I closed down the Washington operation and joined Jim Lake's public relations consulting firm as executive vice president doing strategic communications and consulting. Once again, I was back in the bleachers, watching the game I wanted to be playing.

The biggest regret I have about 1988 is that I didn't wait for Paul Laxalt to make up his mind. He did decide to run and announced in May. It was a short-lived campaign—he pulled out in August because he couldn't raise the money. Even though I have no regrets about being with Jack, I should have gone with Paul. He had been my friend and my mentor, and I wouldn't have survived in 1984 without him. I should have gone over the cliff with him in 1988 because he would have gone over the cliff with me anytime. As I look back I can only say I was too anxious to play the game and I forgot what friendship is all about. Just like Kemp, Paul would have made a great vice president in 1980, and he too would have been the nominee in 1988 if his other friend, Ronald Reagan, had done what was right and chosen him to be his Veep as Reagan so wanted to do.

AT THE SAME time the Kemp campaign was going down the tubes, Lee Atwater's shooting star was finally coming back to earth after a meteoric rise. Lee was a great front man, but he couldn't manage a checkbook, let alone a staff. Ronald Reagan rode to the sound of the guns. In such circumstances, Lee instinctively started looking for the foxholes.

After Dole bloodied Bush in the February 8 Iowa caucuses, Lee melted down. I'd hear stories about him walking around in a daze. By New Hampshire, only eight days later, he'd been relegated to a snowbank. Governor John Sununu took personal charge of the Bush effort in New Hampshire, and with some timely help from Bob Dole's self-destructive tendencies, Bush regained his footing in the Granite State.

Lee's ego had been dealt a body blow, and even his closest allies quietly admitted he was never quite the same. Dole's collapse gave the campaign some breathing room, but it was only a matter of time for Atwater. At Bush's insistence, Jim Baker left Treasury in August to become campaign chairman. For all his talents, Lee still needed adult supervision. He remained in place, but no longer as significant a factor. Nobody wheels and deals on Jim Baker and lives to tell the tale, so Atwater had to tone down his act and be content with keeping his title.

I'd known for a while that Lee was in trouble. In fact, not long after the vice president's comeback win in New Hampshire, Bob Teeter had sent an envoy to see if I'd be willing to jump ship and come work for Bush. Teeter was Bush's pollster and one of his senior strategists, and we'd remained friendly despite my estrangement from his boss. I was told that Atwater's erratic performance had been troubling to Bush, and that Teeter and others believed Lee was in over his head. They were urging Jim Baker to leave Treasury and take over the campaign. Baker was resisting, so Teeter was pursuing alternatives and wanted to know if I was interested.

I knew that Bob hadn't cleared an offer of that magnitude with Bush, and that the odds of such a deal ever happening were next to zero. On the other hand, this sort of thing goes on all the time in campaigns. It wasn't totally far-fetched that I might end up somewhere in the Bush operation, if only for window-dressing. And they all knew that I was a good manager and had good political instincts, commodities always in demand.

Given the bad blood between Atwater and me, getting drafted by the Bushies in any capacity would have been sweet. But I was Jack Kemp's chairman. I told the emissary that if Kemp dropped out I would certainly support Bush, but any conversations about a job at this point were premature. A few days later, Teeter telephoned with the same offer.

"I've recommended to my candidate that he drop out," I told Teeter. "But he's not willing to do that at this point in time, and until he is, I'm uncomfortable talking about this."

Atwater heard about the overture, went nuts, whipped up George Bush, and drove a stake through my heart before the idea got out of the blocks. I doubt Teeter ever owned up to our little conversation, and I don't blame him a bit.

I was sitting out a presidential election for the first time since 1972, and I hated it. At least I didn't have to watch the convention on the tube at home. NBC News rode to the rescue with a paying gig doing commentary for NBC's five owned-and-operated television stations. My dance partner was Chuck Manatt, the former chairman of the Democratic National Committee. At the request of her former boss and my new partner Jim Lake, Sherrie was handling media for the August convention. Our marriage hadn't cost her with the Bush folks.

Two days after arriving in New Orleans I was as shocked as everyone else to learn that Senator Dan Quayle of Indiana had been tapped as George Bush's running mate. It was a sign of ineptitude on the part of Bush's handlers. An appointment as controversial and frankly uninspiring as Quayle's should never be a surprise. It's just bad strategy to blindside a party expecting the Veep nominee to be Bob Dole, Jack Kemp, or someone equally substantial. There was no time to prep the media or the political community. The Dukakis campaign had done it right. Lloyd Bentsen was unveiled beforehand, and by the time the Democrats assembled in Atlanta, his appointment was being acclaimed as pure brilliance.

If Quayle had been announced in Washington three or four days before the convention, the party could have been primed. The weekend talk shows could then be saturated with the likes of Kemp and Dole spinning through their teeth about what a great young leader Quayle was. Springing Quayle was yet another example of the poor political execution that guaranteed the ticket would get off to a rocky start. It was candidate Bush's first big decision, and the way he made it—as well as his choice—proved once again that he values loyalty more highly than competence.

I think the choice had almost nothing to do with electoral politics and everything to do with what Bush likes to dismiss as psychobabble. Give him credit: George Bush had persevered against all odds. In that satisfying moment of triumph, he wasn't about to share the spotlight with Bob Dole or Jack Kemp, two old adversaries who would certainly overshadow him every day of the campaign. He wanted someone subservient and loyal, someone smaller than life; and that's what he got.

Quayle is a classic country club Republican, a good-looking guy of average intelligence who likes to play golf. His Senate colleagues considered him to be a little lazy, but a reliable conservative vote. He was a proven vote getter in Indiana, where he'd knocked off popular incumbents to win his House and Senate seats, but there was nothing compelling about his nomination. I couldn't think of a single state where Quayle could make the difference. When David Broder and Lou Cannon of *The Washington Post* asked me on a hotel escalator what Quayle did to help in California, "Nothing" was my answer.

The day after Quayle's announcement, I was booked at a reporters' breakfast, where I was bombarded with questions about the VP-designate. I tried to be as good a boy as I could without lying, and thought I'd done a fairly good job of ducking and dodging. But the next morning, I heard that the Bush camp was furious that I'd said Quayle brought little if anything to the ticket.

A very irritated Jim Baker encountered my wife at one point and said, "Tell Ed to keep his mouth shut."

"You should call him and tell him that yourself," Sherrie replied, ever so sweetly. He never did.

The next morning, however, I found a note taped to the toilet seat in our hotel room. All week long, Sherrie and I had been like ships passing in the night. She was always long gone by the time I rolled out of bed.

"I'm taking Marilyn Quayle around to do interviews on all the network talk shows," the note said. "You are on opposite her on every one of them. Could you *please* say *something* nice about Dan Quayle?"

Et tu, Sherrie? I tried my best.

But it wasn't just me. There was a strong whiff of disappointment in the convention air. One night I did a radio call-in show from the hotel suite of Arizona Senator John McCain, who had served with Quayle in the House and Senate. Afterwards, McCain's press secretary, Torie Clarke—who would have the same job in the Bush campaign four years later—took issue with a comment McCain had made that Quayle might at least help with women voters.

"Torie," McCain said, "I know three things about Dan Quayle: He's dumber than shit, he's a scratch golfer, and he's good-looking. I went with his strength."

By the end of the convention, it was clear to me that Dan Quayle was one of the poorest choices for vice president in American history. It was a perfect example of computer dating gone wrong. George Bush didn't have the courage to pick someone strong, so he opted for a composite—a midwesterner like Dole, a young conservative like Kemp—and got a pale imitation of what the computer ordered.

Quayle started in a hole and never dug himself out. Ironically, his good looks helped to keep him down. He looked like a boy, not a statesman, especially on television. In the next four years, he was never able to alter his image as an amiable lightweight. I've made scores of speeches in the last eight years, and the question I'm asked most often is why Bush picked Quayle.

I don't have an answer, but I do believe it was a terrible career move for Dan. If he'd stayed in the Senate, he'd now be a committee chairman and on the way to elder statesman status instead of remaining an object of national derision. That aura of ridicule was undoubtedly a powerful factor in his decision not to run in 1996. If he'd entered the race, he'd have been toasted.

From my perspective, the Bush-Quayle ticket looked like a sure loser. Even so, Michael Dukakis was almost too good to be true—an unreconstructed liberal governor from Massachusetts without the star quality or rhetorical firepower of Mario Cuomo—a candidate who preferred intellectual arguments to the emotional jousting of a campaign. His nomination made George Bush's election prospects considerably brighter. But the vice president had his own problems. The conservatives in his own party considered him Reagan Lite, and his general reputation as a Reagan Robot lacking independent conviction or vision kept his negatives uncomfortably high with Democratic and independent voters.

The Bush strategy boiled down to two simple goals: Define Bush as Ronald Reagan's rightful heir, and define Dukakis as a dangerous liberal contemptuous of the traditional values that have made America great. Given the relative vulnerabilities of both candidates, it didn't take a genius to figure out that the low road was the most profitable course for the Bush campaign to pursue.

And who better to blaze the low road than Lee Atwater? I vividly remember the night he began slashing his way through the underbrush.

Four years earlier, as the 1984 campaign was gearing up, a group of us so-called Republican Wise Men started getting together for a monthly dinner to talk shop, exchange ideas, and give informal counsel to the president and the campaign. These dinners were held in a private dining room at the Hay-Adams Hotel, just across Lafayette Square from the White House. The regulars included guys like Lyn Nofziger, Bob Teeter, Ken Duberstein, Dick Cheney, Jim Lake, Charlie Black, Bill Timmons, Tom Korologos, Rick Holt, Stu Spencer when he was in town, Lee Atwater, and me. The dinners became an informal institution, and they continued off and on throughout the Reagan years.

At one of these gatherings in the spring of 1988, we were discussing the likelihood of a Bush-Dukakis matchup in November. Lee burst in, late as usual.

"I got the issue," he chortled. "I'm going to make Willie Horton a household name."

To which Lyn Nofziger replied, "He already *is* a household name—he plays first base for the Pittsburgh Pirates."

Atwater had discovered the hand grenade he planned to drop down Mike Dukakis's chimney. The infamous campaign commercial was actually produced for an independent group, so the Bush campaign had legal deniability. But Lee Atwater was Willie Horton's godfather, and George Bush and Jim Baker looked the other way.

Lee wrote the textbook on negative campaigning. His premise was simple: If you drive an opponent's negatives high enough, he simply cannot recover. Willie Horton was the perfect laboratory rat for a guy who understood southern politics better than anyone I know: A black criminal in a Massachusetts prison for a brutal murder, who'd committed another horrible crime, rape, while on weekend furlough. The very idea offended common sense. But among conservatives, especially southern conservatives, it was a wedge issue that struck at the core of Dukakis's fitness to be president. The issue itself—giving weekend passes to murderers—was absolutely legitimate. But linking it to the sinister mug shot of a black man appealed to the baser instincts of the American character. Lee was no racist, but he played the race card with Willie Horton, and he knew what he was doing. It worked spectacularly well.

Crime was a cutting issue in 1988, and the furlough furor reinforced Dukakis's stereotype as a squishy liberal. But the backlash over the Horton ad tarred the party as closet racists, and ironically made Bush a more timid candidate four years later.

Michael Dukakis ran a fairly effective primary race, but his performance in the fall campaign showed he didn't have a clue about national politics. Admittedly, it's a little hard if you haven't been through the national game before. You spend a year or more of your life tooling around pancake breakfasts and Rotary Clubs in every obscure town in Iowa and New Hampshire and God knows where else, with reporters dogging you much of the way. After three thousand speeches, you naturally assume everyone knows what you stand for when the truth is almost nobody knows what you stand for. In fact, only policy wonks pay any attention to what you stand for until you become the nominee. That's when you have to go back to square one and define yourself all over again.

Immediately after a very strong and effective convention, Mike Dukakis disappeared from the face of the earth. With a seventeen-point lead, he had George Bush on the ropes. He should have capitalized on his momentum as Clinton and Gore would do four years later (they'd obviously learned from Dukakis's gaffe). Instead, he trotted off on a long, lazy victory lap, picking his cabinet and issuing dull issues papers from vacation in the Berkshires. By resting on his laurels, he let Atwater, media consultant Roger Ailes—one of the best campaign ad guys in the country—and the president's surrogates define him as a card-carrying ACLU-er who furloughed rapists, condoned flag-burning, and opposed the death penalty. And he became an object of national disdain when Ailes produced a spot of Dukakis in an M-1 tank that made him look like a hypocritical fool. By the middle of September, it was all over but the voting.

I remembered my 1981 conversation with Nixon many times during 1988, as I watched the presidential election from the peanut gallery. Once again, Nixon's political judgment on George Bush's electoral prowess had been impeccable. The vice president *was* a mediocre campaigner. He ran a terrible race in 1980, and had performed erratically for us in 1984 against a demonstrably weaker and less experienced Geraldine Ferraro. Now, at the top of the ticket, he was campaigning true to form. From start to finish, Bush acted like a candidate who didn't really care if he won. Without a doubt, George Bush was the worst campaigner to actually get elected president in modern times. Even with Ronald Reagan's protective mantle, a better opponent and a better campaign could have beaten him. But in the final analysis, the 1988 election was about Michael Dukakis, not George Bush or Dan Quayle. It had nothing to do with competence; the voters decided they liked Bush better than Dukakis, and were convinced he'd continue on the path Reagan had charted for eight years. Most Americans adopted the attitude that if he's good enough for Reagan, he's good enough for me. And given Dukakis's incredibly inept campaign, even if voters had known that Bush would be anything but Reagan, Bush would still have won.

Only Bob Dole's mistakes in the primaries and Michael Dukakis's greater ineptitude saved Bush from losing in 1988. In the end, he scored a resounding victory, and like most good Republicans I voted for Bush and was pleased he'd won. But I took little pleasure in his triumph. I knew his win sealed the coffin on the Reagan Revolution—and signaled eight long years of estrangement from the party I'd joined with such a sense of hope.

On the last day of his second term, Ronald Reagan watched George Bush take the oath of office succeeding him as president. Then, after a few formalities, he emerged from the East Front of the Capitol to board a helicopter for Andrews Air Force Base, then a plane to his beloved California.

I knew in my soul that history would be kinder to Ronald Reagan than the last two years had been. Reagan had followed four failed predecessors and had made the presidency work again. As Marine One lifted off from Capitol Plaza, I said to myself: Mr. President, you'll never know how much more you *could* have done if you'd had a few more loyal staff members who were interested more in your well-being than theirs. The Gipper lived, but what little was left of his revolution was about to die. I was delighted not to be a part of it.

ROUND 7

IN THE WILDERNESS

ON THAT CHILL January afternoon, Sherrie and I took our seats in the presidential box in front of the White House for the Bush inaugural parade. I've felt like the skunk at a garden party more than once in my life, but never more than on that particular sunny day.

We'd been assigned prime real estate because Sherrie was a member of the inaugural committee. Inaugurals are always days of great joy and hope, but this one was not for me. I felt totally ill at ease.

It was a bittersweet moment for both of us. I'd been on the road from California in 1981 when Reagan was inaugurated, and the 1985 parade had been canceled because of a brutal cold wave, so I was attending my first inaugural parade, in the VIP section, no less. But I couldn't kid myself: I wasn't welcome. All the Bush folks loved Sherrie; they couldn't understand why she'd married that disloyal SOB Ed Rollins, or even worse why he'd gone off and worked against them. As the president's friends and their families filed onto the platform and we exchanged hellos, their eyes all said the same thing: Who the hell let *you* in? An overtone of hostility lay just below a veneer of civility. I was an interloper, and they didn't like it.

My anxieties weren't eased a bit when we bumped into our good friends Jack and Joanne Kemp. "What are *you* doing here?" Jack teased. I wanted to say, "Fuck you, Jack," but restrained myself. Jack was George Bush's new Secretary of Housing and Urban Development. What's more, he was in the process of hiring none other than Sherrie Rollins, my lovely wife, as his Assistant Secretary for Public Affairs.

I remembered how badly I'd wanted to be Secretary of Labor in the second Reagan term. It was small of me, but I couldn't help thinking that if I'd stayed with Bush, I might have been in his cabinet.

I hadn't made too many bright career moves since 1984, but I could still put my head on my pillow at night and say I'd done what I believed was right. I *knew* I was right about one thing: George Bush was no Ronald Reagan, and there was no way his first term was going to be Reagan's third.

That day at the inaugural parade set the tone for everything that followed. A few weeks into the new administration, I ran into Margaret Tutwiler at a social function. As Jim Baker's most trusted confidant and alter ego, she was now ensconced as his Assistant Secretary of State for Public Affairs. We'd gotten along fine when she was the liaison between Baker and the campaign in 1984. Margaret is 100 percent honest; you always know where you stand with her. But she has a well-deserved reputation for taking no prisoners and mincing few words. That evening she made it clear to me that George Bush may have campaigned as Ronald Reagan's designated successor, but things would be different now.

"There are a lot of us who had to suffer during the eight years of Reagan," she said, "and now it's our turn."

In an instant, my mind flashed through the list of people like Bush and Baker and Nick Brady and Darman and Tutwiler and way too many others who had no personal ties to President Reagan and fought him every step to the White House, but whose careers had flourished during his service.

Her remark was all the more galling given the career path of her boss. For more than a decade, Jim Baker led the opposition to Ronald Reagan inside and outside the White House. As President Ford's chief delegate hunter and then campaign chairman, he'd been instrumental in defeating the 1976 Reagan primary challenge. In 1980, he ran George Bush's campaign against Ronald Reagan in the primaries. He was rewarded with the plum job of Reagan's chief of staff. In that position, he constantly undermined the president's revolutionary agenda, in concert with his friend George Bush and against Reaganauts like Cap Weinberger, Ed Meese, Lyn Nofziger, Richard Allen, and Bill Clark. His punishment? Secretary of the Treasury in the second Reagan term. Suffer? I couldn't restrain myself.

"Let me get this straight, Margaret," I smiled. "Jim Baker was Bush's campaign chairman in 1980, and he suffered for it by becoming Reagan's chief of staff. I was Jack Kemp's chairman. I guess that means *I* should be the new chief of staff." She knew I was zinging her patron.

"Well, Mr. Baker is different," she said. "But there are a lot of us who had to take lesser jobs."

A lot of them, I thought, whose candidates had lost in 1980 and who should never have been allowed inside the White House, much less given jobs. But that was the mentality of the new crowd. Reagan was gone, so who needs him?

I watched as history repeated itself in the Bush White House. You can't blame a new president for wanting his own team, but suddenly Reaganites who'd served loyally for eight years or helped in Bush's campaign were purged. The exception was John Sununu, a true Reagan conservative who was nonetheless rewarded for saving Bush's candidacy in New Hampshire by being named White House chief of staff. John and I had become friends during Reagan's second term, when I was the president's liaison to the governors and Sununu had been a staunch Reagan supporter.

But like Don Regan before him, John Sununu's profile was too high, and he would be judged a disaster in the job. A brilliant engineer, he wasn't the first chief of staff to confuse intelligence with political smarts. And like Regan, he sometimes seemed confused about just who was president—he or Bush. One 1992 election book aptly described him as "the poster boy for that locally pandemic disease called the arrogance of power." He mostly surrounded himself with weaklings and sycophants, didn't understand Washington, and suffered fools—by his definition, just about everyone—poorly.

Sununu was particularly inept in his dealings with Congress. He never understood that Capitol Hill is a place where some of the world's greatest buffoons still have one vote, and a few are even committee chairmen who can destroy you or your president's agenda in a heartbeat.

He also had a poor grasp of politics at the national level. In the fall of 1989, for instance, Lee Atwater and I had been invited to lunch with Sununu at the White House Mess to talk about the 1990 mid-term elections.

"There's no reason we can't pick up thirty seats," he predicted.

"John," I replied, "there's two hundred years of history that says we'll be lucky to break even." I reminded him that the party controlling the White House always loses seats between presidential elections.

"That's bullshit," Sununu insisted. I restrained myself from observing that you don't have to be a good politician to get elected governor of New Hampshire. You just have to be a conservative Republican.

At the dawn of the Bush presidency, I was working for my friend Jim Lake. As I had during my 1985 detour into the private sector, I was dabbling in strategic communications and public relations. It wasn't particularly exciting work, but it was extremely lucrative. I was billing clients $50,000 a month for my services, but I was also doling out free advice to any candidate or elected official who walked through my door. The political work was easily more fulfilling than anything else I was doing. It reminded me of what I'd had—and how sorely I missed it.

I tried to tell myself that I was doing just fine, but my frustration with being sidelined came to a boil on March 2, when Sherrie and I were invited to Camp David to celebrate the thirtieth birthday of Margaret Bush, wife of the president's fourth son Marvin. They were among Sherrie's closest friends, and I was now part of the package. I'm sure the president held his nose when he saw my name on *this* guest list.

Sherrie urged me to seize the opportunity and write a letter to the president in hopes of mending fences.

I thought it would be a waste of time, but Sherrie was right: I *was* miserable being out of it, and I'd probably never have another opening like this. In my letter, I said that I wanted to wish him well in spite of our past differences. I also wanted to make him understand that my defection to Jack Kemp hadn't been personal.

"Maybe I can walk some precincts for you in 1992," I concluded.

We arrived at Camp David in the morning and were escorted to the conference center at Laurel Lodge. It was my first time there since Don Regan had assembled the senior staff for a weekend strategy session in 1985. The president greeted me as though we'd been Skull and Bones brothers at Yale. Mrs. Bush was cordial, but not quite as warm.

Then everyone scattered to indulge in the recreational pursuit of their choice. I headed off for the horseshoe pit, where the president was conducting a tutorial. He challenged me to a match. We paired off with a couple of his aides. I got lucky, made a couple of great shots, and my side defeated the president's.

"I didn't know you were a horseshoe player," the president said.

"I'm not. I don't think I've ever played before. It must be beginner's luck." Horseshoes are serious business with George Bush. If looks could kill, I'd be long gone.

We reassembled for lunch, followed by birthday cake and bowling. As we said our good-byes, I pulled my letter from my coat jacket.

"Mr. President, this is just something I wanted to give you personally."

"Okay, that's great," he said. He gave me that crooked smile of his. "See you around."

It had been a wonderful outing. The president and Mrs. Bush, as always, were totally gracious. The journey of a thousand miles begins with a single step, the Chinese say. As we drove down the mountain from the presidential retreat, I thought that perhaps I'd taken a couple of baby steps toward rehabilitation with the new leader of my party.

Later that night, Sherrie got a call from another old friend who was spending the night at Camp David. She was delivering a message from Marvin. He'd appreciate it if we didn't tell anyone that we'd been to Camp David. His father was concerned that some of his closest friends and supporters would be offended if they learned that Ed Rollins had been invited to Camp David before they had. Swine before pearls, I suppose.

I was astonished. The guy's the fricking President of the United States. He doesn't have to justify his guest list to anyone. I'd always believed that his reputation as master of the small gesture was one of his great political assets. Now, he'd outdone himself. This was an unbelievably small gesture. So much for detente.

A few days later, a nice letter arrived from the president, thanking me for my note and saying we should let bygones be bygones. But I was still astonished by the call.

QUITE UNEXPECTEDLY, HOWEVER, another opportunity fell into my lap around the same time. Steve Stockmeyer and Nancy Sinnot, two veteran party operatives, dropped by my office one day. They'd been asked to come up with ideas to revitalize the National Republican Congressional Committee (NRCC), and wanted to pick my brain.

The NRCC is one of the three national Republican committees. The Republican National Committee, which was then headed by Lee Atwater, attempts to build the party at the grass-roots level and is the liaison to state parties. It runs the national convention, which selects the party's nominees for president and vice president. The National Republican Senatorial Committee tries to elect more Republican senators. The NRCC does likewise every two years for the House of Representatives and is the political arm of House Republicans. The

1988 elections had been a particular disappointment for House Republicans. Despite George Bush's impressive victory, the party had actually suffered a net loss of three House seats. There was no question the NRCC needed serious rejuvenation. Even with a huge fund-raising advantage over the Democrats, the committee had been moribund for years.

I told Steve and Nancy that with a strong showing in the 1990 midterm elections, a few breaks from congressional redistricting after the 1990 census, and Bush's reelection in 1992, there was every reason to believe we could elect enough Republicans to rebuild the working majority Ronald Reagan had enjoyed in 1981 and 1982. If we did everything right, there was no reason we couldn't elect a Republican majority in the nineties. But the NRCC had to be more aggressive in recruiting candidates and targeting House races instead of spreading its money around on incumbents who really didn't need it.

They told me that Congressman Guy Vander Jagt of Michigan, who'd run the committee for eighteen years, was feeling the heat from his colleagues to show more results. He was being leaned on particularly hard by his close ally Newt Gingrich, who saw the NRCC as his personal fiefdom.

Vander Jagt wanted a new executive director to breathe some life into the NRCC, preferably a big-time operator. One of the names being floated was Joe Paterno, the Penn State football coach. That was a ridiculous idea, but at least it showed that Vander Jagt was serious about acquiring some star quality—and that he was willing to pay exorbitant sums of money to get it.

"Is there any way we could get you to consider the job?" Stockmeyer asked me, after we'd kicked around some possible candidates. I replied that five years ago I might have been interested, but the $150,000 NRCC salary wouldn't even cover my expenses and the mortgages on my house and country cabin.

Money matters aside, I was simply amazed they'd even come to me. George Bush can be a very forgiving person. He'd overlooked Lee Atwater's meltdown in the 1988 campaign and rewarded him with the party's premier job: chairman of the Republican National Committee. It was just Ed Rollins he couldn't seem to forgive. There was no way Bush or Atwater would ever allow me anywhere near their Republican Party.

A couple of days later, Vander Jagt called and said he'd pay whatever I needed to take the job. He wanted a four-year commitment and offered to give me a guaranteed contract.

"You *can't* pay me what I need," I replied. "I'm making nearly half a million a year."

"Don't be so sure," he shot back. Guy is a superb salesman; in the end, he made me agree to at least think about what kind of salary I'd need to stay whole.

Money has never been that big a deal to me. It's nice to have, but it's not a motivating force in my life. All I remember about money growing up is that there was never enough to go around. So I've always wanted to have just enough not to worry about it. My salary was well above what I needed to pay the bills. What I needed was fulfillment, not financial security.

Sherrie didn't think the job would lead anywhere, but she also knew how much I was chomping at the bit. Several of my friends said it was a major step back. To a certain extent, it was. But I didn't have a lot of options in my profession of choice. George Bush would probably be president for eight years. My Camp David experience told me that he wasn't about to take his tasseled loafer off my neck. If I wanted back in the game, the NRCC was my only shot.

I called Vander Jagt and said I didn't need a contract, but was willing to take the job for four years at a salary of $250,000. He didn't flinch, so I raised the obvious question: How would he explain this to a President of the United States who hated my guts?

"George Bush and I were on Ways and Means together," Guy reassured me. "He's my friend—but this is my committee. Don't worry about the president."

In late February 1989, I visited Vander Jagt to nail down the deal. His office in the Rayburn Building had a stunning view of the Capitol. He wheeled around in his chair and pointed toward the gleaming white dome across Independence Avenue.

"I want you to be inspired," he said. "Your goal is to make us the majority over there." Keynote speaker at the 1980 national convention, Guy was a great orator with a flair for the theatrical.

My appointment as Vander Jagt's co-chairman was announced a few days later, effective March 1, 1989. One of my first congratulatory calls was from Newt Gingrich.

"We'll give you a five-million-dollar bonus if you get us a majority," he promised.

"Safe bet," I laughed. Newt clearly had his eye on becoming the first Republican Speaker of the House in a half century, and he viewed the NRCC as his personal laboratory to find a way to make it happen.

In a matter of hours, my salary leaked. The Democrats gleefully dubbed me "the Million-Dollar Man" and said my appointment demonstrated that the GOP truly was the party of the rich and greedy. I hadn't realized that senior House members like minority leader Bob Michel had been gunning for the NRCC for some time. I was making twice what members earned, and my big salary gave them new fodder to complain about wretched excess. For a while, I couldn't tell who my real opponents were—Republicans or Democrats.

But the guy who screamed loudest was my old friend Lee Atwater, who saw my resurrection as a threat to his supremacy as the party's premier tactician. Atwater went through the roof, and within days he was trashing me all over town. It was a rerun of 1984. This time, though, Atwater had the job I once wanted, and we both knew it.

After the hit job he'd done on me in 1988, I knew this was his modus operandi. I called Charlie Black, Lee's former partner and best friend, to complain. Almost immediately, Lee telephoned me in full denial.

"This is the same old shit," he claimed. "There's nothing to it. We need to let bygones be bygones." I knew him well enough not to be fooled by his pro forma bullshit denials.

As RNC chairman, Lee was back on top of the mountain again, but since the RNC and NRCC shared the same building on Capitol Hill, the guy he thought he'd buried forever was now sitting two floors below him.

I went to see him on my first day in the job. We sat at his conference table for about ninety minutes in our shirtsleeves, Lee at the head, me to one side. It was an awkward reunion. I simply suggested we had to figure out a way to co-exist.

"Let's be adults," I said to break the ice. "Your side won. We don't have to love each other. Let's shoot for a good working relationship."

"I hold no grudges against you," he said, as if I'd been the one trashing him. He stared hard into my eyes, trying to get me to flinch first. That's a fighter's trick, so it did nothing to me. Lee could never beat me at the intimidation game. We knew each other's hot buttons too well. But he was different now. He wasn't the nervous kid who had worked for me anymore. In the four years since he had been my deputy, he had grown in confidence. He didn't need me or my approval. He knew there was nothing I could do to hurt him.

"If you'd have cooperated, I would have taken care of you in the Bush thing," he continued. "But you've always been like the big shark swimming out there alone. Always threatening. Never sure when you might attack. I could never trust you. You always played by your rules. I had to destroy you, and I did."

Well, I thought, at least he's being honest for a change.

"Lee, I treated you like my brother, and you fucked me. We can either work together or apart. I'd like to try and put it back together." We shook hands and agreed we'd try.

With that out of the way, I set about to reverse another potentially poisonous situation I'd inherited. A week after I took the job, we lost Dan Quayle's old House seat in Indiana to the Democrats. On April 4, we lost another seat in Alabama. I played virtually no role in those races, but as Jimmy Carter said, life is unfair. After a month on the job, the Million-Dollar Man was zero-and-two.

I quite naturally compounded my predicament by setting myself up in an interview with the *Washington Times*. The next House race was a Wyoming special election on April 25 to replace Dick Cheney, who'd become Secretary of Defense. I told the *Times* it wasn't fair to blame me for the Indiana and Alabama races, but that Wyoming was definitely on my watch. If we lost there, I said, I was fair game.

The Democrats smelled blood and were committing heavy resources to the race. Their candidate was experienced and had just come within 1,265 votes of upsetting Senator Malcolm Wallop. And our candidate was Craig Thomas, a state senator (now U.S. senator) lacking the personal appeal or the political experience of Dick Cheney, who could have been congressman for life. Dick's wife Lynne was my first choice and could have won just as easily, but she wasn't interested. We had no choice but to carpet-bomb Wyoming with everything we had. I dispatched my executive director Marc Nuttle to take charge of the campaign and budgeted $1 million to hold the seat at all costs.

The hottest issue in the race was taxes. Like every candidate who hadn't taken a stand already, Thomas was counseled by the NRCC to take a pledge not to raise taxes if elected. The instant Thomas signed the pledge, the NRCC would unleash a torrent of direct mail touting his stand. Unfortunately, Alan Simpson, the senior senator from Wyoming and a close friend of the president, was campaigning with him on the very day Thomas was going to take the pledge before a business group. When he learned about the plan, Simpson decreed that Thomas must do nothing of the sort out of loyalty to George Bush. Simpson knew that Bush was then in the process of reneging on his no-tax pledge as part of a budget deal with the Democrats.

I dealt with this threat by ordering Nuttle to make sure Simpson's car got lost on the way to the event so he couldn't brace Thomas again. By the time he caught up, Thomas had already taken the pledge.

The day after the election, the president congratulated Simpson for Craig's victory at a White House leadership meeting.

"It was easy, Mr. President." Simpson grinned. "We just kicked all those goddamn guys from Washington, D.C., out of the state, and ran a good old back-home election." Another nail in my coffin with Bush, I figured.

A few months later, on November 15, 1989, my suspicion was emphatically confirmed when Ronald and Nancy Reagan returned to the White House for the hanging of the former president's official portrait. Sherrie and I were privileged to be invited to the ceremony. Going through the receiving line was one of the most awkward moments of my life. The Reagans couldn't have been more wonderful. But when President Bush saw me, he offered a perfunctory handshake and quickly turned away. And when I thanked Barbara Bush for her hospitality, she looked at me through daggers posing as eyes and said, "You *better* be grateful, because we *were* hospitable." In retrospect, I can't really begrudge them their animosity; to their mind, I was the great defector, and that's something the fiercely proud and loyal Bush clan always takes personally. As for Mrs. Bush, she's a lot less forgiving than her husband.

Having halted the Democrats' winning streak and at least temporarily salvaged my reputation, I turned my attention to the 1990 midterms. At the outset, I thought we had an opportunity to defy the odds and pick up eight or nine seats. We certainly had the financial resources: 1989 had turned out to be a great fund-raising year for Republicans. I concluded that we should be more strategic in allocating those resources. Instead of targeting seventy-five to one hundred House races as my predecessors had done, I decided to concentrate on twenty to thirty where Republican challengers appeared to have a shot, and another ten to fifteen where our incumbents looked to be in trouble.

This strategy put me at odds with Newt Gingrich. Newt was the new Republican whip, succeeding Cheney, and was always spoiling for a fight. My kind of guy, basically. But he wanted me to target 100 to 150 House races and nationalize the elections. He felt that was the only way to take back the House from the Democrats over time. It was a crazy notion. We didn't have the resources or the candidates to be credible in that many districts. I thought I could do it, but not swiftly enough to satisfy Newt's personal ambition.

Gingrich was so annoyed with my unwillingness to knuckle under to his brainchild that he tried to get me fired. He took it to the House Republican leadership and lost. The only vote against me was his.

"I surrender," he told me afterwards. "I feel like I pushed a boulder to the top of the mountain and it just got rolled back over me." After that, he settled down—as much as Newt can ever settle down. True to his word, he was a strong ally, and we worked closely together.

What shattered all my expectations was the holy war within the party over taxes. The Wyoming experience was a microcosm of what was happening throughout the GOP by 1990.

The emotional high point of Bush's acceptance speech at the 1988 convention had been six words: "Read my lips—no new taxes." The phrase was designed to persuade long-skeptical Reaganites that the vice president was in fact a true heir to the Gipper. It did the job— even though subsequent events proved that the pledge was nothing more than a clever sound bite.

It was obvious to a lot of us where the president was heading even earlier. In the fall of 1989, I attended one of the Wise Men dinners at the Hay-Adams Hotel.

"How long do we have to hold the tax pledge?" Bob Teeter asked at one point. "Can we give it up this year?"

"What do you mean, give it up?" I asked, incredulous.

"Well, Darman says the numbers don't work."

"You're going to get killed. This is the most sacred pledge he made. If you raise taxes in this term, he can kiss his ass away in '92, and he's going to take a bunch of House members with him." I think Teeter knew I was right.

I left that dinner convinced it was only a matter of time before my task of electing more Republicans to the House became a ballbreaker. Sure enough, in September 1990, the president agreed to a tax increase as part of a budget compromise package with the Democrats.

The president's decision had divided the party. Congressional leaders like Bob Dole and Bob Michel were backing their leader, while Newt Gingrich and more than a hundred fellow House Republicans were vigorously opposed. This schism was particularly troubling to our House Republican challengers. My advice to them in memo after memo was simple: The tax pledge is the one issue that clearly differentiates us from the Democrats. Take the pledge and contrast yourself with your Democratic opponent.

It was a no-brainer. All our polls showed that the country was in a virulent antitax mood, but I didn't need to spend $25,000 on a poll to know how powerful the issue had become. Since Bush's broken promise, contributions to the party had dropped through the floor. Our mail reflected an angry tone of betrayal. One letter that stuck in my mind was from an elderly longtime small contributor: "Nixon lied to me about Watergate, Reagan lied to me about Iran-Contra, and now Bush is lying to me about taxes." It was only a matter of time before I saw that line on bumper stickers. Just ask Bob Dole about the tax pledge: If he'd signed it in New Hampshire in 1988, he'd probably be finishing his second term as president today.

Even worse, our prospects for November had begun to tank. Early in the year, our data showed that we were poised to pick up eight seats and only eight or nine of our incumbents were in trouble. A month later, those potential new seats had evaporated, and we were in danger of losing thirty to thirty-five seats. And the number of GOP incumbents in trouble had tripled. I smelled the makings of a disaster.

Every candidate was being asked to take a position on taxes, and Bush had made it virtually impossible to straddle. As the calls from nervous candidates piled up, I was asked by the GOP leadership to prepare a definitive memorandum to go out under Vander Jagt's signature recommending the best political course of action for our incumbents and challengers.

Without the slightest hesitation, I had my staff draft a memorandum to candidates urging them to be consistent. If they hadn't taken the tax pledge, they should go with their conscience. But if they had, the memo said, "Do not hesitate to distance yourself from the President."

My political director Charlie Leonard wandered into my office with a draft he'd written. He'd underlined the sentence about breaking with the president. "You know what we're saying here?" Charlie asked.

"Absolutely," I said.

"I don't want to sandbag you here, boss. You know the pricks at the White House will go nuts."

"It's the right counsel. Go with it."

Before issuing them to the field, all such memos were routinely sent to Vander Jagt for clearance; a courtesy copy was also forwarded to the White House political office. I never heard a peep from the White House, but Vander Jagt telephoned me with a small favor to ask. For the first time in his tenure, he didn't want to put his name on a memo.

"Could you sign this one yourself?" he asked. "I know it's what we've gotta do, but the language bothers me. Bush is my friend, and he's gonna go crazy. I may even be forced to vote for his damn taxes." That was fine with me. Guy needed deniability; I'd be blamed anyway, so why not be up front?

The memo went out in October and was quickly leaked to the press. The president came unhinged. I was told that George Bush accused me of insubordination in a Congressional leadership meeting and demanded that I be fired summarily. "I don't know why I ever let that SOB over there," the president fumed. Vander Jagt, of course, didn't tell his friend the president that the House leadership had asked for the memo, or that he'd approved it before it was shipped out.

"Are you guys going to do what Bush wants and can me?" I asked Vander Jagt a couple of days later.

"No," he replied, "you did what we asked you to do. But you better hunker down for a while."

I was unrepentant. My job was electing Republicans to the House. George Bush and his tax deal made that impossible. Now my job was seeing how many we could save. We went into a full court press, and had to abandon most of the challengers to save the incumbents. Guys who didn't think they had a race were all of a sudden fighting for their lives, including Newt Gingrich. If I had to irritate the hell out of the president to help him do his job better, a little tough love was fine by me.

On November 6, 1990, Republican voters stayed home in droves. It was the lowest Republican off-year turnout since Watergate, and it was all because of Bush's tax increase. We had a net loss of nine seats, but I'm convinced that my memo and the heroic salvage operation of my staff saved fifteen incumbent seats that otherwise would have gone down the drain. (Gingrich survived by 974 votes in what should have been a safe district.)

I was proud of my damage control, but bitter that my hopes for a working majority in the House by 1992 had been destroyed by the tax issue. I didn't want to waste another two years of my life winning back those nine seats, and I also knew there was no way the committee could function with me there. George Bush had pasted a scarlet T for traitor on my forehead.

"I don't want to be run out of here," I told Vander Jagt. "I'll stay for two or three months and help you get reelected chairman. Then I'm out of here."

In January 1991, Newt Gingrich and Vin Weber took me out for a beer at a Crystal City bar. Vin was Newt's consigliere and had become my closest friend in the House GOP hierarchy. They told me that Bush's fury was even greater than I'd heard. In a subsequent meeting with Republican leaders, the president had laid down the law: Not even a form letter could be mailed out with his signature if I were running the NRCC. "I'll never do anything for you guys as long as Rollins is up there," he'd said. I knew the memo was the final straw for Bush and me. I figured a graceful exit was the biggest service I could do for my party.

In April 1991, I left the NRCC and returned to consulting with a clear conscience. I'd been true to myself and the principles of the revolution, and I'd busted my butt to salvage a horrendous situation. If we'd lost twenty-five seats as we nearly did, Tom Foley might still be Speaker of the House today and Newt Gingrich would be firing broadsides from the back benches—if he were still a member of Congress.

Of course, that was cold comfort in the face of a President of the United States who considered me public enemy number one. If he'd only been as tough on Saddam Hussein, I thought to myself. Once again, it was time to sort out my life. I had to reconcile myself to the unhappy fact that I'd cemented my reputation as a man without a party.

GEORGE BUSH WOULD be president until 1996. I was on Dan Quayle's shit list, too. He'd never forgiven me for some of the things I'd said about him at the 1988 convention. If Quayle succeeded Bush, which God forbid was at least a reasonable bet, I'd be in the freezer until the end of the century. I was forty-eight years old, and this time we weren't talking temporary furlough. We were talking early retirement. My good old days were gone. It was time for me to make my peace with it, and go on about the bittersweet business of earning a living and playing out the string.

For all my career turmoil, I reminded myself I was far better off than my old partner Lee Atwater. In March 1990, Lee had collapsed while making a speech in Washington. Tests were inconclusive. It was impossible to believe anything was really wrong; he'd never been sick a day in his life, and was a religious jogger and health nut.

The original diagnosis was fatigue, and that sounded right to me. Lee's nervous energy had gotten the better of him, I'd thought. I remembered my stroke in the autumn of 1982. I hoped he'd get the message and dial back on his frenetic life-style.

As it turned out, Lee had spun a story on his own illness. A few days later, however, his closest associates learned the truth: It wasn't fatigue. It wasn't as originally believed a small, benign tumor on the right side of the brain. It was in fact a massive and inoperable malignancy—and it wasn't curable. There was nothing they could do for him except buy some time with radiation and pump him full of steroids.

Lee spent several weeks convalescing, then returned to work for a few hours a day. On his first day back, he asked to see me, and I instantly went up to his office. He looked terrible. Those fierce eyes that had enticed women and intimidated men were full of fear. He was the scared kid I used to know.

"I'm gonna whip this thing," he said, "but I'm gonna need your help. I don't know how much time I'm gonna be able to spend in the building. Would you look out for me and keep things on course?"

I said I'd do whatever I could.

"We've had our differences, but I know I can trust you. You won't fuck me over."

"Absolutely, Lee. You have my word on it."

Most of his responsibilities were taken over by Mary Matalin, his loyal and dedicated chief of staff. Mary frequently asked my advice, and I was glad to help however I could. At the end of each day, I'd go upstairs and see what I could do to lend a hand. We all thought Lee might beat the odds. He was younger and in better health than I'd been when I had my stroke, after all.

But several weeks after he came back to work, I got a frantic telephone call from Mary.

"He's had another seizure," she said. "I've called an ambulance. Can you please come up right away?"

I flew up the stairs to the fourth floor. Lee was lying on the floor, fully conscious, but he couldn't move his arm. I can't remember if he could speak; I don't remember him saying anything. But I do remember he seemed glad to see me. I held his hand until the paramedics arrived. As I helped get him into the ambulance, he squeezed my hand.

"You're gonna be okay, Lee," I told him as he and Mary disappeared into the ambulance. This time, I knew I was wrong.

I'd been angry with Lee for a long time. But now all I wanted was for him to be healthy again—to be the fun-loving, antic character that lurked beneath all the macho horseshit. I wanted my friend to live.

That night, Mary told me that Lee had asked her to thank me for helping out.

"It meant so much to him that you were there," she said. "He said that you'd always been his protector."

After the second seizure, the prospects for bouncing back were grim. Lee's tumor was growing fast. After long deliberations, he opted for a radical type of radiation that involved bombarding his brain with radioactive pellets. The treatment sapped his strength and ravaged his health in a desperate attempt to prolong his life. By now, it was apparent that he wasn't going to make it.

He stayed in George Washington University Hospital for weeks. I went with Mary to see him. It didn't escape my notice that he was in the same VIP room where I'd recovered from my stroke. It had also been Jim Brady's room after he was shot during the 1981 attempt on Reagan's life. The difference is that Brady and I got to go home.

One day, his doctors said that Lee was stable enough for some fresh air. No doubt they acted out of self-defense: Lee was probably hammering the crap out of them to let him loose. They okayed an afternoon outing with a couple of friends, no more. Lee asked to see Lyn Nofziger and me. It's one of my happiest memories of Washington.

The hospital staff put him in a wheelchair and we drove down to Fletcher's Boathouse along the Potomac River. For an hour or so we reminisced about the halcyon days of 1981, when Lee was our go-pher. He wanted us to know how much we'd meant to him then.

"I never would have been in the White House if it weren't for you," he told Lyn.

Turning to me, he added, "And I never would have been *anything* if it weren't for you. You were my mentor and teacher. But more important, you were my real friend." I could feel all the ancient enmities slip away.

A few weeks before the end, Mary Matalin called to say that Lee was going to his cabin for the weekend and had asked to see me. His place was a quarter mile from mine. I'd sung the praises of country life so much that Lee bought a cabin there in 1988. By then I hated his guts, and it drove me nuts to know the guy who'd betrayed me was just down the road. I had fantasies of coming across him jogging some dark night and running him down in my Range Rover.

Such dark thoughts had vanished as his illness progressed. His doctors would let him go to the mountains for the weekends and I'd drop by when I was up there. He was always happy to see me; my visits energized him, but saddened and depressed me. He'd give me his political counsel, sitting there like the Godfather, and he was always right. He'd grown very wise as he lay there dying. George Bush and the party desperately missed him.

Now, as any hope for his recovery dimmed, his wife Sally, his two girls, and I joined Lee for a Tex-Mex dinner in Front Royal, then gathered back at his cabin. After a while, he threw everyone else out and asked me to stay for a while. We sat in the large log living room with a fire roaring. Lee was covered in a wool blanket and his voice was weak, but his mind was clear. He was puffy and terribly deformed, and his hair was gone from the radiotherapy. If I hadn't known it was Lee, I wouldn't have recognized him. He told me he hadn't given up hope, but as he started to tell me what was on his mind, I realized I was hearing his last confession.

"I've gotta do this," he said. "I've gotta tell you all the things I did to you, because I'm ashamed of them all." He began telling me exactly how he'd screwed me with George Bush, Jim Baker, and others. It was a long and rather impressive list of duplicity.

He told me he'd leaked the Ferraro dirty tricks story to Jamie Gangel, and how he'd wanted me damaged but not fired. He told me he always made sure Bush knew the negative things I'd said about him, and actually made up more. I knew most of it, but not all.

But I didn't care. The truth is that I didn't want to hear it. By now I'd put our bitter past behind me.

"Lee, I don't give a fuck what you did to me," I protested. "There was a time when I would have killed you, but at this point it's irrelevant. I knew what you were doing to me, and *you* knew what you were doing to me. And it was like my own brother betraying me. It's over; forget about it. I put it behind us months ago."

"Would you have been my friend if we hadn't worked together? Did you like me?"

"Absolutely," I said. "I might have liked you even better if we hadn't worked together." He smiled, and I suggested he rest.

But he wouldn't stop, so I let him exorcise his demons. After forty-five minutes he started to get exhausted and told me he couldn't go on; he had to rest. He pulled me to him and hugged me. I kissed his deformed head, and tears welled in my eyes. His last words to me were, "I'm sorry. I really love you."

My last words to him were, "Get well. I love you, too."

On March 29, 1991, a year and three weeks after being stricken, Harvey Leroy Atwater died of brain cancer at the age of forty. I was leaving for the office when Sherrie called out the news from upstairs. I know it sounds like a cliché, but it felt like a death in the family: a death I'd known was coming for months, but was no less painful for that.

Five years later, it's still difficult for me to sort out the complex pieces of our tempestuous relationship. At times he was a friend; at others he was more like my kid brother. At times I was his mentor and protector; at others I was his partner. He was my loyal deputy and at one point my most bitter foe. It was the most intense relationship I've ever experienced.

I loved him and I hated him and in the end I loved him again. In all my years in politics, nobody betrayed my trust as badly or served me as effectively as Lee. We were a great team, and we were terrible enemies. But his horrible, lousy death brought a final serenity to the tempest between us.

Lee's funeral couldn't have been any better if he'd scripted it himself—which he probably did. Washington National Cathedral was filled with more than two thousand mourners, including the president, vice president, the cabinet, rock-and-roll singers, saints and sinners. It had the look of a state funeral. Secretary of State Jim Baker delivered one of the eulogies. In testament to Lee's controversial life, his passing was also marked by the presence of many who despised him as well as many who loved and respected him.

Sherrie and I took seats in the middle of the great sanctuary. Before the service, an usher urged us to move up into the VIP section. It was a gracious gesture, but we stayed put. I didn't want to be part of the show; I just wanted to pay my respects and tell him I missed him.

During the funeral, and later at his burial in South Carolina, I remember telling him that if he had to do what he did to me to get what he wanted, that was okay. And as I think back today on his life and his unfair death, I can say with a clear heart that I'm glad Lee got all his dreams—even if it took blowing me up to get them. God knows, in a life as abbreviated as his, he deserved them.

When I was five years old, my dad told me that men don't cry. Ever since, I've cried very little. Having endured thirteen major surgeries and hundreds of fights in and out of the ring, I've developed an ability to absorb a lot of pain. I fought back tears through Lee's two services. But at the 1992 convention, when I was out of favor with the Bush camp after Perot, Sally Atwater asked me to attend a memorial tribute to her husband.

Newt Gingrich was the master of ceremonies. He said something in his introductory remarks that I'll never forget as long as I live.

"There's one person here tonight who was very special to Lee," Gingrich said. "We need to welcome him back into our party. Ed Rollins, would you please stand up?" I almost lost it on the spot.

It was a wonderful tribute. Lee's friend BB King, the rhythm-and-blues great, played his guitar; Lee was a pretty mean musician himself, and had jammed with King and other R&B legends. Then a video was shown of the Lee Atwater I used to know—with all his energy, his vitality, his lust for life. It was the first visual image of Lee I'd seen since his death, and I completely unraveled. In all my life, I've never been so torn up by anything. My entire body was wracked with sobbing over a friend I'd loved and hated, and still miss.

As much as any political consultant, Lee had an enormous impact on the way modern campaigns are run. To the young, hard-charging new conservatives, Lee is a hero. To many in the Democratic Party and the media, he represented everything bad about politics. But in the end, he was neither hero nor villain. He was just a young, insecure, ambitious kid who played the toughest game there is better and more ruthlessly than anyone else.

In a strange way, Lee helped me find my faith again. When first stricken, he tried to find a reason for his illness and began looking for spirituality. He talked to ministers, rabbis, theologians, and priests. He was actually baptized a Catholic before he died, over the objections of some of his Baptist friends. The priest who baptized him was Father John Hargrove, S.J., one of America's premier Catholic theologians. Gary Maloney, who'd been a lieutenant to both Lee and me, arranged for Father Hargrove to visit Lee. Gary brought Father Hargrove by my office one morning after one of those visits. We talked at great length about Lee and about my own lost faith, then the Jesuit suddenly said, "I'm prepared to hear your confession."

"Father, I'm not sure I'm ready." I hadn't been to church in over twenty years.

"You are," he replied. So the lapsed Catholic confessed his many sins to this humble and inspiring priest. The confession was heard in the office where I spent every day trying to figure out how to pound Democrats into oblivion.

I returned to the Church and practiced regularly for the next three years. Then I fell off the wagon during my Perot odyssey, but returned faithfully again after the New Jersey disaster. I truly hope Lee found the religious peace that he sought before he met his maker. Today I pray to St. Dismas, the good thief who died on the Cross alongside Jesus, to take care of another good hooligan, Lee Atwater.

THE SPRING OF 1991 was a time of mourning for me, both for Lee and for my life with the Republican Party. After I left the NRCC, I went to work as the Washington managing partner for Sawyer Miller, a public relations and political consulting firm. David Sawyer was one of the top Democratic media consultants and a good friend. He told me I was the first Republican he'd ever hired.

It will come as zero surprise to learn that my appointment wasn't universally popular within the firm. One of the junior partners was Mandy Grunwald, the daughter of former *Time* magazine executive and ambassador to Austria Henry Anatole Grunwald. She wasn't too popular herself. In fact, many of my new colleagues told me they were happy to see her go. I could see why. She could be insufferably arrogant. She claimed that my arrival had destroyed the firm's integrity, and resigned in protest. She later went on to be one of the ringleaders of Bill Clinton's corps of adolescent know-it-alls.

Sawyer Miller had decided to get out of domestic political consulting and focus on strategic communications about the time I arrived. But international politicking was still a very lucrative sideline. Most of my business was in strategic communications, but I did some foreign political work as well. One of these assignments took me back to my glory years. At the same time, it reminded me maybe I wasn't as smart as I'd thought.

My 1984 experience running the Reagan reelection had taught me that if you want to be a serious strategist, it's essential to stay above the fray. For the first two weeks of a campaign, the manager decides everything from what goes on the bumper stickers to who sits where. From then on, he has to resist being sucked into the minutiae and begin delegating authority to others. In a national campaign, you're managing three hundred people at headquarters, and thousands more in the field. You can't watch every part of it. Ultimately, you have to have confidence that the people you've put in place aren't freelancing. But there's no way to be sure they aren't.

In 1991, Sawyer Miller was involved in the presidential election in the Philippines. I was making my first trip to Manila counseling Ramon Mitra, the speaker of the Philippine house, who was his party's nominee to succeed Corazon Aquino.

I was invited to dinner at the home of a prominent member of the Philippine congress, a real power broker and household name in Philippine politics. He was well educated, sophisticated, and charming. This guy's middle name would be "Operator" in any language. He met me at his home, where I was introduced to his family. He then took me to the home of his mistress for dinner.

We were having a few drinks and telling some war stories when he said to me, "You ran Reagan's campaign, didn't you?"

I nodded my head. I had no idea where this was heading, but his scotch was damn good.

He smiled. "I was the guy who gave the ten million dollars from Marcos to your campaign."

I nearly dropped my drink onto the very expensive Oriental carpet. As Fiorello La Guardia would say, this was a beaut!

I didn't want to insult my host in front of his mistress by suggesting that perhaps he'd had one pop too many. And I didn't want to admit that I had absolutely no clue what the hell he was talking about. But I damn sure wanted to know more about what, if true, was an attempt to make a blatantly illegal contribution from a foreign government to the campaign I'd managed.

"You were the one who gave us that money?"

"Oh, yes," he beamed. "I was the guy who made the arrangements and delivered the cash personally."

Cash? Holy shit, I thought, somebody I know extremely well is walking around Washington one very rich SOB today.

"You know, I can't really remember. It's been seven years. Who did you give the cash to?"

Without batting an eyelash, he gave me the name of a well-known Washington power lobbyist who was involved in the campaign.

"I delivered the suitcase with the cash to him, and helped get it out of the country. He told me he would give it to you for the campaign. It was a personal gift from Marcos to Reagan."

I sat there stunned. Not in a state of total disbelief, though, because I knew the lobbyist well and I had no doubt the money was now in some offshore bank. I wondered if the statute of limitations for illegal campaign contributions was still running. Probably not, I thought.

The guy has made himself quite a fortune as a lobbyist and consultant since 1984. I ran the campaign for $75,000 a year, and this guy got $10 million in cash. At least I earned mine honestly.

The next time Paul Laxalt and I were at our Front Royal cabins the same weekend, I suggested we have dinner. "Paul," I said, "I'm going to tell you a story you will not fucking believe."

I laid out what my Philippine acquaintance had told me. Paul absorbed the story with increasing interest.

"Christ, now it all makes sense."

He explained what he meant. In 1985, President Reagan had sent Laxalt as his personal emissary to Marcos with a warning to clean up his act. He thought that a message from his closest friend in the Senate would carry more stroke than if it were delivered by some striped-pants Foreign Service guy.

"When I was over there cutting off Marcos's nuts, he gave me a hard time. 'How can you do this?' he kept saying to me. 'I gave Reagan ten million dollars. How can he do this to me?'

"I didn't know what the hell he was talking about. Now I get it."

It was a great story. But this flashback quickly rekindled my sense of melancholy. Remembrances of things past served to remind me of what I'd lost, and what I still missed. I was a thoroughbred political animal, put out to pasture. I hated being out of it. As the election season drew closer, I found myself brooding increasingly about the void in my life. My spirits weren't lightened as I watched a party I'd spent my entire adult life helping build careen toward debacle.

IF BUSH'S BROKEN pledge on taxes had wounded us in 1990, it threatened to shoot us dead in 1992. The president's repudiation of his own vow at New Orleans gave Pat Buchanan an excuse to challenge Bush in the primaries, guaranteeing that the party would be fractured along ideological lines heading into the election.

More important, it undermined the president's moral authority. After the 1988 election, Bob Teeter's pollsters had asked people what they remembered Bush saying during the campaign. The runaway winner: "Read my lips." When he went south on the single issue they thought defined him as a candidate, many of them decided he stood for nothing.

I'd seen this disaster coming for a long time. In February 1990, I had invited Pat Caddell and Bob Beckel to come in and talk turkey to all 175 Republican House members. Caddell and Beckel were two of the savviest Democratic strategists around. I thought my troops were getting fat, dumb, and happy about the 1990 elections, and figured two of the enemy's most notorious partisans might shatter their complacency.

Caddell and Beckel argued quite persuasively that while Bush's personal approval rating was close to 70 percent, the number of Americans who believed the country was on the right track was below 30 percent, meaning the president was heading for a fall. They said he was extraordinarily weak and that his popularity was artificial. Caddell predicted that within a year, Bush would start falling.

"And when he starts to slide," Caddell said, "he won't stop until he hits cement."

My House members just blew them off. The consensus seemed to be that barring an economic or foreign crisis, Bush would cruise to reelection.

Now, as 1992 began and the primary season loomed, the accuracy of Caddell's prediction was apparent. After the Persian Gulf War, the president's approval ratings had reached the high 80s, a phenomenal figure. But like those House Republicans, George Bush had let himself get sucked into the euphoria of Desert Storm. It was the highlight of his presidency, and he deserves great credit with history for his courageous conduct of the war. But its domestic political gains were fleeting. Once Saddam Hussein was neutralized, the country turned its attention to everyday concerns. Bush's advantage slipped away as the economy slid toward recession. With American industry laying off tens of thousands of workers, people were scared as hell for themselves, their kids, and their neighbors.

The national psyche began to reflect the very malaise that Jimmy Carter had talked about—with one critical difference. In 1979, Carter was blaming the country. In 1992, the country was blaming the system. And since presidents almost always get both more credit and more blame than they deserve, Bush was far more vulnerable than the Democrats to public wrath. Worse, the country seemed to be coming to the conclusion that their president hadn't a clue about the depths of their fears.

By the spring of 1992, I was convinced the party had already blown it. Pat Buchanan's insurgency had exposed the depth of irritation within the party over Bush's repudiation of the tax pledge. In the New Hampshire primary, Buchanan had embarrassed the man he called "King George" by grabbing 37 percent of the vote. Bush and his handlers had not only kicked away the Reagan coalition; they'd been lulled into complacency about the Gulf War. The political value of a president's foreign policy successes is ephemeral except in times of crisis. And the sense of crisis in the Gulf had long passed.

Bush and his managers also underestimated Bill Clinton, who by then had risen from the dead and was barreling toward the Democratic nomination. I thought the country saw Clinton as a sleaze and didn't want him to be their president. But they weren't mad at him like they were at the president, and he was three times the campaigner Bush was. More to the point, the Democrats were behaving like adults for once instead of ripping themselves to shreds.

I was reminded of this change in their customary habits by my friend Bob Squier, the well-regarded Democratic strategist, who during an informal conversation in the spring of 1992 warned me that Bush was heading for a fall.

"We always kill each other in the primaries and you guys bring an all-star team to the fall campaign," Squier told me. "We've finally learned from our mistakes. Come fall, we're going to have everybody at the table who can contribute, whether they backed the nominee or not."

Meanwhile, the Bush people were still on their search-and-destroy mission. With a few exceptions like Charlie Black, anyone who hadn't been with Bush since 1978 was suspect. (They did make a few smart personnel moves, however; in January 1992, Sherrie Rollins became assistant to the president for public liaison and intergovernmental affairs.)

I was sure of one thing: George Bush wouldn't be reelected. He'd totally lost touch with the electorate, and he and his handlers had systematically squandered the formidable coalition Ronald Reagan handed off to him in 1984. For me, Bush's tepid reaction to the Los Angeles riots in May was the clincher. He confined himself to platitudes and delegated leadership to underlings. It was a classic missed opportunity to assert the moral authority of the office in an ugly situation. It told me that the president was simply oblivious to the reality of the moment.

In different ways, Bill Clinton was equally flawed. Even then he had a reputation for being totally unprincipled, and my friends in the Bush camp dismissed him with a single word when his name was mentioned: "Women." Both candidates were damaged goods.

The time was ripe, once again, for revolution. And for the first time since Ronald Reagan rode into town, another man in a white hat appeared on the horizon, ready to tap into a wellspring of voter disaffection.

ROUND 8

THE CAMPAIGN FROM HELL

IT WAS A glorious Sunday afternoon in May 1992, and I was relaxing at my cabin in the Blue Ridge Mountains. As so often happened since she joined the Bush White House, Sherrie was working. Which was just as well—I was in the process of making what would turn out to be the most difficult, irresponsible, and stupid decision of my life, and I needed time alone to think.

With its panoramic view of the Shenandoah Valley, this was the spot I loved most in the world and where I did my best thinking. After my stroke in 1982, I'd made a vow never to work Sundays again, and I'd spent many peaceful Saturday nights and Sundays there. I've always said that my mortgage on the cabin was in lieu of payments to a shrink; but with hindsight, maybe I should have spent some money on counseling, considering some of the dumb moves I've made in the last decade.

My troubled solitude was broken by the barking of Duke and Dutch, my two Labs, signaling that some intruder was rolling up the driveway. It was James Carville and Mary Matalin, the last two people I expected to see.

Mary and Carville had been an item for at least a year, but had told everyone they weren't seeing each other anymore. It was pure bullshit, a cover story to placate the White House. In the Pennsylvania Senate race, Mary had been accused by Dick Thornburgh's handlers of leaking confidential information to Carville. Mary was now the Bush campaign's political director, and the president himself had complained about her liaison with Clinton's top gun. A lot of her friends were appalled about the relationship for a more basic reason: For all his talent, Carville was a card-carrying eccentric.

His weirdness aside, I respected Carville's political skills. He's a good tactician who brings enormous energy and intensity to a campaign. In fact, he reminded me a lot of Lee Atwater. Neither was a cosmic thinker, but nobody would ever outwork or outscheme them. Two of the best ever to play this game, they were southern, irreverent, unreconstructed mavericks. They understood the changing political culture of the South, and were absolutely charming to women. After a long and frustrating career, Carville had broken out of the pack by masterminding Harris Wofford's upset victory over Thornburgh. He was now Bill Clinton's chief strategist.

I always thought part of Mary's attraction to Carville had something to do with Lee. For the last year of his life, she ran the RNC in his absence, saw him every day, and directed much of his medical care. In many ways, she was as much a wife to him as Sally at the end. I wasn't the only one of her friends to believe that Carville was Lee's surrogate in Mary's eyes.

Mary knew the area well. She'd been a visitor at my place several times over the years, and had made many visits to Lee's cabin during his illness. She explained now that they'd driven out from Washington to look at a nearby cabin that was up for sale. They were both already half in the bag after an afternoon of drinking red wine. Our conversation inevitably turned to politics and their respective candidates. At some point I mentioned the Perot movement, which Carville quickly dismissed as a rich man's egomaniacal folly.

Mary got uncharacteristically quiet when I said I'd been hearing from political pros in California like Stu Spencer that the fervor for Ross Perot was like nothing they'd ever seen. "I take him a little more seriously than most of our colleagues," I said.

"Well, hell," James replied, "*that's* the campaign you ought to go run, since these damn fool Bush people ain't never gonna give you a role in their game."

Carville continued to belittle Perot. "He won't get five percent if he has the guts to run, which I seriously doubt," he predicted. I countered that I believed Perot was running and that he had a strong chance to hold much of his support, which was then around 15 to 18 percent. A wager was quickly arranged. If Perot ran, I'd pay James $200 for every point Perot came in under 10 percent on election day, and he'd pay me $100 for every percentage point over 10. (I'm still waiting for Carville's $900 check to arrive in the mail.)

Within twenty-four hours, I was getting calls from reporters checking out rumors that I was going to run Perot's campaign. I blamed Mary, who's a world-class leaker. She protested her innocence: I didn't believe her. But I learned later that Carville was the culprit and was on his cell phone spilling his guts about our conversation before the two of them were off the mountain.

James was closer to the truth than he knew. What I hadn't told them was that a couple of weeks earlier, one of Ross Perot's chief lieutenants had given me precisely the same advice as Carville, and that I'd been in turmoil ever since.

MY PEROT ODYSSEY actually had its emotional genesis in another double-cross by my erstwhile friends in the Bush camp. In January 1992, I'd been approached by my old friend Bob White, Governor Pete Wilson's chief of staff. The governor had enlisted as George Bush's California chairman and wanted me to be his chief political overseer. My duties would be working the California reapportionment process, the legislative races, congressional campaigns, and the Bush reelection effort.

Once again, I was amazed to be asked. After the NRCC unpleasantness, I was sure the president wouldn't tolerate my presence anywhere in his reelection campaign.

Apparently, I was wrong. In several separate conversations, Bob Teeter and Mary Matalin assured me that they not only wanted me back, but they thought the president could be persuaded to agree.

"We want you here," Mary said in one phone call.

I believed her—until I learned that she and Teeter were telling Wilson's staff that the governor must have been smoking dope to think Bush would countenance such heresy. I called Mary to bitch. She ducked and dodged my accusations.

"I'm trying to do you goddamn guys a favor," I said. "I didn't ask for this job. Your state chairman asked for me."

"Calm down, calm down," Mary cooed. "We're gonna get it fixed."

A couple of days later, Bob White called me back. We'd been friends since our assembly days in Sacramento, and Bob always told it straight.

"Ed, I don't know what they're telling you, but they're telling Pete there's no way you're going to be allowed in this thing." In fact, he added, that had been the reaction from the moment Wilson had first broached my appointment.

I felt utterly betrayed by Teeter and Matalin. Just when I thought I'd risen from the political dead, I was back in the graveyard again.

To make matters worse, Charlie Black, who was a senior counsellor to the Bush campaign, leaked an item to *Time* magazine that I'd turned down *their* generous offer of the California job by haughtily remarking that after managing a fifty-state race, one state was beneath my pay grade. It was a total fabrication, and it fueled my already smoldering sense of embitterment toward my party and my president.

This was the first of many shots fired by Charlie Black into my backside over the next year. He became the campaign's designated Rollins-trasher. That was some irony, since I was the guy who'd brought him back from exile after he'd been fired by Reagan in 1980.

An inside account of the California incident appeared in an Evans and Novak column. Two days later, I got a call from Tom Luce, a senior adviser to Ross Perot.

If the column he'd read was true, Luce drawled, "doesn't look like you're going to be working for Bush. We'd love for you to have a role in the Perot campaign."

I have to admit I was intrigued. From out of nowhere, the Perot movement had swelled into a real force. A lot of old Reaganites who'd become disgusted with Bush were calling me to sing Perot's praises. Even inside the Beltway, all the political chatter was about Perot, not Bush. It was too early to tell whether Perot was for real or whether he was merely the vehicle for a growing discontent with the system. But Perot had definitely tapped into something out there. Except for Reagan's campaigns, I hadn't felt so excited about anything since Jack Kennedy's victory at the 1960 convention.

But it was a nonstarter. "I can't do it," I told Luce. "My wife is the highest-ranking woman in the White House." My joining up with George Bush's arch enemy would be hell for her—not to mention finish me off forever. I told Luce I'd be happy to give some very quiet advice on strategy and staffing as long as I could stay invisible.

There was another reason for my reticence. In March, I'd written a letter to the president apologizing for some things I'd said in an interview that appeared to criticize his children. I'd only said that the Democrats were prepared to make them an issue if the Bush campaign attacked Clinton over the Gennifer Flowers matter. Barbara Bush had gone batshit over my remarks. On April 6, he'd sent me back a conciliatory letter.

"Thanks for your letter and for your generous comments therein," he'd written. "I have never seen such an ugly climate in an election year. Bygones are bygones, and I do appreciate your words of support."

Luce persisted, asking that I hear him out in person. By coincidence, I was scheduled to give a speech to a cable television association in Dallas a week or so later. I told him he was going to be disappointed, but we set a date for breakfast at his home in North Dallas on May 4.

Tom Luce is a very decent man, whose buttoned-down personality is in welcome contrast to his patron's. I'd later discover that he was a weak guy, a yes-man. That's the key to survival with a boss prone to tantrums, I suppose, and Luce had not only survived but flourished. He'd run for governor of Texas in 1990, finishing third in a four-man primary. Because of that, he thought he understood politics. In truth, he knew nothing about the big time.

Breakfast lasted a couple of hours. Luce wanted to know how to put the race together, so I walked him through the basics of organizing a national campaign and recommended several political pros I thought might be interested in working for Perot. I told him the odds were far less than even, but that the mood of the country gave Perot a real shot at being competitive. But it couldn't just be a campaign of volunteers, I remember saying; this was the big leagues.

"Well," he replied, "is there any chance of *your* coming on board?"

"Tom, I really couldn't do that because of my wife. I feel like I'm cheating on her just being here." I knew Sherrie would be upset, so I hadn't told her about our breakfast.

Luce didn't give up easily. The next day, he telephoned me back in Washington to say that he and Mort Meyerson were flying to town later in the week and wanted to meet with me.

Meyerson was Perot's closest business associate. A prominent community leader and philanthropist (the Dallas symphony hall is named after him), Meyerson was widely considered to be the brains behind Perot's business empire, and was his alter ego. Luce told me he'd be Perot's campaign chairman and that Meyerson would be in effect a counsellor without portfolio.

But according to Luce, Meyerson knew nothing about politics (he'd later admit to me that he'd never even voted) and wanted to pick my brain some more. I agreed to dinner at the Park Hyatt Hotel, where Meyerson would be staying. I also wrote a ten-page memo summarizing my blueprint for putting together a credible campaign. Working for Perot was still out of the question, but my professional curiosity had been piqued. Or was it the junkie in me, looking for another fix?

For the better part of three hours, I conducted a Campaign 101 tutorial over dinner. Meyerson repeatedly said Perot was insistent on running an unconventional campaign. I kept saying certain functions are essential regardless.

"You've got to introduce Perot to the public," I said, "describe who he is and why he wants to be president. You've got to have a message. You've got to communicate it on television." They were listening, but they weren't taking notes.

"You need an advance and scheduling operation to move the candidate around. You need to decide whether you want a convention. You'll have one hundred reporters covering you, so, like it or not, you've got to have a press operation to shape what they write. You need to have a professional field operation to utilize the volunteers fully." I paused every once in a while to let my words sink in.

"You're in this mind-set that you aren't going to do it the way they always do it; but these are things you have to do in order to win a war. And a campaign is war." I could see they were uncomfortable with this bottom line. I guess they never got over it.

"We desperately need a campaign manager," Luce interjected, but when I continued to resist, they asked me for other nominations. I'd previously suggested they needed a Democrat and a Republican to lend bipartisan credibility. I'd thrown out Pat Caddell and Bob Beckel, but said I doubted either would be interested. They said Caddell had met with Perot, and it didn't work out.

At one point I mentioned Hamilton Jordan, with whom I'd collaborated on several projects at Sawyer Miller. He was now working for Chris Whittle, the communications tycoon and another eccentric millionaire, and I figured Hamilton might be happy to escape his exile in Knoxville, Tennessee, the Whittle company town. Hamilton had been out of the game a while but was still respected, and as Jimmy Carter's chief strategist in 1976, he'd run the last successful outsider presidential campaign.

Luce and Meyerson looked like kids caught with their fists in the cookie jar. They admitted that Jordan had approached them offering to volunteer.

As the meeting broke up and we said our good-byes, I repeated that I'd be happy to help out, but only on an unofficial, behind-the-scenes basis.

Luce telephoned the next day to ask if I'd meet with him and Meyerson at Hamilton's office in Knoxville the following weekend.

"Mort was very impressed with you," he said. "We had a long

conversation with Perot, and we all agreed this arrangement is crazy. We don't want you behind the scenes. We need you up front. Will you at least have a conversation with Hamilton and us about it?"

I felt my reluctance losing out to my ego and my curiosity, but I still felt this seduction was heading nowhere. I agreed to fly to Knoxville, but I wasn't going to sneak out of town on my wife. It was time to bite the bullet with Sherrie.

I hadn't told her anything so far, and dreaded the conversation. The fatigue from her sixteen-hour work days at the White House was taking the predictable toll. Having spent five years of my life in the same pressure cooker, I understood the stress better than she did. She'd get home at ten o'clock completely frazzled and start again at 6 A.M. There was hardly time to talk, which was just as well. She'd become increasingly secretive about what was happening at the White House.

In her first weeks on the job, she'd asked my advice about various initiatives the administration was pursuing or considering. I thought most of them were pretty stupid and told her so. When race riots erupted in Los Angeles in late April, for example, I told her that Bush needed to get on national television and follow up with an immediate visit to the scene of the looting and destruction. It was an unexpected opportunity to assert some leadership. But instead of going himself or sending Housing Secretary Jack Kemp, the White House formed a task force of departmental deputies to coordinate things, and Sherrie was in the thick of it. As liaison for all outside groups, her office was dealing with all the affected parties, and it was not a fun time. Every smart response she recommended would get bottled up by indecision. Not to help matters any, her know-it-all husband chimed in with remarks like, "How can you people be so stupid? No wonder your boss is going to lose in November."

I never said "I told you so," but I sure thought it. The White House dithered and dawdled, and by the time Bush made it to Los Angeles, Clinton had come and gone and won the public relations battle. It's no wonder Sherrie just quit telling me things. It was better for both our blood pressures. Our conversations had since grown shorter—and more agonized.

The night before I left for Knoxville, I called her at the White House.

"I'm going down for a meeting with Perot's people," I said. "They've asked me for some advice."

Sherrie said she thought the Perot phenomenon was crazy and wished I wouldn't. She didn't explode, mainly because she figured nothing would come of it. I helped that assumption along by putting the most benign spin possible on my visit.

By now, Perot was beginning to gain momentum. Maybe he was a little kooky, but his movement was turning into a full-fledged phenomenon. More to the point, he had a political opening. The afterglow of Desert Storm was ancient history. People were thinking about their own lives now, and they were nervous. The May economic indicators were terrible.

Suddenly, Perot looked for real. In mid-May, a Field Poll in California showed Perot leading Bush by 37 to 31 percent, with Clinton trailing at 25. A Yankelovich national poll found roughly the same split: 33–28–24. It was obvious as hell that Pat Buchanan's insurgency had really exposed the president's vulnerability. Perot had the financial resources to pick up Pat's populist banner. The Reagan Revolution was over—or was it?

During that weekend in Knoxville in late May, Luce, Meyerson, Jordan, and I hashed out all the what-ifs yet another time. For half the time, Hamilton and I tried to explain how you run a big-time campaign. The other half was consumed by them trying to sell us on Perot. Neither Jordan nor I knew much about the guy. From some of his crusades on behalf of U.S. prisoners of war in Vietnam, we knew he was a patriot. We didn't know whether he knew the difference between changing the government and wrecking it. Perot was the genuine article, they insisted, a real American patriot who just wanted to make his country better.

Finally, Luce and Meyerson proposed that we be named co-managers. I knew that wouldn't work. One of us could be the counsellor, but somebody had to make the day-to-day decisions. Jordan suggested that we be co-chairmen, but said it made sense for me to run the campaign because he'd been away from the game for a long time.

I could see that Jordan was a bit farther down this road than I, but there was no way either of us would work for a guy without looking him in the eye first. Jordan and I were pretty much in sync. We both thought Perot would probably run. But if he did, he almost certainly wouldn't do it on our terms. He was too much of a maverick to be managed by hired guns.

The next week, Luce called back to say Perot was interested in going forward and wanted to talk with us. But he and Meyerson wanted one last meeting to walk through just how we'd plan a campaign. We scheduled another four-way in Dallas for Saturday, May 30. Perot would join us afterwards, they promised.

The temptation was still there, but I still hadn't moved my bottom line. I wasn't going to sacrifice my wife's career for my own. "If I weren't married to you," I'd told Sherrie, "I'd do it." She didn't find my disclaimer particularly reassuring.

That was my official line. The truth is, by now my reservations had begun to crumble. Being on the permanently disabled list was eating my insides to pieces. The more I thought about it, the more I found myself saying, "Damn, George Bush is going down, and this guy can win." I believed I could help Perot become a viable candidate, make the two parties more relevant, and change American politics for the better. If ever there was an opportunity to reform American politics in a fundamental way, this might be it. We all have a tendency toward self-delusion, but I thought my motives were fairly decent.

Sherrie repeatedly told me she thought it was madness. "I don't think you know enough about Perot," she argued. "You're destroying everything you've ever worked for. Just be patient and you'll get back in the game."

I tried to explain to her that this wasn't just another campaign. This was a new political movement, and win, lose, or draw, the potential was there to make an important difference. This evolution in my thinking had been helped along by friends like Al Hunt of the *Wall Street Journal,* who'd privately suggested I link up with Perot without knowing I was talking with Luce and Meyerson.

Sherrie and I *had* confided in John Cochran of NBC and Barbara Cohen, then the CBS bureau chief in Washington. We'd all been friends before John and Barbara had gotten married, and I knew they wouldn't break the confidence. Over dinner at the Ashby Inn, our favorite restaurant not far from the cabin, they both agreed that Perot was a genuine phenomenon and didn't discourage me from taking the plunge.

After the Knoxville meeting, I knew things were getting serious and I had better do some clear thinking. My clearest thinking always takes place at the cabin, away from the day-to-day distractions of my office. On Tuesday, May 26, I loaded Duke and Dutch into the Range Rover and headed for the mountains.

I did a lot of thinking and reading at the cabin. I was particularly struck by a passage from one of Winston Churchill's books explaining why he'd decided to leave the Tories and join the Liberal party. It had been a principled decision, Churchill wrote, brought on by his sense that his party had abandoned *him.* Sherrie kept telling me I should bone up on Perot instead of Churchill, but I didn't; and though I'm hardly in Churchill's league, I did find parallels between his decision and the one I was facing.

While I struggled in the mountains over the most difficult decision I'd ever have to make, Sherrie was agonizing as much as I back at the

White House. We both understood the grim reality: Resuscitating my career would complicate hers.

Two days before the Dallas meeting, word began trickling out that I was talking with the Perot camp. The Bush campaign dispatched my old friend and partner Jim Lake to the cabin with an all-is-forgiven offer: The president would be happy to have me in the campaign after all. "You can have any job you want, within reason, of course," Jim said. This from the guys who'd killed me off with Pete Wilson only four months earlier. Jim will always be a friend, but I treated the offer with the contempt it deserved.

"Jim, whether I go with Perot or not, I'm never going to work for George Bush. And even if I did, he's going down in flames and the idiots in the campaign and the White House don't even know it. They think this is only about beating Clinton. This election is about him, and he's already blown it. I know Clinton and his people. This isn't going to be a rematch with Dukakis. These guys know what they're doing."

Jim urged me to give it more thought, and as the clincher, he threw out what he knew was really gnawing at me: "Think of what this will do to Sherrie."

That's all I'd been thinking about all week. If it was just me, I would already be off to Texas. But now it was Sherrie's turn. I resented being reminded of this. Suddenly, the idea of kicking Bush's ass and the butts of all the preppie wimps around him took on enormous appeal.

The same day, Al Hunt had been talking politics with Tim Russert on the Today Show. Russert had made a veiled reference to a prominent Democratic strategist (Jordan) signing on with Perot. Off the air, Russert and Hunt compared notes. Fearful of being scooped on a story he was sitting on out of friendship, Al called and asked me to let him go with his exclusive.

"Al, it's not a done deal," I said. I asked him to sit on it a little longer. But he was adamant. The *Journal* doesn't publish on the weekends. If he didn't write for Friday's paper, he'd be dead in the water until Monday and lose the story.

"Al, you can do what you like," I said, "but I've not met with Perot and this thing might not happen. I wish you'd wait until Monday." He wrote the story accurately, making it sound speculative, but it still made a big splash.

The next day was the longest Friday of Sherrie's life. I was at the cabin, and could easily duck reporters' calls. But she was on Air Force One with the president on a trip to California. All anyone wanted to talk about was that morning's *Journal* piece. We spoke a couple of times during the day. "It's so distracting," she said. "I'm the story at every stop, not the president's event."

Before leaving with the president, Sherrie had asked to see him privately. She wanted to explain why I was in the process of defecting. "Ed has given up on us," she told him. "He doesn't think we can win, and he doesn't think we have an agenda for the next term." She secretly hoped to persuade him to reach out to me and keep me from bolting. It wasn't to be.

"Sherrie," Bush said, "Ed's just flat-out wrong. I know I'll be reelected. I'm the most qualified to be president."

Sherrie told me that he'd been very decent, but had also delivered a warning.

"Ed and Ross will never get along," he predicted. "I know them both. Their egos will get in the way." I couldn't remember her ever being so upset.

I flew down to Dallas early Saturday morning. The four of us met in Meyerson's office. They were all very concerned about the *Journal* piece and couldn't understand how it got out. I tried to explain the incestuous world of Washington, but I might as well have been trying to explain nuclear fission to the Oakland Raiders. We covered the same familiar ground. Hamilton had brought charts and graphs. We talked organization, message, media, field operations, direct mail, a convention, a running mate—the works. And this time, we spent a lot of time talking money.

If Perot was serious, I said, we'd need to spend $150 million to be credible, and because billionaires don't have much success raising money, most of it would have to come from his personal fortune.

"Let's not start this thing if he's not going to commit the resources," I said.

"Ross has never swum across the river halfway," Meyerson assured us. The money would be there; but, he confided, there was a more serious problem: Perot still wasn't entirely sure I was the right guy.

"You know, Perot has got some real concerns about you," Meyerson said. He was nervous about taking on someone whose wife was a senior White House official, which was understandable. My stroke had raised some questions in his mind about my health, which was also fair despite the fact that I hadn't had a recurrence in nearly ten years.

"And," he continued, "this is your second marriage. He wouldn't want to do anything to jeopardize this one. And he's hearing in Washington that your wife's very unhappy about this."

I was stunned. It wasn't a state secret that I'd been married for a little over a year in the late seventies, but maybe a hundred people on the planet knew that Sherrie wasn't my first wife. All of a sudden it dawned on me—these guys had done a full-scale shoot on me. And how the hell did they know how unhappy my wife was unless their investigaton was checking on her, too?

I told them my health was fine and so was my marriage. "Let's get something straight," I said. "I'm putting a gun to my head politically even sitting here. You asked me to do this. I didn't volunteer. You're the ones who've pushed it. If Perot has serious reservations, let's be honest about it and let me get on a plane and get the fuck out of here."

It was my first direct exposure to what might be charitably described as the dark side of Ross Perot. I was irritated at their snooping. Any campaign manager worth a damn checks out his own candidate for vulnerabilities; this was the first time I'd heard of the candidate investigating the campaign manager. Perot's espionage told me the guy was more serious about running than I'd thought.

Luce and Meyerson both reassured me that Perot was simply showing his compassionate side. He was only concerned about my marriage and my health.

We moved on to the substance of my recommendations. The vibes were contradictory. Perot seemed ready to jump, but he still wasn't sold on our blueprint.

"I'm not sure Ross is gonna buy into all of this," Meyerson said. "You're describing a conventional campaign. He's not a conventional person."

"Mort, what I'm describing is a *campaign*. Conventional or unconventional, this is how you win a national race. Volunteers won't do it. They're a tremendous asset nobody else has, but this is not a petition drive."

They wanted to brief Perot before we went any further. They'd see him that night, and if it was a go we'd have our first audience in the morning.

Hamilton and I walked out convinced the mating ritual was over. "He ain't buying into this thing," Hamilton said. I called Sherrie and told her not to worry, it wasn't happening.

"Get on a plane and get out of there," she pleaded. "Your instincts are right. It's not good." Much to her dismay, I told her I'd decided to stay another day to have dinner with Charlie Leonard, my former deputy at the NRCC, who was already on Perot's payroll.

In one of our previous conversations, Luce had said he needed a first-rate political operative to run the field operation, and I recommended Charlie. Luce met with him and hired him on the spot.

Charlie and I found a place close by to my hotel for dinner. As soon as we were seated, he started to spill. His short time in Dallas sounded like something out of Dante's *Inferno*.

"The place is in chaos," he said. "There are fifty people wandering around with cell phones, but nobody knows what they're doing. They have no clue what it takes to run a campaign. If you're coming down here, you better do it fast. You want to be here before it collapses."

Charlie had already crossed the line, and was in Perot's sights simply for trying to create order out of the chaos. As an experienced campaign manager, he knew what to do and how little time they had to do it.

I hoped it wasn't that bad, but Charlie has never been an alarmist. Before coming down, I was open to doing the campaign if the circumstances were right. Charlie's downbeat assessment on top of today's meeting was making me very nervous. I called Sherrie again to say I wasn't going to take the job even if Perot offered it. "You can sleep tonight," I assured her, adding that I'd try to get an early plane back to Washington. She was incredibly relieved to hear I'd finally come to my senses.

The next morning, Meyerson called to say he and Luce were meeting with Perot again and they'd get back to us. This thing is nuts, I thought. But I was curious to meet the man, and decided to hang around to see him up close and render my own judgment. Around noon, Luce called.

"Perot wants to meet with you at one o'clock," he said. "Everything's a go." I was still dubious.

The four of us assembled in Meyerson's office, an elegantly furnished high-tech suite in a downtown office tower. We were all dressed casually, sports jackets and polo shorts. Five minutes later, Perot walked in. He was wearing his uniform: dark suit, white shirt, collar pin.

"Boys," he said, "I'm glad to have you here. I'm looking forward to working with you. Tom and Mort tell me you've had some good discussions. Let's sit down and get to work. Tell me what we need to do." Even though neither Hamilton nor I had agreed to sign on, Perot acted like it was a done deal. Sandwiches were ordered in, and we took off our coats and waded in. He really *is* a no-nonsense guy, I thought.

He had a compact body and was very fit. He was high-energy, with an outrageous laugh. His eyes were alert and mean, but he was downright charming. Jordan and I were his customers, and he was going to make a sale. It didn't matter what we said; he was going to agree and get us to sign on the dotted line. Details could be worked out later.

For the next four hours, we hashed over our scenario yet again. He listened politely, but wasn't really interested in the nitty-gritty of electioneering. It was apparent Perot had already made up his mind.

It was also apparent that while we knew what he was getting into, *he* didn't have a clue. I tried to sensitize him to the reality of the modern campaign. It didn't matter who he was or how much money he had to throw around. Fair or not, he was going to get the living crap beat out of him for the next five months. I told him a presidential campaign was like war: You didn't get killed, but you could get badly wounded. He got indignant over this statement.

"You may think this is war," he shot back, "but I've known real men who have been in *real* wars. They've lost limbs and friends and have been badly wounded. This may be the closest you've come to war, but it's kid's stuff compared to the real thing."

I thought to myself, Let's see if you still think it's kid's stuff in about thirty days.

"I've been fired at before." He smiled. "I've been around heroes all my life. I can handle it."

I kept waiting for the catch, some comment or raised eyebrow to tip me that he wasn't really committed. It never happened. I was utterly shocked: Perot agreed to everything, including our insistence that we be allowed to teach him the way government operated. Jordan and I wanted to change what was wrong in Washington, but neither of us wanted to destroy the system.

"You guys are the Dream Team," he said, his charm offensive in overdrive. "I need some pros; there is no way I can do this thing without you." Money was no object, he said. If $150 million was what it took, he'd spend it.

We quickly sorted out a tentative organizational structure. As chairman, Luce would be the campaign spokesman. Meyerson was the chief troubleshooter and counsellor to the candidate. Jordan would be in charge of the message. I'd be the chief operating officer.

It didn't take a genius to recognize that this meeting was really about taking the measure of one another. It was a classic blind date. If we were all going to climb into the sack together, we needed to find some basic compatibility.

I walked out thinking I'd seen pieces of Richard Nixon and Ronald Reagan in this guy. He had Nixon's toughness and razor-sharp mind, and some of Reagan's charm and patriotism.

I called Sherrie from the airport and told her I'd said I'd think it over for a couple of days.

"Oh, God, you're going to do this, aren't you?" she asked.

"Well, I'm not sure, but he's a pretty fascinating guy. And I think he can win." As she'd feared might happen if I stayed around, I'd been swayed by Perot's sweet talk.

"If I had to make a list of my top five candidates, he wouldn't be on it," I said. "But he might be on a list of the five people with the leadership abilities to be president today."

As I checked in for my flight home, a young guy standing in line introduced himself as a friend of George W. Bush, the president's son.

"I guess I know why you're here," he said. "Are you gonna do it?"

"I don't mean to be rude, but I don't know you and I don't think I want to have this conversation."

"Don't do it. I'm from Dallas. You don't know Perot. He's a nut case."

During the flight, one of the pilots wandered down the aisle and delivered a contrary opinion.

"I hope you're going to do it," he said. "Go kick George Bush's ass. I voted for him last time, but he's been a disappointment."

My plane was delayed two hours. By the time I got home, Sherrie had abandoned all hope.

"I know you're going to do it," she said.

"Let's both think it over and give ourselves twenty-four more hours to make the decision," I said.

The next day, June 1, a Monday, Sherrie and I had dinner at the Jefferson Hotel in Washington.

"If it weren't for you, I *would* do it," I said. "But I'm not going to do it because of you."

"I think you're a fool," she said. "This is going to blow up in your face, and I don't want you to do it. But if the only reason you're not going to do it is because of me, you've got to do it, because you'll always resent not having done it." She was as adamant as I've ever seen her.

"Even though I think this is a stupid idea, and even though you won't admit your ego is involved, I do think in your heart and soul you believe it's in the best interest of the country to do it. So I'm going to go in tomorrow and resign."

It was my turn to tell Sherrie she was nuts. "You don't have to resign," I argued. "You're a Bushie. You have every right to be there. Your being there has nothing to do with me. If they're smart, Bush will hold a press conference and say, 'Listen, I've got the best Rollins on my staff, and if her idiot husband wants to go off with that idiot Texan, then so be it.' " In fact, they should have made her the chief campaign surrogate for the president. That would have been a public relations coup.

Sherrie had made up her mind. She'd concluded that it was simply too great a conflict of interest for her to stay if I went with Perot. She'd also be compromised and less effective.

"I don't want to be excluded from strategy meetings because people are suspicious of me," she said. "And I don't want to sit through meetings where people are dumping on you, either." As usual, she was right. Her position *was* untenable—thanks to me.

On Tuesday morning, I called Luce and said I was in. Perot called me to sprinkle holy water.

"I'm pleased with your decision," he said. "I think we'll make a great team."

The next morning, June 3, Sherrie resigned after the senior staff meeting. They went crazy. All except the president, who was totally gracious, told her she didn't have to leave, and asked her to reconsider.

The Bush campaign went into overdrive. Understanding they needed to make an example of me to make sure nobody else of prominence in the party defected, they abused me wall-to-wall. The heaviest trashers were Jim Lake and Charlie Black—both of whom I'd brought back from the dead in 1984 after they'd been fired by the Reagan campaign in 1980—and Mary Matalin, whose hand I'd held every day at the RNC during Lee Atwater's long illness. Like they say, no good deed goes unpunished.

We'd planned a press conference in Dallas the next afternoon, but it made no sense to wait now that the networks were reporting that Sherrie had resigned and that my deal was done. I called Sherrie to tell her how sorry I was and that I was flying to Dallas to do a hurried-up press conference. I caught the next plane out, and the new co-chairmen of the Perot campaign met reporters that afternoon at his headquarters in North Dallas. The conference room was crammed with people, which seemed to shock Hamilton.

"I can't believe there's this kind of interest in this," he said to me just before the press conference.

I found his remark disquieting. Perot was the hottest story in America. It told me that Hamilton was far more removed from the current political scene than I'd realized.

Contrary to some published reports spread by the Bush team, I didn't do it for the money; I was paid exactly what I was earning in the private sector. And I told myself that revenge wasn't a factor, either. I know today, of course, that I was deluding myself. In fact, lust for payback was central to my motivation. I was bitter about my treatment by the Bush crowd, and wanted to stick it to them, pure and simple, to show them they'd been fools to spurn my talents.

I knew I was staring over the edge of the abyss. By going with Perot, I'd shut the door forever on my career as a Republican operative. But if George Bush and Dan Quayle were now the Republican Party, it wasn't a party I would have ever joined in the first place. The bottom line was that every time I thought about how it would feel being a bystander, I became more willing to roll the dice. The more my interest was piqued, the more excited I got. And like a compulsive gambler, I thought only about the next deal, not the long haul—or the damage I was inflicting on my loved ones.

I STARTED TO work immediately after the press conference. Jordan didn't begin for almost another couple of weeks. A cancer survivor, Hamilton had a prior commitment to spend some time at a kid's cancer camp he'd founded. Until he arrived on June 15, I had the candidate all to myself. I came away from these early encounters believing that despite our rich man–poor man pedigrees, we had some common ground.

In one of our early meetings, I told Perot that I was as much a maverick as he. "Ross, I just have to make it very clear that I don't intimidate easily," I said. "If you want a yes-man, I'm not your guy. The fact that you've got three billion dollars is totally irrelevant to me. I've worked for three presidents and tried to give them the best counsel I could. I'll do the same for you, and you may not like everything I tell you, but you need to know it won't be out of disrespect."

"I've got plenty of yes-people," he assured me. "I don't want any more yes-people." At the time, I believed him.

Ross Perot is an extremely complicated personality, but he's nobody's fool. He's a man of enormous contradictions. I mean, here's a guy who owns four jet planes and God knows how many helicopters with all the trappings, and he'll serve you coffee in a Styrofoam cup. He'd spend fortunes on things that didn't matter, but when an expenditure really counted, he'd treat nickels like they were manhole covers. He considered campaign necessities like direct mail, advertising, and television pointless extravagances, yet he'd spend hundreds of thousands on offices and computers and electronic gadgets that weren't really useful.

He compartmentalizes everything; work is a compartment, as are family and politics, and in his opinion none of the compartments should ever intersect. One of the telling things I discovered early on was that he didn't want his family involved in the campaign. His wife Margo was a fabulous asset and had done a terrific interview with Barbara Walters. With Barbara Bush such a strong plus for her husband, it made even more sense to utilize Margo.

"It's not going to happen," he told me. "That's the last time she's going to do anything in this campaign. My wife and my family are not involved in this campaign." I argued that in the television age, candidates' families were inevitably part of the calculation.

"I don't care," he said. "They're out of play. You don't understand; I've had death threats on my children before. I've always been afraid they'd be kidnapped." This obsession with his family's security was misguided but genuine. He wouldn't allow the press office to release any information on his family, which was absurd. In fact, one of his daughters worked as a volunteer in the campaign using her mother's maiden name so nobody would know she was a Perot.

He suffers from a small man's complex, which includes an enormous need for ego gratification. This partially explains his tendency to spin tall tales, all of which place him squarely at the center of a paranoid and delusional universe. His staff has invented a verb to describe Perot's tendency to make stuff up: "Rossing."

The best example of Rossing on my watch was an incident in which Perot claimed to have foiled a Black Panther attack on his home in the 1970s. When police officials said there wasn't any evidence to support the claim, I checked with one of Perot's security guys, who told me it never happened. I warned Luce that when the national media caught up with this story, Perot's credibility would be in the toilet.

"Ross ran them off himself," Luce explained. According to Perot, his security dogs alerted him to the Panthers, and he and his dogs scared them away. I double-checked this new and improved version of events with the security man, who told me Perot hates dogs and doesn't have any.

"We call them the Stealth dogs," he chuckled. Afterwards, we'd joke that the Perot presidency could save tax dollars by dispensing with the Secret Service. The Stealth dogs would protect Perot.

These whoppers had earned Perot a reputation for quirkiness that I knew could become a political liability. In my first private session with him the first week on the job, I'd raised the issue indirectly.

"You're going to be scrutinized in a way you've never been before," I said, "so it's very important that we know everything there is to know. Let us make the judgments on what is politically dangerous. You and no other candidate can make that kind of a judgment."

"My life is an open book," he replied. "There's nothing there anywhere."

It didn't take me long to size up the "big little man," as he was called around the office. What I originally took to be an admirable complexity I soon saw was a bundle of crippling contradictions. He stubbornly adhered to principles that were idiosyncratic at best, and certainly were not in tune with many of his supporters. And he was shortsighted and narrow-minded to a breathtaking degree.

He can be extremely personable, but not to his top staff. He was patronizing to the women and ruthless to the men. One of his closest advisers once told me, "He's the kind of a guy who walks into the company cafeteria and five hundred people call him 'Ross,' but he walks into his boardroom and his ten closest aides call him 'Mr. Perot.'"

He's very intolerant and excessively judgmental. He once told me that George Bush was weak and his kids were crooks—just like that. And if your life-style didn't match his, you were immediately suspect.

The day I agreed to join up, for example, he caught me by surprise. "Of course, you're not going to be able to keep that beard," he said matter-of-factly.

"Ross, I've had a beard for sixteen years. Nobody would recognize me without it. Shaving it off isn't even an option."

"Well, I've never had anyone work for me with a beard."

Some time later on the Today Show, Katie Couric provided Perot with an opportunity to deliver a misleading postscript to this exchange when she asked him about a former employee he'd fired for having a beard. It wasn't true, he replied. After all, his campaign manager had a beard.

Another illustration of Perot's disdain for alternative life-styles involved Willie Nelson. Perot was obsessed with a gala lunch he was throwing for his state coordinators and top supporters in late June. There was a long list of crucial decisions we needed him to make, including the choice of a running mate, but he wasn't interested in anything except this stupid-ass lunch.

A couple of days before the event, Perot was micromanaging the guest list. When he saw Willie's name, he exploded. "He's a dope smoker and doesn't pay his taxes," he said. "I don't want him here."

I could see the headline: "CANDIDATE SNUBS ONE OF HIS BIGGEST SUPPORTERS." I told him that uninviting Willie would prove the exception to the rule that there's no such thing as bad publicity.

"Ross, I guarantee you Willie Nelson has more fans than you, George Bush, and Bill Clinton combined."

"I don't care," he said. "I want him uninvited."

I ignored the order, but at least once a day he'd asked me if I'd deep-sixed Willie yet.

"You're going to do yourself real political damage," I warned, and said he'd have to do it himself.

Finally, we had the lunch, and as I predicted, the media was swarming all over Willie, who was saying wonderful things about the candidate. But the candidate was beside himself when he took in the scene. He ordered me to get Willie away from the press.

"Ross, I wouldn't worry too much about Willie," I reported. "He's telling them he thinks you're the guy who can save the country."

"You know what he represents—drug users and tax dodgers!"

"Ross, if you're going to try and get elected by eliminating people who haven't smoked dope in their lifetime, there aren't enough votes left."

Perot's cavalier treatment of former Treasury Secretary William Simon was a classic case of Perot's tunnel vision. Simon was flirting with endorsing Perot, but like all political animals, he wanted something in return. His payback was quite modest: an hour or two with the great man to talk economics and schmooze. Simon's endorsement would have lent a powerful aura of legitimacy to the campaign. I thought Perot would leap at the chance.

"Is this that right-wing kook from California?" he asked.

"Ross, Bill Simon is one of the most highly respected Treasury secretaries in my lifetime." I told him Simon's endorsement would pay huge dividends on Wall Street and elsewhere. Moreover, Simon would be joined by Marty Anderson, Ronald Reagan's longtime domestic adviser. Anderson's approval would serve us well with the Reagan conservatives we wanted to attract.

"I already got a Treasury secretary," Perot replied, "I got [John] Connally. What do I need two for?" I argued for a while longer, but Perot was adamant.

"I'm not going to spend a couple of hours with anybody," he said. "There's nothing he can tell me I don't already know." Simon could meet with his staff, and he'd drop in for five minutes. I knew that would be a disaster. Simon, justifiably insulted, would walk out and tell the first reporter he met that he'd just spent five minutes with a simpleton who doesn't know anything about the economy.

I called Simon and told him as apologetically as I could that the candidate didn't want to meet with him. That was the end of what might have been a very important endorsement.

When Perot wasn't ignoring the right people, he was paying attention to the wrong ones. One day, Katharine Hepburn, who was on the campaign's national advisory committee, sent a memo detailing how unhappy she was with how things were going in New York. High points of the "important memo" included:

Perot is going down the drain here.
He is self-destructing.
He is breaking people's hearts.
It's disappointing, horrible, and shocking.
Those who were for Perot are switching to Clinton.
He should have new speeches.
The commercials should be out by now.

I didn't disagree with anything she'd written—I'd been saying the same things myself internally—but Luce and Meyerson stupidly took this memo right to the top. Sure enough, it took the better part of an afternoon to reassure the candidate that, the distinguished Miss Hepburn's "analysis" aside, the carpetbaggers he'd hired hadn't screwed up New York. But that was vintage Perot. He ignored his political professionals, but gave the opinion of a famous nonprofessional—or an inexperienced volunteer—the credence of a papal edict.

Reduced to basics, Perot is the ultimate control freak. And that's where he and I ended up knocking heads. Politics is a world full of things you can't control; what you have to do is manage them. That's why politicians hire experts, and why smart politicians listen to them. Perot wasn't a smart politician. He was a lion out of his jungle. He wanted to play in a world he didn't understand and couldn't dominate—but he couldn't bring himself to relinquish the control necessary to compensate for his ignorance. In the end, it proved lethal.

AT THE START, Perot was a bona fide contender. By mid-June, he was leading in California, Texas, and several other states. He was a strong second in Ohio and Michigan. And in a three-way race, 36 or 37 percent of the vote might be enough to translate into 270 electoral votes. Perot's national numbers were between 31 and 34 percent. We were within striking distance, and we hadn't spent a dime.

"Jesus, we're going to elect this guy president," Bob Barkin, the campaign's creative director, said to me one day.

"Yeah," I replied, "but do we really want to?"

At the time, I was kidding.

I assumed Bush would get the eastern establishment Republicans, Clinton the traditional Democrats. Perot's target voters were the disaffected from both parties—conservative Republicans and blue-collar Democrats, the same universe of voters Ronald Reagan appealed to in 1984. There was no reason to think we couldn't put the same coalition together that worked for Reagan. After Atwater's death, Bush and his people never understood the coalitions that Reagan had handed down to them. They did everything possible to piss them off, and those votes were now up for grabs.

The key to holding Perot's base and adding the extra handful of percentage points to give him a plurality was coming up with a clear message. Nobody knew much about the candidate except that he was this quirky short guy from Texas with a crewcut and a squeaky voice. We had to define him before the opposition did.

In mid-June, Jordan and I had put together a message strategy with three distinct planks. The first would emphasize a little-known aspect of Perot's persona: his humanitarianism. Over the years, he has done hundreds of good deeds, most of them for fellow citizens he's never met. Only a few of them, like his efforts on behalf of Vietnam POWs and MIAs, have ever been publicly disclosed. He's sent money to strangers. He's paid tens of thousands of dollars for special surgeries the Veterans Administration wouldn't perform on injured veterans because of the cost. Beneath that flinty exterior beats the heart of a Good Samaritan. We aimed to tell this good and real story.

Our second theme would stress Perot's can-do spirit. The rags-to-riches story of his rise from IBM salesman to megabillionaire was the stuff of American folklore. Because of his strong work ethic and self-made success, Perot's wealth was actually a powerful draw for the blue-collar voters he needed to attract.

Once we persuaded voters that this was a guy they should like and admire, we'd hammer home the theme that Ross Perot was no traditional politician. The country was sick of politics as usual. Perot was the prescription for a cynical electorate precisely because he hadn't spent a day of his career in Washington.

While Perot was riding high, we'd come in with a heavy wave of national media buys to define this image. While we reinforced his positives and softened his negatives, we'd let Bush and Clinton chew each other up. It all seemed perfectly sensible to me. What I didn't count on was Perot's bullheadedness.

Most candidates think they're smarter about politics than their handlers. Sometimes they're right, but most of the time they're not. One of the little appreciated but most demanding skills of the campaign consultant is being able to convince your principal that he may not be as brilliant as he thinks.

This is arduous duty; the disdain most office seekers feel for their operatives is crystallized in one of George Bush's favorite lines: "If you're so smart, why aren't you president?" (In Bush's case, the answer today is, "Because Ronald Reagan didn't hand it to me on a silver platter.")

But at least most candidates know the territory. The great emotional struggle of the entire Perot campaign was trying to find a way to tell the candidate he simply didn't know what the hell he was doing.

Given his Napoleon complex, I couldn't say what all of us were thinking: "Ross, sit down and shut the fuck up. This is how you run a campaign, and this is your role. This is not like anything else you've ever done in your life. That's understandable, but you don't have a clue. If you'll let us, we can save you from yourself."

If I'd made that speech, I'd probably have been on the next one-way coach ticket back to Washington. Maybe I should have done just that. But the truth is that despite some glimpses into Perot's occasionally bizarre character, in the early days I was totally energized by the outpouring of support for the guy. And all day long, or so it seemed, another former congressman, former Reagan White House aide, or state chairman was calling to offer help.

Just as suddenly, reality began to rear its ugly head. In my second week on the job, I was taken to task by Perot for my hiring practices.

"I can't believe all the people you have here," he told me. "You're building the Pentagon."

In fact, Perot himself was the empire builder. I'd assembled a team of a dozen or so operatives, but on any given day there were several dozen Perot people wandering around campaign headquarters, installing computers and telephones and generally tripping all over themselves. Most headquarters are rather spartan, so I wasn't prepared for the luxury I found when I arrived. This amazing physical complex was crammed with every piece of sophisticated office technology known to mankind. We must have had 150 portable telephones at the headquarters alone. What was missing was any sense of how the hardware related to getting Perot elected.

Nobody was in charge of Perot's people—least of all me. I had this weird idea I was the campaign manager, yet every time I'd give one of them an order, I'd find out later they'd gone to Luce for an okay. One day I complained to one of the office administrators because I hadn't gotten a television hookup for ten days.

"You know," she said, "you political people think this whole thing revolves around you."

"Fine," I replied. "You go and tell Mr. Perot how to win the presidency after you get my damn television set hooked up. I know it might sound unreasonable to you, but as the campaign manager I would like to know what the networks are saying about us before this fucking campaign's over."

The Perot loyalists were abetted in this xenophobia by Jim Squires, the campaign spokesman. Squires was a well-respected reporter and bureau chief who'd flamed out as editor of the *Chicago Tribune*. He'd been squeezed out and was breeding horses in Kentucky when Luce hired him well before I arrived.

I've never thought reporters make good press secretaries; they prefer breaking stories to flacking them. Squires was even worse, a disgruntled former journalist who'd soured on his profession. He really hated television journalists and didn't think much better of the new breed of print reporters who came along post-Watergate. He was the perfect match for Perot, who detested the press. Their ideal press operation would have been an answering machine that never called back.

When he wasn't making enemies for Perot by ignoring reporters' phone calls, Squires was spewing poison about me. He thought I was the antithesis of everything Perot stood for, and he opposed virtually everything Jordan and I wanted to do.

"You're the best in the business," he told me in one of our first conversations. "But it's a shit business." That said it all.

He constantly undermined me with his old Washington press pals, notably Jack Nelson of the *Los Angeles Times*. When you have a reputation as a leaker, it's child's play for your enemies to spread stuff and pin it on you. Squires was a master of this game. He did a constant number on me with Perot, Luce, and Meyerson. He did more press leaking than all my staff combined—then blamed it all on me. Perot believed all the crap Squires shoveled his way, especially Squires's thesis that he could ignore the media assigned to cover his campaign in favor of the network talk shows and pay no price.

A more troubling clue to Perot's tin ear soon emerged over the campaign budget. When I arrived, money was flying out the door with no rhyme or reason, so I sat down with my staff and we quickly put together a budget of $147 million—$3 million less than Perot had pledged. The vast majority was earmarked for television. We all knew that unlike the Democrats and Republicans, whose candidates were better known and had the luxury of a convention to tell their stories, we had to be up heavy on television in July and August defining our message.

Luce and Meyerson said the budget looked reasonable, but they'd run it by Perot first. I thought that was my job, I told them. This was the first campaign I'd been in where the manager didn't brief the candidate on something as critical as budget.

"Well," Luce smiled, "when it comes to money, Ross is never going to let anybody he doesn't know spend his money."

They took the budget over, and came back with their tails between their legs. "He isn't buying any of this," Meyerson reported. "He thinks it's absurd—way too much money." Perot didn't think a penny for direct mail made any sense, and he'd crossed off the entire $3 to $4 million for issues research. I said that we needed another session so Hamilton and I could justify the numbers to Perot personally.

The four of us went over to Perot's office, which looks like a museum of Americana—Norman Rockwell originals, Frederic Remington bronzes, unique historical pieces, and military paraphernalia and armaments of all sorts and sizes. I tried to explain the financial imperatives. Most presidential campaigns don't budget a lot on direct mail, because the DNC and RNC spend millions on it that doesn't count against spending limits. We didn't have that luxury. The direct-mail budget was partly to respond to the 4 million people who'd called his toll-free number offering to help. The Perot people had entered their names on computer files, but never got back to them.

"And you can't run a campaign without a research operation," I said, refraining from pointing out that we needed to spend more in this area because he was a guy who knew damn near nothing about policy or issues. Now, he wanted to eliminate the very people who could get him up to speed.

"I don't need these people," Perot complained. "All they keep doing is bringing me big thick books. This thing here on health care is almost six hundred pages. There's not any reason you can't get all the facts that are important on one page."

Perot axed $2 million for polling, saying he had all the polls he needed in the newspapers. Trying to run a national campaign without polling is like flying an airplane without instruments. We subsequently hid the money under "media research." We'd lumped other essential functions under "volunteer activities" to get them past Perot's blue pencil. It didn't work. Perot thought the budget was exorbitant and arbitrarily cut it in half, to about $75 million. Much of the money we'd earmarked for direct communication with the voters—media, direct mail, field operations—had been slashed.

He thought it made more sense to husband resources until the very end. I argued he was being penny-wise and dollar-foolish. It was like building a luxury office tower with a cheap foundation. He couldn't be swayed.

I walked out of the meeting convinced that Perot was like most rich candidates: They always say they'll spend whatever it takes, but when the time comes to sign the checks, they develop rigor mortis. What he didn't realize was that he'd already wasted a fortune. Luce had vendors selling him junk that wouldn't be used in a dog catcher's race, and they were stealing him blind by charging far more than what they got from more experienced campaign organizations. Perot is a very generous person by instinct, but when other people try to spend his money, he turns into an incredible tightwad. And every decision we urged on him cost money—lots of it.

But the problem went well beyond dollars. The candidate simply didn't grasp what it took to run a major league campaign. Every mistake you could make in starting up a presidential race had already been made.

The first blunder was designating a person who knew nothing about politics as his campaign point man. Tom Luce was less equipped to be involved in politics than most anyone I've ever met. His whole life had been built around kissing Ross Perot's ass, and he'd made millions doing it. Tom served as Perot's lawyer and political gofer in Austin for years. By the time Hamilton and I got to Dallas, he was so far over his head he didn't know whether to swim or go blind. He was operating in a total state of delusion both about the campaign and his candidate. Tom was already envisioning himself as the next Attorney General of the United States in President Perot's administration.

My suspicions that I was managing a candidate who couldn't be managed soon escalated. In May, Perot had gone on *Meet the Press* and got his clock cleaned by Tim Russert. During a budget discussion, Perot demonstrated his ignorance about even the most fundamental aspects of the subject. After my arrival, I'd urged him to stay off the talk shows until he could bone up on those issues books he loved to malign. He agreed.

A couple of days later, I was watching the *MacNeil/Lehrer News-Hour*. Much to my surprise, my boss appeared on the screen. I called Tom Luce.

"Tom, am I mistaken, or did Ross agree two days ago not to do any more television interviews?"

"Of course he did. Why are you asking?"

"Turn on *MacNeil/Lehrer*." Pause.

"It must be taped."

"Nope, it's live and in person, from New York."

"That's nonsense," Luce insisted. "He's in his office."

As usual, Ross had scheduled himself, flown to New York on one of his private jets, and didn't bother to tell anyone in his campaign. I've been in many campaigns where I didn't know what the candidate would say at a given moment. Ross was the first candidate where I didn't know where he'd *be* on a given day. He kept his own schedule, made his own appointments, controlled his own movements, and didn't think it was anybody's business where he was.

One eccentricity invariably led to another. I'd been told by Luce and Meyerson that when Perot started raving, his minions had learned to stall for time and ride out the storm. In a campaign, there's no time to wait for the boss to regain his sanity. Every day is critical, so we had to try to force Perot to make decisions. But he was resistant to practically everything we brought him. Even more important, he wouldn't let us make decisions for him. Every other day or so, I'd send him a memo reminding him there was a deadline around the corner and that if he didn't do something today, it wouldn't happen.

Perot was usually able to deal with something that required immediate attention, like signing a check or renting a volunteer office. But he had an utter inability to think strategically. He was convinced he didn't have to get serious until October. "They run thirty-day campaigns in Europe," he'd complain. "Why can't we?"

"Because we're not in Paris, Ross."

I tried to explain that even five months wasn't long enough when your opposition has been running for two years, but it never took.

The generally amateurish attitude of Perot and his two lieutenants crippled one of the most important policy decisions of the campaign: picking a running mate. To meet the requirements of getting on some state ballots in time, we had to have a vice presidential "nominee"— and soon. James B. Stockdale, a retired admiral, was always supposed to be only a temporary surrogate. (We had until the middle of August to make a change.)

Perot is a tireless supporter of Vietnam-era POWs and MIAs. During the years Jim was a prisoner in North Vietnam, Perot and Sybil Stockdale were frequent allies in the POW/MIA cause. Perot is also the ultimate military star-fucker. After graduating from the Naval Academy, he got out of the service the instant his commitment was up, and he had a reputation as a crybaby the whole time he was in. The truth of the matter is Perot didn't like taking orders then any more than he does today. But he has a genuine affection for the uniform. He had great respect for Jim Stockdale, a fellow Annapolis graduate, as well he should. As a stopgap solution, Jim was an obvious choice.

We all knew that we'd ultimately need a brand name on the ticket with Perot. Jordan and I argued that a VP of national prominence would add credibility to Perot's outsider status, and with his poll numbers close to 40 percent at the outset, we could attract somebody of stature if we moved quickly.

The process of attracting a permanent running mate, however, was worthy of the Marx Brothers.

Luce and Meyerson circulated a list of maybe one hundred names recommended by various sources. My first thought was that William French Smith, Reagan's first Attorney General, perhaps should be removed, since he'd been dead for a couple of years. After a while it became obvious they were seriously considering a woman, and their prime candidate was Elizabeth Dole. Liddy and I were very close allies in the White House, and as the wife of the Senate Republican leader, I knew she wasn't going to jump the Republican Party. But the morons marched on, and continued to waste valuable time. Luce had met with her twice and was very impressed, but she said she knew the question he had on his mind—and please don't ask.

Then they got intrigued with Senator Nancy Kassebaum of Kansas. I said that was stupid. Nancy was very close to Bob Dole, and her father Alf Landon had been the Republican nominee for president in 1936. Then, after reading a *New York Times Magazine* piece about her, they got excited about Bernadette Healy, head of the National Institutes of Health. More wasted time.

Out of the blue one day, Luce walked into my office and said, "What would you think of Cokie Roberts as a VP choice?" She'd interviewed him for an ABC piece on Perot, and Tom had come away dazzled. He had the dazzle part right, but he didn't seem to know she was the daughter of the late former House majority leader Hale Boggs of Louisiana and Congresswoman Lindy Boggs, and the sister of one of the Democratic Party's most prominent fixers, attorney-lobbyist Tommy Boggs.

"I'm a big fan of Cokie's myself, Tom," I said, "but we'd be laughed out of town, and Cokie would laugh the loudest." That didn't stop someone from floating her name, and we looked like fools.

In the end, we never got serious or met the deadlines. With all the screwing around, we could never attract the kind of running mate we needed. By the time Perot was ready to pick a running mate, the campaign was already in such trouble that nobody of political stature was willing to run with him. When Perot returned to the race in

October, Jim Stockdale was stuck on the ticket, and when he came across as rattled and somewhat confused during the VP debate in October, Perot's credibility as a plausible alternative to Bush and Clinton was compromised.

Of all the political injustices in my lifetime, what happened to Jim Stockdale was the greatest. Congress should pass a law requiring every person who laughed at him during the vice-presidential debate to read the citation that explains why Stockdale received the Medal of Honor for his conduct as a senior prisoner of war in Hanoi for more than eight years. This man is a great academic scholar, a true war hero, and a wonderful human being—the best the military and this country have to offer. He deserved better.

As if there weren't enough problems to say grace over, my co-chairman took a dive after less than a month on the job. In late June, Hamilton was over at Perot's office showing him a very rough cut of the campaign documentary film. The candidate exploded in rage over what he considered an inferior product. Luce and I arrived late, while Ross was in the middle of a tirade. The first words I remember hearing are, "You've just wasted my money on this crap! I thought you were a professional." Perot didn't know enough about television to realize that this footage was a long way from a finished product.

Actually, Perot had authorized the spending, but reason was always a waste of time during one of his tantrums. Hamilton isn't a screamer, and wasn't used to that sort of abuse. On our way back to headquarters, he began sweating profusely. By the time we arrived, he was having a full-blown anxiety attack. We got him down on the floor of his office, but he refused an ambulance. We thought he was having a heart attack.

"I've had these before," he said. "If I can rest for an hour, I'll be all right." Once his condition stabilized, he went straight home.

The next morning, he told me he'd decided to resign. "You worked for a lot of candidates and you might be used to this crap," he explained. "I've only worked for one—Jimmy Carter. I had a wonderful relationship with Carter. He always treated me like a gentleman, and I've never been talked to like this by anyone."

He said that the guy was nuts and I should get out of there, too. "Quitting's not an option for me," I told him. "I recruited some all-star talent and they're depending on me to get them through this shitstorm."

He went to tell Perot he was leaving, but came back from his audience subdued and ashen. Hamilton stumbled around in a daze for a few days after that, the realization apparently dawning that it would be humiliating to withdraw so soon, and besides, he probably needed his salary. He'd quit his job with Whittle and was in the process of moving his family to Dallas. After accepting Jordan's resignation, Perot himself must have realized that losing his campaign co-chairman would be a serious embarrassment. They let each other off the hook, though I have no idea what actually transpired. Nothing was ever said, but the result was that he kept his title and turned in his portfolio. Hamilton played tennis, took his kids to amusement parks, and hid out in his office. That left me the only guy in Perot's face. I could tell he was liking that less and less.

IT WAS EARLY July, and the wheels were coming off. Our budget had been trashed. We couldn't attract a big-deal running mate. Perot's polling numbers were heading south. The candidate was scheduling himself. My co-chairman was missing in action. Our organization was in chaos. A perfect example of the state of affairs was the fact that Perot had given my authority over field operations to Mark Blahnik, an ex-Marine officer who handled Perot's security and schedule. He knew nothing about politics and seemed to be in a constant state of shellshock. A guy who wears four beepers on his belt makes me a little nervous.

Time was ebbing away, and Perot still was avoiding decisions. The morale of my staff was in the sewer. They knew what needed to be done, and like me were powerless to do anything about it. Along with my other duties, I tried to be the morale officer. The best I could do was appeal to their sense of professionalism. The slogan I scrawled across the top of my office blackboard became our rallying cry: *"Fort Alamo—There Is No Back Door Here."* Maybe Perot would finally wake up, and maybe he wouldn't, but we all needed to suck it up and soldier on. The Alamo's commander, Colonel William Barrett Travis, had taken as his motto "Victory or Death." By now there were no illusions inside my bunker which way this battle would end up.

Since media strategy had always been the biggest source of friction between the candidate and his handlers, it was only fitting that the beginning of the end was over television. Back in the glory days of mid-June, when I was still starry-eyed and had a functioning co-chairman, Jordan and I spent a lot of time honing our message. The plan was to get a strong bunch of ads on television no later than July 1. Perot had grudgingly approved a $6.5 million media buy beginning July 1, but later refused to release the money, so our spots never ran.

Perot had been so successful in sweet-talking his way onto talk shows that he thought that's all he needed in the way of a media policy. Jordan and I had argued with him a dozen times. If we weren't on television by July 1 defining Perot, the opposition would define him at their conventions—and destroy his credibility in the process. But nothing we said could persuade him. He thought spending money to get his message on TV was stupid.

"Why do I have to pay for it," he'd always say, "if I can get on *Larry King*?" He considered *Larry King Live* his personal forum. Any time he wanted on, the show was his. The Today Show was his favorite breakfast treat, until Katie and Bryant Gumbel started roughing him up.

We never bridged the gulf on media. "I don't understand why you guys can't get a commercial on TV in two days if I can send a rescue team to Iran in twenty-four hours," he frequently complained.

His solution was to send one of the best media guys in the business around the country shooting footage of Perot communing with volunteers at rallies. Basically, he thought shooting spots was like covering a fire: You point the camera and interview eyewitnesses.

Hal Riney is one of the most creative advertising guys around. His feel-good commercials for Gallo wines, Saturn automobiles, and Alamo rental cars are widely acclaimed in the industry. He was a principal architect of the "Morning in America" ads in the 1984 Reagan campaign. He also did their narration; Riney's soothing, modulated cadence is the best voice-over in the business. Listen to an Alamo ad and you'll know what I mean.

I was amazed and delighted that Riney was willing to come into a campaign as high-risk as Perot's. But like many Americans, he'd become frustrated with the political system. He had an infant child from a new and happy marriage. Like Hamilton Jordan, who also had young children, Hal was worried about his baby's future. He thought Perot could be the answer.

From the start, Riney and Perot were on different planets. Perot had no concept of marketing or advertising. He'd made his billions by having a brilliant concept at the right time—automatic data processing—not with public relations. He thought he had all the answers. His attitude to every issue was simple: It's my money, you do it my way.

Even though he knew nothing about television or any other media, he thought he did. He drafted a script for his own documentary. Riney took one look at it and said it was fine but it would take about eight hours to cover it all.

Like a good soldier, Riney produced some volunteer-in-the-street ads to Perot's specifications. We all agreed with Hal that they were pitiful—canned, boring, utterly ordinary. Perot was the only guy who thought they were any good. The campaign was about volunteers, he said, so let's get a lot of volunteers. That was the message: Volunteers are nice people.

"I don't want to be judged on the garbage I've been shooting," Riney said one day. So without shooting another foot of tape, he put together two commercials that were just incredible. They captured the magic of our old "Morning" campaign. And he did the voice-over himself. They *were* the Perot movement. Even Perot liked them. "This is what I'm talking about," he purred after Hal screened them.

On July 7, we showed them at a big lunch for Perot's state coordinators, and they were very excited. Then one guy stood up and said something to the effect that the spots were good but looked like ads Clinton or Bush would run, and he thought Ross was going to run a different campaign.

The next morning, I saw Perot. "Well," he drawled, "you saw the reaction. Those things were crap. They're out." They were great spots, but they never ran—except on CNN and *Nightline,* after I released them in disgust after the campaign.

Perot's new plan was for Riney to bring in all the raw footage and splice the frames he liked into commercials. It was a dumb idea, like trying to make a photo album from undeveloped film. Riney and I brought the rough cuts over to Perot's office. To nobody's surprise, he hated them.

"Is this what I'm paying all this money for, this crap?" Perot snarled.

"This is not how you do commercials," Riney told him. In layman's terms, and with admirable patience, Hal tried to explain the finer points of message, concepts, scripts, and storyboards. "First you have to decide what it is you're going to sell," he said.

Then he started to explain the cost of camera crews, lighting, and everything else that goes into making a commercial. Perot stopped him short.

"You're telling me it costs sixty thousand dollars a day to have all those long-hair college dropouts with gold earrings stand around and do nothing all day but play with cameras?"

"What makes you think these guys are college dropouts? The people I use are graduates of some of the best film and art schools in the country."

"That may be your idea of an artist," Perot replied. "It's not mine. I just see a lot of people standing around wasting time and my money." Riney was incredulous.

"Hal, is it true that you once spent one hundred thousand dollars of hard-earned money to put a goat on top of a mountain?"

"Who told you that, Ross?" Hal challenged. "That's absurd."

"Well, let's just say a little birdie."

It wasn't a little birdie, I thought to myself, but an old vulture by the name of Jim Squires. I was in the room when the prick told Perot that bullshit story.

It went downhill from there. All Perot wanted to know was how much it would cost. "Without knowing more about what you want, it's impossible to say," Riney replied.

"I've never had a salesman say he couldn't tell me what his product costs," Perot protested. Riney said that most network commercials cost between $450,000 and $800,000 to produce. Sometimes, the costs break $1 million.

"We've made a terrible mistake here," Perot snapped. "You want to build a Rolls-Royce; I want to build a Volkswagen."

Riney explained that campaign spots weren't as expensive as selling Saturns. On average it shouldn't cost more than $75,000 to $80,000, he guessed. "You could do it for less. But if you're going to spend over one hundred thousand dollars a minute to run them, you want people to watch them."

Perot went crazy, practically coming out of his chair. "This is just nuts," he countered. "Even your lower rate is way too much. I don't think we should make a commercial that costs more than five thousand dollars. And I am not going to spend that kind of money to buy time when I can get it free on *Larry King*."

Somehow, Riney swallowed his disgust. "Well, I can set up a video camera in your office, and you can talk into it, and we'll just put that right on network television," he said. "Now, will anybody watch it? I don't think so. And do I want to be part of that? I don't think so. Those are not my talents."

Hal and I both knew there was no way to jump this chasm. As we walked out, Perot flung his arm around me.

"Now, Ed," he soothed, "I know this isn't your fault. You and Hal figure out how to make it work."

On the ten-minute drive back to the headquarters, Riney was fuming. "I've had only one other client like this in my life," he said. "I was just starting out. It was my biggest account, and I didn't have many others at the time. But I quit that account because the client was nuts. And this guy's nuts, too. I'm wasting my time. This thing isn't going to work." I asked him to give me a chance to put it back together.

I saw Luce as soon as we got to the headquarters. "I hear the meeting was terrible," he said. I knew damn well where he'd heard that.

"Well, Ross wants him out," he went on. "Do you want me to do it?"

"No, I'll do it," I angrily replied.

I was stunned by Perot's duplicity. He'd decided to fire Riney *before* he'd led me to believe we could sort things out. But I knew he was right. There was no way to square Hal's creative brilliance with Perot's know-nothing penny-pinching. I went back to my office and broke the news to Riney. You don't sugar-coat bad news with pros like Hal. I told him that it just wasn't going to work and that Perot had pulled the plug.

"I don't know how I could have done it any different," he said. "I'm sorry to have let you down." A class act to the end.

"I'm more than a million dollars out of pocket," Riney added. "Do you think he'll pay me?"

"I'll make sure he does," I said, without much assurance I could keep my pledge. (Months later, Riney got back most of his out-of-pocket costs from Perot—but none of his professional fees.)

"Hal, this is the end of the campaign," I said. "This thing is in meltdown. You can tell your kids you were there the day the Perot campaign came apart."

I had no way of knowing it, but Riney's last meeting with Ross turned out to be mine as well. The date was July 8.

I called Sherrie that night in Bali, where she was vacationing after leaving the White House, and told her that, as usual, she'd been right from the start.

"You know, I've finally come to the conclusion this guy is nuts and wouldn't make a good president."

"Then how can you rationalize working for him?"

"Fortunately, he's never going to listen to me or anyone else, so there's no chance he'll ever be president."

In a matter of hours, word got around that Riney had been canned. I knew I was the next target; Squires was leaking on me like a sieve, so I'd stopped taking any press calls. Liz Noyer, a former Bush press aide I'd just recruited as the campaign's press assistant, asked me to make an exception and talk to the *Wall Street Journal.* Squires was trashing Riney when he needed a break from hosing me. Somebody, she pleaded, had to say something nice about Hal. So I called the *Journal* reporter and said: "I'm sorry it didn't work out. Hal Riney is the best in the business." The story, with my quote, ran on July 10.

As soon as he saw it, Perot went berserk, telling Luce and Meyerson I'd leaked the story and had taken sides against him by praising Riney. My loyalty was now suspect, they told me. I knew it was just a matter of time—for the campaign and for me.

Luce certainly had to know I was a dead man. The day the *Journal* piece ran, he invited me to dinner at his house. Tom couldn't have been more solicitous. A teetotaler himself, he even went out and bought a pint of Cutty Sark for me.

It was mainly social. We didn't talk much business, and Tom barely had time to eat. About every fifteen minutes, Perot would call in a swivet. He was batshit over a story ABC had about how he'd broken up an affair between one of his daughters and a college professor. The man was married, but separated from his wife. He also happened to be Jewish. According to press reports, when Ross found out about it, he confronted the professor and threatened to ruin him. He said he didn't want his daughter involved with a Jew. He also set up a surveillance team across from the man's house and had him followed.

When Ross first told me this story, he said ABC was going after his daughter because she'd had an affair with a married man in college. I replied no legitimate news agency cared about some college kid involved with a professor. He then told me he'd had them under surveillance for a while.

"*That's* a story, Ross," I told him. "A *big* story."

I hadn't exaggerated to Riney. By now, the campaign *was* over. Perot's poll ratings had dropped from 39 percent to 17 percent, and his negatives were the worst of anyone in the race.

The day after the *Journal* article, Perot threw away the speech we'd prepared for him and made his boneheaded remarks about "you people" at the NAACP convention in Nashville. He compounded the damage by calling Bernie Shaw of CNN without consulting any of us and doing a follow-up interview that gave the story legs and reinforced his ignorance of racial issues. Perot was now defining his own message in earnest: Wacko.

Ross Perot, Jr., had been in my office the day the poll numbers came in. I explained to him that as bad as the numbers were, they would only get worse when the Democrats started bashing him at their convention. Our only recourse was to get on television with our spots—fast. The problem was that Ross was dithering, and we were out of time. Besides, with Riney gone, we didn't have much in the way of spots.

"You must explain this to my dad," he urged me. I said his father wasn't listening to me or anyone else anymore, and unless someone could get to him, "we're going to hit the cement and not be able to get back up." Ross Junior said he and his dad were having dinner alone that evening, and he asked me for a copy of the polling data.

At 11:00 P.M., the candidate called me at my apartment. "You are not to use my children against me ever again," he ranted. "Your behavior is outrageous and disloyal. You are never to speak to anyone in my family again." He slammed down the phone before I could say anything.

The next morning, Ross Junior called to apologize, adding sheepishly that his father had ordered him not to come into the campaign headquarters again. A very capable and decent man in his mid-thirties was being treated like a wayward schoolboy by his paranoid and domineering father. I said to myself that this ship was sinking faster than the *Titanic,* its captain was nuttier than Captain Queeg, and I'd been a fool to book passage in the first place.

Three days after my dinner with Luce, Perot didn't show for the Monday 8:00 A.M. senior staff meeting. Before Perot's secretary called to say he wasn't coming, Squires and Luce accused me of leaking stories about disarray and morale problems inside the bunker. In this environment, I wasn't talking to anyone—particularly reporters. I told them they were crazy. If they didn't like bad stories, I said, they'd better fasten their seat belts. The Democratic Convention had just convened, and Bill Clinton's boys were going to have a field day with us.

"Leaks aren't why this ship is sinking," I said.

We reassembled at 10:00 A.M. Meyerson said Perot was unhappy with the strategy.

"There has to be another way to do this," he said.

"Mort, there *isn't* another way. I'm not the only guy with a magic formula. This is how you run a campaign."

"Well, Ross just isn't gonna buy into it. Why don't you go back and see if we can put together a scaled-down version."

It was pointless, I knew, but I did the memo. I gave it to them that afternoon.

"We have three options," I told them, summarizing the memo. "We can quit and put together an exit strategy that preserves some credibility. We can continue on the path we're on, but we've lost twelve points in three weeks, and when the Democrats finish with us this week and the Republicans pound on us at their convention, there'll be nothing left of this campaign. Or we can *run* a campaign, Ross can make the damn decisions we've been sending to him, and we can get ourselves back in the game." I didn't need to hear back to know what the answer would be.

We sat around most of the next day, waiting for the kangaroo court to come in with its verdict. The silence was overpowering. By now, any semblance of civility was hanging by a thread. At one point, Hamilton made a crack about my guys leaking like an old tub. I blew up.

"I saw Jimmy Carter on *Crossfire* last night," I said. "He said he'd heard that Hamilton Jordan was very unhappy and was thinking of quitting. I've never talked to Jimmy Carter in my fucking life and I don't think any of my guys have, either. Now where do you suppose he heard that?" Hamilton sheepishly didn't respond.

"All the stories are coming out of the Democratic Convention, Hamilton," I couldn't resist adding. "That's your party last time I looked."

That afternoon, Luce and Meyerson walked into my office and shut the door.

"Ross doesn't want to do it your way," Luce told me.

"Well, there's no sense wasting your money keeping me here," I said. "If you're not going to run a real campaign, you don't need any of us."

Meyerson appeared stricken at the prospect that I'd take a hike instead of saluting. "The problem is that you want to run a traditional campaign," he repeated for what seemed like the hundredth time in the ten weeks I'd known him.

I'd finally had it with these two well-meaning political nitwits. "I don't want to run a traditional campaign," I shouted, "I just want to run a fucking *campaign*! You go on television, you tell your message, you identify your voters, you get them to the polls, you have debates. This is what you do in any campaign."

"Well," Luce said, "there has to be another solution." As usual, they couldn't tell me what that might be. We had a candidate with no clue who wouldn't decide anything, and two water carriers with empty buckets.

After they left, I assembled my staff. "This thing is over," I told them. "I'm sure tomorrow's my last day."

The next day, Wednesday, July 15, the morning papers were filled with stories about the disarray in Dallas. I was wondering what the morning staff meeting would be like when my assistant Susie Farris told me it had been canceled but Luce and Meyerson would like to take me to lunch. We went to a nearby Tex-Mex joint. The coup de grâce was at hand.

"This thing is just not going to work," Luce said, handing me the Luger.

"Fine, I'll get out of here. What about my people?"

"He wants them all gone, too. All the professionals."

I tried to make them understand that no new "professionals" would be stupid enough to sign up as replacements after word of this debacle got around.

"He doesn't want any professionals," Luce said. "He thinks you guys are the problem. He wants to go back to an all-volunteer campaign."

"Ross never trusted you," Meyerson chimed in. "He thought you were part of the Republican dirty tricks squad. He's just gotten extremely paranoid in the last week that you've been sent down here to destroy this campaign."

By now, I was beside myself. "I've been working sixteen hours a day trying to make this thing work," I exploded. I could tell my blood pressure was rising. "It's my guys' plans that aren't being acted upon. *I'm* not the one sitting around on my butt not making the decisions. It's the Big Little Man who can't cut it, and you're his co-conspirators." I took a quick breath and plunged ahead.

"I've walked away from a party I spent twenty years helping to build because I thought this guy could change the system. And let me remind you that I didn't fucking volunteer to come down here—you recruited me. How can this guy be so stupid as to think I'm trying to sabotage his campaign? I have no future."

"We talked about that," Meyerson replied, "and he thinks maybe the CIA put you on a contract for life." Perot's theory was that as a former head of the CIA, George Bush knew how to do these things and had put me on a lifetime CIA retainer to cause Perot trouble. Even by Perot's goofball standards, this was absurd. Perot's crack investigators had discovered I'd been married twice, but they apparently hadn't learned just how deep I was in the Bush family doghouse. If George Bush *had* approached the CIA about me, it would have been to put out a different kind of contract.

My anger steadily rising, I told them even the best CIA and KGB operatives combined couldn't have done a better job sabotaging the campaign than Perot and the two of them had. "This is fucking nuts. I don't have the stomach to eat," I said. "Let's get out of here." The inmates really *had* taken over the asylum. I wasn't so angry about being fired, because I'd pretty much forced the issue, but I was furious with myself for being suckered by such rank amateurs.

I walked back to the headquarters, gathered my team, gave them the news, and told them Luce had promised to take care of them financially. Then I went to see Jordan, who already knew all about it. I asked if he was going out with me.

"Well," he replied sheepishly, "he wants me to stay." He confessed that he didn't want to be run off with the rest of us and was about to see Perot.

Everything had come full circle: Hamilton had been hiding under his bed for the better part of a month, and now he wanted to stay on as a Potemkin campaign manager to make me the fall guy. What little respect I had left for the guy went right out the window.

Around 2:30 P.M., Hamilton reported on his meeting with Perot, who'd assured him none of this had been his fault. He wasn't going to do it our way, but he wanted Jordan to stay on. "Do whatever the fuck you want to do," I said, and walked out.

Shortly thereafter, I was visited by Perot's son-in-law, Clay Mulford. Clay was out of his element, but had become the in-house prick. He had a nervous smile that looked like someone had stuck a coat hanger in his mouth. He was always smiling at the wrong moments—like now. He handed me a sealed envelope. Inside was what lawyers call a confidentiality agreement. During Watergate, they called it hush money.

When Perot hired me, I'd asked for a one-year contract. "I'm not giving any contracts," Luce told me he'd said, "but my word is good."

If I signed this document, I'd get my year's pay, but the price was steep: even for $600,000 severance pay. I had to agree never to discuss Perot or my experiences in Dallas. And I'd need their permission before talking to any reporter about Perot for the rest of my life.

I walked over to Tom Luce's office.

"Tom, this is fucking bullshit."

"Well, that's the deal."

"I'm not going to give up my First Amendment rights for something Perot already promised me. There's no deal. I didn't come here for your fucking money."

I was paid for the month of June. Perot still owes me for two weeks in July. Most of my staff got two weeks' salary instead of the generous severance they were promised. Maybe the checks are in the mail.

A couple of lawyers told me later that I had a strong lawsuit. Several big names even offered to take my case for free just for the opportunity to get a shot at Perot. But I knew any victory would be Pyrrhic. "I have one hundred sixty lawyers working full time for me," Perot had boasted to me once. "If anybody wants to sue me, they'll earn their money." I didn't want to be dragged through the courts for two years and get paid less than my legal fees.

And I hadn't done this for the money. I really thought Perot could make a difference. Ironically, he did. He made Americans even more cynical about our crazy political process.

I don't fault Luce entirely for behaving poorly at the end. I was told by several staffers that he left the headquarters later that day in tears after being verbally abused by the Little Emperor. Tom's weak, but he's a decent guy. Like most everyone around Perot, he deserved better.

At my 4:00 P.M. press conference, I didn't say what I really thought about the king and his court jesters. If there's anything I've learned over thirty years in politics, it's that you always take the high road out of town.

"Changing the grass-roots movement into a full presidential campaign has caused some difference of opinion," I said, "and I have decided it is in the best interest of the campaign and the movement that I resign effective today.

"I continue to believe in the basic ideals of the movement and of the Perot candidacy and I wish Mr. Perot well. Ross Perot and his people have treated me fairly."

I also said I'd enjoyed working with Hamilton, Tom, and Mort, and wished them "the very best." The omission of Jim Squires's name was definitely not an oversight. The guy was a devious bastard.

As I was leaving, a CNN reporter asked me if I had any regrets.

"My biggest regret is I now have to listen to my wife for the next thirty years telling me I told you so."

I took my staff to dinner that night and picked up the tab. The mood was a lot less funereal than you'd expect under the circumstances. The truth is, we were all so relieved to have had our life sentences commuted, we did a lot more drinking than eating. I was feeling lousy for having dragged down a lot of folks who deserved better from me. What hurt the most was that nobody would ever know just how capable a team we'd assembled on the fly. It would have given either Bush or Clinton a run for their money.

There were plenty of toasts, and even a few tears. I especially wanted to say something to the kids on my staff, the gofers who picked us up at the airport, took care of our laundry, did our filing, and in a lot of other small ways kept us all sane.

"This will probably be my last campaign," I said in my toast. "Don't let it be yours. The future belongs to you. Please don't be discouraged. This campaign proved there's a place for vision and dreams in this business. If you want to change the system, you can. Don't give up because of what's happened here."

I was at my apartment packing the next morning when Joe Canzeri, my scheduling and advance guy, called to say Perot was on television. I turned on the set and was stunned to hear him drop out of the race.

In a way, I was relieved. It was all over for everybody, not just me and my guys. I was also right. I knew the guy didn't have the guts to stay in when the bullets started flying. I wondered if he wanted to repeat his little lecture about campaigns not being like war now. After the press conference, I walked across the street to headquarters and into Hamilton's office. He seemed dazed.

"Did you know?" he asked.

"I quit yesterday," I reminded him. "You're the campaign manager."

"I walked in here this morning thinking I was the campaign manager," he said, "and now I learn it's over."

I had absolutely no sympathy. The day before, he'd been prepared to stay on and hang me out to dry. His reward for that was he got to stay twelve hours longer than the rest of us. He also got to tell the press that as campaign manager he found out Perot had quit from CNN like everybody else in America.

As Perot's press conference ended, a squad of Ross wannabes—bad haircuts, white shirts, polyester ties, cell phones—fanned out through the headquarters. Each of my staff was assigned a personal storm trooper watching their every move. Amazingly, none of our computer passwords worked any longer.

Joe Canzeri walked down from his office at the other end of the floor swaggering like a Nazi officer.

"Zee trains for Auschwitz over zis vay," Canzeri barked. "You vill all obey orders!"

I went back to my office to gather up my belongings, my personal escort at the ready. Squires told *The Washington Post* that I cried in my office. It was a total fabrication, the usual from Squires. I shed no tears. But I did recall an exchange with Perot that first Sunday afternoon forty-six days earlier.

"Ross, don't do this if you're not serious about it. All those people who see you as a savior will be even more disenchanted with the system if you let them down."

"I'm not gonna let anybody down," he said.

I had a clear conscience. I'd given it my best shot. I took Perot's abrupt withdrawal as a personal vindication. In the end, Ross Perot talked a good game, but he wasn't serious. *Newsweek*'s cover story had it right: "Quitter." *Sic semper tyrannis.*

I did less due diligence on Ross Perot than any candidate I've ever worked for. I should have read the books about Perot. The more I learned about him, the less I liked him. When it was over, I read some of those books and found them extraordinarily accurate. But even if I had known more about him, I wanted to be a player again so badly that I probably would have done it anyway.

There's no doubt in my mind that until he tossed it away, he had a legitimate shot at being elected. The country was absolutely ready for an outsider, and his message had great resonance. At one point, he was at 39 percent in the polls. If our campaign had done anything right, he could have finished in the mid-30s. As it was, we did nothing right, and he still finished with 19. The potential existed for 40 percent or more, which was good enough to win. Perot had promised his beloved volunteers "a world-class campaign"; instead, he gave them the world's worst.

A couple of years after the election, I ran into Mort Meyerson at a business conference in Colorado. "I've known Ross Perot for many years," Meyerson told me. "The Ross Perot I saw during that period was a total stranger, a man I never knew."

Perhaps. I choose to believe that the Ross Perot I encountered was the real Perot. There's no doubt he's done a lot of remarkable things in his life. He's a natural leader, a skilled communicator, and a wonderful father with a marvelous wife and beautiful family. But he's also an extremely dangerous demagogue with delusions of adequacy who would have been a disaster in the White House.

A good president has to be secure with himself, and Perot is insecurity incarnate. Presidents need to be tough, and Perot can't take a punch. And he has no clue about how Washington works. As our issues guy, John White, now Bill Clinton's Deputy Secretary of Defense, told me in frustration one day in Dallas, "Do you know how little this guy knows? He knows nothing about anything in government."

"It's not going to matter," I replied, "because he'll never be running the government."

He has zero appreciation for the constitutional role of Congress; from day one, he would have been at war with Capitol Hill. His government would have been a managerial disaster. The presidency is the premier inspirational job in the country, not the top management job. Perot is chemically incapable of delegating authority. One week he'd play Secretary of Commerce, the next Secretary of the Interior, routinely making decisions assistant secretaries should be handling. He'd have been a little dictator, ruling over a government in chaos. A Perot presidency would have set back the cause of an independent presidential candidacy for a generation.

In the halcyon days, when we were still having civilized conversations about "message," I'd told Perot that I wanted him to tape the words "KOOK" and "HOPE" on his bathroom mirror.

"Every single day," I told him, "your opponents are going to make you into a *kook*. If they do that, or if anything you do makes you look like a kook, you lose. You have to be the candidate of hope. If you can keep people focusing on *hope*, you can win this thing." In the end, he did exactly the reverse. The candidate of hope had taken the "KOOK" label and stuck it to his forehead.

That's not to say he didn't provide valuable service to the country he loves so much. Like Ronald Reagan, he offered a message of hope to voters disenchanted with traditional politics. More than any other politician, he educated Americans on the evils of budget deficits and campaign spending. And he showed that in an era of political fragmentation, an independent candidacy *can* be successful. Ross Perot proved himself to be the wrong man at the right time. The country, happily, is clearly a better place for that.

Incidentally, he's still Rossing. He told Larry King after the election that he barely knew me.

IF THE PEROT campaign went up in flames, the Bush effort was more like one of those underground mine fires that smolder along without anyone realizing that the ground is about to give out beneath them. In a little over two years, the hero of Desert Storm went from 89 percent in a Gallup Poll to 38 percent on election day. You've got to be worse than bad to fall that far that fast.

From my unenviable position in universal exile, I was able to watch the rest of the campaign play out with some detachment, if not equanimity. Picking over the smoking wreckage, I could see a lot of things clearly.

Without a doubt, the 1992 Bush campaign was the worst performance by an incumbent president in modern political history. Bush came stumbling out of the Republican Convention, and he never regained his balance. A president who's never been a strong campaigner was backed up by the weakest political team in memory. The cast of characters was a bunch of well-meaning guys who hadn't a clue how to win an election.

It's hard to believe, but Sam Skinner was even worse than John Sununu as White House chief of staff. Sam was far less arrogant than Sununu, but not nearly as competent in the job. He was hopelessly in over his head. Bush lost confidence in him almost immediately, and finally replaced him with Jim Baker.

There's no nicer man in politics than former Commerce Secretary Bob Mosbacher, and no better fundraiser. Bob was the first general chairman of the Bush campaign committee, and had a finger on the pulse of the business community and the economy, but his words of caution fell on deaf ears.

Bob Teeter was totally miscast as campaign chairman. Bob is a seasoned, savvy professional. If I ever do a campaign again, I'd want him on my team. But he's a terrible manager, and couldn't make decisions or crack skulls, which is what an effective chairman has to do.

Either of the Bobs should have been the Republican national chairman, where they could have kept the party faithful inspired and given the counsel Bush might not have wanted to hear but needed.

Fred Malek, the campaign manager, had been a Nixon administration aide. A former Marriott hotel executive, he was a good manager but lacked the political experience. For the most part, the rest of the senior campaign staff was a joke. The line that says it all was uttered by Marty Puris, an advertising superstar who, like so many other good men and women, deserved better from their association with Bush-Quayle '92: "Who do I have to sleep with to get *off* this campaign?"

It may have all looked good on paper, but it didn't work. But it hardly mattered who ran the campaign; it was clear to me that George Bush was going to lose—and lose big—the day the convention opened in Houston on August 17.

That was the last best chance to get back in the game for the campaign, but it was blown by convention director Craig Fuller, possibly the most overrated guy in Republican political circles. Fuller and his team should have been headquartered down the road at NASA, because they spent their time on another planet. They actually thought Pat Buchanan's fire-and-brimstone speech was a political plus. They lost control of the convention because they were too busy placating Buchanan to think about a message for Bush. The message that came out of Houston was that the party of Abraham Lincoln was a mean-spirited bunch of bigots. It was the worst-run political convention I've ever seen.

After Houston, George Bush was dead in the water. People had tuned him out, written him off. His only shot at redemption was to do something that would make the American public give him a second look. There were several things he could do to make voters believe he'd learned his lessons in the first term and would be a different president in a second. But the most important one was to dump Dan Quayle.

He could have replaced Quayle with just about anyone of stature—Dick Cheney, Colin Powell, Jack Kemp, Bob Dole, even his friend Jim Baker. The mere act of change would have been sufficient to make the point. The entire country knew Quayle had been a mistake. Psychologically, Bush would have signaled what politicians hate to do most—admit they've blown a big one. It would have been an enormous plus for his prospects. And the party would have gone along without a whimper. Senator Bob Kasten of Wisconsin, a Quayle friend, told me that he and several other senators were prepared to approach Quayle and tell him he must withdraw from the ticket for the good of the party. That message was passed along to the president, who refused to authorize the mission.

I think George Bush would have been willing to dump Quayle at the end, but only if Quayle came to him. And Quayle was shrewd enough to preempt Bush by going into the Oval Office and telling him the rumors of his demise were everywhere. That forced Bush to announce he was fully behind Quayle. I'm not sure he would have pulled the trigger anyway. He should have—and if he had, he'd probably still be president. In the end, he proved once again that he valued loyalty over competence, and he paid for it. Now they're both out of a job.

By Labor Day, it was all over but the balloting. In desperation, Bush had forced Secretary of State Jim Baker to give up a job he loved and return as White House chief of staff and de facto campaign manager. Bush and Baker are close friends, but it's a love-hate relationship with an incredible competition thrown in. Forty years later, they're still like two kids snapping wet towels in the locker room. It must have been galling for Bush to admit to the world he needed Jimmy to bail him out.

Baker was a definite improvement over Skinner. The trains ran on time, meetings were focused, and decisions actually got made. But Bush was too far gone, and Baker made sure the world knew that by the way he sat on his hands from the moment he left the State Department. Baker is relentless at distancing himself from trouble, and he knew he'd be tarred when his friend went down. The only way to limit the damage was to separate himself symbolically from the Campaign from Hell. So one of the great leakers in Washington, a man so good at schmoozing reporters that he had more media credibility than the President of the United States, never briefed the press, on or off the record. He may as well have worn a sandwich board reading: "DON'T BLAME ME."

The truth of the matter is that Baker *shouldn't* be blamed—except for going AWOL in spirit. One of Baker's closest aides tells the story that not long after returning to the White House in August, Baker told the president that the White House staff and the campaign were hopelessly screwed up. At a minimum, the campaign needed an infusion of professional talent. He suggested bringing in Stu Spencer and me. "I'd rather lose than have that happen," the president reportedly said, and it sure sounds like him.

When Baker persisted, Bush dusted off a favorite line which infuriates Baker: "If you're so smart, Jimmy, how come I'm president and you're on that side of the desk?" At that point, Baker knew it was hopeless and gave up the fight. At that point, it's hard to blame him.

George Bush was the beneficiary of the greatest baton pass in presidential history in 1988, and he and his people tossed it away. The truth is, if Ronald Reagan had picked Jack Kemp as his running mate in 1980, Bush probably wouldn't even have been a delegate to the 1988 convention, much less the nominee.

In the history of the Republican Party, only one of its presidential candidates—William Howard Taft—has drawn a lower percentage of the vote. In 1912, President Taft concluded there was no way he could beat Woodrow Wilson or Teddy Roosevelt, so he essentially stopped campaigning on Labor Day and started packing his belongings. Eight years after inheriting the greatest electoral landslide in history, Bush lost one-third of the Republican base vote. Even Barry Goldwater attracted more support in the Johnson landslide of 1964.

There's no question this dismal showing was partly the result of Ross Perot's candidacy, but the bottom line was that 29 percent of Republican voters refused to support a former chairman of the Republican National Committee. Republicans, not Clinton and Perot, defeated George Bush. If the Republicans who went with Bill Clinton had stuck with Bush, he'd be in the eighth year of his presidency as I write these words. The hero of Desert Storm even lost the veterans' vote to a draft dodger. That may be the greatest indictment of all.

George Bush was an extraordinarily decent man who simply had no business being in the Oval Office. He was even more of an accidental president than Jerry Ford. Neither would ever have been president in their own right if not appointed vice president. He was a competent appointed official who made no waves and a perfectly cast vice president, but he had absolutely no vision, no core ideological values, and no real electoral strengths. In his amiable, slightly eccentric way, he did more than any other Republican to roll back the Reagan Revolution. Worst of all, he gave the country he loved to Bill Clinton.

ROUND 9

BONFIRE OF THE VANITIES

AFTER THE SIX most miserable weeks of my life with Ross Perot, I knew I'd be scrambling to make a living. I'd severed my ties to Sawyer Miller when I left for Dallas, so that door was shut. My new notoriety landed me a few dozen speech bookings over the upcoming six months, but I knew that gravy train wouldn't last. I hoped to put together a public relations consulting firm of my own. I had the contacts and clients to make it work. It wouldn't be as glamorous as the political game, but it's a more respectable living, and you don't take such a beating, either.

I didn't care about getting back in the ring. I wasn't sure where my life was going, but I knew I was done as a political consultant. When I made the decision to go to Perot, it was with the realization that I was signing up for my last campaign. When it blew up, I knew for sure that was the end for me. As it turned out, I was wrong—thanks to Christine Todd Whitman.

In early 1992, Lyn Nofziger had called to ask if I might be willing to lend a hand to Christie Whitman, who was planning to run against New Jersey Governor James Florio in 1993. Lyn had close ties to the Todd family and was an unofficial head-hunter for Christie. I was still in the Bush doghouse, but anxious to keep my hand in the game. I said I was interested, and Christie and I had a couple of conversations. I agreed to sign on as a consultant beginning later in the year.

Then the Perot flirtation intervened. I called her to say I'd decided to go with Ross. "I wish you weren't," she politely replied. I assumed she thought, as did I, that working for Perot was the end of me as a Republican campaign operative.

Much to my amazement, Lyn called shortly after that debacle to say Christie was still interested in having my help. It was a particularly generous gesture on her part given the fact that by then I was an even blacker sheep in her party and mine. If she was willing to stick her neck out for me, I damn sure wanted to help her. Besides, I wanted to prove that Perot notwithstanding I was still good at this game.

We met in her Houston hotel suite during the Republican Convention in August. She teased me about my Perot interlude, but said she was still interested if I was. I said I was, and we agreed to talk further. A couple of weeks later, I met with Christie, her husband John, and Lyn at the Whitman estate in Somerset County. The essence of my advice was that she should expect a tough primary the following June and an even tougher general election. No incumbent New Jersey governor had ever been defeated in a general election, and this one wasn't going down without a fight. I agreed to be her chief strategist and give her two days a week of my time. I also agreed to put her campaign team together and oversee the primary operation. I'd chair Monday morning strategy meetings to set the agenda and schedule for the week. We both agreed I'd keep a low profile to avoid raising the ire of Bush Republicans, whose support she'd need.

My Bush problem aside, she and I made pretty strange bedfellows. Christine Todd Whitman's patrician background couldn't have been more different than mine. She was born to money and power, and married into still more. Christie proudly described herself as a Rockefeller Republican, a term not often used in a party dominated by conservatives.

She was the youngest child of Elinor and Webster Todd; he was a giant in the construction business and New Jersey Republican politics. He'd been the builder for the Rockefeller family. His construction projects included the restoration of Colonial Williamsburg, Rockefeller Center in New York, Newark Airport, and many other public works projects in the Northeast. For more than two decades, Webster Todd controlled the New Jersey Republican Party as its chairman and chief financial benefactor. He was one of the key early backers of Dwight Eisenhower, and counted among his friends every major Republican figure of the past forty years. His daughter had grown up in New Jersey horse country, gone to the best schools, and graduated from Wheaton College in Massachusetts. She'd married John Whitman, an investment banker whose grandfather had been governor of New York.

Christie was one of a long line of New Jersey's privileged classes to serve in state government. She was the female equivalent of George Bush in background, style, philosophy, and temperament.

I quickly learned that keeping a low profile was a good defensive move on my part. The Whitman team was a small-time operation, riddled with problems large and small. The campaign apparatus was basically Christie, her arrogant husband John, and a handful of none-too-professional state operatives. I was able to import some heavier hitters, but even they didn't manage to make much of a dent.

The basic problem was overconfidence. The candidate, her family, and most of her supporters were convinced she couldn't lose—the primary and the governor's mansion were hers, they were certain. They based this false optimism on her surprisingly close showing against Bill Bradley in the 1990 senatorial race. In fact, she'd been a sacrificial lamb, the only candidate crazy enough to run against Bradley. They didn't realize that her narrow loss was not a show of real strength: Disgruntled voters had used her to send a message through Bradley to Jim Florio, telling him they didn't like Florio's tax increases, the largest in state history. That race had given Christie major name identification and a tremendous leg up in the 1993 primary. But she was such a long shot that she hadn't been really scrutinized by the press or attacked by Bradley. Florio wouldn't be so easy. Neither were her two primary challengers, Cary Edwards and Jim Wallwork, who treated her like one of the boys and beat the daylights out of her. As June 8 approached, Whitman was battered and damaged, and her rivals were closing in for the kill. Her own missteps had turned it into a very close race.

As so often happens when a campaign isn't going well, the campaign team gets blamed. But it wasn't the staff's fault the Whitmans had hired illegal aliens as nannies, had a special tax exemption allowing them to pay minimal property taxes on their two palatial estates, or that Christie had missed voting in a local school election the same day she was announcing her education plan, or that as a member of the Somerset Board of Freeholders she'd voted twenty-eight times to raise taxes and double spending.

She was hammered by her opponents and the press for these vulnerabilities. Some of the attacks weren't fair, but that's the campaign biz. We could have counterattacked and knocked both opponents back to the Stone Age, but she wanted to focus on issues. To her credit, she didn't want to run a negative campaign, and resisted my counsel to go on the offensive.

A week before the election, I finally put the gun to her head.

"If you don't let me attack Cary Edwards in this last week," I said, "you're going to lose this thing. You don't have to attack him personally, but we've got to fight back on television."

She relented at last and we fired back. The commercial we aired wouldn't win any Atwater awards; its message was that there wasn't a dime's worth of difference between Florio and Edwards, a moderate Republican. The truth of the matter is the same spot could have been used on Christie. There wasn't much philosophical distance between her and Florio, either. But the ad got the job done; Christie won the primary, getting 40 percent of the vote to Edwards's 33.

WITH THE PRIMARY behind us, the real work lay ahead. But first the Whitman brain trust, which included her husband and her brother Dan, had to get in their licks. They promptly invoked the mantra of most successful candidates: "If it weren't for us, the staff would have lost this thing." Instead of a relieved thank you to the folks who bailed her out after she'd made almost every available blunder possible, Christie cashiered them wholesale. The campaign manager, pollster, media team, and press secretary were fired, and they probably would have canned me as well if they hadn't worried that would make a bigger story.

They also needed me to do their dirty work. I got to fire the team I'd hired. These were first-rate people, and I resented it. The media team, Russo-Marsh, showed their talent a year later by helping Senator Al D'Amato come from behind to win reelection. In 1994, they helped George Pataki upset Mario Cuomo. Pollster Dick Wirthlin and I had our differences in the 1984 Reagan campaign, but he's one of the country's premier numbers-crunchers. She also asked me to fire her longtime chief of staff, Kayla Bergeron, whom I liked and thought had the best feel for what was going on in the state.

In the end, instead of firing me, the Whitmans simply froze me out. I don't think I talked to Christie four times over the entire summer of 1993. My Monday morning strategy meetings were canceled. If I had any pride, I would have packed my bags and walked on the Whitman Amateur Hour. But I owed Christie. If she hadn't come to me, I never would have done another campaign. Then she'd stuck by me after the Perot fiasco and took a lot of heat for it. With all the baggage I was already toting around, walking away from this race would sink me forever as a Republican consultant. And I'll be honest—I was especially excited at the prospect of going *mano a mano* with Bill Clinton's Ragin' Cajun, James Carville, who was running Florio's campaign. Besides, I liked Christie personally, and I knew before this race was over she'd need all the help she could get. Somebody had to save her from her husband and brother, who were locked in a close race to see who'd get the prize as the most pompous, abrasive, and cocky asshole in New Jersey.

The campaign was taken over by Dan Todd, a Montana rancher who'd moved back to New Jersey to help his little sister. Danny had never managed a real campaign, but that didn't stop him. Like his brother-in-law, he thought he knew everything there was to know about politics. He didn't.

Danny wasn't a bad guy, but he definitely wasn't cut out to manage people or a modern campaign. He was very secretive and refused to delegate. He locked himself in his office all day and was seldom seen by the staff. He controlled the schedule, tried to write her speeches, and micromanaged every other minor detail in the campaign.

Todd saw this race as a means to resurrect his own political aspirations. He'd served one term in the New Jersey state assembly before his father called in a chit with his pal Dick Nixon and got his oldest, ne'er-do-well son a second-tier political job in Washington. After serving without distinction, Dan went off to Montana to run his ranch and squander his inheritance. Now, he'd get his kid sister elected governor, become state party chairman like his father before him, then run for statewide office himself; or so the plan went.

As I watched from my vantage point away from the action, the summer and early fall campaign was a disaster. Dan and his minions were truly the gang who couldn't shoot straight. Every mistake that could be made was. Example: When she should have been working the vacation crowds at state beaches, Christie went off on an ill-advised ten-day biking trip to Idaho. A week after the primary, Christie had been neck-and-neck with Florio, but by mid-September she'd slipped far behind.

She wasn't a bad campaigner, but she wasn't turning on crowds or even attracting them. She was putting thousands of miles on her car driving around the state, winning converts one by one. Meanwhile, Florio's campaign was outmaneuvering and outcampaigning us.

I'd watched and grudgingly admired Jim Florio for a long time. He was a member of that huge freshman class of House Democrats swept in by angry voters in the election of 1974 and known forever after as the "Watergate Babies." I first met him in 1975, when I was working congressional relations for the Nixon Department of Transportation. He'd been named to the energy and commerce commit-tee, and eventually chaired the subcommittee with oversight over the nation's railroads. He also authored the 1980 Superfund legislation to clean up America's toxic waste dumps. He was a young, handsome rising star in the Democratic liberal wing.

In 1981, when I was in the Reagan White House, he lost the New Jersey governorship to Tom Kean by 1,797 votes. Over the next sev-eral years, I watched him fine-tune his organization for another try. He studied and meticulously corrected every mistake his 1981 cam-paign had made. In 1989, he became governor with 61 percent of the vote. Florio was intense, hardworking, calculating, and ambitious. I was sure that Drumthwacket, the governor's residence near Prince-ton, wasn't the only white mansion he had in his sights. The gover-norship of New Jersey is the country's most powerful. The governor is the only elected state official. He appoints the attorney general and all other statewide officers. Such power in a single executive is an even greater leg up toward reelection than the normal advantages of incumbency.

Our life stories were remarkably similar. We were both Catholics, and had lived in public housing. Our fathers were shipyard workers. We'd both boxed for the Navy. He went to Trenton State College, I went to Chico State College. He's tough, and a loner. I'm also a loner, and some people think I'm tough. The difference between us is obvious: We both started out as Kennedy Democrats, but he still carries the flame.

I could relate to Florio's scrappiness, and admired what he had accomplished from modest beginnings. Now I was trying to end his political career.

For all his personal appeal and vote-getting ability, Florio had handed me the gun in 1990, when he'd broken his pledge not to raise taxes. Practically overnight, the largest tax increase in New Jersey history had made Florio a profoundly unpopular governor. I knew he could be had. But it wouldn't be easy. Florio knew he'd need top talent to win reelection. The man he hired was none other than James Carville.

Carville had been the principal strategist for President Clinton's 1992 victory. As a result, he was now the hottest political consultant in the country. He and his fiancée Mary Matalin sold their memoirs for $1 million. In a single year, he and Mary pulled in almost another million on the speech circuit. Like most consultants, Carville had toiled in the business for a long time with limited success before winning the 1991 Pennsylvania Senate race for Harris Wofford and hitting the jackpot with Clinton.

A week after Clinton's election, Florio had hired Carville and his partner Paul Begala as the general consultants for his 1993 reelection campaign, creating glee in the Democratic camp and sending a shock down every Republican spine. Carville knew the state well, having run Frank Lautenberg's decisive 1988 Senate victory over Pete Dawkins, the former West Point All-American, Rhodes Scholar, and Army general.

If the Whitman-Florio contest was a clash of cultures, the Rollins-Carville face-off was the battle of the super-consultants. James and I weren't doing anything to hype it, but never before had two high-profile consultants who'd each helped elect a president gone head to head.

It's fair to say I've attained a certain celebrity in the political world. Such status usually results not from how good you are but from your visibility in the media, especially television. There are plenty of consultants better than either Carville or me who just don't have our visibility. During the late eighties and early nineties, Lee Atwater and I were probably the most visible Republican operatives in the country. In addition to having managed successful presidential campaigns, we were colorful, tough, and quotable. Carville now fills that role for the Democrats. He's just more eccentric than either Lee or me.

The Florio team not only had Carville and Begala but also some of the best political talent in New Jersey. Led by campaign manager Jim Andrews and press secretary Jo Astrid Glading, they'd turned this race around. Carville and his troops managed to take a referendum on the most unpopular governor in recent years and turn it into a campaign about Whitman and our screwups. The question they'd skillfully planted in voters' minds was whether Christie was up to the job. In tough coverage and editorials, the press was answering it for Florio with a resounding no. Their strategy was simple: If you think Florio's so bad, just look at her. And it was working.

The Florio campaign was relentless. Every time we made a move, they'd counterattack. They had a video crew dog Christie everywhere she went. They'd tape what she said, and analyze and rebut it before we arrived at the next stop. They obviously had spies in our campaign, because they knew our every move. At one point, Carville somehow got a confidential memo off my desk and released it as a Florio press release. The memo contained suggestions for tactics we should use in the closing weeks of the campaign. Getting inside our heads and distracting us was a major part of their efforts. That was working, too.

While Christie was losing ground, brother Dan was irritating every Republican in the state. Not to be outdone, her high-strung husband was driving everyone else in the campaign nuts. John Whitman was a multimillionaire investment banker who was running his own prosperous business from an office at Pontefract (Broken Bridge, in French), the family farm. He'd read the morning newspapers, go batshit, and call Christie's press secretary Carl Golden to holler because Florio was getting better press. Then he'd show up later at campaign headquarters and second-guess what everybody was doing. Even worse, he was messing with the candidate's head every night, when she'd come home wiped from a long day on the campaign trail. After a bottle of expensive French wine, John would start in on her about how the campaign was screwed up and why she wasn't doing this or that to counteract Florio. Danny was also living in their house, along with three or four other young campaign workers. It was like a frat house. Christie never got to escape the campaign. After a while, her nerves started to fray.

Mine were intact, but my frustration level was rising. On August 19, I sent Christie a memo asking her to define my role more precisely. I wrote that I felt "totally detached from this campaign since the primary and . . . totally underutilized." I didn't want to add to her troubles; I thought I could alleviate them.

"I have never been in a campaign where I've had so little control or felt so out of the decision loop, but yet taken such public blame. But that's politics."

I offered her five options for my services, ranging from greater involvement to volunteer status. We agreed on a middle course: I'd move to New Jersey after Labor Day and travel with her as a personal counsellor.

In early September, Carville also moved to New Jersey full time and began an all-out assault. Despite their growing lead, Florio's team knew the numbers would eventually close, and whoever made the last mistake would likely lose. So they kept up the pressure. They couldn't wage the campaign on Florio's big-tax record; instead, they cleverly zeroed in on making voters believe Christie was no more than a rich dilettante who, despite her distinguished political pedigree, simply wasn't up to the job.

Our campaign reached its nadir on the morning of Monday, September 27, when the *New York Times* ran a front-page poll showing Florio kicking our butts 51–30. Our own polls had us seriously behind, but not by that wide a margin. Panic erupted within the campaign and state party circles. Our phones were ringing off the hook with complaints. The finance people, who thought we'd blown it, weren't interested in raising any more money. Republican legislators also on the ballot began to think Christie was jeopardizing their races. The brunt of all this anger was aimed at Danny. That afternoon, I typed out an eyes-only six-page memo designed to make Christie understand she was on the verge of kissing it goodbye.

"This campaign is at the critical point and if drastic steps are not taken immediately, you will lose and possibly by a far greater margin than ever anticipated," I wrote. "The old Japanese proverb, 'Let's fix the problem, not the blame,' is appropriate to our situation."

I laid out the steps she'd have to take immediately to get back in the race. The first would be the toughest—ditching her brother as the day-to-day manager. "As painful as this may be to you, no decision in this campaign (or if you get elected governor) will ever be more difficult or critical." I also recommended major changes in scheduling, press, surrogate, and fund-raising operations.

"Every campaign makes mistakes. The most serious one is that we have let Florio set the terms of debate." We could still win it, I told her, if we ran "a near-perfect campaign," which meant getting the focus back on Florio and his lousy record as governor. "We must make every voter fearful of four more years of Florio," I wrote, adding that it would mean taking some risks on our part.

That evening, Christie went to Washington for a fundraiser at the home of her sister Kate. The next morning, several advisers met in her sister's kitchen to review the bidding. I wasn't the only one at the table suggesting Danny had to be replaced.

I'd offered to drive her to the Holocaust Museum, which she wanted to visit as a gesture to New Jersey's Jewish voters. On the twenty-minute ride from Northwest to the museum, she read my memo. I told her that it made the most sense for me to succeed Danny. It was too late to bring in anyone new, and I already knew all the players. I didn't want to take over day-to-day management, but there was nobody else to do it.

"At this point," I told her, "you've got to do something bold in order to get people to take a second look at your campaign. Changing managers will make everyone think something new is happening. Danny can't cut it, and if you don't replace him you're both going down the tubes."

Christie looked stricken. She knew I was right, but it was painful medicine.

"Isn't there any other way to do it with Danny?"

"Christie, if you want to win, Danny's gotta go."

She wanted me to tell Danny.

"Christie, I can't fire your brother. You've got to do it."

"All right, I'll take care of it."

The other thing we had to do, I told her, was go negative—and fast. To her credit, that wasn't the campaign she wanted to run. Now she had no choice. The Florio team's barrage of negative spots had worked; voters now viewed her more unfavorably than a very unpopular opponent.

Two days later, I was the campaign manager, although she continued to avoid confirming it to the press for a day or two longer. Inside the campaign there was new energy. I had thirty-three days to put this derailed train back on track. It wasn't going to be easy, but I still felt it could be done.

I'm not a particularly good detail man. My skill is getting talented people around a table, delegating responsibility, and making quick decisions. There are many people much better at this game, but I can lead a good team as well as anyone and make sure their talents are used to the fullest. And now I had a first-rate bunch of professionals at my disposal.

Mike Murphy was our media consultant—a brash, fun-loving, and extremely talented young man who had a knack for getting the best out of Christie. Ed Goeas and Dave Sackett, our pollsters from the Tarrance Group, had worked New Jersey GOP races for years. They proved to be the best I've ever worked with. Carl Golden was a top-notch press secretary who had worked eight years for former Governor Tom Kean. I moved Jamie Moore, a rising young star, over from the state party to be my deputy. I needed him to cover the little stuff that kills you if it doesn't get done. We may not have had as much high-priced talent as Florio or as much bench strength, but the first team was as good as any in the game.

First we had to alter the negative psychological mind-set that had infected the entire state party structure after the September 27 *Times* poll. On October 2, the campaign summoned the cream of the Jersey GOP to a pep rally at the Princeton Hyatt. The audience included all the county chairmen and most of Christie's biggest financial boosters. We unveiled Murphy's newest attack ad, which showed a clip of Florio saying he wasn't going to raise taxes and opining that he "may be the worst governor New Jersey's ever had." Our message was simple: We're back, and it's doable. Don't bail out on us.

Unbeknownst to me, James Carville was up to his usual mind games. He and several of his Florio pals were holding forth with reporters at a mezzanine bar a few steps away from our closed-door meeting. As usual, Carville was spinning like crazy. He claimed he'd be more nervous if I were the candidate, not the campaign manager.

"The spokes change, the flat tire is still there," Carville drawled dismissively.

As our meeting concluded, somebody told me about Carville's ambush. Time for a little psy-war of our own. I walked over to the bar and shook Carville's hand. He was wearing a blue United Steelworkers jacket, and seemed a little nervous that I'd joined his parade. We sparred with reporters for four or five minutes, trading respectful comments about our patrons.

As I walked from the bar, a reporter asked me if Whitman was still a viable candidate.

"Sure she's still viable," I replied. "But if you're asking me the same question ten days from now, she won't be." I had exactly thirty days left to prove I wasn't just spinning like Carville.

MOST PEOPLE DON'T know what a campaign manager actually does. As the day-to-day operations officer, you work from a twelve-by twelve-foot windowless office that becomes the campaign's command center. You sit in there alone and make decisions based on information others feed you. You read polls. You talk on the phone for hours on end. And all day long, people come in and tell you how fucked up things are. The candidate calls in from the road and usually complains that the last event was totally screwed up, or the crowd wasn't big enough. Inside your command bubble, you don't see how the candidate's performing or the crowd's reacting. Everything you do is based on the input of others. But in the end, it's only you in that small room. You alone make the tactical decisions that win or lose the race. You alone make the calls on how to spend millions of dollars. You alone figure out where the candidate will or won't appear. You alone decide which commercials to run. And every call you make is picked apart as fast as you make it—by the candidate, the spouse, the fundraisers, party officials, key supporters, and most of all the media. You constantly field questions like, "Why didn't he come to my event?" "Why didn't she do my fundraiser?" "How could you run that stupid commercial?"

The most important qualities a campaign manager must have are a sense of confidence and an ability to make quick decisions. Everyone else in the operation watches the manager. If he (or she) is decisive and projects confidence, everyone else will follow. If he's downbeat, the troops pick it up in an instant, and morale craters.

My private view of reality was a bit less bullish than my game face projected. I hadn't been in day-to-day control of a campaign since Reagan's in 1984 and wasn't looking forward to the task. But I felt confident enough about my own skills and the quality of my team. I was reasonably sure we could get Whitman back into contention. With a month to go, I figured the odds were 60–40 that we'd lose, but by a much closer margin than anyone suspected.

It was a tough campaign because the other side was so good. I've never faced a team that responded as quickly or attacked as ruthlessly as the Florio–Carville–Begala team. They seemed to anticipate our every move.

Meanwhile, John Whitman was becoming more of a pain in the ass by the day—especially to the candidate. He'd almost unnerved her at the first campaign debate, which took place in a Trenton television studio on October 6. Five minutes before air time, Florio approached the podium with papers in his hand. John freaked out and came running up from the back of the stage in a state of total panic.

"There are to be no notes!" he screamed. "He's cheating. There are to be no notes!"

Christie was nervous to begin with, but being forced to hose down her hysterical husband moments before debating the governor live in front of millions of viewers wasn't part of the preflight checklist. Mike Murphy and I tried to get John to chill out, to no avail. He rushed up to his wife with a stack of briefing notes.

"Goddamnit," he shouted, "if *he* can have notes, so will she!"

I worried that this idiotic distraction might unnerve the candidate. But Christie's one cool lady, and once the debate started she really rose to the occasion, despite her bonkers husband. She more than held her own with Florio. In debates, it's always critical for the challenger to come off as the equal of an incumbent. Our polling that night showed that viewers thought she was concerned, knowledgeable, and confident. Christie had passed a critical psychological threshold: She looked like a governor.

At the end of the debate, she challenged Florio to take a pledge to stop the negative campaigning and "stop the distortions and half-truths that have been projected on the airwaves about me. . . . We need to change both the way we govern and the way we campaign. You talk about your record and what you're going to do in the future, and I'll talk about my economic plan."

Florio and Carville ignored her invitation, as we knew they would. If he'd accepted Christie's challenge, we were sunk; we had to run negative attacks to get back in the race.

With three weeks to go, the Florio campaign was about to add yet another dimension to their attack campaign: the candidate's husband. When Christie ran for the Senate in 1990, she'd released her taxes for 1988 and 1989. This time she'd released her taxes for 1991 and 1992, but the Florio campaign insisted on seeing the returns for 1990. The Whitmans refused, breaking one of the cardinal rules of damage control: If you've got nothing to hide, don't behave like you do. Given a wonderful opening, Florio's camp started implying that John had been involved in shady Wall Street deals. They also told reporters he'd been involved with Ivan Boesky, the convicted Wall Street inside trader. It was all rumor, but it was stirring up a fuss.

We got word that Florio was preparing to hold a press conference to attack John and demand the missing 1990 tax information. They had an ad prepared to run that same evening going public with their vague charges.

On the morning of October 12, Christie asked me to talk to John. In no time, the tension that had been growing between the two of us came to a head. In a meeting with a group of senior aides and supporters, I pleaded with him once again to release the information. I didn't want another negative issue distracting us, I said, warning that this kind of attack, whether true or not, would only raise more doubts.

"Where do you draw the line?" he replied. "If you give them this, they'll keep coming back for more."

"This will defuse the issue once and for all."

"Goddamnit, they'll just demand more stuff next week."

"This is *the* issue, John. If you want to spend the rest of this campaign talking about it, we'll never get this thing back on track."

At first he'd argued it was a simple matter of principle with him. But as he began to absorb the gist of my message—that he was about to torpedo the campaign—he turned personal.

"Your strategy hasn't worked so far," he said, "and your advice hasn't been any damn good."

I bolted out of my chair, swatting my coffee off the conference table in a total rage.

"Goddamnit, John, I'm the only thing standing between your wife and the abyss. I don't spend nights on a fancy farm with a tennis court. I stay at a forty-four-dollar-a-night room at the Ramada. If you think you can do any better, you take this fucking campaign over."

I completely lost my cool and came embarrassingly close to punching him out. My behavior was totally inappropriate—especially because it took place in front of about a dozen onlookers who watched in stunned silence.

John asked everyone else to leave, and after we traded apologies, we went back at it, absent the histrionics. We each made clear just exactly what we couldn't stand about the other, which took longer than either of us wanted, but seemed to make us both feel a lot better. After fifteen minutes, we agreed on a truce we both knew wouldn't last a minute longer than the campaign: He agreed to my request that he stay away from the headquarters for the rest of the campaign.

I didn't tell him that his constant bitching had driven his wife so nuts that a few days earlier she'd called me and plaintively said, "You've got to get John off my back." What I said was that she needed his support and loving care more than ever now.

"John, your job from here on out is to be your wife's greatest cheerleader," I said. "You've got to become her comfort zone. When she gets home every night, you have to throw your arms around her and tell her how fabulous she's been doing. The single most important thing in this race is whether she performs in a confident manner the rest of the way. If she doesn't, she'll lose. If she does, she'll win this thing." To his credit, he was a very supportive husband for Christie the rest of the way.

Campaigns are always murder on spouses. There's seldom a defined role for them. They hurt when their partner is attacked and usually want to fight back. They're so personally wrapped up in the race that they're always looking for someone to blame for every stumble in the road. For a manager, dealing with the candidate is a full-time job and more, but dealing with a candidate *and* an unhappy, aggressive spouse is an impossible task.

At the last possible moment, John Whitman did the right thing for his wife. In a matter of hours, we released the 1990 returns. They showed, like his previously released returns, that he'd made a shitload of money and paid plenty in taxes. So what? Florio's press conference was a bust. They couldn't run their tough tax commercial, and lost an issue they'd planned to exploit for an entire week of media spots. Even worse, they'd lost their momentum for the first time in the race. It was a crucial setback for them, and the turning point for our campaign.

On Wednesday, October 20, a *New York Times* poll showed Florio ahead by only fifteen points. The next day, we put Christie on a bus and toured the state. *The Wheels of Change,* as we named it, was highly visible but protective. Christie was comfortable with it because she was reinforced by the presence of some key advisers and old friends, including her brother Dan and Lyn Nofziger. The bus trip was the idea of our advance man Keith Nahigian, who had worked for Dan Quayle. It was a great concept; it had worked for Bill Clinton and Al Gore after the 1992 Democratic Convention, and it worked for us.

The Florio team responded by hiring an eighteen-wheel semi emblazoned with billboard-sized Florio posters to follow the bus everywhere. This damn truck was driving us crazy until Keith came up with a solution. As we entered a turnpike tollbooth, he had a car strategically positioned to pull in front of the truck, then break down. That enabled our bus to move away smartly while the truck sat helplessly until the stalled car was towed away. In retaliation, every night for the last two weeks of the campaign Florio's merry pranksters set off the fire alarms in the hotel where I and several other campaign staffers were staying. It's a little hard to get back to sleep after being evacuated at four-thirty in the morning. Our campaign rocked along more or less smoothly the rest of the way, steadily closing the gap.

As the final weekend approached, the Florio campaign made a fatal error. Their polls had them ahead by a mere four to six points, ours showed it almost even. Florio had some very powerful negative ads. One which quoted critical editorial comments about Christie from the state's major newspapers was devastating. But in the end, he wanted to finish on a positive note, and started running ads praising himself. In a minor classic of campaign disinformation, we faked Carville into believing we too planned to finish on the high road. We put together an endorsement spot by former Governor Tom Kean and held a press conference to flack it. The deception was laid; in fact, the ad ran once in the New York market on *60 Minutes.* Everything else was hardball. We attacked Florio for raising taxes and misappropriating funds, for corruption in his administration, and for being an ineffective governor. Our ads were better, and more believable.

Election day—November 2—was a killer. I wanted to vote in the Virginia gubernatorial race, so I took an early flight out to Washington and returned at midday. Sherrie was coming in on a later flight. I checked with Jamie Moore to see what was going on and stopped by headquarters. I'd gotten a report that Carville and Begala were predicting a six- to eight-point victory for Florio and hosting a group of reporters at a midtown restaurant in New York for a little pre-victory celebration dinner. A little premature, I thought to myself. I had a quiet confidence we were going to pull this out. All the big public polls had us losing badly, but our nightly tracking polls showed the race moving our way. And even though it was still dead even, I thought the undecideds would break for Christie, since they usually go against the incumbent. As Carl Golden would later say, Carville and Begala spiked the ball on the two-yard line instead of waiting until they crossed the goal.

Christie had really caught fire, and in the closing weeks she stood toe to toe with Florio in two more debates and gave better than she got. She also didn't make a single mistake. Even though she was exhausted, she'd been spectacular. I've never been prouder of a candidate. I was also confident that the get-out-the-vote effort run by the state party would be more effective than Florio's.

The Whitmans hosted a small dinner for their families and close friends that night at the Scanticon Conference Center. Over the course of the evening, nearly everyone in the room took me aside to ask if she really had a shot. I kept saying the momentum had shifted our way in the last week, and everything I knew about politics told me she was going to win. Christie spoke and thanked everyone. In my toast to her, I said that next to Ronald Reagan, she'd been my favorite candidate.

"And next to Nancy Reagan, John has been my favorite candidate's spouse." Even he laughed.

The most touching moment of the evening was when their fifteen-year-old daughter Kate spoke. She teared up and said she really had mixed emotions. She wanted her mom to win because she had worked so hard and would be a great governor, but she was really sad because she knew if she did win, she'd lose her as a mom.

Later that evening the group moved the election watch to the Princeton Hyatt, where we'd set up a war room to monitor the results. By ten o'clock, Christie had a lead of about 40,000 votes. It would be another hour before we knew the results for sure. I was going nuts from the tension. It was Tuesday night and time for my favorite TV show, so I went upstairs to my room to watch *N.Y.P.D. Blue*. At the ten-thirty news break, a newscaster announced Whitman's lead was down to 15,000 and I started getting real nervous. I watched about ten more minutes of cops and robbers, couldn't stand the suspense any longer, and bolted down to the war room. Everyone was looking even more nervous than I felt. I asked for a reading from Jack Carbone, an election law specialist in charge of our ballot security—a critical facet of any New Jersey election, especially a close one like this.

"It's getting close and we'd better go into full alert," he said. That meant we sent our lawyers and marshals into the key urban precincts and made sure Florio didn't steal the election.

"What's the most votes they can steal?" I asked Carbone.

"If we keep our margin above ten thousand, we're all right. If it goes below that, it's trouble."

At that moment, we got word that the results in Essex and Camden counties had been delayed. Then we heard that because the election clerks in those counties hadn't been authorized overtime pay, the count wouldn't be finished until the next morning. It was a moment from Hell: Those two counties were Democratic strongholds, and the Florio machine owned the clerks' offices.

As the eleven o'clock local newscasts reported it was too close to call, I ordered Carbone to deploy his troops. Our lawyers were on the phones with Florio's planning a recount. I headed up to Christie's suite on the top floor. It was a mob scene and I could hardly squeeze in the door. I told her aide to get her into the back bedroom, which was also too jammed to talk, so I pulled her into the bathroom. Crowding in there with us were John, Danny, Tom Kean, and a handful of others.

I did my best to get her attention in the crush of bodies. "Christie, this is real important. We can't let them steal it," I said. "I want you to go downstairs to the ballroom. Get onstage with the cameras on you, and demand they finish the count tonight. You must urge Florio to send out the highway patrol to protect the ballot boxes. Remind people what happened twelve years ago when Tom beat Florio by less than eighteen hundred votes and it took weeks to certify a winner."

As she worked her way to the door of her suite, somebody yelled out, "It's the Governor on the phone." She froze for an instant, then headed for the telephone.

"Ask him to finish it tonight," I reminded. Surrounded by dozens of relatives and hangers-on, she picked up the receiver. I heard her say, "Thank you, Governor." Then she started beaming and gave me a thumbs-up.

"Florio has just conceded," she yelled. In the instant before the room went crazy, I thought to myself, We don't know whose votes are still out there, but he does. It's his machine and he knows she won.

I can't remember a more exciting rush in my life. I'd taken over a candidate twenty-one points behind and left for dead. In a month, I'd guided her to victory over an incumbent governor and a team of the best political consultants in the country. It was the biggest upset of the year and certainly one of the biggest in New Jersey history. It was also a defeat for President Clinton, who had campaigned hard for Florio. For me personally, it was one of my greatest wins. After the Perot debacle, it was my comeback, my redemption. Once again I was The Sandman, King of the Ring. I was ten feet off the ground.

Christie hugged me and thanked me. She grabbed John and kissed him.

"Let's go down and declare ourselves the winners," I shouted into the pandemonium.

The ballroom erupted as she walked to the stage. I grabbed Sherrie, whom I hadn't seen for two hours and who had just arrived, and gave her a big hug. I was being pounded on and congratulated by everyone. People were pulling us toward the stage, but I resisted. "Let's get to the back of the room and watch," I told Sherrie.

Christie made her acceptance speech, then she and her family exited out the side door, now escorted by state troopers. "Let's us get out of here, too," I told Sherrie. That was one of the happiest nights of my life and I didn't want to spend it in a hotel ballroom with a bunch of drunks.

It was also the last time I ever saw Christie Whitman.

THE NEXT SEVERAL days were a blur of encore celebrations for me, each more satisfying than the next. After my reversals with Kemp and Perot and my troubles with Bush, I reveled in the pleasure of the moment. To me, this victory was a resounding vindication of my professional and personal worth. As the old hymn says: "I once was lost, but now am found." I was back on the mountaintop, and savoring every sweet moment.

The morning after the election, I left early for two paid postmortem analysis speeches in Pennsylvania that had been booked for months. I spent the night at Penn State, then flew back Thursday for a campaign postmortem at Princeton University with Danny and our Florio counterparts. I was surprised to see that Carville didn't show. I had a brief catchup call with Christie, who'd already announced several appointments. That night, I took my staff out for a victory dinner. On Friday morning, I cleaned out my office and flew back to Washington, where I was interviewed by the *New York Times* for a glowing profile and did John McLaughlin's *One on One* on tape and *Crossfire* live.

Sherrie was out of town, so I drove out to my cabin with the dogs late Saturday afternoon. On the way out to dinner that evening with Rollie and Kay Evans, I decided to pay a call on my vanquished colleague and neighbor. Carville and Mary Matalin had bought a cabin on the mountain only two hundred yards up the road from me the year before, and I figured he'd be holed up there licking his wounds. I was taught to be a good loser but also a gracious winner. After all, the guy was now my next-door neighbor. Besides, he and

Mary were getting married the following week—her third or fourth (but who's counting), his first.

My old friend Mary was considerably less than enthused to see me. I explained that I just wanted to tip my hat to a great effort.

"How's he doing? He ran a great campaign."

"He's asleep," she said, but let me in nevertheless. We walked downstairs to a darkened basement, where Mary roused her husband-to-be.

"We'll never talk about this again," I said, "but I want you to know it was the best campaign anyone's ever run against me."

James tried to be hospitable, but he was clearly in one enormous funk and didn't appreciate my imposition. He mumbled something and managed to offer me a drink. By then I knew my decent gesture was for naught. I'd always heard Carville goes into deep depressions after a loss. I'd intruded on his privacy and invaded his space. I finished my drink, and got the hell out of there.

I slept in on Sunday, then drove back to town on Monday in time for a dinner party at the home of Arianna Huffington. I left early to do *Larry King Live,* but Arianna beat on me until I agreed to return after the show. Mike Murphy and I were the guests of honor, and Arianna wasn't about to let one of her conquering heroes off that easy. I dragged myself home around 1:30 in the morning, then set the alarm for 5:00 A.M. to get to NBC's studios in time for an interview on the first hour of the Today Show. I was exhausted, but still flying high, when I showed up at 8:00 A.M. for one of Godfrey Sperling's breakfast meetings with reporters.

For over a decade, I've appeared at Sperling breakfasts once or twice a year to discuss the national political scene. Budge Sperling is Washington bureau chief emeritus of the *Christian Science Monitor,* and his breakfasts have been a Washington institution for thirty years. A couple of times a week, print reporters gather to grill a newsmaker at the Carlton Hotel, a couple of blocks north of the White House across Lafayette Park. The number of reporters attending depends on the importance of the guest, and the traditional fare is so unhealthy that one guest long ago dubbed these breakfasts "Cholesterol Gulch." The setting is casual and informal, and the guest is always on the record. Anything you say can and may well be seen in print the next morning.

That morning they treated me like the resident political guru, peppering me for comments about various hot topics of the hour. The last question, from Sperling himself, was a softball about how I beat Florio. For a couple of minutes, I delivered a stream-of-consciousness dissertation about some of the key reasons for our victory, especially Christie's surprising strength among African-American voters. It was a courtesy question, a free shot to strut my stuff and relish my moment in the sun in exchange for cutting into my sack time. Then it was over. Exactly one week after the election, I left for my Georgetown office on an absolute roll.

At 4:00 P.M., I was staring at my cluttered desk, with more than five weeks of unopened mail stacked up in piles. I couldn't decide whether to begin by sorting mail or by returning the hundreds of calls in my phone logs from friends offering their congratulations. I'd ignored my public relations clients for months. I knew I needed to focus on business, but I was having trouble coming down from my Jersey high.

My longtime assistant, Susie Farris, poked her head in the door and said Carl Golden was on the phone. I hadn't talked to Carl since election night.

"Rollins, what the fuck did you tell a bunch of reporters this morning about us buying black ministers?" he demanded.

His words felt like a kick in the stomach. I quickly tried to recall precisely what I'd said at breakfast—a little Clinton, a lot of politics. And I *had* said something about black ministers, but just at the moment I couldn't remember what.

"Carl, I don't know exactly what you're talking about, but I certainly didn't say we bought black ministers."

"Well, the phone's ringing off the hook. Every reporter in the state is calling. *The Washington Post* is moving a story on the wires that says something like that and we're getting bombarded. Other than that, how the hell are you?"

All of a sudden the blow to my stomach turned to nausea. Whatever I said, I'd obviously screwed up again. Would I ever learn to watch my mouth when talking to the press?

Carl said he'd keep me posted and hung up. I left a short time later and told Susie to call me at home if she heard anything.

Sherrie had just returned from her trip, and I didn't say anything to her about the breakfast. I turned on CNN to watch Ross Perot debate Vice President Gore about NAFTA on *Larry King Live*. The night before, I'd said on Larry's show that the White House was stupid to give Perot another forum to debate NAFTA and that I'd never put the vice president into that role if he were my client. I was dead wrong. Gore wiped the floor with Perot. That's the problem with doing live television commentary. I always call them as I see them, but sometimes I miss by a mile. My discomfort at being proven wrong was mitigated by my satisfaction in seeing Ross Perot self-destruct before millions of viewers.

In the middle of the debate, I got a call from *New York Times* reporter Rick Berke about the *Post* story. Halfway through the conversation, I knew I was in deep shit.

By now I remembered some of what I'd said in those final minutes at the breakfast, but as I tried to explain myself, I could tell Berke wasn't listening. He already had his story written and was just going through the motions so he could write that he'd given me a chance to comment. I knew from the tone of his queries that I'd be giving Perot and Gore a run for their money for the next day's headlines. I still couldn't believe it. Sperling's question was a throwaway, for crying out loud.

I told Sherrie about Golden's call, and as I explained what I thought had happened, I could see her eyes cloud with pain. She didn't say anything, but didn't need to. It was all there in her eyes. I felt like a total jerk for letting her down again. I tossed and turned for a few hours and finally quit trying to sleep. I knew the *Post* would be delivered about 5:00 A.M., so I turned on the tube and just waited. Finally I heard it land on my doorstep. The headline on Tom Edsall's front-page piece—dated Wednesday, November 10—shattered what little hope remained that the hurricane might blow past without much damage.

Rollins: GOP Cash Suppressed Black Vote; Manager Says Whitman Campaign Paid N.J. Ministers, Democrats

As I started to read the story, my hands began to tremble.

> Republican political consultant Edward J. Rollins said yesterday that the successful gubernatorial campaign of Christine Todd Whitman in New Jersey spent roughly $500,000 in "walking around money" largely to suppress black voter turnout.
>
> Rollins, who managed the Whitman campaign, said much of the money was paid to politically active African American ministers and to city Democratic political workers. In both cases, the recipients, whom Rollins declined to identify, were asked to minimize or stop get-out-the-vote activities in behalf of Democratic incumbent Gov. Jim Florio.

Oh, fuck, I thought, I've really done it this time. I'd been playing Russian roulette for so long, and this was finally the fatal bullet.

I walked upstairs. Sherrie was awake, and she asked me how the story had come out.

"It's bad, real bad." I read her the headline. I was suddenly having a hard time breathing.

"I've just got to get out of here," I said. "I'm going to the cabin."

I'm a fighter, but at that instant, I had to escape. I just instinctively knew it was going to be horrible, and Sherrie's silence said she knew it too. I wasn't sure I had any fight left in me. I remembered the disgust I had for Roberto Duran, one of the greatest welterweight champions of all time, when he quit against Sugar Ray Leonard. He wasn't hurt and was still on his feet, but he just stopped fighting and said, "No más. No más." Suddenly I identified with Duran. No more. No more. I couldn't handle any more controversy.

Sherrie ran out to the driveway; she urged me not to go and wait until I knew more. "Please drive carefully," she said. "And don't do anything foolish. Call me as soon as you get there."

The one-hour drive west to the cabin usually relaxes me, but not this time. The more I thought about the story, the more agitated I became. I called Sherrie as soon as I got there. She's the best public relations strategist I know. Her instincts are always on target. She felt I had to take the offensive immediately and explain what I'd meant. Unfortunately, I didn't follow her counsel, a mistake I've made too many times before.

I called my office. Susie said the phones were ringing off the hook. Most calls were from reporters, but some were from friends offering to help. Charlie Leonard, my former partner and great friend, called to offer a hand. He'd helped me set up the campaign and knew all the players. He'd already been in contact with the Whitman people. They wanted me to keep my mouth shut and simply issue a retraction. I wasn't comfortable with that.

I knew instinctively what I would advise a client to do. I should hold a press conference, explain my mistake, and offer a heartfelt mea culpa. But I also knew this was more complicated. It wasn't just about me. I'd dragged Christie into the muck and I had to respect her wishes. She was the governor-elect and I'd just thrown her election into question. I knew I could clear it up with one press conference. It would be uncomfortable, but it would be over, a two-day story. But if they didn't want me doing that, I owed it to Christie to defer.

Besides, there was a complication. John Whitman and Danny Todd were up to their eyeballs in the street operation I'd talked about at the breakfast. There was nothing about their actions that I knew to be illegal, but this was neither the time nor the place to attract more attention to Christie by involving her husband and brother. Charlie offered to draft a press release and coordinate it with the Whitman camp. I told him to go ahead, but I needed some time to think before I made any decisions.

Then I made the call I dreaded most. It took a little while to get through, but we finally connected.

"Christie, I can't tell you how sorry I am. This is certainly not what I intended to do."

To call her tone frosty would be a gross understatement. You'd think we'd never met. She was angry as hell, but I also heard fear in her voice. "What you suggested is illegal," she said. The implication was clear: If I were telling the truth, the Democrats could move to invalidate the election.

She told me she was going to hold a press conference in an hour and wanted my retraction to read to the press. She said something about this possibly putting the whole election in jeopardy.

"Feel free to shoot me publicly," I offered.

"I'm not the one to shoot you publicly; you've got to shoot yourself."

After all the hours, days, and months I'd spent helping her get elected, I feel badly that these would turn out to be our last words. It was certainly all my fault, and I was prepared to put the revolver in my mouth. But I was just as miserable over the loss of the relationship. I'd come to admire her and was proud that I'd helped get someone of her caliber in public service. I also knew she could use my counsel in putting together her administration. She'd be getting it elsewhere now, I realized. I was a leper in New Jersey.

Over the next hour, Charlie Leonard and Carl Golden worked out the wording for Christie's statement to the press. Their draft made it clear she intended to hang me out to dry. She could have distanced herself effectively without kicking the corpse so hard, but in the end I just said, "Screw it. Let them have what they want."

Christie kicked me even harder at her press conference. I was disappointed by some of the things she said about me during this crisis and long afterwards. She had every right to cut me loose, but I hadn't expected her to pile it on like that. Too often, candidates forget they're not the only ones making sacrifices in a campaign. For the five weeks I managed her race, I worked sixteen to eighteen hours a day. I didn't see my wife for more than a few hours each week. I flew home Sunday nights at 7:00 P.M. and returned the next morning on a seven o'clock flight. During the last two weeks, I didn't go home at all. I lived in a hotel room across the street from the campaign headquarters, and ate meals at my desk. I handled all the unpleasant tasks for her, including cutting her husband and her brother out of her campaign. I helped restore confidence in a campaign that was dead and gone.

Goddamnit, I'd helped her win. But I'd watched her discard a longtime associate after the primary, and I guess I was stupid to have expected anything better. I didn't think she could be that ruthless. I realized I was wallowing in self-pity. I'd bitten the bullet, but my wounds still hurt.

I bundled myself up in a heavy jacket and went out on the deck overlooking the majestic Shenandoah Valley. The view from the 2,000-foot elevation was breathtaking as always. It was the middle of November and the cold wind felt good against my face.

After Perot, the whisperers said Rollins would never work in politics again. I'd proven them all wrong, and then tripped myself up. The stupid thing about this business is we get too much credit when things work and way too much blame when they don't. A campaign manager is like a jockey: The best jockey can't make a county fair nag win the Preakness, and the worst can't lose with Secretariat. We just try to make the horse run as well as it can. We know the track and the competition. And the most valuable thing we bring to the track is the experience of having seen it all before.

I was so angry at myself. I still wanted to believe that what was reported wasn't what I'd said. Even if it was, it certainly wasn't what I'd intended to say. But I learned a long time ago that what's printed in *The Washington Post* or the *New York Times* are your words forever.

As I stared out over the valley, I became as depressed as I've ever been in my life. I thought about Sherrie and what she was going through. I thought about my parents and the heartache and humiliation that I knew they had to be suffering. I knew my career in a second blood sport was finished. Twenty-five years ago, a savage knockout ended my boxing career; this time I'd won the fight, then disqualified myself. Twenty years in Washington had taught me that people living there cheer for two things: The Redskins to win, and whoever's up to fall.

What I didn't know was just how ugly it was about to become. I soon learned that the Justice Department (and presumably the Clinton White House) had already set out to destroy me. Later that afternoon I got a call from Michael Carvin, an attorney friend who'd been a major player in the Reagan Justice Department. Carvin told me his most reliable sources in Justice had tipped him that they were launching a full-scale investigation into New Jersey. This had been approved by Attorney General Janet Reno, who'd campaigned for Florio in September. I assumed the White House was behind this attack, although later I found out that they were very nervous because of allegations that Clinton's 1990 gubernatorial campaign had paid get-out-the-vote money to black ministers in Arkansas.

It was critical, he cautioned, that I not say anything to anyone until we could talk in person. He urged me to lie low and stay away from both my house and cabin. He was trying to protect me from the press, who had my house and office staked out, and from federal marshals, who he feared would subpoena me and my records. His plan was that I would voluntarily cooperate with every investigation, but he wanted first to know if I was a criminal target of their investigation.

Sherrie and I rendezvoused that night with some friends and hid out the next day at their Chesapeake Bay cottage. I talked to Carvin several times during the day and he kept me informed of the legal maelstrom swirling around me. We agreed to meet the next morning, a Friday, in his Washington office at Shaw, Pittman.

IN PREPARATION for that meeting, I spent many hours trying to reconstruct my comments at the Sperling breakfast and recall the events that led up to them. But I didn't yet have a transcript of the interview; besides, I was still so upset that I wasn't thinking very well. And in the traumatic days and weeks that followed, events moved so quickly that I never did get the breathing space I needed to sort out my thoughts and recollections with an absolutely clear head. Only much later—in fact, only as I prepared to write this book—was I able to pull together all the pieces of this complicated puzzle. Now, with the advantage of reflection and hindsight, I can finally provide a more precise account of what happened during the campaign and a full explanation of my unfortunate comments to Godfrey Sperling.

The breakfast that day had started out like all the others I'd appeared at over the years, except I was probably more exhausted this time. I wasn't there to discuss the Whitman campaign, which for daily journalists was already ancient history. I certainly didn't expect to make news, and I suspect most of the fifteen to twenty reporters there didn't expect much, either. Most of the hour-long discussion was about the president, the disarray in the White House, and that evening's upcoming debate between Vice President Gore and my old boss Ross Perot.

By tradition, Sperling usually closes with the last question. "In fairness to you," he said, "I guess we need to let you tell us how you won the Whitman campaign."

I gave a quick gloss on our strategy, and then I uttered the words that turned my life upside down.

> I think the last three weeks in the campaign we had better television. We had our candidate perform better. And I think in the end

the thing that surprised a lot of people was we really had a better ground operation. . . .

I think the thing that a lot of people didn't see is that we mailed out two and a half million pieces of mail. They mailed no mail. We made one million paid phone calls to identify our voters. They made, to the best of my knowledge, no calls. We had 400,000 get-out-the-vote phone calls. We had about 15,000 coordinators.

For the first time, at least in my history, we had walking-around money, which is legal. And it's amazing to me in New Jersey, with a very tight election law, there's a title in there which is called "Walking-around Money." And you have to report some, not who you give it to or what you do with it. We had a substantial amount of walking-around money, which is a different game.

Q: How much?

Somewhere in the neighborhood of half a million dollars. And here's how we used it. We went into black churches and we basically said to ministers who had endorsed Florio, "Do you have a special project?" And they said, "We've already endorsed Florio." We said, "That's fine. Don't get up in the Sunday pulpits and preach. We know you've endorsed it, but don't get up there and say, 'It's your moral obligation that you go on Tuesday to vote for Jim Florio.' "

Equally as important, in some places we . . . said to some of their key workers, "How much have they paid you to do your normal duty? . . . Well, here's . . . We'll match it. Go home, sit and watch television." And I think to a certain extent we suppressed their vote, suppressed it in a very positive—

Q: You talked to the black ministers. And if they don't say something, they get something in the way of money?

No. We made contributions to their favorite charity, which usually is some special project. I mean, what we did, I think for the first time, is we played the game the way the game is played in New Jersey or elsewhere. And I think to a certain extent our game plan was not to have this intensified [pro-Florio black] vote in the areas that we couldn't obviously make up . . .

Q: Did [the contribution] vary depending on the size of the church?

I'm sure it did. I mean, those are our community people, who obviously knew what they needed to do and where they needed to do it . . . We were street-smart this time. . . . In the end it was a fairly smart campaign, and we knew what we had to do.

To tell the story behind these words and put my comments in their proper context, I should begin by describing what academics might call the psychic surround of the big-city campaign. Every campaign is rife with rumors and misinformation; disinformation, in fact, is always part of the strategy. You try to conceal what you're really up to, and persuade the opposition you're doing something else.

There are always hangers-on in campaigns, people with undefined roles who play a small part in the effort. They may be the precinct chairman, ward boss, or block captain. They always want to convince you nothing happens in their turf without their say so. In some cases that may be true. Most of the time, it's pure bullshit. The exaggeration factor in campaigns is always enormous at the street level.

When a hired-gun consultant turns up in a state or congressional district, the locals always say, "We do things differently here. You may understand the national game, but you have to do it our way here or you'll lose." There's a little truth and a lot of fiction in that assertion. You don't want to alienate the locals, so you listen to them, but in the end the basic campaign techniques are the same everywhere.

Wherever I went during the short time I ran Whitman's campaign, some character would come up and introduce himself and the two goons with him. They'd always say they were in charge of this precinct or that, and that Christie was going to win their area big—but don't forget the walking-around money. That was the term they always used.

The small fry weren't the only ones looking for a handout; in at least one case I knew of, one of the state's major players also took a keen interest in walking-around money. In early October, I sat in on a meeting with Bret Schundler, the Republican mayor of Jersey City. His town was a Democratic stronghold, but he felt he could peel off significant numbers of black Democrats with some strategic financial help from us.

The mayor's chief political aide put a fine point on the request. "We need $30,000 in walking-around money," he said. We gave it to them, and I have no doubt that whatever purposes it was used for helped Christie run stronger in Jersey City than Republicans usually do.

Which isn't to suggest that the mayor did anything wrong. In New Jersey, a state with publicly financed general elections, walking-around money is legal. It's used by the state parties to get people to the polls. It can go to just about anyone—Little League coaches, party retainers, school bus drivers, church bus drivers, maybe even black ministers—you name it. In the three months that Christie's brother Danny ran the campaign, a lot of promises were made to pass this money around. Danny kept those promises in a binder that he carried everywhere.

When I came on board, I was repeatedly asked by people in the party's county organizations to make sure I was going to live up to Danny's commitments. Being perfectly honest, I didn't give a damn about walking-around money or Danny's promises. Unlike Danny, I wasn't a volunteer worker, and as I understood it, by state law there was a wall between what the state party was doing and my operation. Besides, I've never been in a campaign where any of that street crap really mattered, and when you're twenty-one points behind, street money is a real low priority.

Instead, I was focusing on much bigger issues, such as the fact that there was no vote to get out. Christie Whitman, a pro-choice woman, was getting clobbered among women voters. That's the sort of thing I needed to fix. My priorities were getting our television commercials on the air with a sharper message, getting her ready for debates, and turning the spotlight off our missteps and back on Florio and his pitiful record. Most of all, I had to rebuild the confidence of the candidate and her supporters. Anyone who asked me about the street program was told to go see Danny. That was still his baby even after I replaced him as the manager.

Because of public financing, we didn't need any more money anyway. But the state party *did* need to build up a fund to finance get-out-the-vote efforts. In the closing weeks, Michael Francis, the Whitman finance chairman, Cliff Sobel, the state party's finance chairman, and John Whitman held several meetings in the campaign conference room to talk about how much they needed to raise for street-money commitments. Danny Todd and Frank Holman, a crusty old pro who'd been the party chairman during the Kean years, also sat in on these meetings.

I was asked to attend these meetings, but I always declined. I had better things to do, and in any case, I didn't care how they raised the money, or where it went. I'd been told by Todd and Holman that the figure committed for street money was in the neighborhood of $200,000, presumably all in cash. John Whitman was apparently the rainmaker; Francis and Sobel led me to believe that if John didn't make the pitch, people weren't going to give.

Meanwhile, in the closing weeks of the campaign, the Florio camp was focusing heavy attention on the African-American community in the urban centers. Florio had neglected them during his term, and their leadership was furious. If he didn't do well there, he couldn't get reelected. Carville turned up the heat. Jesse Jackson came in to campaign for Florio, as did members of the Congressional Black Caucus.

Naturally, we responded in kind. Christie had already made many efforts to reach out to the black community and had received a number of endorsements from African-American leaders and ministers. But Lana Hooks, the prominent black attorney who was handling our outreach to the community, was starting to get worried about the Florio effort. She met with Jamie Moore and me and asked for suggestions. My primary concern was hanging on to black leaders who'd already endorsed Christie. Lana said the Florio people were threatening to cut off state grants for their child care projects and other favorite state-sponsored ventures. I told her to say we could help raise money to keep those projects alive if Florio pulled the plug. The critical point was to keep the dialogue going. I didn't want the African-American ministers getting up in their pulpits and urging their congregations to please go vote for Jim Florio, as Carville and Jesse Jackson were telling them to do.

I have no doubt that our efforts to reach out to the black community had some effect. But after the election, when I took a close look at the numbers, I was astonished to see that Christie drew 25 percent of the minority vote, an unheard-of number for a New Jersey Republican. Our outreach could explain part of the surge, but in my opinion not all of it. The only other likely explanation was that the street organization built with the walking-around money had had a substantial impact.

My suspicion grew stronger two days after the election, when I rode back from the Princeton seminar to campaign headquarters with Danny Todd. It was the first chance we'd had to compare notes on our victory. Danny was ten feet off the ground, and he had every right to be. He volunteered to me that the street operation was largely responsible for the inroads Christie had made into traditional Democratic voter blocs. "We ran a good shoe-leather campaign like my father used to," he told me. "We had the money and we had the best operation ever. The walking-around money did the job in the black community."

He wasn't more specific than that, and he definitely didn't mention black ministers. But I recall at one point during the seminar, in the context of explaining his sister's strength among black voters, he seemed to say the word "suppression" before stopping himself in mid-word. (Later, during my grand jury appearance, U.S. Attorney Michael Chertoff played a videotape of Danny's truncated remark. Again, it seemed obvious that he had been about to say "suppression.") And as the seminar was breaking up, Florio's chief political adviser, Doug Berman, conceded that our campaign had done better in the inner city than theirs.

None of this proves that black ministers were paid off. But years of cloakroom talk, my experience in other campaigns, and what I heard about the walking-around money during and after this campaign led me to believe that it probably had happened. After all, in just about every big city in America, election day is payday for a lot of voters.

In other words, there was some generalized basis for the words I spoke at the Sperling breakfast—though that hardly excuses what I did. Politically, it was incredibly stupid to raise the subject in the first place, but my more serious mistake was to present as fact what I had only guessed at. The truth is, I had absolutely no direct knowledge of any voter suppression, any payments to ministers or their favorite projects or charities, or any illegal or unethical conduct by anyone allied with the Whitman campaign. It was worse than talking out of school—I was maligning people based on hunch and supposition. I was talking about events I thought had occurred but didn't know to have occurred. I never wanted to fool or mislead anyone, but in the vernacular of the street, I was talking trash.

To top it all off, the $500,000 figure I mentioned at breakfast was flat-out wrong. That was the total amount spent on our get-out-the-vote effort, including phone banks and direct mail. The walking-around money piece of that pie was probably about $200,000.

There's no escaping the harsh truth: I gave an inaccurate account of what went on in our campaign. Sometimes I have a weakness for grandstanding, and I enjoy being the center of attention perhaps a little too much. In the flush of victory, I spun myself out of control.

The bottom line is, I still don't know precisely what went on in the mean streets of New Jersey in 1993. I'm sure some people do—Democrat and Republican alike—but they're not talking. Nevertheless, more than two years later I believe in my gut that someone did pay people in the black community to help Christie Whitman become governor. I'm also convinced that someone did the same for Jim Florio—and, amazingly, in New Jersey, all of it happens to be perfectly legal.

MY PERSPECTIVE on this disastrous episode is clear now, but when I met with my lawyers two days after the scandal broke, I was only just beginning to try to make sense of what had happened. Soon after I arrived at Shaw, Pittman that Friday, Mike Carvin and I were joined by Ben Ginsberg, another friend and former general counsel of the Republican National Committee. Ben was now a partner in the prestigious Democratic law firm of Patton, Boggs. They agreed to serve as my co-counsels throughout the upcoming ordeal. I sure as hell needed them. Before it was over, I'd be facing a federal investigation led by the Attorney General of the United States, a state investigation, a Democratic party inquisition, and a frivolous $500 million civil suit by Jesse Jackson and Al Sharpton.

Mike handed me a partial transcript of the breakfast, which he'd gotten from a reporter. I quickly read through the critical pages, and upon seeing my somewhat garbled remarks in black and white, I understood for the first time why I was in so much trouble: My words clearly suggested that I knew for a fact that the Whitman campaign had bought the silence of some black ministers. In truth, I knew nothing of the sort. Now more distressed than ever, I proceeded to tell them the entire tale as best I could remember it.

When I finished talking, Carvin and Ginsberg offered their assessment. "From what you've told us," Mike said, "you have nothing to worry about from a criminal standpoint. You did something stupid, but nothing wrong or criminal." The danger, he added, was that I was about to be dragged through multiple investigations. If I changed my story anywhere along the line, I could be nailed for perjury. It was critical, Mike and Ben warned me, to tell the entire truth, even if it completely contradicted my breakfast remarks—and to tell it consistently every time I repeated it. They also emphasized the importance of keeping in mind the legal definition of "knowledge." If I saw it or did it, they explained, I had knowledge. If I heard about something or had a suspicion about something, that was hearsay or speculation.

When I got home from the meeting, I discovered that my voice-mail had blown a gasket. Ninety calls were backed up. In the trying days ahead, four hundred well-wishers would telephone. Many of them were people I hadn't heard from since high school. Some, like former Canadian Prime Minister Brian Mulroney, I'd never met.

"Ed, I've been reading about you in the *Times*," he said. "I think you're being too hard on yourself. My impression is that you've always been an honorable man. Get back up and go on with your life." It was a wonderfully generous call, totally out of the blue.

Within the next few days, Barbara Walters and Senator John Warner insisted on taking Sherrie and me to brunch at the Watergate Hotel, a very public place. Bob Beckel, the 1984 manager for Walter Mondale and a dear friend since that campaign, offered to organize a legal defense fund. William Bennett called to say that I shouldn't hunker down like a felon. "I want to take you to lunch publicly," he said. And he did. His brother Bob, the Democratic superlawyer, offered to defend me—for free.

One of the first to call was Julius Hunter, my old pal from the barricades of Washington University. "This is all horseshit," the first black anchor on St. Louis television reassured me. He offered to get on a plane that night to help, and called every couple of days to hold my hand.

Vernon Jordan and my old boss, former Transportation Secretary Bill Coleman, also offered their support and counsel. But the irrepressible Vernon wasn't to be outdone. He invited Sherrie to lunch one day and laid it on the line.

"Have you slept with your man lately?" he inquired. "Now's when he *needs* you." (Three days later, Vernon and I happened to find ourselves on the same airplane. "Have you been laid lately?" he asked with a smile, draping his arm around my shoulder. "Because if you have, I'm responsible.")

As usual, my dad found a way to put it all in perspective. "It's not like you're a parish priest who's molested altar boys," he said.

Not everyone was so understanding. The wife of one of network television's most prominent Washington fixtures told several friends that she bet that Sherrie would leave me and should have done it years ago. Roger Stone, who worked for me in 1984 but thought I was behind Whitman's insistence that he have nothing to do with her campaign, hired a press agent to get him on television to bad-mouth me. He said I was "radioactive" and would never work in politics again.

The enormity of what I'd done to myself was horrendous, but I felt badly for Sherrie, too. She was now working for *U.S. News & World Report*; once again, she was a member of the media at a moment when I was in the news. For the second time in as many years, she was put in an awkward position professionally, solely because she was married to me.

As Sherrie and I tried to sleep the night after my meeting with the lawyers, we both knew I'd touched off a firestorm that was gathering force and heading straight at us.

ON SUNDAY, NOVEMBER 14, I met with two FBI agents from New Jersey for four hours and answered all their questions. They subpoenaed my campaign records, my computer and disks, and various other personal and business records. At the end of the interview, one of them handed me a subpoena to appear before a federal grand jury in Newark on the 18th.

My lawyers and I flew up the night before and stayed at a Marriott hotel near the airport. Leaving the airport, bystanders started pointing me out. I felt like John Gotti and didn't like it one damn bit. I ordered room service, watched a movie, and tried in vain to get some sleep.

I've been the target of plenty of big media stakeouts, but I wasn't prepared for the mob scene as we approached the federal court-house next morning. There were television vans everywhere, and dozens of reporters and camera crews. A federal police officer kept the press at bay as we raced inside. Unfortunately, I needed better advance work. We were in the wrong building. Somebody pointed across the street to the building where the U.S. Attorney's office was located.

Utterly trapped, we waded back through the media throngs. Mike Carvin instructed me to say nothing and keep walking. I followed his orders almost perfectly, except for one quip: "I wish I'd stayed home and had breakfast with my wife," which of course led all the news-casts. Finally, my lawyers wedged out an opening through the media gauntlet, and we were inside.

Michael Chertoff was the U.S. Attorney for New Jersey. He was a Bush appointee and, I assumed, a Republican. They put me in a holding room while Carvin and Chertoff discussed the procedures for my grand jury testimony, at which my lawyers wouldn't be pres-ent. Chertoff again assured Carvin I wasn't a target of the probe. He did say he'd question me himself. Not a good sign, I thought. This guy wants to keep his job with the Democrats. Maybe I'm his meal ticket.

As we were leaving Chertoff's office, Carvin asked for a U.S. marshal to escort us. Chertoff admonished us not to overreact. He said he'd tried a bunch of Mafia dons and seen lots of press before, and he'd get us through. When we got to the front door, his tune changed.

"Holy shit," he exclaimed. "Get us some marshals!"

One of my lawyers shoved Chertoff toward the press, and as they engulfed him, we sprinted across the street, led by a marshal on one side and the limited blocking skills of my lawyers on the other. One reporter grabbed me as I was going in the door and asked if I had anything to say. "Yes, I wish I had bigger lawyers." My feeble at-tempt at gallows humor did nothing to stop the churning in my stom-ach.

Before we began, Carvin told me, "Be careful, be honest, and think through your answers. And if at any time it sounds like you're being accused of anything or if Chertoff uses the word 'target,' ask for a break and come talk to me."

The jury room was old, high-ceilinged, dark and wood-paneled. I was sworn in by the foreman, then told to sit in a witness chair facing the grand jury, which may have been eighteen persons, fairly evenly mixed by race and gender.

Chertoff was a very serious guy—aggressive and argumentative. He peppered me with questions for over five hours. One of his favorite openings was "Do you expect us to believe, Mr. Rollins? . . ." I wouldn't want this guy after me if I were guilty of something. Two years later, I'd be chuckling at the poetic justice of politics as I watched Chertoff, now the chief counsel of Al D'Amato's Senate Whitewater Committee, grilling the same White House crowd I assume had sicced him on me.

Fortunately, there were a few moments of levity during my day in court. After a couple of hours of intense questioning, the court stenographer stopped and hollered out to the prosecutor, "I've got to take a pee break." The aristocratic Chertoff didn't quite know how to handle it. After rolling his eyes, he called a ten-minute recess.

Later, during the lunch break, she asked if I could help her spell some of the names I'd mentioned.

"How do you spell James Carville?" she asked me.

"A-S-S-H-O-L-E," I replied with a straight face. She wrote it down and spelled it back to me before realizing what I'd done.

That's also when I learned there *is* such a thing as a free lunch. One of my lawyers went out for sandwiches. When he came back, he reported that lunch was pro bono. The street vendor said this was the best day he'd ever had; he didn't know the poor guy being tried, but he was making a fortune off the press. When my lawyer said the guy was his client, the vendor said lunch was on him.

We finished up at 6:00 P.M., after seven hours of testimony. Chertoff told the steno he needed the transcripts by the weekend. "No way," she replied. "I'm not working this weekend, and next week's Thanksgiving and I was going to take a few days off." I went back to Washington grateful to have survived, but feeling pretty goddamned battered and completely unnerved.

Chertoff had been a tough inquisitor, but at least he'd been professional. The interrogation I faced the next morning at a Washington law firm was another matter entirely. In a totally partisan charade, the New Jersey Democratic Party had gotten a ruling that my breakfast comments might constitute evidence that Republicans had violated the terms of a 1981 restraining order. The order had been obtained by the Democrats, who had charged voter suppression in the 1981 Kean-Florio race.

There were sixteen lawyers in the room, and most of them were out-and-out partisan jerks. The questioning was deeply biased and outrageously hostile. For seven hours, I was hammered about my motives. Why had I said these things? Did it really happen? What was it like to be in a race with Carville? Wasn't it all lies?

In what added up to nearly three hundred pages of transcripts, I talked about a lot of things, but only one item was reported—the piece of testimony in which I asserted that I'd made up the whole story to get back at Carville, who'd been telling reporters that I'd stolen the election instead of conceding that he'd lost it fair and square.

"The bottom line was this was an act of fiction that was sort of a psychological warfare," I testified. "It was one-upmanship, and it backfired, and the ultimate revenge was Carville got to me. I jumped to his bait [and] said two minutes of words that I wish and will wish for the rest of my life I could take back."

I sure as hell wish I'd left James out of it. It's true that the campaign's mind games had continued after the election, as so often happens. But to suggest that my Sperling breakfast remarks were entirely the result of our rivalry was a gross exaggeration. After several hours of relentless badgering, I was tired and just wanted it to be done. So I in effect allowed these jerks to lead the witness and create a sideshow. I was goaded into answers which, while truthful, made a much bigger deal of the competitive aspect than was appropriate.

Predictably, the lawyers who grilled me that day distorted the truth. One of them walked out early to catch a plane and couldn't wait to tell the horde of reporters waiting for me outside, "He made it all up." That became the headline.

About three weeks later, I was dragged before the Newark grand jury one more time as their final witness. Shortly after my testimony, Chertoff released a report saying the grand jury had found no evidence of illegal activity. Next to me, the most relieved people in America were the Democrat ward bosses in New Jersey who *really* know how to run a street operation. In their zeal to nail me, the Clinton crowd had set off a backlash in their own camp by sending several dozen FBI agents into New Jersey to investigate street operations. The Democratic pols started yelling to Washington about cutting a little too close to the bone, and it wasn't long before the FBI was called off the chase.

On January 18, 1994, Christie Whitman was sworn in as governor. Not surprisingly, I wasn't invited to her grand inaugural. I don't like inaugurals, but I'd have shown up at this one. Obviously, I knew it wasn't in the cards. I did feel better when someone told me she'd said it was a shame that the one guy who should have been there wasn't.

When I was a kid, we used to say, "Sticks and stones will break my bones, but words will never hurt me." Grownups know that words are by far the deadlier weapon. My careless words hurt Christie Whitman and tarnished her great victory. They caused embarrassment and pain to many good, God-fearing African-American ministers who were stereotyped by my insensitivity. They insulted many African-American citizens of New Jersey who vote honestly and diligently. They hurt my party, which has made significant gains in the numbers of African Americans who vote for Republicans across the country.

But in the end, they hurt me the most. Those words spoken out of careless bravado over breakfast cost me what it had taken a quarter of a century to build. The financial repercussions were enormous. Although I was never charged with anything more than gross stupidity, my legal bills exceeded $100,000. I lost several clients, and put my business in jeopardy. I also lost my job as a regular commentator on the Today Show. But that was the least of it. The thing I cared most about, my reputation, was shredded. My integrity and my racial sensitivity had been questioned. Of all the repercussions of these self-inflicted wounds, nothing pains me more than having been called a liar and a racist. My parents raised me to be honest and racially sensitive, and I've spent my entire life trying to live up to their high standards.

In spite of the pain and hurt, some good came out of this miserable chapter in my life. My marriage got stronger because my wonderful wife stood by me, loved me, and comforted me. I found out who my real friends are, and they are many and faithful. The rest, as Don Regan loved to say, are known to management. I reacquainted myself with humility, an elusive quality in the heady atmosphere of Washington. Pride is one of the seven deadly sins for a reason—and it *does* go before a fall. And most important, I found my faith again.

In my darkest hour, I again turned back to my Catholic religion. When I was at my lowest point, I walked into St. Matthew's Cathedral and found forgiveness from the only one who matters. After being away from the religion of my boyhood for so long, I'm grateful that I could return. The Good Lord still has a long way to go in shaping up this sinner, but I do believe I'm a wiser and better person for being tested by these events.

Several months after Governor Whitman took office, in June 1994, I went back to Trenton. In a church a few blocks from the state capitol, I apologized in person to a group of African-American ministers representing the New Jersey Black Ministers' Council. In more than two hours of dialogue, plenty of anger and compassion were expressed on all sides.

"What do you Republicans really think of us?" one of them asked me at one point.

"Well, being perfectly honest," I replied, "we think of you as Democrat operatives." This comment was received with "amens" by some, and more anger by others.

Then, just before the meeting ended, the bishop suggested to his fellow men of God that they should perhaps at least privately acknowledge that my remarks at the Sperling breakfast, repugnant though they were to the assembled, had in fact touched on a truth about some of the ugly things that happen in politics.

The church fell silent as the bishop let his comments sink in. Then I heard a new smattering of "amens."

The bishop called the meeting to an end with these generous words of conciliation:

"This man has come to us asking for forgiveness. Let he who has not sinned cast the first stone." He ended by leading a prayer as we all stood and held hands.

The ministers were most kind, and I cherish their forgiveness. But as one said afterwards to the ever present reporters outside, "Let it be understood by all that forgiveness is not forgetting."

I won't forget, either.

FOR THE FIRST time in my life, when I stared into the abyss, I saw myself down there. Since leaving the NRCC under a cloud in early 1991, I'd essentially been semiretired in the political game except for my Perot lunacy and the Whitman campaign. Inside the Beltway, however, I'd remained a significant character. I was still on the social A-list, which I could care less about, and in heavy demand on the lecture circuit. Talk show producers still called me with booking requests. The best tables at power restaurants like The Palm and Sam & Harry's came my way automatically. I was definitely in the deep freeze with my own party, but one of my Democrat friends anointed me Washington's favorite Republican. That was a pretty sweet consolation prize.

But now even that was evaporating. The bookers stopped calling, the speeches tailed off. My public relations consulting business was in shambles—nobody wanted to hire a guy whose personal P.R. strategy had proven so utterly disastrous. I had confessed to being an admitted liar, and in the minds of many people, a closet racist. Several potential clients told me the racial element of the controversy alone made it impossible to hire me: The potential for backlash in the black community was simply too great. Much as I hated to admit it, my old nemesis Roger Stone had been right. I *was* radioactive.

It didn't bother me so much that my social invitations had taken a conspicuous dive. I'd been a controversial figure for a dozen years, but this was the first time I'd ever felt genuinely embarrassed by my behavior. The truth was, I didn't want to go anywhere. I couldn't bear to be seen and whispered about. Encountering black friends was unbelievably painful. It triggered a Pavlovian reaction: I couldn't stop myself from insisting I *wasn't* a racist to people who certainly knew it.

The only thing that felt comfortable—that genuinely kept me whole—was going to church. My daily visits to St. Matthew's Cathedral renewed me and forced me to reflect on how I'd lost my way. Pride is one of the seven deadly sins, and I was truly guilty of it more than once. My reawakened spirituality pushed me out of self-pity and into survival mode. I made a strategic decision to reorient my business toward international consulting, with specific focus on the enormous untapped potential of the Chinese market. Rollins International would never be confused with Kissinger Associates, but the Chinese business and political leaders I met in Nanjing and Beijing that winter were totally unconcerned about my notoriety and eager to engage.

Then, from out of nowhere, another political temptation was offered me in December 1993. My new potential benefactor, George Nethercutt of Spokane, Washington, was a close friend of more than twenty years. When he was chief of staff to Ted Stevens, Alaska's senior senator, George was one of the first people I met after arriving in the nation's capital in 1973. For years we played touch football and softball in the Capitol Hill League. I had enormous respect and admiration for him. Unlike so many intoxicated by the Washington power game, George had walked away from his job in the late seventies and returned to Spokane. He'd just gotten married, and he told me he wanted to raise his family in a community with traditional values, far from the corridors of power. In addition, his father was ill, and George was needed at home to help run his dad's law firm. We stayed in touch over the years and usually got together once or twice a year, when they passed through D.C. on their way to South Carolina to visit Mary Beth's folks.

In December 1993, not long before Christmas, George had called to say he and Mary Beth were coming east for the holidays and wanted to have lunch. We met at Sam & Harry's. Its plush green leather booths attracted many of Washington's most influential wheelers and dealers. If any of them had overheard our conversation that day, they would have called it Rollins's Folly.

We spent the first twenty minutes catching up. They wanted to know if I was surviving the "New Jersey Incident," as my friends called it, usually while gazing at the carpeting. The Nethercutts had reached out to me immediately after the storm broke. I shrugged, trying to convey a sense of detachment they must have realized was a bit of a stretch. Then George explained why he'd been more eager than usual to get together.

He'd recently been approached by a number of local party activists about challenging the local congressman, who also happened to be Speaker of the U.S. House of Representatives. Although he was the Spokane County Republican chairman, George said he'd never had political ambitions.

"But I think Tom Foley is vulnerable this time," he ventured. "What do you think, Ed?"

I've never been in the habit of bullshitting potential clients, and I wasn't about to start by misleading a dear friend. I explained it would be an extremely tough race at best, and even if Foley were having trouble back home (as some published reports were suggesting), the Democrats would commit enormous resources to save him. Incumbency and the money it attracts are the most powerful weapons in every politician's arsenal. It's no accident that 95 percent of all challengers lose.

"George, nobody beats a Speaker," I said as gently as I could.

"You probably haven't paid a lot of attention to what's happening out here," he replied, reminding me that Foley had hurt himself seriously by supporting a lawsuit to overturn the term limits Washington State voters had recently approved. It smacked of arrogance and proved Foley was out of touch with his constituents, George argued.

While it was obvious they were tempted, George and Mary Beth were clearly struggling with the decision. As their friend, I wanted to be sure I helped them make the correct one. I suggested we look hard at the race and take a few weeks to come to a decision. I also suggested that he commission a poll to find out how vulnerable the Speaker really was, so we could reach a judgment with some empirical data.

"If I ran," George asked, "would you help me?"

"George, I'm the last guy in the world you want involved. Foley would surely make me a campaign issue."

I said I'd do everything possible behind the scenes. I'd help them put together a strategy and assemble a strong political team. But any direct involvement would be suicidal for his chances.

"I think you're the best in the country," he said as we got up to leave, "and you're my friend. If I run, I want you there, regardless of the controversy."

I walked out onto Nineteenth Street into the cold December wind thinking to myself, I'd love to do this fucking race. George would make a great candidate and congressman, and beating the Speaker would be a nice way for me to finish my career. Then I came to my senses. I *couldn't* do this race. My presence would guarantee needless trouble for an utterly uncontroversial candidate. Once again, I realized how much damage I'd done to myself and people I cared about with those careless words at the Sperling breakfast. As I drove home, I was caught in a tangle of mixed emotions. I was happy my friend wanted to run, and the gambler in me hoped he would. I was bitter as hell that I couldn't do anything but whisper from the shadows. And I thought he had a 30 percent chance of winning at best.

I was amazed, therefore, when George telephoned me a few weeks later to report the poll results had come back surprisingly positive. Tom Foley *had* apparently lost touch with his district. The data suggested Foley was vulnerable to a conservative challenge if his opponent wasn't a right-wing extremist, as Foley's last two challengers had been. I knew from experience that vulnerability in a January poll is a far cry from losing in November. But the numbers said George had another important asset: Although he wasn't well known in the district, he fit perfectly the profile of the kind of candidate who could give Foley trouble.

In early February 1994, two months after our Washington lunch, George called to say that he and Mary Beth had made up their minds. I told them that was the easy part. They'd now committed themselves and their family to the most excruciating year of their lives.

"I'm going to do this," he said. "Will you help me?"

I said again that I was trouble he didn't need, but I'd be happy to do whatever I could quietly as a volunteer.

"No, I want to pay you," he said. "Besides, if I lose because you were involved, I deserve to lose."

Mr. Nethercutt Goes to Washington. How could I say no?

I flew out to Spokane for our first planning session on March 10. We met on a Saturday in the home of Rich Kueling, a prominent lawyer active in local Republican politics who'd been the Bush state chairman in 1992. The level of enthusiasm in the room was high. The level of reality—what was going to happen to all their lives over the next seven months—was low. At least Mary Beth had the good sense to be nervous. Win or lose, no one's routine would be changed as dramatically as hers. Her life at that moment was story-book perfect. The mother of two young children, she had a great career, was a marathon runner who jogged every day, served as PTA president, and was active in the community. There was no way George's running wouldn't rock that boat.

She'd been one of my favorite people from the moment I met her. When she was working on Capitol Hill as an aide to Congressman Charlie Wilson of Texas, she was a show-stopper—beautiful, charming, petite, blonde, smart, and very southern. The intervening years and motherhood had been very kind. Five weeks after the birth of their first child, she began law school. The in-laws cared for the baby during the day, and George took over at night. After Mary Beth graduated summa cum laude, she had her pick of Spokane's prestigious firms, but joined her husband in his family practice.

George and Mary Beth have a true partnership, as professionals and as parents. She sends the kids off to school and then heads to the office. At 3:00 P.M., she's home to meet them. After they're in bed, she works on legal briefs. If she's tied up in court, George comes home to take care of the children after school.

My mission at that first strategy session was convincing everyone George had a chance to win. I quickly added that George was a decided underdog. While the Washington political gurus still didn't have a clue that we were gunning for Foley's seat, his local backers would soon start smelling trouble and send up a warning flare. Any chance of sneaking up on Foley was wishful thinking.

We agreed that every effort would be made to keep me out of the headlines and behind the scenes. If the spotlight found me, I warned George, I might have to disappear in a hurry for his own good.

A chance encounter in the lobby of the Capital Hilton Hotel blew my cover. About a week after I got back from Spokane, I was attending the annual dinner of the Gridiron Club. The Gridiron is one of official Washington's most durable fixtures, a white-tie event for six hundred VIPs hosted by the elite of the national press corps. The guest list is a *Who's Who* in D.C., beginning with the president. It's a long night of drinks, dinner, and skits by the club's members, who dress up in ridiculous costumes and sing songs spoofing many of the powers-that-be in the audience. It was the last place on earth I wanted to be spending my fifty-first birthday, but Sherrie had persuaded me I needed to show my tattered battle flag. I may have been bucking for the glutton-for-punishment trophy, but I'd agreed to attend as the guest of Godfrey Sperling. I'd been forewarned I'd be the butt of some of the satire that night. Laughter may be the best medicine, but I was cringing beneath my frozen smile.

Exiting as fast as I could, I ran smack into Tom Foley and his wife Heather. Having spent the preceding weekend in his backyard planning his political demise, I felt a little guilty. He stopped and asked how I was doing and made a point of saying he hoped all was going well. It was a touching gesture of humanity from a very decent man. I said I was doing fine and planned to run a few campaigns that year.

As he turned toward his limousine, I felt obligated to be honest with him. "Mr. Speaker, I'm helping an old friend of mine, George Nethercutt, who's going to run against you this year. I just wanted you to hear it from me and no one else."

He looked a little taken aback. "I really don't know George, but I've heard nice things about him," he said. "I won't wish you luck," he added with a weak smile, "but I appreciate hearing it from you in person."

At that point I noticed that Meg Greenfield, editorial page editor of *The Washington Post,* was getting into the limo with Heather. By Monday, I knew, the word would be all over town that I was running the campaign against the Speaker. That was big news.

I've always come at competitors straight on, not behind their backs. If I hadn't told Foley, I would have felt like a duplicitous jerk. I'd done the right thing, but I also knew I was a marked man. I had to hope my old friend wouldn't suffer for my notoriety.

Working for the Nethercutts in the spring of 1994 was a tonic. It was the way it's supposed to be, the way it *was* once upon a time. As we quietly plotted our assault on the seemingly impregnable Speaker of the House, I felt my spirits reviving. At the twilight of my career, two old friends had given me one last chance to play the game the right way, for the right reasons, with the right clients. Come what may, at least I'd be taking the high road out of Dodge City.

But my delight at finding spiritual and professional redemption in Spokane were increasingly tempered by an unpleasant reality. I was broke. My New Jersey legal bills were close to $100,000, and my consulting business was in shambles. I honestly didn't want to, but I had to try to drum up some other campaign work this year. Otherwise, my cash flow would dry up and my next stop was probably bankruptcy.

GIVEN MY TARNISHED reputation, I didn't expect to land consulting jobs with any Republican heavyweights. But much to my surprise, in early summer opportunity came knocking in the form of California Congressman Michael Huffington. A year earlier, when my business was still prospering and I was working for Christie Whitman, Huffington had called me to say he was considering a Senate race against Dianne Feinstein in 1994 and wanted to know what I thought about his prospects.

Huffington was the Houston millionaire who had moved to California, announced his candidacy, scared off more credible opponents in the primary with his wealth, and with the help of his personal fortune had won the most expensive House race in American history the previous year. Feinstein was the former mayor of San Francisco, an entrenched and popular incumbent.

"If you're willing to spend the money," I'd told him, "you'd have a shot. I doubt you can beat Feinstein, but who knows? And if you lose, you'll still be first in line to run against Barbara Boxer." The junior senator from California, Boxer was an easier mark than Feinstein and would be up for reelection in 1998.

Huffington asked me to consider being his chief consultant. I said I'd be glad to talk about it but that I had a commitment to the Whitman campaign. I didn't want to consider other races until New Jersey was finished.

"I don't ever make these decisions alone," he replied. "I'd like you to meet my wife Arianna."

The following month, Sherrie joined us for dinner at Citronelle in Georgetown, during which I mentioned my frustrations with the Whitman operation.

"I can't understand why you don't quit and come work for us," Huffington said.

"I don't quit campaigns," I replied—words that would come back to haunt me later.

I came away from dinner impressed with her, but not with him. Arianna dominated the conversation. When she wasn't seducing me, she was bossing him around. He sat there for the most part like a bump on a log.

As I subsequently learned, Michael Huffington is an odd duck. He can't relate to average people or their problems. He is awkward, shy, and painfully poor at small talk and public speaking. Huffington is as much an oddity in the monied set as in the political world. The sad part is how very few people really like him. I'm sure he's been socially isolated for years—at Culver Military Academy, for instance, he turned in his roommate for being late and was thereafter despised by his fellow cadets.

I didn't expect to hear from them again, and especially not after the Whitman fiasco. To my surprise, Michael and Arianna were among those who called. I appreciated their kindness; I also understood that they wouldn't be wanting my assistance anymore. Six months later, I couldn't be more surprised when Arianna's secretary called. Michael had just won the June 1994 California primary after spending $10 million; now, he was gaining fast on Feinstein. The primary had been a cakewalk, and as the main event approached, the question was whether he was ready for prime time. They wanted to have dinner and solicit some advice.

I wasn't sure I wanted to do this race, and Sherrie warned me not to go near them. She has far better people instincts than I do, and just as with Ross Perot, something told her this wasn't a couple I'd click with. "You have nothing in common with either of them," she said. "It will never work." Unfortunately, once again I didn't pay attention to my wife. I was listening to the wrong woman.

A few days later, I joined the Huffingtons for dinner. Arianna was at the top of her game that night. "Creator and Destroyer" are the words she used as the subtitle for her best-selling biography of Pablo Picasso. She should have saved them for her own autobiography. In the thirty years I've been around national politics, I've never met anyone more cunning than Arianna Huffington. She's truly unstoppable. Her motto, she once told me, is "Strike first, strike fast, and strike hard"—the same rules any good street fighter would use. Maybe that's why I liked her.

She can also be utterly charming, and that night she focused her charm on me. Some femmes fatales play to a man's sexuality, some to their intelligence, but she just played to my damn ego, and that was enough. Jess Unruh had warned me every man has a price. Arianna had found mine.

At that point, I'd been kicked from one side of the political ring to the other, by friends and foes alike. She made me feel like I was needed again in an important race back in my home state of California.

As the dinner progressed, several warning signs flashed, but I was too dazzled by Arianna to connect the dots. At one point I made a comment in passing that I'd always thought Michael's father would make a superb candidate for public office and I'd love to run his campaign. Big Roy Huffington was a legend in the oil business, a self-made man who served as President Reagan's ambassador to Austria. He filled any room he walked into. I thought his son would be flattered by my remark, but as I finished my thought I could practically see the hair on Michael's neck rise.

"Why would you say that?" he challenged, obviously irritated by my remark. "*I'm* the candidate."

I quickly changed the subject. It was pretty clear this insecure only son didn't enjoy walking in Daddy's very big footprints.

When the conversation turned to the inevitable topic of finances, Huffington's reaction was equally revealing. I asked him how much more of his own money he was prepared to put into the race. He said he'd already put in more than he'd planned for the whole campaign, and asked how much I thought the fall campaign would cost. I said it was too early to tell, "but it's at least ten to fifteen million for television alone." He turned ashen.

I was surprised, since it was clear to me that Michael thought a campaign consisted only of television commercials. He and Larry McCarthy, his media guru, seemed content to hide out in a production studio and fire-bomb Feinstein. But bombs cost money, and given what he'd already spent on media, he should have known it.

I volunteered to fly out to California for a few days and assess the condition of his campaign. That way I'd have a better sense of what it would cost. I wasn't ready to commit yet, but this was a good way to get a fix on whether it would be worth my time.

"I'll do the consultation for free," I said. "It will only cost you a first-class roundtrip ticket to California." I expected him to be grateful. His answer took me aback.

"Nobody flies first-class in my campaign, not even Arianna," he said. This was a candidate who'd already spent over $10 million without a serious primary opponent and had just been told the price tag for the fall would be substantially more. I wasn't about to be nickel-and-dimed over a freebie.

"Mike, that's Arianna's problem. I'm a fat old man, and at this point in my life, I only fly first-class."

"It's not negotiable," he insisted.

"I agree, it's not negotiable." A few days later, I had my first-class ticket. But the real message, which was broadcast loud and clear, was that Huffington was another Ross Perot: a guy who'd spend millions promiscuously on things he wanted, but would cut corners on the items that could make a genuine difference, like direct mail and get-out-the-vote efforts.

If these two exchanges weren't enough of an omen, the evening ended with another sign from above that I should thank them for a pleasant dinner and go my way.

Sherrie had just begun a new job as senior vice president with the ABC television network in New York and had left that morning for the city. My dinner with the Huffingtons ran longer than planned, and the parking lot attendant had locked up my car and, more importantly, my house keys. I took a cab home, assuming I could get into the house somehow. I should have realized that my ever efficient wife had locked the place up tighter than a drum. I hopped the back fence—not easily, I might add—and attempted to crawl through the dog door. Undignified, to be sure, but it was my only chance. After much effort and even more swearing, I finally managed to get my head and shoulders through the door, only to be greeted by my two lovable Labs: Duke and Dutch proceeded to lick my bald head with great vigor and a lot of saliva.

Like most overweight, middle-aged men, I still imagine myself looking about like I did when I was playing football in high school. I assumed once I got my shoulders through the door, my hips would follow. Wrong. For the better part of the next two hours, I banged, cursed, struggled, and damn near drowned in dog drool while attempting to squeeze through the fucking door. Off and on during the whole time, of course, the phone is ringing and I know it's my frantic wife calling from her apartment in New York, wondering where the hell I am and what I'm doing there. I tried to remember what day the maid came in and wondered if I'd still be alive when she found me. At long last, I managed to break down the frame around the dog door and drag myself into the house, exhausted and relieved. I could imagine *The Washington Post* headline: "Controversial Political Consultant Ed Rollins Dies of Heart Attack While Thwarted by Labs Breaking into Missing Wife's Home."

In spite of all these warning signs, I told the Huffingtons I'd do their race a few days later. Now, there were four races to juggle; in addition to George Nethercutt, by this time I was advising Bruce Benson and Bernadette Castro, who were running, respectively, for governor of Colorado and U.S. senator from New York. Thanks to Huffington, my cash flow problems were eased. And there was another advantage: Michael's deep pockets could help subsidize the shoestring Nethercutt race by paying the air freight to get me to the West Coast.

In early July, I started to run a Texas millionaire's campaign for the second time in three years. The first one I did because I thought my candidate could change the country. The second one I did for the dough. One thing that I quickly discovered from both of them: Rich people *are* different from the rest of us. And rich Texans are even more different. Fool me once, shame on you. Fool me twice, shame on me.

My old boxing coach Mike Denton would tell a fighter after a loss, "Shut your mouth, get back in the gym and train harder than ever, and win the next one." I had to win the next one if I ever wanted to get out of this rat race. It was becoming a vicious circle. I did Perot to prove to the Bush people I still had the right stuff. I did Whitman to show up all those who said I would never work in this town again. I'd do Huffington to pay off my debts after Whitman. But when this one was over—win, lose, or draw—I was out of there.

THE FIRST FEW weeks on the Huffington campaign were actually kind of fun. The professionals were old friends or former colleagues, and I had great respect for them. It was a formidable team, one of the most experienced and expensive in campaign history, and yet we didn't have a serious disagreement throughout.

Dick Wirthlin had been Reagan's pollster and chief strategist in 1980, and my numbers guy in 1984. Ken Khachigian was one of California's premier conservative consultants, headed Reagan's White House speechwriting team, and was a veteran of the Nixon White House. Larry McCarthy's hard-hitting primary commercials had already made Huffington a serious contender to unseat Feinstein. We'd worked together at the NRCC, and I'd hired him for George Nethercutt's race. I wasn't the only political junkie who considered McCarthy the best negative-media man around. Bruce Nestande, my consigliere, was an old pal from the 1972 Nixon campaign, when we'd both worked for Lyn Nofziger. We'd also run around together in Sacramento when Bruce was an assemblyman from Orange County. A former chairman of the Orange County Board of Supervisors, Bruce had managed Huffington's congressional victory two years earlier, and of all the advisers he had the best personal relationship with the candidate. We kept each other sane throughout this whole exercise in futility.

I was the chief strategist and oversaw the daily operations. I'd brought in Jamie Moore, who'd worked for me at the NRCC and with Whitman, to run the daily operation. While I shuttled between Spokane and my other races, he stayed back at the campaign headquarters in Orange County to keep everything on track.

The first order of business was producing a budget. Unlike Michael's congressional race or the Senate primary, where he'd simply kept signing checks, we needed a budget for the fall campaign. Jamie and I prepared one for him that came to a little over $16 million, much of it for television and radio buys. Michael went nuts; there was no way he was going to spend that kind of money, he insisted. He'd pretty much given up fund-raising because he didn't like to grovel for cash. Big contributors want to be tapped by the candidate, in person or at least on the phone. Mike wasn't willing to do either. He announced he'd spend only another $7 million of his own money—at least $10 million short of what he needed. It was déjà vu all over again, Texas-style. We put together an alternative budget, but warned him he'd lose his financial advantage over Feinstein and diminish his chance to win.

His solution was to install rigid expenditure controls, including a hiring freeze. Those controls were constantly overridden by his wife, who hired people left and right. When I complained about her budget-busting, she'd tell me not to worry, she'd take it up with Mike. She once hired three new staffers and told Mike they were volunteers. When he wouldn't give her more money, she'd run to his father. Roy would do anything for Arianna, and I'm sure she would have loved to pull some scams with her father-in-law's checkbook I didn't know about. The problem was that by law, Mike could spend all he wanted of his money, but his father by law was good for only $1,000, like any other contributor. The long and short of it was that I spent too much time going to the lawyers to make sure we weren't violating federal election law. The strategic problem I had to juggle was that he'd wasted so much in the primary that we had to cut important things in the fall, like voter outreach and field operations.

On one of my first working trips to California in July, Arianna invited me to spend the weekend at their Santa Barbara estate. The drive up the coast from the campaign headquarters in Orange County brought back many wonderful memories of summers past. President Reagan spent most of every August at his ranch north of Santa Barbara, and his senior staff would hole up at the Biltmore, a world-famous hotel overlooking the Pacific. It was always wonderful R&R. The workload was light, usually not much more than standby duty.

Over those five summers, I developed some close friendships in the local Republican community, which was now badly split over the Huffingtons. Nobody much liked either of them; the two camps were divided between neutrals and haters. The latter were longtime supporters of Bob Lagomarsino, who'd represented the area in the state Senate and as congressman for eighteen years. We'd been neighbors during the Reagan years, and Bob and his wife Norma were beloved by many, including me. In 1992, Huffington had challenged Bob in a Republican primary six months after he moved to California and spent millions of dollars bombarding Lagomarsino with negative commercials. Mike spent at least $5.6 million to win the primary and the general election—the most money ever spent in a congressional race in U.S. history.

The bitterness he engendered among many of the locals he now represented hadn't abated with time. The community feud grew worse when Huffington decided after six months in Congress that he wanted to run for the Senate. He was so unpopular that he'd lost his home county in the just-concluded Senate primary. David Garth, executive director of the San Luis Obispo chamber of commerce, told the story of how Huffington didn't renew his chamber membership a few months after getting elected to Congress. Garth wrote asking for an explanation, saying the business community would be terribly offended and feel they'd been used in the campaign. In a telephone conversation a few days later, Huffington told Garth, "I'm running for the Senate, and I don't need you anymore." Asked why he wanted to move up so quickly, Huffington replied, "I really hate being a congressman because all it is is constituent service." In fact, he seldom visited the district, preferring his L.A. apartment to the Montecito mansion. Arianna and the kids lived in the beach house two hours away in Newport Beach.

The Huffington estate in Montecito is one of the most beautiful homes I've ever seen. It sits on ten acres overlooking the Pacific Ocean near Santa Barbara. As Michael was showing me the property, I told him there were two issues of business I wanted to address: the release of his tax information, and the need to repair the damage he'd done himself in his new hometown. Many longtime Republican activists were openly supporting Feinstein. I suggested he commit the money and organization for a major rehabilitation effort. He said he'd think about it.

Then there were his tax returns. By refusing to release them, he was vulnerable to Feinstein's charges that he'd paid no taxes and had, in fact, avoided them by remaining a resident of Texas until he ran for Congress. He told me there was no way he'd ever release them and, in fact, he *couldn't.*

He didn't explain why, and I didn't ask, but as we walked across his estate he told me this story: Before he married Arianna, he didn't own a house. He lived in an apartment in Houston and was very happy. After the wedding, they'd looked for over a year at more than a hundred homes around Los Angeles and purchased this one for over $4 million.

"We spent another fortune redoing it," he said. "Then I get elected to Congress and Arianna needs a house in Washington, so we buy another one for five million. She then spends another fortune redoing *it.*

"No one but my accountants and I know how much I'm worth. The press has estimated it at seventy to seventy-five million, based on my disclosure forms. That's way low, but it's fine if that's the figure they want to use. It's more like double that amount. If I disclose my taxes, then Arianna will figure out how much I'm worth and try to spend it all."

Now I understood, and I almost felt something like sympathy for him. Not releasing his tax returns would become an explosive issue, but one that I never raised with him again.

We retired to his spacious office and library after a rather unpleasant dinner in a downtown restaurant. Michael and Arianna had fought over the campaign and every other thing on her very long list. She kept arguing that he had to spend more money and we couldn't let up now. He insisted he was not going to have that discussion in a public place and was quite tired of her constant nagging. The tension between the two made me very uncomfortable.

After she went up to bed, Michael and I again talked about how much the campaign was going to cost. From the paneled shelves behind his desk, he took down a plastic model of a corporate jet. It looked like a Gulfstream IV, a very expensive plane. He explained that he loved flying and travel. Then he said wistfully, "If I had my way, I'd be spending my money on one of these."

This confirmed my suspicion that the race he'd hired me to run was the obsession of his upwardly mobile wife, not his. A few years earlier, she'd dated Jerry Brown and tried to elect him president; Michael was her latest target of opportunity. It was a twenty-four-hour-a-day, seven-day-a-week obsession for Arianna, and an excuse for an occasional obligatory drop-by for the candidate. He'd spent nearly $6 million to buy a congressional job he hated, and there was no evidence he was going to like the one he was now seeking any better.

I left him there alone and went upstairs to my room. This poor bastard wants to be a senator about as bad as I want to be the Pope, I thought to myself. He hated all of this. I'd soon learn that he hated fund-raising, he hated giving speeches, he hated the press, he hated campaigning, he hated meeting constituents, and if he got elected, he'd hate being a U.S. senator. What Michael Huffington really wanted in July 1994 was to spend his $30 million on a private jet and fly away.

Before long, what was flying was rumors. It began relatively tamely with innuendos about his sexual proclivities and took off from there. My first whiff of it came shortly after I'd joined up. I received a case of condoms from an old friend—industrialist Barney Klinger, a longtime Reagan supporter I'd gotten to know during those August trips with the president.

"If you're going to sleep with the enemy," Barney said, "use protection. Remember when you're around Mike, protect your ass at all times." It was a not-so-subtle hint to the whispers that Michael was gay—rumors Barney took great delight in spreading. I raised the subject pointblank one day in a meeting.

"Do you think I'm gay?" Michael asked.

"It's totally irrelevant what I think, and I truly couldn't care one way or another. But the stories are all over New York, Houston, and Washington, and the press is starting to pick up on them. We're getting questions about it every day. If there are any bombshells out there, it's better to be prepared for them in advance. If there's any truth to any of it, the Feinstein camp will be the first to know."

"I'm not going to answer any questions like that from you or anybody else," he said, and the meeting was over. It was the most bizarre answer I'd ever gotten from a candidate. There was no sense of outrage at such a personal query. It wasn't that he protested too much; he didn't protest at all.

He did react to a similar inquiry of mine after a story appeared in which a former staff member complained Huffington was always hugging him. He told me he always hugged his employees. I kiddingly responded that he'd never hugged me. "You're too short," he replied. I've never been more relieved to be short in my life.

After that, I pushed Arianna to travel with Michael as often as possible. There was no better way to put to rest malicious rumors than to see a man with his attractive wife and two adorable children. But she bored easily when she wasn't the center of attention.

I soon realized that I was trying to manage two candidates—and the truth of the matter is she truly was the better one. She's very bright, incredibly fast on her feet, a good people person, and a tremendous debater. In the primary, Michael had been missing-in-action and Arianna was an eager stand-in. She actually debated his primary opponent six times, Michael none.

Her mind was like a steel trap, abetted by her Day-Timer, a large black binder in which she organized her life and thoughts. Days after a conversation, she'd pull out her binder and say: "You said you would do this by this date. What is the progress?" No matter what else was going on, that stupid book drove her and everyone else's agenda.

I was learning that the Huffingtons were a classic example of how a candidate's character and life-style can carry over and sometimes overwhelm the daily operations of a campaign. From the moment of my involvement, this was a bizarre, chaotic odyssey in which the three principals were frequently in separate orbits, if not galaxies.

In mid-August, for example, I arrived back in Los Angeles late on a Sunday evening and took a shuttle to the Orange County headquarters. The next morning, the Today Show aired dramatic footage of a devastating forest fire that was blazing out of control in Atascadero. I wasn't paying that much attention until I realized the inferno was in Huffington's district. Michael was getting killed in Feinstein's commercials and the Santa Barbara press for ignoring the district. She was reminding voters that he'd actually been stupid enough to say, "I want a government that does nothing. What's great is what's private." The forest fire gave us an opening to show that the candidate in fact paid attention to the home front.

I called Bruce Nestande, who was already on the case. Governor Pete Wilson had announced he was going to the fire scene. We all agreed Mike needed to drop everything and go to the district, so we tracked him down in San Diego, where he was preparing for a rare campaign appearance.

He was amazingly reluctant, saying he wanted to make an afternoon flight back to Washington. I suggested we charter a jet, fly him to the district to meet the governor and local officials, assess the damage, and then fly back to L.A. in time for a red-eye that would get him to Washington early the next morning. Assuming he'd agree, I chartered the jet at a cost of about $2,500 for the day while Michael was speaking. It was the only way to get him there in time for Wilson's press conference.

When he came out of his San Diego speech and learned about the schedule change, he went ballistic. He wanted to know who the hell had authorized the jet, which he immediately canceled. He wasn't sure if he'd go to the district, but he sure as hell wouldn't be taking a jet if he did.

I got on the phone and told him he absolutely had to go. It was one of those events that could make or break a campaign, I said. His answer was emphatic. He hung up without a word.

Not quite able to figure what was going on in this guy's head, I located Brian Lungren, the traveling press secretary. His first words told me all I needed to know.

"It was a fucking disaster, boss, a fucking disaster." Then he gave me all the gory details.

Michael had been invited to make a luncheon address to the Catfish Club, a nonpartisan African-American business group. I'd killed this event weeks ago, but in my absence, Arianna had slipped it back on the schedule. As it happens, Arianna had just written a book called *Fourth Instinct,* which proposed abolishing all government welfare programs and replacing them with voluntary charity. She'd been trying to make volunteerism the overarching theme of the campaign since long before I arrived, but had gotten as lukewarm a response from the pros as from the public. Her book was a flop and so was the campaign theme. (The only volunteer events she turned up at were the ones being covered by TV crews.) Nonetheless, she was insistent that Michael address the subject, and she thought an all-black audience would be perfect. This black audience, however, consisted of successful entrepreneurs. A speech about getting off welfare was clearly an insult and was sure to be viewed as pandering.

Michael arrived at the Christ United Presbyterian Church with a camera crew in tow because he wanted to film this speech for a TV commercial, his preferred means of communication with voters. He arrived forty-five minutes late, and the audience was rather restless, to say the least. Instead of apologizing and starting his remarks immediately, he made matters worse by disappearing into a holding room for another twenty minutes to have his makeup applied. Meanwhile, Larry McCarthy was setting up his lights and cameras, making it obvious to the audience that they were being used merely as a backdrop for the commercial. Several people walked out. They were the lucky ones.

Michael finally began reading his text, but stopped in the middle and started ad-libbing such idiotic sound bites as "We have to care about our little boys and little girls because, after all, God put us on this planet not to take care of ourselves but to take care of others."

And: "I'm not a politician. I'm a businessman, I'm a father, I'm a brother, I'm a son."

And then the best one: "I'd like to see us reinstitute school prayer so that our young children have some moral beliefs, they have some principles." The guy was making George Bush sound eloquent.

He then stopped abruptly, and getting no applause from the enraged audience, left by a side door with the press in pursuit.

As I'm thinking this can't get worse, Thessen tells me:

"Then a guy from KSDO radio asks Mike if his wife has ever been an ordained minister in a cult called Movement of Inner Spiritual Awareness [MISA, pronounced "Messiah"]. His response is, 'Not that I know of.' Unfortunately, at the same time Arianna is telling the traveling reporters yes, she was ordained as a MISA minister. The follow-up question from a reporter is of course, 'How could your husband never know?' 'We've never discussed it,' she says. 'It's never come up.' "

I was still shaking my head in disbelief over Lungren's report when Huffington's driver called in to say he was driving the boss to the district, and that Mr. Huffington didn't want to be disturbed or to talk to anyone in the campaign. I called the car immediately, but he'd disconnected the car phone and turned off the portables.

It was now about 2:00 P.M. The governor's press conference was set for three. The drive from San Diego to Atascadero is about four hours. This is why candidates make lousy advance men.

Just when I thought this story couldn't possibly get any more bizarre, the advance guys told me Arianna had commandeered the jet I'd chartered and was flying to the scene with a photographer from *People* magazine who'd been following her around. Before leaving, she'd gotten a call from someone who'd heard on the radio that the firefighters needed drinking water. So she ordered ten cases of Evian to hand out when she got there. I hope she remembered the limes.

Arianna arrived in time for the governor's press conference, distributed her celebrity water, and was featured prominently on all the local television stations. The candidate arrived well after the film crews and everyone else had disappeared. He got a quick tour of the fire scene from a park ranger, drove back to L.A., then flew to Washington. Except for the ranger, nobody in the district knew our candidate had been near the place. We didn't hear from him for another week. Then Congress adjourned for the summer and Huffington, who'd made only two campaign appearances since the June primary, went to Hawaii for two weeks' vacation. He wanted Arianna to join him, but she was too busy campaigning for her Senate seat.

DESPITE MICHAEL'S DEFECTS as a campaigner, the gap was narrowing. By Labor Day, what had once been a thirty-point deficit was down to about eighteen. Like many other Republican candidates, Michael was riding the wave of a strong anti-Washington mood, accelerated by voter disapproval of President Clinton's job performance. I began to believe that maybe we'd be able to pull this one out.

Predictably, the fall became a battle of negative ads. We'd go nuclear on DiFi, and she'd fire back on us. Adding to our troubles, the national and local news media were hammering on Arianna daily. They had uncovered her MISA identity. One magazine reported that on her wedding night she'd gone off minus her new husband with her spiritual guru named John-Roger—the kook who got his heavenly inspiration while suffering from a kidney stone in the seventies—to give an impassioned speech that brought the two hundred seekers of the way to their feet. Just goes to show she'd rather talk than do what most normal people do on their honeymoon. I was convinced the Feinstein camp was going to bomb us with a cult-priestess spot any day, and I didn't have a clue how to respond. Even by California standards, this was totally off the wall.

The bad press was wearing Arianna down. In September, she was obsessed with reports she'd been getting about a piece that Maureen Orth was working on for *Vanity Fair*. Orth's husband is Tim Russert,

Washington bureau chief for NBC News and the moderator of *Meet the Press. Vanity Fair* had done a piece on Arianna once before that she didn't think was fair, and she wasn't anxious to get blasted again—especially by a magazine that was a must-read among her Park Avenue friends.

One day, I walked into her office to chat and overheard her saying something about getting "the detective's report on Maureen Orth." When she got off the phone, I let her have it.

"I hope I heard that wrong, Arianna, but if you've got a private detective looking into Maureen Orth, you're fucking nuts! Are you out of your mind? If the media ever finds out you're hiring private eyes to follow reporters, we're all dead."

I could tell by the defiant look on her face that she wasn't getting the message, so I added, "If you don't call this off now, I'm outta here." She hurriedly changed the subject.

I asked her later that day if she'd stopped the investigation; she coolly said she had. Her evasiveness convinced me she was lying. I know she had another private investigation going on at the same time, this one presumably designed to discredit Peter McWilliams, another MISA "minister," who was coming out with a book that linked her to the cult and a lot of other weird stuff. When I raised concerns about that investigation, she said it had nothing to do with the campaign and she was paying for it out of her own funds. I later happened to see a check to the private investigator, which was drawn to the "Huffington household account." Hiring private eyes out of the grocery money certainly was a new one on me.

Things were getting so negative on both sides that I decided it was time to shift gears and make for the high road. In early September, I brought in Sig Rogich, the media guru who'd been so effective for Reagan in 1984 and Bush in 1988, to help us do some positive spots. It was another bizarre day on the trail. We shot the commercials at the Santa Barbara mansion. Even though Arianna was going to appear only in the background with the kids, you'd have thought she was Elizabeth Taylor filming *Cleopatra.* She had multiple changes of clothes, her own makeup artist, plus the usual entourage of cooks, nannies, and her own masseuse. (We were the only campaign in history with an in-house masseuse and personal chef, but no get-out-the-vote effort or field staff.)

Arianna kept bugging Sig to write lines for her to say on camera, which wasn't part of the plan. Meanwhile, she was trying to sneak a photographer into the house to do interior shots for a *People* magazine layout. Michael's a security nut and has never permitted photos of the inside of his home, so he wanted the photographer thrown off the property. Naturally, Arianna lied and said it was my idea, then tried to sweet-talk me into sneaking the photographer in the back way while Sig was off shooting Michael.

Michael got pissed and ordered me to throw the guy out. I told him I was neither his private security guard nor the fucking referee between him and his wife.

Incredibly, the day ended without bloodshed, and Sig got some great footage of Michael for the commercial. Mike proudly proclaimed that Ronald Reagan couldn't have done the last shot better than he just had.

I thought to myself, Ten years after Reagan's dead and buried he'll do the shot better than you, Michael. What a man will put up with for money. (Arianna managed to sneak the photographer in, and Mike blew a gasket when he saw the *People* spread.)

Our walk along the high road was brief. In early October, the Huffingtons assembled their senior staff for an afternoon strategy session in a fifteenth-floor suite of the Clift Hotel in San Francisco. With four weeks to go, the battle was fully engaged, and the air war was vicious. We were bombarding Feinstein with TV and radio commercials, and she was fighting back furiously with broadsides of her own. The mood in the room was tense. We were nearly even in the polls, but my staff and I knew the worst lay ahead. Feinstein's attack ads would only get more relentless, and the national news media was beginning to get their licks in, too; it was as if they felt some sacred duty to stop this power-crazed pair.

By now, Arianna and I weren't getting along at all. I'd been her ally early on and now I was her nemesis, the guy who had to tell her no. I felt at times like an arms negotiator running back and forth between the two of them. I'd told Michael a few weeks ago that it wasn't my job to be their goddamn marriage counsellor and that he had better start telling her no and sticking with it.

After we'd talked strategy for an hour, Wirthlin presented his polling numbers. They weren't good. Even though the race had closed, Michael and Arianna's unfavorable ratings were in the stratosphere. This news notwithstanding, the candidate was cocky because he'd beaten Feinstein in the campaign's one and only debate on *Larry King Live* earlier in the week. Arianna, on the other hand, was terribly distracted. She kept going into the bathroom to talk on the phone with her chief spy in the campaign, Jennifer Grossman, and each time she came out more agitated.

Jennifer was the press secretary, and she was in way over her head. She'd worked as a speech researcher in the Bush White House. She was bright and worked hard, but it was preposterous for a major campaign in a media state like California to have a press secretary who'd never worked a campaign or dealt with the press before. But she was an Arianna wannabe and worshipped the ground the Greek goddess walked on. Michael couldn't stand her and wanted Jennifer out, but Arianna had run off two good press secretaries and insisted on Jennifer.

The *Los Angeles Times* hated our guts and was preparing another hatchet job on Arianna for the next day's edition. The story was how she'd fired several staffers and was essentially running the campaign herself. The fired aides were obviously bad-mouthing her. I'd never seen a campaign with such staff turnover. Every time I looked up, Arianna had a new scheduler, a new secretary, even a new nanny. Anyone who crossed her was soon gone. Now, she wanted me to take the fall by telling the *Times* I'd fired them all for incompetence. I said no way to that.

During her next bathroom phone break, I turned to Mike. "You've got to help me with her," I said.

"I already *have* helped you this week by beating Dianne Feinstein in the debate." He had been living on another planet; now he seemed poised for a new solar system.

She came back into the room, and this time she was crying. She started right after me, screaming that it was all my fault. "You're a liar!" she screeched in a hysterical fury at one point. That was Arianna's favorite epithet in a fight.

I stood up and turned to Michael. "I'm not putting up with her bullshit any more," I said. I stormed out of the room and waited in the hall to cool down. The meeting disintegrated.

Just as Michael and Arianna got on the elevator, I grabbed the elevator door. "Mike, we got three choices here. I can quit and go take care of my other races. I can go back to Washington and you can call me for advice on the telephone. Or I can stay here and try to win this thing for you. But if I stay, I don't want to have a fucking thing to do with your wife the rest of this campaign. Nobody calls me a liar."

"Please don't swear at my wife," he replied. "Calm down and let's get this fixed."

He was right. I shouldn't have sworn at Arianna. I should have decked her, and if she were a man, maybe I would have. As the elevator doors closed, she was pleading with me to talk to her. I rejoined my astonished colleagues, who couldn't believe what had just happened. The phone rang. It was Arianna, calling from the lobby.

"Please, darling, we must talk. I won't go to the fundraiser if we can just talk." I caved, and Mike went on to the fundraiser in Monterey without her. Why he bothered is still beyond me. We were the only campaign in history that lost money on our fund-raising operation. That was another area Arianna supervised.

For two hours at the bar, I let her have it, and she argued, cajoled, and sweet-talked me. In the end, I said, "I'm the lifeguard, and you're drowning five hundred yards from shore. If you let me save you, I can. If you struggle with me, you and your husband will both drown."

Predictably, she then turned on the charm machine. "I'm worried about you," she purred. "It must be miserable being away from Sherrie and living in a terrible hotel. You need to be nurtured so you can think strategically." She insisted on getting me a suite at the Four Seasons in Newport Beach and having her personal masseuse give me a daily massage. She asked me if everything was all right with Sherrie and me; if it wasn't, she'd be happy to supply me with "company." I assured her my wife and I were doing just fine, thanks, and I didn't need any company. I was astonished. Arianna would go to any lengths.

In the end, we formed a truce. But I knew I'd be lucky if it lasted forty-eight hours. Didn't someone once say, "Beware of Greeks bearing gifts"?

For all our internal chaos, particularly the constant interference of the indefatigable and ruthless Arianna, we'd actually roared past Feinstein with less than two weeks to election day. Then, on October 27, the roof fell in. When the *Los Angeles Times* broke the story of the Huffingtons' illegal alien nanny, the voters of California decided they'd had enough of Michael and Arianna Huffington. So did Ed Rollins. I was on a plane to Spokane before the week was out.

Ironically, Michael Huffington had introduced only two bills during his one term in Congress. One would have given a bigger tax deduction to millionaires for charitable contributions. The other would have made it illegal to transport an illegal worker across state lines. He and Arianna had violated the spirit of that bill when they brought their nanny to Washington with them. When asked about that, he said the bill didn't pass.

I still believe that public office is a sacred trust. But trust was one resource Huffington's checkbook couldn't buy. Those of us who worked for him couldn't trust him or his wife; they couldn't trust each other; and ultimately the public didn't trust either of them. Who could blame them? The campaign's first commercial, ironically, had quoted Bill Bennett's *Book of Virtues*. The last spot called Dianne Feinstein a liar.

THE 5TH DISTRICT in eastern Washington is the largest congressional district in the state and one of the largest in the country. For the past thirty years, the 5th had been represented by Tom Foley. Since the Civil War, no sitting Speaker had been defeated, and Foley was not going down without a fight. His defeat would be far more than a crushing blow to the Democratic Party. It would be the final nail in the liberal agenda he'd faithfully supported since he was elected in the Johnson landslide of 1964. It would also be a huge embarrassment to Bill Clinton and the Democratic Party. To save Foley, his party was preparing to pull out all the stops. It would be the showcase congressional race in the country.

We knew he'd capitalize on his power and prestige to the hilt by delivering the pork in the months ahead. Federal dollars would roll into Spokane in ever-increasing amounts, and the Speaker would get the credit. The local newspaper publisher loved Old Tom, and before long editorials would appear raising the obvious question: Why should we give up all this for some inexperienced nobody?

Because of what his clout in Washington delivered to the district, we couldn't make a frontal attack on the Speaker or paint him as a big-spending liberal. Our strategy instead was to neutralize that power and pork by arguing that it—and Foley himself—was precisely what was wrong with Congress. Foley and his cronies had lost touch with the district because he didn't live there anymore and came home infrequently. He didn't know it yet, but Tom Foley was about to become the local poster boy for everything American voters didn't like about their government. Our strategy was to treat the Speaker with respect, thank him for his thirty years of splendid service, and give him his gold watch. The Nethercutt slogan made the point succinctly: "What this district needs is a listener, not a Speaker."

One reason that slogan struck a chord was because George Nethercutt epitomized what the 1994 elections were all about. Across the country, voters felt that Washington didn't understand what was going on in their lives. On the other hand, George is Mr. Main Street U.S.A. He's a friendly, articulate guy, well liked by his friends and neighbors. I've never heard him say an unkind word about anyone, and vice versa. He has deep roots in his community. Despite his opponent's prestige and power, George Nethercutt was closer to his community than the absentee Speaker.

Our first challenge was getting George into the runoff. Washington State has a unique primary process. Not only is it the last one held, in mid-September, but it's an open primary. That means everyone gets to vote for the candidate of their choice regardless of party. The top Republican and Democratic vote getters then face off in the general election.

On April 21, George launched his campaign with a "Breakfast of Champions" fundraiser in Spokane. It wasn't exactly a power breakfast: Wheaties and orange juice at $10 apiece. But one thousand people filled every available seat, and another two hundred spilled over into the hallways of the auditorium. I'd supervised hundreds of congressional races in my White House and NRCC years, and I'd never seen a turnout like this—even in heavily urban districts.

Our campaign was volunteer-driven. Hundreds of people signed up to work the phone banks and walk precincts. The downtown headquarters was always packed with people—ordinary folks who just wanted to help. This race had all the makings of a grass-roots crusade.

On one of my regular trips to Spokane from Orange County, a television crew was waiting at the arrival gate. I panicked, afraid that my low profile was about to be blown. As I was trying to think of what to say, they rushed right past me. It turned out they were waiting for the Speaker and his wife, who were arriving on a flight from Washington a few minutes later. George met me at the gate, and as I was getting my bags, back came the camera crew. They'd finished with Foley and realized they had another story.

They interviewed George for a while, then stuck a mike in my face as I struggled to pull my bag off the line. The lead on the eleven o'clock news was: Big-time Washington consultant comes to Spokane to help friend beat Foley. The piece was straightforward and omitted my usual middle names, like "Controversial" and "Ruthless." The closing was interesting, though. It was a shot of the Speaker and Heather standing at the curb waiting for their car. The voice-over said Tom Foley was coming home for what may be his last congressional campaign. I liked the sound of that.

A few weeks before the primary, our internal polls showed George running third behind the two other Republicans. They were both well funded but each had run unsuccessfully against Foley in earlier elections. Both men were viewed as more conservative than George and had been attacking him from the right.

The issue that separated them was abortion. His two opponents were strongly pro-life; George was pro-choice. He and Mary Beth were both personally opposed to abortion but felt it was the woman's right to make that decision. George had a unique added qualification in this issue. He was the top adoption lawyer in the state. He and his wife had arranged for hundreds of adoptions and charged only a minimal fee. It was hard to make the usual baby-killer attack on someone who's spent much of his life working on alternatives to abortion.

George also supported fetal-tissue research, another hot issue for the pro-life movement. I thought he defused the issue brilliantly when challenged in a debate about it. He pointed out that he was president of the local diabetes association and that his oldest daughter had been afflicted with the disease since childhood. How could he ever be against any medical research that might someday save his daughter's life?

Since George was performing well on the stump and we were raising enough money to run our race, our internal polls didn't bother me at that point. I assumed the numbers were merely the result of his primary opponents having more name identification from their earlier races. Once we started our television campaign, we'd be fine. However, the polls sent shock waves through our troops and had a chilling effect on the Nethercutt household.

I was due back in L.A. that night, and Mary Beth asked if she could drive me to the airport so that we could talk. As we sat in the small waiting area, she let down her guard, telling me how worried they were and asking if I thought they might lose. They weren't wealthy and had loaned the campaign most of their savings.

"Mary Beth, you can always lose," I said, "but we're not going to lose." That small reassurance was all she needed, and she gave me a hug as I got on the plane. I wasn't bullshitting her. By now my skepticism had vanished. I was confident we'd win the primary and still felt we had a good shot at Foley. Her trust gave me a real boost.

Mary Beth was the perfect candidate's wife, a welcome change from Arianna. Although justifiably nervous at times, she pretty much stayed out of the way and helped maintain some normalcy in George's life in the midst of the chaos of the campaign. Their marriage, like their law practice, was a genuine partnership. Mary Beth was secure enough, and their relationship was strong enough, for them to make changes under tough conditions. As the campaign heated up, George was able to be a full-time candidate. This meant Mary Beth had to take on more responsibility at home and with their teen-aged kids, who were very involved in school, sports, and social activities. It also meant that, in addition to putting supper on the table, she had to keep the law practice going and the clients happy in case the campaign didn't work out. She juggled two jobs, which allowed him to do one well.

As she drove away, I watched her out the window and thought to myself what a crappy business this is, how much we put our candidates through, and, more important, how much we put their families through. Over the years I'd watched so many lives and families destroyed by trying to get elected.

On the flight back to Orange County, I reexamined our strategy and was sure it would still work. We had the better candidate, the better team, and the better organization. In every campaign I run, I always hold back my resources and save the heaviest TV and direct mail for the end. That's the way the Unruh team taught me back in my early California days: Communicate with the voters when they're paying attention, which is in the closing days of the race. Voters think campaigns are too long, and they tune out to most of what's going on until the very end. But political junkies watch and react to every little part of it. They watch all the opposition's commercials, read everything in the newspaper, and tend to panic easily. My strategy takes discipline, but it works.

George won the Republican nomination easily, with 30 percent of the total vote. Running unopposed, Foley got only 35 percent. It was the lowest vote he'd ever gotten in a primary, and he knew he was in for the fight of his life.

George turned out to be a natural candidate who had a message from the outset that was his own. He had great political instincts and never needed to be scripted. He relied on his own words and his own thoughts, and he believed in them. For a novice, his performance on the campaign trail was impressively mistake-free. The guy making the mistakes was the Speaker.

Aside from abortion, the other major issues in the campaign were term limits and gun control—the latter a particularly sensitive button in the wake of the tragic shooting at Fairchild Air Force Base in Spokane in June. A few weeks after Congress had narrowly passed a ban on assault weapons, a madman had killed four people and wounded twenty-three others at the base. As was customary for a Speaker, Foley abstained from voting but was unable to duck the issue back home. The local press pushed the Speaker to say how he would have voted. After days of hemming and hawing, Foley retreated from his thirty-year record of opposition to gun control and came out publicly in support of the ban. The National Rifle Association (NRA), which had previously supported Foley, launched an all-out assault on the Speaker and gave enormous support to George, who opposed the ban.

Even though the NRA was crucial to George's prospects, its attacks caused us a lot of internal heartburn. The NRA television spots targeted Foley personally, something George didn't want to do.

Many people in the community were very unhappy about the ads and blamed George.

As he'd done on the abortion issue, George tried to make clear that his position was a matter of principle. Despite the horror at Fairchild, he believed that the right to own weapons was constitutionally guaranteed by the Second Amendment. I was confident that his clear stand, in contrast with Foley's muddled one, would help give us what he needed to win.

As George had suggested in our first conversation about this race in December 1993, Foley had given us a huge break when he joined in a lawsuit to overturn congressional term limits, which voters had passed overwhelmingly. It was yet another example of this Washington insider being out of touch with the mood of his constituents.

The six-week campaign from the September primary to election day in early November was incredibly intense. I was shuttling back and forth between Southern California and Spokane, and trying to keep in touch with George and Mary Beth by phone daily despite the distraction of Arianna and her histrionics. More than once I was struck by the contrast between my two main candidates.

Back in Spokane, the national Democrats pulled out all the stops, pouring in money and hired guns. Foley and his party ended up outspending us two to one and by more than a million bucks. The consulting firm of David Doak and Bob Shrum, two of the top Democrat operatives, was retained to prop up the Speaker. In this same election, they would bring Virginia Senator Chuck Robb back from the dead against Ollie North, and pull Ted Kennedy through what many felt was his toughest race. It was only a matter of time, according to the conventional wisdom, before George Nethercutt also succumbed to their talents.

Unfortunately for them, there was no dirt to find on George. He was squeaky clean. But that didn't mean they couldn't attempt to blast him out of the water with negative commercials. Newt Gingrich's Contract with America became the issue he had to defend against their attacks—and they were effective. George was accused of wanting to cut money for education, polio immunization shots, and Medicare for the elderly. George had never said he wanted to do any of those things, but Doak and Shrum put a magnifying glass on the Contract's fine print and blew it all up to billboard size. They also tried to make George look like a Washington insider and professional pol, citing his years in Washington in the seventies and his volunteer stint as the county party leader. They attacked him for supporting the sale of assault weapons and charged that Fairchild Air Force Base would close if George were elected. More than the specific charges, it was the amount of money spent on the attacks that did the damage. You couldn't turn on the television without seeing a Foley spot.

Our first poll right after the primary had George winning 54–38. Two weeks later, it was down to 46–42. A third poll, with two weeks to go, showed Foley had retaken a slight lead, 48–46. His ads were working. Respondents in our polls started to quote Foley allegations back at us.

Larry McCarthy, the media maestro I was using for both Huffington and Nethercutt, came up with a brilliant spot to stem the damage. It showed George sitting in his kitchen talking straight into the camera. It responded directly to Foley's accusations. George said, "Why would I want to cut education, when I'm the one with two children in public schools? I'm the one whose sister is a teacher, and it's my wife who is president of the PTA. Tom Foley will say a lot of untruths about me." The camera then moved to a shot of George with his arm around his golden retriever. "Next, Tom Foley's probably going to tell you I kick my dog. But, Chessie, you know I'll never kick you."

Through it all, George stayed calm and performed well. The harder the Foley camp attacked, the madder he got and the harder he fought back—hard, but clean. What a handicap that was. George didn't want to go negative. We had good stuff on Foley's voting record and his extensive travel paid for by lobbyists, but George wouldn't let us use it.

There were six debates over the course of the campaign. All drew large audiences, and most were televised. Foley was very knowledgeable about federal issues, but George more than held his own. The polls were seesawing and driving us all nuts. One night we'd be ahead; the next Foley would go back on top.

"I'm not going to give you nightly numbers anymore," I told George and Mary Beth during one of our phone calls. "They'll only drive you insane. You just keep doing what you have to do and let me worry about the numbers."

By then the Huffington race had blown up in my face, and I was getting to Spokane less often than I wanted to. The Nethercutts were understanding, but one night on the phone I felt a pang of guilt when Mary Beth said, "I know we're not the Huffingtons, but don't forget us. We're in trouble." Her voice was as sweet as it could be, but I got the message. There was no doubt in my mind that I was going to spend the last weekend before the election in Spokane, where my skills could make a difference—and in a race that mattered to me.

As I was checking into my hotel, a stranger approached me.

"Do you think your man is going to do it?" he asked.

"It's very close, but I think we're going to pull it out."

"Well, I'm for the other guy, but it's been one hell of a campaign."
I thought nothing of it until I found out he was Foley's press guy
from Washington.

Sunday morning, I went to early mass at the Cathedral of Our
Lady of Lourdes. As I knelt in the beautiful old building, my
thoughts went out to Tom Foley. I knew Tom was a Catholic and he
must have worshipped here on many occasions. I couldn't pray for
his defeat here. I only asked the Good Lord that His will be done. I
truly hoped that if we were successful on Tuesday, Tom Foley would
find peace in knowing that he had served his state and his nation with
honor and dignity for thirty years.

The last debate was that Sunday afternoon. George appeared
calm at the podium, but I could tell he was really nervous beforehand. The race was neck-and-neck. The debate was being televised
live after the Seattle Seahawks football game, guaranteeing a large
audience. It would be the last chance for voters to see what had
become the biggest shootout in congressional history. Foley had been
hammering away on the assault weapons issue in the earlier debates
and George still didn't think he had a good answer. He couldn't
waffle because the NRA supporters were too important. He also
believed in his position, but he knew he needed to respond on an
emotional level.

I drove over to the hotel where the debate was being held with
him and Mary Beth. As we stepped out onto the snow-covered parking lot, Tom and Heather Foley drove up. Tom was driving the car
himself and seemed a little uncertain behind the wheel. It seemed so
strange to see this big bear of a man behind the steering wheel of a
car. The Speaker has a limo the size of the president's, and I'm sure
he hadn't driven himself much in decades. For more than twenty
years, Tom Foley had been one of the most important leaders in
Congress. In Washington, the biggest perk of all is a car and driver. I
chuckled to myself. Our spot had worked. One of our first spots was
about the Speaker and his big, black limo.

As Tom got out of the car, he and George shook hands, and then
he shook mine. "Have you been up here much?" he asked.

"A few times," I said.

"More than just a few, I hear from my people." He smiled.

"Spokane's a lovely community." I smiled back. Then we all
walked off to our respective holding rooms. A little later, the
Speaker and Heather, accompanied by the debate moderator, came

to George's room to discuss the rules. I was asked to flip the coin to see who went first. George called heads, and heads won.

The debate was a donnybrook. The Speaker was aggressive and knew his issues. George was equally effective, and I thought he won. He nailed the assault ban question by talking passionately about the tragedy of those families who lost their loved ones at Fairchild. He said he would do anything if he thought it would have made a difference. I thought George exceeded expectations and came off as the more likable. I was really proud of him.

My pleasure in George's performance was short-lived because I had to fly back into the Orange County whirlwind that night. I didn't want to, but Huffington had called me that morning and threatened to withhold the last $25,000 he owed me if I didn't come back to hold Arianna's hand. I don't know why, since that race was lost. I wanted to tell him to screw himself, but I needed the paycheck.

Mary Beth drove me to the airport again. She was nervous, and didn't think George had done as well as I thought. It was a perfectly common reaction, but she was wrong: He'd done great. She couldn't thank me enough for all I'd done for them. But it was I who should have been thanking them: They'd made it fun for me again. The two of them had created a candidacy I could believe in again.

I wanted to end my career right here. I wanted to drive voters to the polls on election day and go door to door turning out Nethercutt voters. I didn't want to fly to Orange County that night. As I looked back over the Spokane skyline, my thoughts were warm and fuzzy. Whatever the outcome on Tuesday, these wonderfully ordinary people had restored my faith in my profession. Maybe democracy does work pretty well after all.

IN THE EARLY-MORNING hours of Wednesday, November 9, I was home alone in Virginia and couldn't sleep. I'd been tossing and turning for hours. After running on adrenaline for weeks, I couldn't shut it off.

I'd returned to Orange County in the face of Michael Huffington's extortionate demand, but I went through the motions. Normally I might have hung around campaign headquarters and checked on how the get-out-the-vote operation was working, but Huffington had no such operation. So two hours after the polls opened in California, I'd left behind the last campaign I ever want to run.

Election day was now over, but the outcome of my two West Coast campaigns was still in doubt. The television was on in the bedroom and CNN was giving updates. It appeared that Bill Clinton and his Democrats had gotten their butts kicked. This defeat would be almost as big as the one he'd handed George Bush two years earlier.

The California Senate race was closer than I'd thought, but I knew in my gut that the Huffingtons had lost. I was pleased that Arianna's scheming and manipulation had come to naught, but I'd never been convinced her husband really wanted to win. This suspicion was confirmed a few weeks after the election, during a conversation about the Huffingtons with the California industrialist who hosted their post-campaign Caribbean cruise. His brand-new, 200-foot, triple-deck luxury yacht was truly spectacular, with spacious bedroom suites and mahogany and marble everywhere. It could comfortably sleep fourteen guests, pampered by a crew of ten. The ship's owner told me that after touring the ship, Michael asked how much it had cost him to build. The answer was $28 million. "That's what it cost for my Senate race," Michael observed gloomily.

During the campaign, I'd come up with a line for a speech to justify the huge sums of his own money Michael was spending on this race: "Other rich men spend this kind of money on yachts and jet airplanes; I'm investing this money in California for the future well-being of my kids and your kids." At the time, I didn't understand that what Michael Huffington really wanted was to spend his money like most rich men—on yachts and other grownup toys.

As I lay in bed listening to the buzz from CNN, I thought: This is it. No more of this insanity. No more dumb-fuck candidates yelling at me, no more candidates' wives making my life miserable. After today, it's over.

Ironically, it was a year ago to the day that I'd come close to destroying my political career with my dumbass remarks at the Sperling breakfast. I'd pulled out of it by throwing myself into the hard work of running several campaigns at once. I'd pushed myself to the limit—physically and emotionally. It had been the longest and most difficult year of my life, filled with reflection, regret, and remorse.

In the course of the year, I'd worked on six different races. Three had failed to raise any money and therefore couldn't wage viable campaigns. Two of those were for African-American candidates—Joe Watkins in Pennsylvania and Teresa Doggett in Texas—whose races I did for free. Both were outstanding candidates who were essentially abandoned by our party. Some day, the Republican Party will get serious about black outreach and support candidates like Joe and Teresa. The third candidate, Bernadette Castro, was running in New York against the formidable Daniel Patrick Moynihan. No one would help her because they thought she couldn't win. Despite being outspent five to one, she held Moynihan to 55 percent of the vote, and did it without a statewide television campaign.

The fourth race was destroyed when my candidate's divorce records were released to the media. Bruce Benson was a self-made oil millionaire who'd been the Republican state chairman in Colorado. He was newly married to Marcy Head, my former executive assistant in the White House. Bruce was actually leading Governor Roy Romer over the summer, but then a local television station went into court and asked to have his divorce records unsealed. In a gross invasion of privacy, the court agreed, and every ugly detail of a long, painful divorce proceeding was made public. Benson never recovered. When he was thinking about running, they asked me if I thought Bruce's messy recent divorce would hurt. I said no, and have never been more wrong on any counsel I've ever given. I'm not sure he's forgiven me. Friendships often suffer in this business.

But it was the two West Coast campaigns that crystallized my feelings about what I—and politics as we know it—had come to. On the one hand, there are candidates like George Nethercutt: honest and decent people who want to serve their communities and continue to be part of them. On the other, there are the Michael Huffingtons: arrogant seekers of power who don't understand the purpose of government, the value of public trust, or their own responsibilities as caretakers of democracy. Such predators with unlimited resources pervert the political process. They can hire the best talent, and if they listen to it, can redefine themselves, and in most cases win. There are also a lot of George Nethercutts out there, but lacking both money and good campaign help, they usually lose. Happily, two of my races broke the mold.

As dawn arrived and the results from California and Spokane became certain, I was suspended between a sort of political alpha and omega. George Nethercutt had won; Michael Huffington had lost. George represented everything good and hopeful about American politics; Michael represented the system at its cynical worst. I'd never been prouder to lend a hand to one campaign; I'd never been more ashamed by my association with the other. One I did for friendship; the other I did for money.

Charles Dickens had it right: "It was the best of times, it was the worst of times. . . ."

ROUND 11
NO MÁS, NO MÁS

WHILE I WAS consumed with managing the Huffington and Nethercutt campaigns, a Republican earthquake was realigning the American political landscape. When Republicans swept the House, the Senate, and most of the nation's governorships in November 1994, I was as surprised as anyone at the size of the victory. I knew Republican gains could be significant and thought there was a real chance of recapturing the Senate, but I felt it would take another election to go over the top in the House. I sensed the country's mood shifting against Clinton and the Democrats, but I never anticipated it would be so dramatic and so swift.

I applauded the new revolution enthusiastically. But it wasn't *my* revolution. I was there when the foundation was laid, but when I decided to leave the NRCC after the 1990 elections, I'd walked away from it. I suppose I could have joined up again at some point, but along came Perot, and then New Jersey. Meanwhile, Newt Gingrich and his lieutenants did just fine without me.

After the stunning Republican mid-term victory, though, I could have easily jumped back into the middle of things. I'd been the campaign manager for a winning presidential campaign and the chief political adviser to the House Republicans, so I knew how both ends of Pennsylvania Avenue worked. More recently, I'd been the chief strategist for the first challenger to unseat a Speaker of the House since the Civil War. And nobody blamed me for the Huffington loss.

To the contrary, party leaders told me they were amazed I was able to keep it close. As Bob Squier told me a few days after the election, "You have the best of both worlds. You showed you could still win a big race—and you don't have to spend the next six years making excuses for Senator Huffington and her husband."

I still wasn't welcome in every Republican household, but I felt I'd redeemed myself somewhat with my party after the New Jersey fiasco. The new Speaker had been an ally, and several of my closest friends in the House were now powerful committee chairmen. My phone started ringing with calls from candidates who wanted to talk to me about running their races. Among the presidential hopefuls, Bob Dole and Pete Wilson sent out feelers to see if I'd consider working for them.

I'd said repeatedly during the grueling mid-term year that I was finished as of 1995. I knew in my heart that I wanted out of the campaign trade, which had become an increasingly brutal business. Years earlier, I'd made a decision to box one more time—and ended my career as a loser. I was a little smarter now, and I knew that it was time to say good-bye. Thanks to George Nethercutt, I could leave a winner.

Once again, I had to decide what I wanted to do next. With the Republicans now controlling both congressional chambers for the first time in nearly fifty years, there were plenty of opportunities for lobbying. But lobbying wasn't what I wanted to do. I don't have a supplicant's personality; I'd rather do something for someone than ask them for a favor. I knew I wouldn't be able to stomach sitting outside members' offices, waiting to grovel, or standing in the halls outside committee rooms jockeying for a seat at hearings. I learned from my Sacramento experience that to be an effective lobbyist, you have to practically live at fund-raising breakfasts, lunches, dinners, and receptions. I don't like to schmooze, and I hate fundraisers most of all. As my wife will attest, I can usually be found at Washington parties exactly where she left me—riveted to a corner. And I'm terrible at ass-kissing, another reason I'd be a pathetic lobbyist.

Instead, I began thinking about what it would take to rebuild my business, and by now international consulting seemed even more appealing to me. In the late eighties, I'd become intrigued by Asia, in part because of several business trips I'd taken to Japan after leaving the Reagan White House. I had also provided strategic counsel for Roh Tae Woo's successful 1988 presidential race in South Korea. But I was especially fascinated by China. In 1988, as a member of a bipartisan delegation, I had spent ten days in China at the invitation of the government. That visit had persuaded me that China had the most potential of any nation in Asia, and it was easily the most interesting.

I returned to China in January 1994 after the New Jersey debacle, and I liked what I saw. For one thing, one billion Chinese had never heard of Ed Rollins or New Jersey. More to the point, economic development had escalated dramatically since my 1988 visit. Over the next two years I would return ten more times.

But before I could leave behind political consulting for good, I needed to discharge an obligation to Jack Kemp, the final link to my own personal revolution. For my money, Jack was still the heir to the Reagan Revolution. Despite the disappointment of his 1988 presidential campaign we'd remained friends, and I wanted to help him if he ran again in 1996.

Jack and I met just before Christmas in his office at Empower America, the conservative think tank he founded in 1993 that was viewed by many as the launching pad for another presidential effort in 1996. Jack had said he wanted to talk with me, but I knew he was dreading it all the same.

I've always been a reality check for Jack, and I think he trusts my political judgment as much as anyone's. I'd also been an enormous pain in his butt when I'd chaired his campaign in 1988, trying and usually failing to get him to do things he didn't want or wasn't ready to do. He hadn't run the kind of campaign he should have in 1988, and I didn't want history to repeat itself for my friend. I'd been nagging him for more than a year to get started if he was going to be a serious candidate in 1996.

In 1991, when Jack was HUD secretary, we'd gotten into it over dinner at the home of Frank Keating, who was HUD general counsel and is now governor of Oklahoma. I'd urged Jack to resign from the cabinet, move back to his original home state of California, and run for one of the two Senate seats that were open in 1992. Governor Pete Wilson and every Republican in the California House delegation would have supported him. He would have wiped the floor with Barbara Boxer. Always the party's favorite true believer, Senator Kemp would have emerged as the GOP front-runner for the 1996 presidential race.

But he didn't want to do it and left dinner early to escape my badgering. "I know you're right," he admitted, "but it's not what I want to do."

Now, three years later, we both knew he wasn't going to go for it. Still, we went through the motions. He outlined his reasons for staying out of the race, and they were all logical. He'd left government after twenty-two years; now, for the past two years, he was finally making some real money. He was devoted to Joanne and their four kids, and wanted to spend more time with them and several new grandchildren. He wasn't needed as the messenger anymore; his allies Newt Gingrich and Trent Lott, now the Senate Republican whip, would see that his ideas were pushed.

Besides, Jack had never liked the campaign grind, and he was now even more resistant to the prospect of spending two hundred nights on the road over the next year raising the more than $20 million he'd need. He talked for more than an hour, and I listened. When he finished, he asked for my counsel.

"Jack, you've made up your mind," I said. "Why should I add to the difficulty by trying to convince you otherwise? I'm first and foremost your friend, and if you don't want to go spend every waking moment of the next two years running for President, you won't make it anyway." We shook hands, and that was that.

He'd decided matters for both of us. I was now free to pursue other options without being drawn into another catfight for the presidency. But I was disappointed Jack wouldn't be the candidate of hope and opportunity the party and the country needed. For the next generation of young conservatives, Jack could have been what Ronald Reagan was for me. Ironically, 1996 might very well have been his year.

So now I could quit the political game—and believe me, there were no regrets. I had never intended to run campaigns for a living. As a young man, I considered governing the real work; campaigning was just something you did to get your boss reelected so you could continue to serve. But I'd come to love the rough and tumble of a hard-fought race, and for the most part the political consulting business had been very good to me. Now, at age 51, I couldn't take the physical punishment anymore. But the deeper problem was that I was sick of the life.

Few people have any sense for what it's really like to run a campaign. As George Bush would say, the job is wall-to-wall Tension City. You're constantly hounded by the candidate, his or her spouse, the opposition, your staff, and the media. Before one fire burns out, another is smoldering. Long-range planning is tomorrow's crisis. Between juggling the demands of six races and my business, I spent twenty nights in my own bed in 1994, and there were plenty of times I literally couldn't remember the name of the hotel where I was staying. It got to the point where I lived for airplanes just so I could sleep for two hours without hearing a phone ring. And it's not just telephones—the cellular phone, the fax machine, and the relentlessly buzzing pager are now part of the consultant's standard operating equipment.

If you're physically present in a campaign only a day or two a week, the candidate and his staff want every minute of your time. The pressure is unbelievable, and it only gets worse as election day approaches. You work eighteen or twenty hours a day, and if you can't handle stress and make quick decisions, you're a goner. You can't delay a decision, because another critical one will be facing you shortly. You never forget that one bad call on a commercial can waste a million dollars and cost your candidate the election.

Meanwhile, your other campaigns still want you making the decisions and offering guidance, so even when you're elsewhere, you're talking on the phone constantly to them. After all, if you do your job well, the candidate becomes addicted to you and needs your daily counsel.

As for money, the only guys who get rich are the premier media consultants, who can pull down 5 to 15 percent of a campaign's television buy. A statewide race can earn these guys up to $400,000, and they do three or four races at a time. And if you're one of the few people good enough or lucky enough to cut spots for a presidential campaign, you can become a multimillionaire virtually overnight. But only a handful of practitioners are good enough to charge these rates. Like pro athletes, only the elite can play at that level. Most consultants struggle to make a decent living, and many starve in the off years. Then, too, making ends meet would be a lot easier if our bills always got paid, but the fact is that there's not a consultant in the game who doesn't have former clients owing them huge sums that will never be collected.

Adding insult to injury, our public image isn't exactly terrific. Most people seem to think political consultants are a bunch of unprincipled hired guns engaged in a glamorous profession that makes us rich and famous. They're not just wrong about the money—they're wrong on all counts. The vast majority of consultants start in politics because they believe in somebody or a cause. But after a while, we see our new client or opponent make the same mistakes we watched another guy make two or four or eight years ago. With each election cycle, we lose patience and become more hardened and cynical. Maybe that's why so many of us eat too much, smoke too much, and drink too much. Add these vices to the fact that we spend too many nights alone in motels in far-off cities and you've got a lot of ulcers, coronaries, and divorces waiting to happen.

Every campaign consultant's worst nightmare is to end up like the late Paul Tully. He was one of the good guys in this business—among other things, he'd been the political director for the Mondale campaign in 1984 and the Democratic National Committee's political director in 1992. Six weeks before Bill Clinton's election, he died of a massive heart attack at age forty-eight alone in his Little Rock hotel room. For over a year, Tully had worked the states and watched the polling numbers; he was convinced that a Democrat was going to beat George Bush. He was a lonely messenger for a long time; he gave it his all, and then died before his man won.

So is the life of a political consultant exciting? Absolutely. But glamorous? Forget about it!

But consultants (including me) really shouldn't complain—hell, until fairly recently our job didn't even exist. Thirty years ago, when I started out in this business, campaigns were managed by political or personal confidants. Nixon's 1960 campaign was run by Bob Finch, his former administrative assistant. Ted Sorenson was Jack Kennedy's aide and speechwriter. Those days are gone. The modern campaign is the bailiwick of hired guns—political gypsies skilled in the mechanics of polling, fund-raising, media buys, and driving a message. The process has become so complex that anyone who tries to do it without people like me is a fool. George Nethercutt, for one, could never have beaten Tom Foley in 1994 without me and the professionals I put around him. And Speaker Foley, even after winning fifteen previous elections, wouldn't have made it competitive without his imported hired guns.

Of course, what caused the role of the manager to change was the evolving nature of campaigns. Not long ago, for instance, the typical congressional race looked something like this: The candidate was a mayor, state legislator, or city councilman. His campaign was run by his administrative assistant, who might double up as the press secretary. The manager didn't need a pollster. Opposition research would cost $3,000 for a private detective—half to investigate the opponent, half to check out the candidate's public records. Two or three direct-mail hits were plenty; if you needed to take the low road, you might add another mailer at the last moment. Ten billboards scattered around the district and one snappy radio spot took care of advertising. Television ads? Why bother? If you felt like splurging a little, the whole thing might cost $50,000. The typical campaign lasted three or four months, and you had days to react to an opponent's charges.

The modern campaign, by contrast, is a high-tech, high-maintenance, high-anxiety, high-concept monstrosity where response time is instant. The candidate may have never held office. The manager is a professional political consultant who may be juggling three other races. The pollster samples public opinion every night for weeks. The press is frantically looking for dirt on the candidate and his or her every relative, dead or alive. The television budget may be larger than the gross national product of Niger. And if your ads don't slash and burn, you'll lose.

There's no such thing as a cheap campaign anymore. The $1,000 limit on contributions has remained the same for more than two decades. It's the only number that hasn't exploded. The costs of mail, polling, phone banks, television commercials, even what it costs to raise that puny $1,000, have mushroomed. The average congressional race cost over $500,000 in 1994, the competitive ones much more. Several cost over a million dollars. The average Senate race in that same election averaged $4.5 million. Statewide races in California and New York can cost a million dollars a week for television buys alone just to stay in the hunt. And money's just one part of the story, which starts, as always, with the candidates themselves.

In the old days, candidates for federal offices worked their way up through the local political chain of command—mayor, state representative, state senator. Today, anybody can run. In fact, having *no* experience is a major asset these days. A fresh and independent face is usually much more appealing to voters sick of politicians.

If you have your own money—real money—so much the better. Wealthy people have always been attracted to public office—Jack Kennedy, Herb Kohl, Ross Perot, Frank Lautenberg, Howard Metzenbaum, Jay Rockefeller—but if you've got a truly massive personal fortune and are committed to watching it disappear, you can bypass the process. You don't need to kiss ass with political leaders, or to pay any dues with the party organization.

Michael Huffington, for instance, would never have made it to the starting blocks if he didn't have his own deep pockets to raid. This phenomenon isn't new, but it's growing and becoming more dangerous. If rich people looking for a little drama in their lives buy up television air time and hire the best consultants, they can become significant players in American political life. Even if they don't always win, they can alter the course of the political dialogue. They can also discourage more qualified candidates from running who can't compete financially. They can even scare off candidates far more qualified or deserving.

Huffington didn't listen to his handlers and had a wife who proved a major liability; even so, he almost bought himself a Senate seat. There are plenty more Huffingtons out there, salivating to be senators, governors, and even president. Someday, somebody like Michael Huffington or Ross Perot won't fail.

Money is a huge part of winning an election; party affiliation and the issues play a role, too, of course. But in the end, someone has to like your guy before they'll vote for him. Ronald Reagan's great strength as a candidate was that there wasn't a mean bone in his body. George Bush ran a mediocre campaign in 1988, but in the final analysis he won because voters liked him better than Michael Dukakis. Not so in 1992; Bush lost in part because he came across as too shrill. Incidents like calling Al Gore "Ozone Man," for example, made voters feel maybe Bush *wasn't* all that likable.

Sometimes you can make people like your candidate. But you can always make them dislike the other guy; inevitably, that's what you set out to do. Negative campaigning is getting a lot of attention at the moment, but it's always been around. In the old days, if your guy was in trouble, you'd flood mailboxes with a character attack two days before the election so your victim didn't have time to recover. Now it's a mainstream technique, one you have to use whether you like it or not.

The 1978 North Carolina Senate race let this genie out of the bottle. Jim Hunt was the incumbent governor, the most popular politician in Tarheel history. Jesse Helms had no chance—until he started trashing Hunt and kept up the drumbeat for a year. By the end of that campaign, there was nothing left of Hunt's reputation, and Helms won.

It took a while for the message that crime pays to reach the presidential level. Richard Nixon's gutter campaign against Helen Gahagan Douglas in 1950 tarred him as a dirty politician. But Hubert Humphrey and George McGovern weren't victims of character assassination on television in 1968 and 1972. In 1984, the most negative spot we ran simply said Walter Mondale was going to raise taxes. Big deal; he'd volunteered that in his acceptance speech at the convention. In 1988, the Bush campaign elevated negative campaigning to a lethal art form with their complicity in the Willie Horton spot.

Polling has gotten totally out of hand as well. You could once run a congressional race with three polls—one at the start of the campaign, another around Labor Day, and the last about three weeks before the voting to see if your message needed a mid-course correction. Today, late in a campaign, polling is an almost daily occurrence in any statewide or national race. News organizations are also obsessed with polling. There's seldom a week goes by when a television network or major newspaper isn't running its own poll. This forces voters to focus too much on the horse race instead of the substance of the campaign. And the addiction to polls doesn't end when the campaign is over. These days, Bill Clinton doesn't make a decision unless his poll results say it's okay. After the Branch Davidian firestorm in Waco, Texas, for example, Clinton didn't react publicly until an overnight poll told him what to think.

The trouble with polls is that they've turned pollsters into strategists—but most pollsters don't have the nerves for the task. Many pollsters aren't thinkers; they're analysts. They're driven by numbers, not instinct. It's next to impossible to get one of them to say, "Here's what I feel, here's what I think." They don't *know* what to think until 1,500 scientifically selected citizens tell them. Polls have become ubiquitous, so that it's hard to persuade the candidate to ignore them. I've been in campaigns where great television spots got pulled prematurely because the daily tracking polls said they weren't working. Sometimes it takes more than a few days for your message to resonate, but when you're a slave to the polls, perspective and common sense go out the window. Politics is still a game where a good manager's instinct is usually right. Polls don't always mirror your gut feeling about what voters are really thinking. When that happens, I make the pollster do another sample.

Another increasingly tricky issue for campaign managers is the candidate's spouse. In the old days, politicians' wives were simply ornaments—part of the sideshow, trotted out at election time and never heard or seen again until the next campaign. Jess Unruh had a wife, but she was invisible. Jacqueline Kennedy was a tremendous asset to her husband, but she wouldn't have dreamed of involving herself in campaign strategy. Pat Nixon and Betty Ford are other examples of the classic model for political wives: devoted spouse and mother, taking care of the kids while the breadwinner hits the rubber-chicken circuit two hundred days a year. These women and their generation weren't a problem for the campaign manager, or an issue with the voters.

Those Ozzie and Harriet days are gone forever. In the modern political era, spouses are an inevitable piece of the political power game. Some of them are constructive influences on the electoral fortunes of their mates (Nancy Reagan, Marilyn Quayle). Others aren't (Arianna Huffington, John Zaccaro, John Whitman). Hillary Clinton is both. And if Alma hadn't objected, Colin Powell might be running for president today. The common thread that binds them is that they've all become players, and therefore, justly or not, fair game for the media and the political opposition.

These days, a campaign manager who doesn't scrutinize a spouse just as mercilessly as the candidate is asking for unpleasant surprises. There's no such thing as separate identities anymore. If a spouse has any baggage at all, it's sure to be wrapped around the neck of the candidate. Even if there's no dirty laundry, spouses are still labor-intensive. You have to prepare them for the turmoil they're about to encounter. And it's essential to make them partners in the race. You need them on your side; after all, if they're not happy with what's happening to their mate, they can undo everything you've done in the course of a day with some well-timed pillow talk.

In extreme cases, the manager ends up playing marriage counsellor. In the Huffington campaign, "You tell my wife" was the candidate's stock refrain. The same thing happened in the Whitman campaign, with John Whitman reducing his wife to tears with his constant second-guessing. She pleaded with me several times to get him off her butt. He drove her nuts, and at times made her a less effective candidate.

Regardless of their individual differences, political spouses are enormously influential. I'm absolutely convinced Ronald Reagan would have retired back to his ranch after losing to President Ford in the 1976 primaries if it hadn't been for his wife. Nancy pushed him to run again in 1980, and provided the constant encouragement and emotional support that turned a reluctant candidate into a two-term president.

Barbara Bush's grandmotherly persona masks a very tough woman. She's frankly a lot more hard-knuckled than her husband— particularly when you've screwed up. You can cross George Bush and live to tell your grandchildren about it. I'm not so sure about Barbara. After Bush was embarrassed by Bob Dole in the 1988 Iowa caucuses, Barbara was on Rich Bond's case like white on rice. She let it be known that she was suspicious of Lee Atwater's loyalties and was particularly displeased with an *Esquire* article for which Lee posed in boxer shorts. It's an open secret in Republican circles that she still thinks Jim Baker is a lot more loyal to himself than to her husband. And it goes without saying that in this life, I'm not on her Christmas card list.

Hillary Clinton, too, is tougher and a lot smarter than her husband. Her intervention in the 1992 campaign helped him get elected. She brought focus and discipline to the campaign, qualities alien to her husband. She cracked heads in the campaign hierarchy, and centralized power in James Carville. And I'm convinced her stoic performance on the famous *60 Minutes* interview put the issue of Clinton's philandering to rest for the remainder of the campaign. Hillary did what she had to do—stonewall the truth. If she'd shown any emotion, any hint of her private hurt and pain, it would have been all over for him. She's been a political liability for much of his presidency, and if he's reelected it will be in spite of her. But he never would have won in the first place without her, and he knows it.

In general, I've found that spouses are the haters. It's always personal with them. If you ignore them, they'll make your life miserable. If you cross their partner, you're slime—even if you're working your guts out and ruining your health to get the spouse elected. The bottom line is simple: Unless it means the difference between winning and losing, never, ever go to war with the person who sleeps with the candidate.

I SPENT 1995 tending to my international consulting business, and when the 1996 election cycle rolled around I was content to watch from the sidelines. At first, I wasn't sure I'd feel that way; after all, I'd been involved in every presidential election since 1968. But I knew I'd be all right when I went out to Iowa in February to be a guest analyst on Larry King's show about the caucuses. I thought analyzing the vote would be like watching a heavyweight fight from a skybox, or being an election observer in a third-world country: Glad to be Here, but Something's Wrong with this Picture. In fact, I was amazed how little I missed it.

What happened during the Republican primaries only confirmed my sense that I was better off out of it. Most everything that's wrong with American politics today was on ugly display in the 1996 Republican primaries. All five of the leading contenders went negative, and it worked. Lamar Alexander's spots helped drive Pete Wilson out of the race before the first vote was cast. Steve Forbes's mean-spirited spots helped beat Bob Dole in New Hampshire. All the contenders engaged in a blistering campaign against Pat Buchanan, and to varying degrees they all resorted to spreading rumor and innuendo about each other through elaborate phone banks. Alexander's plaid shirts and marketing gimmicks ("Lamar!") were utterly phony and cynical. Hired guns were more ubiquitous than ever. And the Forbes phenomenon was a fresh reminder of the power of money to create a candidate. Phil Gramm may be gone, but he'll be remembered for one memorable phrase: "A candidate's best friend is ready money."

The only real revolutionary in the field was Pat Buchanan. People forget that Pat was the communications director in Reagan's second term; he's continued the struggle begun by Reagan and both furthered and diminished by Newt Gingrich. Like Reagan, Buchanan was running against the party establishment and attracting the same clientele—true believers, former blue-collar Democrats, single-issue voters, the religious right. If Reagan or Jack Kemp had run this time,

Pat would have been lucky to get 5 percent of the vote. But as the radical outsider, he offered the only hope for many conservatives and disenchanted voters.

Pat has no casual thoughts, only deep convictions, and he can articulate his message better than anyone else because he believes what he's saying. By tapping into the anger and alienation voters feel today, he's made a lot of converts. He may lay claim to be Reagan's political heir, but he's also the successor to the growing legions of the disaffected who marched to the siren songs of George Wallace and Ross Perot.

And like it or not, he's still a Republican. Some party leaders have made a serious error in deciding to "save the party from Buchanan." But it's time for the queasy Republican establishment to pay attention to him, his message, and his followers. If voters who support Pat don't have a place in the Republican Party, we'll be a minority party again well into the foreseeable future. Like many Republicans, I disagree with some of his ideas, particularly in the areas of foreign policy and trade, but I don't make the mistake of believing he's not speaking for a lot of worried Americans—not to mention Republicans.

In 1992, the Bush team gave Buchanan prime time at the Houston convention, then ignored him and his following the rest of the way. Many of them sat it out, and their apathy helped retire George Bush. If the party makes the same mistake again and gives Pat and his followers short shrift, Republicans can forget about winning in November.

Now the man who must forge that victory is Bob Dole, an old-style political insider who first came onto the national scene in 1976 as Gerald Ford's running mate—not exactly a revolutionary pedigree. Fairly or not, Bob Dole is viewed by many conservative Republicans as having fought the Reagan Revolution at every step of his career. If William Pitt was the Great Commoner, Bob Dole is the Great Parliamentarian. He's a classic midwestern Republican, in the Jerry Ford–Bob Michel tradition, although a bit more of a maverick than the Eastern Establishment types like Bush. But even his most ardent fans know he's not in favor of dismantling anything. The most depressing moment of Campaign '96 to date for this Reagan Revolutionary was the front-page picture in the March 7 *New York Times* showing Senator Dole sharing a few laughs with George Bush as he picked up the former president's endorsement. Not exactly my vision of the Republican party I joined more than two decades ago.

Bob Dole has been running for president for twenty years, and this is his last hurrah. Dole's reward for winning the primary race on his fourth try is that he now faces the most difficult challenge of any Republican nominee since Barry Goldwater in 1964. Unlike Goldwater, who offered the country an alternative to Lyndon Johnson's big government, Dole isn't offering the voters a different vision of America. And trying to beat Bill Clinton on experience is absurd. Dole may have been around for three decades, but Clinton is no longer a rookie president, and at the moment many voters don't think he's doing such a bad job. Dole has to create contrast between himself and Clinton by reminding voters why they didn't like Clinton two years ago and by making the case that Clinton is a superlative campaigner but a lousy leader. At the same time, he has to make people like him and respect him while he's attacking a flawed but fairly popular incumbent. That's no easy task.

First on his list ought to be finding a way to showcase his most important advantage over Clinton: the ability to govern and get things done. In his thirty years in Congress, Dole has demonstrated time and again that he knows how to build coalitions and make government work. But many voters aren't yet convinced of that, and seem to be worrying that a Dole presidency would be a Bush 1988 rerun. In 1992, voters decided they'd had enough of a visionless, leaderless administration. In November, the voters will reject Dole also—unless he can convince them in the next few months that he's a leader with the vision to take the country into the next century.

The truth is that as matters now stand—in the spring of 1996— Bob Dole faces an uphill but not impossible task to be elected president. The Clinton lead in public opinion polls is today as significant as Ronald Reagan's at a similar period in 1984. If those numbers don't close by Labor Day, it will take a small miracle for Dole to win. As a Christian, I believe in miracles, and they sometimes do happen in politics. After all, after the 1992 New Hampshire primary, even I declared that Bill Clinton was a corpse. I do believe his resurrection had more to do with Ross Perot and the ineptitude of the Bush campaign than divine intervention. Even so, the hurdles to Dole's election, large and small, are formidable.

If he does get elected, though, he'd make an excellent president. Unlike Clinton, he doesn't need adult supervision and knows how to get the job done. I'm absolutely certain he could make the tough decisions that always fall to a president.

Unfortunately for Dole, his party as well as his leader on the other side of the Capitol, Newt Gingrich, are starting to be a drag on him. Voters currently see Republicans more negatively than they have in years, and the Speaker is viewed more unfavorably than any congressional leader in modern times. Certainly the Clinton team will try to make this election a referendum between Newt's views of the world and Clinton's. The Dole team can't let that happen and have any hope for success.

Meanwhile, even before the first skirmishes of the primary season, it was clear the other real revolutionary would sit this one out. After too much coy hemming and hawing, the Speaker of the House decided to pass up the race for president he'll surely make in 2000 or 2004.

Newt Gingrich is one of the most complex men I've encountered in government. He's a true visionary—brilliant and articulate; he can also be very charming. That's when he's not being ruthless, petty, careless, and cunning. His intensity is awesome: I've never met a political animal so committed to his goals. Newt's whole adult life has revolved around getting elected. He ran three times for Congress before winning a seat. A protégé of Jack Kemp and Trent Lott, he's always been something of a gadfly, and for years his Republican colleagues didn't consider him a serious potential leader. He was too busy throwing bombs.

Newt has one characteristic alien to most politicians: He's willing to be hated to achieve his goals. Unfortunately, sometimes he's too good at it. As the accuser who almost singlehandedly drove Speaker Jim Wright out of Congress, Gingrich was the most despised member of the minority. Now the Democrats are preparing to demonize him again during the 1996 presidential race.

For all his flaws, there's no doubt Gingrich was the catalyst for the astonishing mid-term victory in 1994. Many other circumstances contributed, but he was both the spiritual leader and the field general who led his troops over the top. It simply couldn't have happened without his efforts. Moreover, no other leader could have accomplished as much in the first one hundred days of the 1995 legislative session. He organized the House brilliantly, and drove himself, his team, and the GOP freshmen to implement the Contract with America. On the other hand, Newt has often let his ego and sharp tongue get out of control to the detriment of his party's interests. He's been sloppy about his financial dealings and the appearance of conflict of interest with some of his contributors and supporters. His multi-million-dollar book deal was a public relations disaster for himself and the party.

Our politics today are driven by personality. Most of the time, the messenger merges with his message to become one and the same. Gingrich is in danger of becoming the message himself. He deserves full credit for launching his revolution, but I give him low marks as a communicator. He's allowed himself to become the focal point for

Democratic attacks instead of forcing debate on his issues. He risks letting his stridency taint his agenda as well. Newt Gingrich needs new rhetoric and a new communications strategy. But it's foolish to underestimate him. He's a force to be reckoned with well into the next century, and if Dole loses the presidency, the Republican party is his for the foreseeable future.

As for that other compulsively ambitious, bright, and articulate southern politician, I always thought Bill Clinton would have made a great salesman for a Fortune 100 company. Though getting better, he's largely been a third-rate president. But make no mistake, he's a world-class campaigner. To win in November, Republicans must sharpen the contrasts with him and remind voters why they repudiated him and his lackluster leadership so decisively in November 1994.

Though Clinton was elected in 1992 by a razor-thin majority, he came into office with a very powerful ally: hope. By inauguration day, virtually everyone wanted him to succeed, because the alternative was just too dismal to contemplate. But almost immediately, Clinton began to squander his reservoir of good will. Through his own political ineptitude, his lack of an articulated vision, and an uninspired administration riddled with amateurs and hobbled by no sense of direction, he contributed as much to the uneasiness of the people as the situations he pledged to correct—perhaps even more. Two years into his term, the country still didn't have the set of priorities it so badly needed (and isn't likely to get one from this president). His wife's bungling of health care reform, the biggest policy debacle in a generation, reinforced the impression that Clinton hadn't figured out that governing isn't the same as running. Clinton seemed to be many things, but a leader wasn't among them.

Now, only two years after voters repudiated him wholesale, Clinton is in a surprisingly strong position for reelection. As Congress becomes more polarized between liberal Democrats and conservative Republicans, Clinton has effectively cast himself as the voice of reason. There's a vacuum in the center, and he's positioning himself to fill it. He's promising to check the Republican excesses and block their spending cuts he paints as draconian. He's also abandoning his own congressional Democrats—who detest him, incidentally. And he's busily positioning himself as the champion of the elderly, the environment, and school kids. At this moment, he's well on the way to another term.

If you hang around Washington long enough, history repeats itself. I've seen this movie before, only the leading roles are switched. I never thought I'd hear a liberal Democrat president say, "The era of big government is over"—though Clinton clearly doesn't believe it. I also thought I'd never see the Republicans attacking big business and deploring corporate greed. Or that the GOP primary winner in New Hampshire would run on a platform of isolationism.

So I guess I shouldn't be surprised that Bill Clinton is trying to run as a younger version of Ronald Reagan this time around. Clinton's 1996 campaign is the exact same one I ran in 1984. His strategy, themes, and events this year are straight out of our old playbook of balloon drops, whistle-stops, and appealing photo ops. At a moment when the Dole campaign is still struggling to find its center, the Clinton team has already settled on a strategy and knows exactly how it will run this race months in advance. As Reagan's 1984 manager, I've racked my brains to figure out how I could have beaten us that year. I can't see it yet.

But Clinton can get away with this duplicity only if Republicans let him. And so far we have. At the moment, we're playing Fritz Mondale to Clinton's ersatz Gipper. Instead, we should be highlighting Clinton's political hypocrisy and flexible principles, while reminding voters that Republicans are the champions of individual freedom, limited government, and economic opportunity. My party also needs to focus on issues that touch people's lives—the economy, environment, and education. These are the core concerns for most Americans, and our response to them will decide whether we flourish in the next century.

If Republicans can breathe some credibility into this agenda, voters will then take a harder look at the character issue, and that's a big net minus for Clinton. But if Bob Dole doesn't find his voice as the Republican nominee, and if Buchanan keeps lobbing hand grenades at Dole, we're going to get our butts kicked by an unprincipled guy who's stolen the Reagan agenda and won't implement it. This election is definitely more winnable than the conventional wisdom suggests—but it won't be handed to us on a platter, and if we don't fight at the top of our game, my party will be back in the wilderness again at the dawn of the twenty-first century.

MODERN CAMPAIGNS ARE tough on the people who run them, but they're toughest on the candidates themselves. That's why the once-noble profession of politics has had so much trouble attracting—and keeping—good people.

Look at the distinguished list of Republicans who chose not to run for president this time—several of whom might make a better president than either Bill Clinton or Bob Dole. And look at the roster of prominent senators from both parties who have chosen to retire in 1996. Many of them delivered the same valedictory: They're sick of gridlock, sick of the rat race, and sick of the system.

Let's face it—nobody's happy with what's happening to our political process. Politicians and the people who elect them sense that things have gone haywire. The electorate in particular is disgusted with what passes for politics in this country today.

When running for federal office is such miserable duty that the best and the brightest abandon ship in droves—or aren't even interested in booking passage—we're careening toward disaster. In my opinion, here are the six most significant factors why the system is currently dysfunctional.

Attack ads. Negative commercials are the biggest problem in politics today. Negative-media campaigns are destroying politics. Unlike any other business, in which you try to convince the consumer your product is superior, the essence of campaigning today is winning by destroying the opponent and being the lesser of two evils. Think about it: If every oil company talked about how their business rivals polluted the environment and every carrier in the airline industry ran commercials about how many people were killed in competitors' plane crashes—and the competition responded in kind—nobody would feel safe driving or flying anywhere. That's not much different from what's happening in politics today.

Here's the ugly truth they never teach you in civics class: Negative ads work. It's easier to defeat your opponent than to get elected yourself. Not all that long ago, campaigns were issue-driven. Now they're character-driven. Party labels are essentially meaningless. Issues don't matter as much as the message, and the message doesn't count anywhere near as much the messenger. So the campaign trains its sights on the messenger. You go out and tarnish their personality; you run ads that beat the living daylights out of them.

The name of the game is proving that your opponent is dishonest or has some character flaw. These attack ads go well beyond setting the record straight or laying out policy differences. And unfortunately, American voters have now been conditioned to believe the worst, which is why negative ads are so effective. The 1994 California Senate race was the first I've ever seen where the negative ratings of *both* candidates went over 50 percent.

The worst part of it is watching candidates who deserve better get trashed and even destroyed. George Nethercutt was so clean he squeaked, but Tom Foley's campaign spent six weeks telling voters Nethercutt wanted to cut Medicare, Social Security, and aid to schools, and Nethercutt's negatives exploded. Families get dragged into the muck, too. If a candidate has a daughter who's had an abortion or has a son who's a homosexual, the opposition will know about it, and somebody will probably print it. I've encountered several good potential candidates who decided not to run because their kids had been picked up for smoking marijuana or driving while intoxicated. And there's no statute of limitations. Candidates get nailed for not paying their nanny's Social Security taxes twenty years ago. A spouse's tax shelters and business dealings—not to mention the messy divorce from a previous marriage—are all fair game.

The idea is to put a thought or phrase into the voter's head that reinforces preconceived ideas: Bob Dole's been around so long he's obviously part of the problem; Bill Clinton's so smooth and slick he's probably dishonest.

Nasty things have been said about office seekers since the beginning of our democracy. The difference from those early whispering campaigns is TV. Television reaches huge numbers of consumers directly and can pound home a negative message in millions of living rooms night after night. That's the up-front technique—the sneak attacks now come by way of telephone banks. A typical example is calling a senior citizen's home under the guise of doing a poll and slipping in this message: "Are you aware that Candidate X is for abolishing Social Security?" It happens all the time.

I'm not so naive as to think negative ads will go away. The 1994 elections and the early Republican primaries this year were as negative as any in recent history. But there was a time in our history when politics had *some* rules. The only way to stop gutter politics is to make the candidates deliver every negative attack personally. It's easier to get away with disembodied words. If you're slinging the mud yourself, you'll be more careful. But don't count on anything that sensible happening. Willie Horton has become the norm, not the extreme. He'll be back.

The insatiable media. The fundamental difference between the old and new ways of campaigning is the crushing intensity of electronic coverage and the incredible cost of competing on television. When I started out, television was a fairly new phenomenon. Now, even podunk stations have two or three hours of news programming to fill every day. The networks are even hungrier, and CNN never sleeps.

Fifteen years ago, we'd say that overnight is a lifetime in politics—and that was before cable. Nowadays, if CNN has it, you damn well better have your response in an hour, or your candidate has lost the war of the visuals. Television is such a staple of modern society that for most voters, it's not real until it's on the tube. Unfortunately, scandal and sensationalism are the order of the day. And of all the media, television has most avidly bought into the notion that people running for office either aren't honest or have something to hide.

The print media isn't far behind. There's a whole new breed of reporter out there who went to journalism school in the post-Watergate period. These hotshots are activists. They don't want to report the news; they want to be participants in the process. They know it's increasingly harder to get into print without a "holy shit" story, as it's known in the trade. They also know that if you can make a splash with your stories, you'll get invited onto the network talking-head shows. From there, it's a short distance to fat speaking fees. A surprising number of reporters make more on the lecture circuit than they do on their day jobs. Reporting pays the grocery bill, but being a celebrity journalist can pay for your kid's college tuition and a condo in Ocean City.

The bottom line is that these new-age reporters are willing to push the envelope—so they'll bite on a bullshit tip more readily. When I hear reporters talk about stories "too good to check," I know they're not joking.

Political reporters are also far more partisan than they used to be. The vast majority of them think they're objective. But as a breed, most are liberal and Democratic—and absolutely biased against Republicans, culturally and ideologically. Consequently, there's a shared mind-set among most reporters. Their value systems are in lockstep, so even when a reporter is trying to be balanced, the subtle influence of his (or her) peers means that he's probably still going to be slanted. And it's human nature for a reporter to give more weight to the side of a story that's closer to his own beliefs.

In 1992, for example, several prominent reporters made little effort to conceal their affection for Bill Clinton. And even when reporters weren't kissing Clinton's ass or encouraging their editors to bury negative information about him on page nineteen, many of them were quietly leading cheers for him from the sidelines. Why? Because he was one of them. They liked him and didn't like Bush, which was obvious to anyone mixing and mingling with them.

Here's a perfect example from the 1993 New Jersey governor's race. In the final days of the campaign, the race had closed to a dead heat. I did several background interviews with reporters and predicted that Christie Whitman would win. I could tell from their questions they thought I was nuts, despite my reputation for not bullshitting the press. When James Carville backgrounded those same reporters, they all believed him when he said Jim Florio was eight to ten points up. Those reporters may have been "objective," but they gave Carville the benefit of the doubt because they shared his political beliefs and wanted his candidate to win. You'll never convince me the attitude of the media doesn't contribute to skewed coverage.

I'm not one of those media critics who think journalistic ethics is an oxymoron. But I do think some reporters are less principled than they used to be, and it's bound to get worse before it gets better—if it ever gets better.

Dysfunctional campaign financing. When I was recruiting candidates at the White House and the NRCC, the first question most of them asked was how much money they needed to win. I'd always say that while no amount of cash can guarantee a victory, the amount needed to be viable was larger than they thought.

The sticker shock only gets worse. Several credible candidates decided not to run for president this year because they weren't sure they could raise the $20 million to $30 million needed to be a serious contender. The unrelenting and ever-growing need for money has put our politicians in the position of succumbing to the siren song of well-heeled special interests and the cynical process of constant fundraising. In particular, the bottomless need for more money helps keep the power of political action committees intact. Unfortunately, the PAC system is an incumbent's best friend. The ease by which an incumbent can fatten his campaign war chest without going more than a few blocks from the Capitol to a PAC fundraiser is appalling. When the Democrats ran Congress, most of the PAC money went to them. Now the Republicans demand the same largesse—and get it.

The irony is that PACs came about out of a desire to reform the system by limiting the huge sums that individuals or corporations could previously give to candidates. In the end, the voters get screwed. Most incumbents raise at least half their campaign money from PACs. A great deal of that money is controlled by the lobbyists peddling their influence on Capitol Hill. Is there any wonder that the larger PACs have enormous influence over the drafting and passage of legislation?

Genuine campaign finance reform will only occur through a constitutional amendment eliminating PACs and prohibiting wealthy individuals to spend their own fortunes. If it doesn't happen soon, the system will only get more corrupt and fewer challengers will be competitive.

Confrontational politics. Since this Congress convened, confrontational politics has been the order of the day. It's the ugliest climate I've ever seen on Capitol Hill. The truth is, voters are sick of it.

When I came to Washington in 1973, there was still a sense of order and civility to the political process. You fought as partisans during the day, but called a truce at nightfall. Now, with the election of a Republican House and the elevation of Newt Gingrich to Speaker, partisan warfare is the rule and fraternization with the enemy is a near-capital offense.

Serious polarization is the inevitable result. In the House, Democrats are fewer and more liberal; Republicans are greater in number and far more conservative. To the seventy-three freshman GOP members, ending the era of big government is a sacred duty. Yet the solutions to resolving many of our most serious problems lie in the center, and require bipartisan support.

Gingrich is a street fighter of the first order and is loath to compromise. The Democrat leadership is equally partisan and ruthless in trying to save the old order. But Newt and his often intemperate rhetoric set the tone. The last Speaker as mean and partisan was Jim Wright. Gingrich brought him down and sent him back to Texas in disgrace. The Democrats will be satisfied with nothing less for Gingrich. Live by the sword, die by the sword.

When I worked for President Reagan, the Democrats were just as partisan, and divided government didn't work much better then than it does now. But people *thought* it worked. No matter how bitterly they fought one another on issues of substance, Reagan and Speaker Tip O'Neill always seemed to be standing in the Rose Garden to celebrate signing some bill. That was reassuring to the country. The opposite is true today: It's not working, and it doesn't look like it's working, either. The public doesn't trust Clinton and they don't like Gingrich. And as the campaign heats up, it's bound to get worse.

The power of special interests. As the clout of political parties has diminished in the last several decades, special interest groups have risen to fill the void in the political process. Organizations as diverse as labor unions, church groups, and hunting clubs now affect campaigns as much as the old ward bosses of Boston and Chicago. The single issue that such groups support can become the litmus test that mobilizes the membership on election day.

The conservative religious movement is now a critical part of the coalition for any successful Republican candidate. Labor unions fill the same role for Democrats. Candidates endorsed by such organizations are increasingly expected to march in lockstep or pay a heavy price. In the future, the power of these groups will continue to grow. Big labor plans to spend upward of $35 million to defeat Republican House candidates in the fall. Small business groups are planning a similar blitz for Republicans. To try to get elected without the support of single-issue groups like these is becoming damn near impossible.

The lack of term limits. Every place I go, people ask me why better people don't run for office. The truth is good people do run, and some good ones win. But the vast majority lose, because the power of money and incumbency stacks the system against challengers. Once in a generation, as in 1974 and 1994, a frustrated public will decide on radical change and throw a lot of incumbents out. But year in and year out, many good people don't stand a chance of winning.

Turnover in politics is healthy. Making a career of holding office isn't. More than one person in a congressional district of 600,000 people can represent the community's views. If we don't make politics more competitive, more good people will decide not to bother. That's why I support a twelve-year limit for congressional membership, but I wouldn't stop there. We should change the Constitution to create a four-year term for House members and require all members to run in the presidential election year. That would cut down on the cost and duration of campaigning, and eliminate year-round fundraising. Today we get one year of governing and one year of campaigning in a two-year term. This way we'd get three and one. Congress could take more time studying complex issues and could enact multiyear budgets. And if every member had to run with his party's nominee, party platforms would have more relevance, and members would be more accountable to a president's agenda.

THE CUMULATIVE EFFECT of these six factors is that voters don't like or trust *any* of the people they send to Washington. They believe instead that politicians and parties have developed tin ears—and they're right. Our representatives don't listen to the people as they're charged to do; instead, they heed the loudest and most seductive voices. Even the most highly regarded officeholders are deemed long on rhetoric and short on substance. They don't seem to have the best long-term interests of the country uppermost in their minds.

No wonder people are always asking me, Where have all our leaders gone?

That's the crucial question, because leadership is what the American people really want. When they're angry with the status quo, they want a Newt Gingrich or Ross Perot to break some furniture. But what they want for the long haul is a *leader*—a unifying figure like Ronald Reagan or Colin Powell who is capable of blending pragmatism and idealism. Unfortunately, the American public doesn't yet seem to see a true leader in this year's presidential race.

Another question I'm often asked is, What are the characteristics of the ideal presidential candidate? Here's what I see:

A successful candidate for president and ultimately a good president must have a strong sense of self. Certainly, he must be able to communicate on television effectively and know the direction in which he hopes to lead the country. He must have high energy and strong discipline. He must be able to motivate others and make decisive judgments. And perhaps most important, he must believe in a higher purpose than merely his own place in history.

Of all the might-have-beens, the politician who comes closest to my dream candidate is Dick Cheney. He would have made a superb president. But to my mind, the perfect president is a composite: He'd combine the leadership ability and inspirational talents of Colin Powell; the passion, compassion, and ideas of Jack Kemp; the intellectual force and breadth of experience of Dick Lugar; the charm of Elizabeth Dole and the courage, integrity, and pragmatism of her husband; the core beliefs, intellectual firepower, and the ability to communicate of Bill Bennett; the tenacity and charm of Christie Whitman; the managerial skills of Pete Wilson and John Engler; and the bulldog determination of Rudy Giuliani.

My party doesn't have a monopoly on virtue, however. The best Democratic president would blend the intellectual integrity of Bill Bradley; the centrist philosophy of Sam Nunn; the personal charm and inspirational life story of Bob Kerrey; the commitment and good looks of Al Gore; the passion and oratory of Mario Cuomo; the campaign and communicative skills of Bill Clinton; and the tenacity of John Dingell.

As important as the message is, the messenger is even more critical in this age of cynicism. The extremes dominate the debate and capture the headlines, but most Americans are firmly rooted in the political middle. What's needed is a leader who believes in the center and speaks for the center. The country is frankly disgusted with the demonization of the liberals by Newt Gingrich and his partisans over the last three years. When this campaign is over, they'll be just as disgusted with the demonization of conservatives by Bill Clinton and his partisans in 1996.

That will be a shame, because our great country deserves better. I've been a fighter and a partisan all my life, but as I close out my career in politics, I am absolutely certain that for the good of the process and our people, it's time for healing and common ground. Every member of the party of Abraham Lincoln—and all Americans, for that matter—would do well to remember the words spoken by Lincoln in 1854 at a far more perilous moment in our country's history:

"Our republican robe is soiled and trailed in the dust. Let us turn and wash it white in the spirit, if not the blood, of the Revolution. . . . Let us readopt the Declaration of Independence. . . . Let north and south, let all Americans . . . join in the great and good work. If we do this, we shall not only have saved the Union; we shall have so saved it as to make, and to keep it, forever worthy of the saving. We shall have so saved it that the succeeding millions of free happy people the world over shall rise up and call us blessed, to the latest generations."

EPILOGUE

ON MARCH 13, 1995, my life changed forever. I'd left my office in the Old Town section of Alexandria and was standing on the corner waiting to be picked up by one of my staffers. It was around six-thirty in the evening, and it was cold and snowy. All of a sudden, standing in front of me, was the most beautiful little Chinese girl I'd ever seen. She was three years old, very shy, and there was a doll-like quality about her. I couldn't pull my eyes away.

Her father, a former California Democratic consultant, recognized me, introduced himself, and then introduced me to Diana. He told me he and his wife had adopted her as an infant. I was curious about the process, and he kindly filled in the blanks.

In an instant, I was smitten. I thought about Diana for days. It was Lent and I was trying to go to mass every day. Coming out of church three days later, I unexpectedly ran into Diana and her dad going into the preschool next door. I decided then and there that adopting a Chinese baby was my destiny. I called Sherrie, who was back at ABC Television in New York, and asked her what she thought. "What happened between Monday morning when I left for New York on the shuttle and today? We've never discussed adoption." After I explained the story to her, she laughed at her crazy husband, and our great baby adventure began.

Two weeks later, at a dinner at my home, I confided my intentions to my Chinese business partners. I told them I hoped this wouldn't be considered an insult; instead, they were honored, and offered to help. Within two weeks, one of my partners telephoned me from Beijing: "We have found a very special baby for you in Nanjing."

As it turned out, my little girl was born eight days after I met Diana. On Easter Sunday, April 19, she'd been abandoned on the Nanjing Bridge over the Yangtze River, found by some high school kids and delivered to the local orphanage. A note left in the basket with her said that her mother was an unwed college student who hoped that someone would provide her baby with a good home. When we heard this story after learning the baby would become ours, we decided to call her Lily after the Easter flower. Sherrie and I will always be grateful to the mother who gave her life.

We began the long process of making the adoption formal, and two months into it I finally had the opportunity to visit her. I saw Lily for the first time in the Nanjing municipal orphanage on July 2, and this is what I wrote in my diary:

> July 2, 1995; 10:40 A.M. Nanjing, China; Central Hotel: I have just returned from seeing my baby, Lily, for the first time. I don't think I have ever experienced anything more meaningful in my life. She is the most beautiful child I've ever seen. Holding her in my arms and knowing that she was my child excited me beyond my capacity to explain. I held her for twenty minutes and it seemed like the most natural thing in the world to do. She has a beautiful face and her skin is exquisite.
>
> Every part of her was perfect. Her little nose and lips and tiny fingers were so well formed that she far exceeded anything that I could have expected. The pictures we have seen of her just don't do her justice. When the nurse put her in my arms for the first time, I could have not gotten more excited. When I held her little fingers and she squeezed my finger, it was about as good as it gets. She laughed and smiled and looked everywhere with the most beautiful and alert eyes anyone has ever seen. You can't take your eyes off of her. I didn't want to let her go and I didn't want to leave her behind.

But I couldn't take her back with me. She was barely three months old, and the Chinese government won't allow adoptions until an infant is at least four months old. I was in Nanjing on business for a week and visited Xiao Xiao (her Chinese name, which means "Thing of Beauty") every day for an hour. Leaving her behind was heart-wrenching. The only compensation was the love and affection the nurses had for her and the four hundred other children who lived in the center. I've seen a lot of sensational stories in the media about the mistreatment of babies in Chinese orphanages. Having made ten trips to China in the last two years, I know it's foolish to generalize about a country with 1.3 billion people. But the experience I had with the orphanage in Nanjing was incredible, and the love and care given those children in my presence was heartwarming. Love is love, and my baby was loved in the orphanage. I saw nurses and doctors tending to sick babies day and night. I saw nurses take the older children home for weekends and overnights. These kind people have dedicated their lives to taking care of these poor babies and older children, and Sherrie and I will never forget them.

We did everything in our power to expedite the process, and with the help of Chinese and American friends we were able to obtain quick approval. We flew to China in August 1995, and when Sherrie, Lily, and I left the orphanage, everyone was in tears.

With a new infant joining the family, our commuter marriage was out of the question. So in mid-October, Sherrie, Lily, Duke, Dutch, and I moved to Bronxville, New York. The Washington phase of my life was over. For almost a quarter century, it had become more than the place I lived. Washington, D.C., is also a state of mind. It's where I climbed the tallest mountain and fell off. It's where I made some of the most wonderful friends and powerful enemies imaginable. It's where I fell in love, got married, became both famous and notorious, served my country, and maybe even lost my perspective.

In Washington, D.C., you're not just a person. You're who your title says you are. You're either somebody, an assistant to somebody, or an assistant to somebody who *thinks* he's somebody. I've left Washington behind, but I'm still who my title says I am. I'm Lily's daddy. That makes me somebody, and I've never been happier with any title.

FOR THE FIRST time in nearly thirty years, I can honestly say that I'm at peace with myself. I have nothing to prove to myself or to anyone else. It hasn't always been so. Politics was an addiction. In an instant, and at the slightest pretense, I'd quit everything else to jump back in. No matter how many times I intended to quit, I always went back. And as with any addiction, politics consumed me. It was my mistress, the center of my universe. It cost me a fortune, ruined friendships, destroyed one marriage, and would have destroyed a second if Sherrie hadn't been the unbelievably tolerant and supportive person she is.

I didn't set out to spend my life this way. My early goals were to go into teaching or coaching. But from my first job in the California legislature, I was hooked. Unlike many people in politics, I actually like government. This will sound crazy to people who know me only by reputation, but I'm much more interested in public policy than partisan politics. I've made my reputation, of course, in the arena of competitive politics. The only reason I ended up in the competitive business of campaigns is because I decided early on that I didn't want to run for office myself but instead help others who did.

My political career was as unusual as any I know. I pride myself on staunch loyalty to the principles of my adopted party, though often as not I found it damn near impossible to give absolute loyalty to the party itself. Even more important, I've never blindly followed any of the men or women that I've worked for, no matter how much I respected or admired them. I've always given the counsel I thought was right, which wasn't necessarily what my candidates wanted to hear. For that I have sometimes paid a price.

I've been damned and praised; I've had moments of brilliance and colossal stupidity. But through it all, like the fighter I was trained to be, I gave it the best I had, and I tried to make a difference by winning. Unlike sports, politics awards no medals for second place. If you win, you govern. Lose and you go home humiliated, even ridiculed, and more often than not in debt. Bill Clinton became president with 42 percent of the vote. In 1984, Walter Mondale got 1 percent less and went home with one of the worst defeats in history, barely carrying his home state. Four years later, Michael Dukakis won more votes than either Mondale or Clinton, and was lucky to find a job teaching at the Kennedy School at Harvard.

I believe deeply in what I've tried to do over these thirty years as a political warrior. I have strong convictions, and so do most of the people who practice my trade. Political consultants aren't merely the cynical mercenaries depicted in the media. Everyone starts in this business because they believe in someone or something. Very few get rich at it, and nobody I know does it just for the money. If your candidate wins, he gets the credit and the job. If he loses, it's your fault. Like my friends in the media, consultants can't help but get a little cynical when they've seen it all before. Human frailties up close are never pretty. Campaigns bring out the worst in people—even good people—and it's not often that I've respected my candidate more at the end of the race than I did at the beginning. I'm sure some of them feel exactly the same way about me.

At my core, I'm like most Americans: libertarian on many social and behavioral issues, conservative on most fiscal and economic ones. I believe we must each take responsibility for our own lives. But I also believe any great society, even an opportunity society, must take care of its sick, poor, downtrodden, disadvantaged, and elderly, and most of all its children. How we do that and at what cost will be hotly debated as long as there's an America. But as we consider how and how much, let's not forget why.

I believe deeply in our democratic system. In Guatemala, I watched peasants stand in line for six hours to vote despite threats against their lives. In Colombia, I helped politicians who have given their lives fighting for justice. In my career, I've taken on the most powerful people in government, from speakers to presidents—including the president of my own party. But I've never been physically threatened or beaten up. I've never been audited by the Internal Revenue Service, or wiretapped by the FBI. I've never even had anyone take a swing at me, although I'm sure some would relish the prospect. We live under a wonderful system, the envy of the world. I'm proud my baby daughter will have the opportunity to savor its blessings. I know she'll grow and prosper under the freedoms that we all hold so dear and too often take for granted.

So NOW I'M hanging up the gloves. These thirty years in the political ring have been incredible. I've been in places and situations most people in this game never see. I've learned from and worked beside some of the most talented people in politics and government. I was in the room when great people made important decisions. In some cases, I'd like to think I helped those decisions get made. In the process, my nose has been bloodied by some of the finest political fighters in the ring, but I'm still standing. I gave as good as I got, and then some. I've made enemies and friends, and each one changed my life in an important way.

My story is uniquely American. As an adolescent, my only goal in life was not to work in the shipyard like my father. Nowhere else could a wiseass, street-smart, pugnacious kid from a small, blue-collar Navy town have had the kinds of opportunities I've written about in these pages. What I have to give back are the lessons of my experiences, and what I can say with great confidence is that the sort of good fortune I've had is available to anyone who pursues his or her goals with diligence and cherishes the blessed country that makes dreams possible.

The good and the bad, the wins and the losses, the draws and the knockouts—I wouldn't trade a second of my life. These days, I'm smarter and maybe wiser. I'm definitely more battered and bruised. But I'm not broken. For this blessing, and for many others, I consider myself a very lucky man.

APPENDIX

ROLLINS'S RULES OF CAMPAIGN COMBAT

1. Always fire first.
2. Always assume that your candidate hasn't told you everything and that what he hasn't told you will leak out.
3. If your candidate says, "Don't worry, I can raise the money," worry—and demand to be paid up front.
4. The most important hire is your candidate's press secretary.
5. Define your candidate before your opponent does it for you.
6. If it's not on television, it barely matters.
7. An attack made on television must be responded to on television.
8. Don't let the polls drive you nuts. And if you don't believe the numbers, order a new poll.
9. In boxing you must win the rounds; in campaigns you must win the weeks.
10. Election day is the ultimate deadline; a day lost is gone forever.
11. Campaigns aren't democracies; don't be afraid to ignore all committees and rule like a petty tyrant.
12. Don't tell your candidate what to believe; tell him how to say it.
13. If your candidate doesn't believe in anything, don't do the campaign; he's going to lose.
14. If your candidate doesn't listen to you, quit; he's a goner.

15. Never let your candidate go on vacation in the middle of the campaign; it's an invitation to disaster.
16. Never let your candidate control the spending—especially if it's his own money.
17. Never let your candidate sit in the headquarters. Don't give him an office—don't even give him a chair.
18. Be the first and last person your candidate talks to every day.
19. If you think things can't get worse, relax; they can and they will.
20. Never get into a pissing match with the person or persons who sleep with your candidate.

ROLLINS'S RANKINGS,
1964-1996

Best Presidents
Ronald Reagan
Richard Nixon; Lyndon Johnson
 (tie)

Worst Presidents
Jimmy Carter
George Bush

Best White House Chiefs of Staff
Dick Cheney (Ford)
Ken Duberstein (Reagan)
Bob Haldeman (Nixon)
Don Rumsfeld (Ford)

Worst White House Chiefs of Staff
Sam Skinner (Bush)
Don Regan (Reagan)
Mack McLarty (Clinton)
Hamilton Jordan (Carter)

**Best White House Press
 Secretaries**
Jody Powell (Carter)
Mike McCurry (Clinton)

**Worst White House Press
 Secretaries**
Dee Dee Myers (Clinton)
Ron Nessen (Ford)

**Most Effective Congressional
 Leaders**
Robert Byrd
Bob Dole
Newt Gingrich
Tip O'Neill

**Least Effective Congressional
 Leaders**
Carl Albert
Tom Foley
Tom Daschle
Jim Wright

Best Congressional Press Secretaries
Chris Matthews (Tip O'Neill)
Mark Johnson (Jim Wright, Tony Coelho, Dick Gephardt)
Walt Riker (Bob Dole)
Linda Peek (Robert Byrd)

Best Campaign Press Secretaries
Lyn Nofziger (Reagan 1980)
Jody Powell (Carter 1976)
John Buckley (Kemp 1988)
Kathy Bushkin (Hart 1984)

Best Modern Presidential Campaigns
Reagan 1984
Johnson 1964
Clinton 1992
Carter 1976

Worst Modern Presidential Campaigns
Bush 1992
Dukakis 1988
Ford 1976
Bush 1988 (even though he won)

Guys I Want in the Foxhole with Me if I'm Ever Stupid Enough to Run Another Presidential Campaign
General Strategist—Art Finkelstein
Media Strategists—Roger Ailes, Stuart Stevens
Ad Team—Tony Marsh, Larry McCarthy, Mike Murphy, Don Sipple, Greg Stevens
Manager—Kieran Mahoney
Political Director—Sal Russo
Fundraisers—Bob Mosbacher, Joe Rogers
Pollster—Ed Goeas
Speechwriter/issues—Ken Khachigian
Press Secretary—John Buckley
Communications Director—Bill Greener Jr.
Opposition Research—Richard Billmire, Gary Maloney
Coalitions—Paul Weyrich
Senior Advisers—Marc Nuttle, Lyn Nofziger, Sig Rogich, Vin Weber

Guys I Never Want to See Lobbing Grenades at Me Again
General Strategist—Tony Coelho
Media Strategists—Bob Squier, Bill Knapp, Tom Ochs
Ad Team—David Axelrod, Frank Greer, Clint Reilly
Manager—Les Francis
Political Director—Bill Carrick
Pollsters—Mark Penn, Doug Schone
Fundraisers—Peter Kelly, Terry McAuliffe
Speechwriter/issues—Bob Shrum
Press Secretary—Mark Johnson
Communications Director—Paul Begala
Opposition Research—Phil Noble, Tony Podesta
Coalitions—Ann Lewis
Senior Advisers—Bob Beckel, Pat Caddell, James Carville, David Garth

AUTHOR'S NOTE

As I was completing this manuscript, a man I admired immensely and regarded as a friend, Ron Brown, died in a tragic plane crash in Croatia. Ron epitomized the best of American politics. Over the years, we were on the opposite sides of many battles, but I always came away from those encounters with great respect for him as a man and as a leader. Although he was passionate about his politics, it was never personal with him. He knew that whatever our partisan persuasion, we were all Americans and together we had to find solutions to the significant problems facing our nation. For the next generation of people in politics, there is no finer role model than Ron Brown. The Clinton administration, the Democratic Party, and this country are diminished by his passing. We shall all miss him.

ACKNOWLEDGMENTS

LIKE MUCH of my life, writing this book has been a great adventure. As a first-time author, I could never have completed this undertaking without the encouragement and assistance of many wonderful friends, former co-workers, and family members. As in many of the winning campaigns I managed, much of the success of this endeavor is because of the efforts of others.

I have singled out a few individuals in the following paragraphs who were the catalysts and in some instances the inspiration for this memoir. It's an impossible task to note only a handful of people when so many have contributed to my life and to this book; if I've left out a name I shouldn't have, know that you aren't forgotten. I'll always remember the legion of people who have been kind, fair, and honest to me throughout my lifetime.

Allen Weinstein, president of the Center for Democracy and a dear friend, provided early encouragement for this book and helped get me started.

My agent, Michael Carlisle of William Morris, convinced me I could write this book, never gave up on me, and most important of all put the deal together with Broadway Books to make it happen. I'll always be grateful for his great negotiating skills and his friendship.

This book could never have been written without the extraordinary efforts of Tom DeFrank, my collaborator and co-writer. I admired Tom from my years working in the White House, where he was regarded as one of the best and most trustworthy journalists on the beat. In his twenty-five years as a White House correspondent for *Newsweek*, he established himself as a great reporter and phenomenal writer. Among his many contributions, he took my rambling words and made them more readable. Working with him on his project has only heightened my respect and regard for him.

Many friends were particularly helpful in filling the gaps in my recollections. Gary Maloney and Richard Billmire, the two best political researchers in the business, gave me valuable assistance on facts and events. Michele Davis, my executive assistant in the White House and the 1984 Reagan campaign, provided remembrances of long past events. John Roberts, an associate from the Reagan days and after, helped with many ideas and thoughts and also provided invaluable notes from meetings that occurred years ago. Jamie Moore, who worked closely with me in the Whitman, Huffington, and Nethercutt campaigns, provided a plethora of detail from those campaigns and the events that followed them.

Mike McManus, Bill Sittmann, and Rick Ahearn, friends and colleagues from the White House, offered their insights and recollections. Charlie Leonard, my ally at the Perot campaign and the National Republican Congressional Committee, did the same for those incarnations. Lyn Nofziger, my friend, mentor, and colleague over more than a quarter century, not only made many of the experiences chronicled in this book possible but also helped me remember them accurately.

A special thanks goes to William Sandy, my brother-in-law, who moved in with me for four months and served as my in-house editor. Without his friendship and talents, I never would have made it through this enterprise. Another special effort was provided by my friend and business partner Bob Barkin, who helped me strategize this book and gave me some of the best thoughts in it. His constant encouragement also kept me going.

I'm also indebted to Paul Locigno, my partner at Rollins International, who kept my business going while I took several months off to give this project my uninterrupted attention. My able young assistant Matt Cochran served double duty, juggling a variety of tasks to make my life easier and also serving as the book's researcher-in-chief. Holly Hopkins, cheerful as always, handled the unenviable chore of transcribing hours of interviews. The library staffs at Washington University in St. Louis, the American University of Washington, D.C., and the Reagan Library in California provided valuable research services.

This book could never have been launched or consummated without the tremendous efforts of Broadway Books. Under the steady leadership and vision of Publisher and President Bill Shinker, they turned my concept into a reality. John Sterling, Broadway's editor-in-chief, brilliantly edited the manuscript with a deft hand, keen mind, and the patience of Job. He was my taskmaster, architect, instructor, and cheerleader; without him, there would be no book. Barbara Ravage, a gifted freelance editor, did a superb job of line-editing the manuscript. Stuart Applebaum of Bantam Doubleday Dell generously lent his prodigious talents as a publicist to the project. Thanks also to many others at Broadway, especially Victoria Andros, Lauren Field, and Rebecca Holland.

Finally, I want to thank the people I love most in the world—my wonderful family. My parents, Ed and Mary Rollins, my brother Michael, and sisters Nancy, Donna, and Marian have had to put up with me for a lifetime. Their love and support over the years have always made my life full.

My wife, Sherrie, deserves special credit for this book. Not only has she given me her total support and love, but she took on the added burdens of moving into a new house and adopting a baby during the months I was writing this book full-time. With little or no assistance from her pseudo-author husband, she managed to make it all happen smoothly and with minimal disruption. Her patience has been truly astonishing. Her editorial suggestions were also important to the finished product—although she bears no responsibility for my controversial or colorful language or for my conclusions.

My inspiration throughout was my infant daughter, Lily. Without these two beautiful women in my life, this book would hardly have been worth writing.

I guess I should also thank the boys who have lived this life with me—my many dogs who provided friendship and company through thick and thin: Sampson (St. Bernard), Chaucer (Old English), Goldie (Golden Retriever), Rocky and Ranger (Huskies), Bear (Newfoundland), and Duke and Dutch (Labs).

Harry Truman once observed, "If you want a friend in Washington, get a dog." I've been privileged to have some great friends, and also some great dogs.

E.R.
Bronxville, New York
May 1996

INDEX